THE LEARNING RAINFOREST

FIELDBOOK

TOM SHERRINGTON

ILLUSTRATIONS BY OLIVER CAVIGLIOLI

JOHN CATT

30 CASE STUDIES FROM THE UK AND AROUND THE WORLD

First Published 2019

by John Catt Educational Ltd,
15 Riduna Park, Station Road,
Melton, Woodbridge IP12 1QT

Tel: +44 (0) 1394 389850
Email: enquiries@johncatt.com
Website: www.johncatt.com

ISBN: 978 1 912906 28 4

Set and designed by John Catt Educational Limited

CONTENTS

PREFACE TO THE LEARNING RAINFOREST FIELDBOOK

The greatest thing by far is to be a master of metaphor. It is the one thing that cannot be learnt from others; and it is also a sign of genius. – ARISTOTLE

I first 'met' Tom Sherrington at about 8.30 am on the 27th of October 2012. It would have been my dad's 85th birthday; and within a minute of each other, Tom and I posted very personal essays about our deceased dads. The connection was instant. A month later I was waiting on my own for the doors to open for the *London Festival of Education* when this bloke sidled up to me; by pure chance it was Tom, and we have been close friends ever since. Throughout our own personal and professional ups and downs we have been there for each other. It has been a joy to watch Tom's influence grow these past few years, to have batted about his initial ideas for his book *The Learning Rainforest*; and it is a genuine privilege to write the preface for this follow-up, *The Learning Rainforest Fieldbook*.

One of my favourite poets, the wise American Robert Frost, once remarked that 'an idea is a feat of association, and the height of it is a good metaphor'. Well, Tom's idea to associate learning with organic growth and to embody that idea in his Learning Rainforest metaphor was a moment of genius. Tom's metaphor, so clearly articulated in his introduction to this *Fieldbook*, has given literally thousands of teachers across the world a framework to reflect upon, and consequently improve, their teaching.

What I like about the metaphor most is its inclusivity. It has space for new ideas which grow from what we already know. It has common sense roots, a trunk packed with knowledge and a canopy of infinite variety, where new learning occurs. Tom's ideas synthesise research evidence and practitioners' experience in equal measure. As the teaching profession begins to build upon what we know has the best chance of working, Tom's Learning Rainforest metaphor has helped teachers use their existing knowledge and experience to translate research evidence into classroom practice, pretty much the teaching profession's Holy Grail.

In the Gordonstoun case study, Caroline McCallum talks about how so much CPD can be a 'bang then a whimper'. What is remarkable about Tom's book *The Learning Rainforest* is that its influence has been strong and steady since its publication; in fact, it is increasingly influential. I learned only very recently that Katy Potts, the ITT coordinator at Huntington School where I am headteacher, bases her whole training programme upon Tom's book. All our trainees receive a copy at the outset of their programme with us. It is fitting, then, that this new *Fieldbook* reports back on the influence of *The Learning Rainforest*, from the perspective of both the classroom practitioner and the learner.

Tom's unbridled sense of curiosity is at the root of his respect for all those voices featured in this book. He loves to work with classroom teachers, both to enable them to grow and to extend his own thinking about this ridiculously complex thing called teaching and learning. In this *Fieldbook* you will find the authentic voices of teachers and students reflecting upon their own teaching and learning through the lens of the learning forest metaphor, laid out with aesthetically pleasing clarity.

So, I suggest you sit down with a decent coffee or a glass of fine wine, arm yourself with a pencil and annotate heavily as you dip into the *Fieldbook's* individual case studies. The featured schools cover a wide range of contexts: independent/state; academy/LA; Ofsted 'outstanding'/'requiring improvement'. You will discover nuggets of wisdom on every page. I expect the 30 schools featured here will soon be inundated with requests from other schools to pay them a visit, as the influence of Tom's Learning Rainforest grows exponentially, way beyond his control!

John Tomsett, 27th of August 2019

CHAPTER 1: INTRODUCING THE LEARNING RAINFOREST FIELDBOOK

When I set out to write *The Learning Rainforest* two years ago, it was clear that in seeking to capture the essence of 'Great teaching in real classrooms', I was never going to be writing an objective manual based entirely around formal evidence. It was a personal journey from the very beginning. I felt I needed to start with an account of my own life as a student and then as a teacher in order to provide readers with some perspective for the values and beliefs that inform the rest of the book. In doing so – although not entirely deliberately – I was also modelling a process of professional reflection. For all teachers and school leaders there is a back-story, a set of personal experiences that shape values and attitudes to their professional lives. Teaching is a deeply human, social process where knowledge in all its forms is exchanged and shaped through interpersonal communication and personal experience, a complex array of interactions with the environment and with other people. This is a major element in both the joy and the challenge of teaching well. The interplay of my own values and my personal engagement with research evidence lies at the centre of the Learning Rainforest that I tried to depict in the book.

In parallel with narrating my own thoughts about teaching, structured around the three elements of the Learning Rainforest – revisited in the section below – I was starting out in the world of consultancy, visiting schools, meeting leaders and teachers, observing lessons and running training sessions in a very wide range of contexts. As a new entrant to this competitive world, I decided early on to accept any offer of work, however far it took me from home. By the end of this year I will have visited well over 200 schools, travelled to the many corners of the UK and the Channel Islands, and delivered training in 20 countries. It's been an incredible experience. I feel that I have been on a global adventure – I've seen the Learning Rainforest made real.

One of my conclusions has been that schools and teachers have a great deal in common wherever you go. People everywhere – from primary to further education, state comprehensive to selective independent schools, special and mainstream, in cities and towns in the UK and around the world – have

a common sense of purpose, deal with common questions and face common challenges:

- What kind of young people are we trying to nurture? What values and characteristics do we value and celebrate?

- What should we teach? And, therefore, what do we not teach? How do we slice up the time that we have?

- How do we enact the curriculum such that the teaching maximises learning? Do we all agree and does this matter?

- What constitutes excellence? How do we know what the standards are and how do we communicate them to students?

- How do we motivate reluctant or struggling learners? To what extent do students have agency? A voice? Should they have more?

- How do we teach groups of students with a wide range of prior attainment so that they all achieve excellence?

- How do we continue to develop as professionals, learning more about our subjects, more about the evidence from research and more about how our particular students respond to feedback?

But for all they have in common, each school, every teacher, and every school leader is unique and that is what makes the world of education so fabulously fascinating. In this book's first incarnation, I pitched the idea to Alex Sharratt at John Catt that I could tell the story of my journey around the schools I visited; working title: 'School Trip'. The cornerstone of the idea was the richness of the dialogues I have with headteachers and principals when they show me around their schools. It's always a special moment, a genuine privilege as I hear the stories being told. I'm not sure whether having been a headteacher myself before – with mixed fortunes presenting no reputational threat!   allows my hosts to be more open than normal, but I don't ever feel I'm getting a whitewashed, airbrushed account. There's almost always a confessional air – a tale of trials and tribulations – blended with the warm glow of pride and satisfaction at what has been achieved. I find it quite humbling actually. So many of the people I meet seem like the unsung

heroes of our education system and, understandably, they value a visit from someone who is not there to judge them but understands the pressures they've faced and why even small gains can feel like triumphs.

However, beyond the honesty and humility, very often the triumphs are actually simply astonishing. I visit the most fabulous schools with inspiring leaders, talented teachers teeming with ideas and students producing exceptional work. The energy behind all of this is what I wanted to capture. I just wasn't sure how.

The Learning Rainforest was published in October 2017, more or less at the same time that I decided to commit to working as a freelance consultant on a permanent basis. Having started to enjoy the freedom and the opportunity to visit lots of different schools, it became impossible to imagine going back to school leadership. As my consultancy work started to grow, to my great joy, *The Learning Rainforest* also began to gain traction. It was never at the top of any charts, never a best-seller, but sales have chugged along nicely and, long after the launch, people still seemed to be picking it up. I was contacted by some schools telling me that they were using it as a key resource for their in-house professional development programmes and I was inundated by people sending me images of their newly arrived copies. I'm sure my Twitter followers grew tired of seeing them!

Then, in April 2018, Dylan Wiliam tweeted a positive review comment: '*The Learning Rainforest* … is an extraordinarily good book (and I'm not just saying that because he says nice things about me). It covers a huge range of important issues in teaching in depth. Impressive, and highly recommended.'

This was my 'back of the net' moment. *My all-time edu-hero likes my book!*

Dylan then, very kindly, went on to provide a fabulous foreword for the US Dylan Wiliam Center edition of the book where he says:

> To design a bridge, the engineer needs to know about strength of steel and stone in compression and in tension, but this says nothing about what the bridge should look like. In the same way, to create great schools, we need to take account of the research evidence, where it

exists, but we need to go beyond that, and embrace the fact that great schools are about people, and this is why Tom Sherrington's book is such an extraordinary achievement.

When I picked up *The Learning Rainforest* – which I read in a single day – I was struck by the parallels between Tom Sherrington's career and my own. We studied high school science from the same textbooks (A.F. Abbott's *Ordinary Level Physics*, and D.G. Mackean's *Introduction to Biology*), started teaching as a way of financing playing in a band (both bass guitarists by the way) and taught math in high schools two miles apart, using the same math scheme (though he hated it, and I loved it). But what really stunned me about this book is the way that Tom has taken the research evidence that does exist, and woven it into a powerful vision of how education can transform lives, even in the most challenging settings. I know of many books that do a great job of summarizing the research on reading, on memory, on assessment, on feedback, and so on.

I do not know of a single other book that addresses so well all the threads that have to be woven together to create great schools, in such a readable way. *The Learning Rainforest* addresses head on the complexity of teaching 'in real classrooms', sure-footedly building on the research where it exists, and, where it does not, providing the wisdom of someone who has successfully led outstanding schools. A particularly powerful feature of the book is that for all of the complexity of the issues discussed, Tom has managed to distil his wisdom into a series of powerful precepts about establishing the conditions for effective teaching and learning, building the knowledge structure that is needed for students to succeed, and then using this as a base for exploring future possibilities.

With Dylan's confidence-boosting endorsement, I began to think that I could and should make more of the Learning Rainforest structure itself – and this is when I heard from Caroline Derbyshire, executive headteacher at Saffron Walden County High School. She sent a message suggesting that I made a return visit to SWCHS, a school I've visited a few times now, because, having read *The Learning Rainforest*, she felt that the ideas in the book resonated strongly for her and her colleagues. She also suggested that perhaps a book along the lines of *The Learning Rainforest* 'in practice' or 'in action' might be a good idea – and one she'd like to contribute to. Immediately I realised that this was how to get the ideas in 'School Trip' across. Rather than being a different book, this was just 'School Trip' re-imagined. Instead of me telling my story about visiting the schools as an outsider looking in, I would ask the schools to tell their own stories. Instead of my voice, readers would hear a range of voices, in the true style of Rainforest diversity.

I made a list of schools that I had worked with or visited or that were led by people I wanted to get on board, giving top priority to the schools I've worked with most extensively. I have tried to get a balance in terms of geography, age range, school sectors and stages of development, both in school improvement terms and their history. The result is the collection of 30 schools and colleges[1] presented in this book. It's a special group of institutions as far as I'm concerned. Each case study begins with my personal introduction where I explain my connection to the school and the reason I wanted to include them.

The *Fieldbook* title entered the frame once Oliver Caviglioli came on board to help with the design and illustration. He suggested that a 'fieldbook' had a pedigree in a researcher's vernacular and I absolutely loved the image: a researcher out in the field, out in the Learning Rainforest, capturing data, taking testimony, making notes in a travel-worn fieldbook.

In shaping the template for each school entry, I wanted to make it easy for schools to tell their stories without too much structure to inhibit them. For this reason, the way schools have told their stories is very diverse. Some read like project evaluations; others are personal histories. Some are focused on the details of classroom interactions whilst others focus on broad vision and ethos. Also, there is no neat subject categorisation. Some schools have focused on curriculum, some on assessment, some on teaching and learning, some on professional development – and often a combination. These themes overlap with the three-part structure of the Learning Rainforest – establishing conditions, building knowledge and exploring possibilities – and I asked contributors to highlight any direct links that can be made.

From the outset I was determined that the children – the students – at the heart of all of these ideas should have a voice. A key theme in the metaphor is that the trees in the rainforest represent the students and their learning. The lush rainforest canopy represents the possibilities for excellence that individual students can achieve and, to ensure we always keep that in mind, each school has provided student profiles where aspects of their learning are exemplified. They are brief snapshots but collectively add so much in terms of the spirit of the Learning Rainforest.

The Learning Rainforest metaphor revisited

Before diving into the *Fieldbook* case studies, to help make sense of the references, it will help to revisit the key themes in *The Learning Rainforest*, not least for any readers coming directly to *Fieldbook* without having read the original book. There are four main aspects that seem to resonate with people the most – based on what they tell me:

1. Plantation Thinking vs Rainforest Thinking

Here's how I introduced the metaphor that drives the whole Learning Rainforest concept:

> The Plantation: It is important for all specimens to reach certain minimum standards but there is little or no room for diversity. This tendency towards a monoculture with a narrow gene pool halts natural evolution and increases vulnerability to long-term or sudden environmental change. There is uniformity, conformity and an emphasis on control. The plantation managers are typically risk averse and, where

---

1. Importantly Oldham College, a Further Education (FE) institution is included and makes a major contribution. At various points in the book I refer to 'schools' as a shorthand for 'schools and colleges' but Oldham College is implicitly included in my thinking throughout.

improvements are needed, have a predisposition to seek out tried and tested methods with predictable outcomes.

In a school context, Plantation Thinking is the school manifestation of this emphasis on conformity and control:

- School culture is dominated by the notion that there is a right way to do things; the scheme of learning is non-negotiable.

- School leaders are driven, to a great extent, by compliance with standards set by external bodies and accountability regimes.

- The curriculum and learning are heavily driven by what can be easily examined.

- Professional learning is standardised to ensure no one falls through the net.

- Data has very high status.

- Interventions with students are heavily focused on short-term gains prior to examinations.

- Any new ideas or initiatives that are believed to be beneficial are elevated to the status of a rule or become a standard requirement.

Conversely, this is how I tried to capture the Rainforest alternative:

The Rainforest: There is enormous variety in the range of trees and plants that are thriving in the environment; it is lush, exotic, awe inspiring, unpredictable, non-linear, evolving, daunting. Each specimen is magnificent in its own right with different organisms occupying their niche in an environment that is self-nourishing. Without the need for external artificial interventions, the soil is fertile and the process of evolution is continuous. Whilst each plant has distinctive features and unique requirements, they all co-exist in an equilibrium that develops organically over time in response to changing conditions.

For schools, Rainforest Thinking suggests the following:

- The dominant mindset of leaders is to nurture the individual talents of staff and students, providing nourishment and creating a culture that

is motivational and rewarding to operate in but not to control or micro-manage the processes or predetermine the outcomes.

- There is a high-trust/high-challenge culture.

- Teachers and leaders recognise that the learning process is complex and, to a large extent, unknowable on an individual basis. There is, therefore, great variety in the approaches adopted over time.

- Where teachers are thriving, delivering excellent lessons and securing student outcomes, there is a high level of autonomy.

- Data is recognised as providing a rough guide to some aspects of learning – in a complex and non-linear fashion.

- It is understood that there is no 'right way' for most things we do in schools. There is still a recognition that there are aspects of bad practice – things that rarely or never seem to work – but, in the main, all kinds of teaching approaches can be effective in different contexts.

- The effectiveness research that promotes certain approaches is evaluated in context and is understood as suggesting an average general pattern with fuzzy edges, not an absolute truth.

- Professional Development is highly personalised – on the basis that it is counterproductive and demotivating to impose a uniform model on every teacher.

- Performance Management is to nurture self-driven reflection and professional learning – not to satisfy external accountability pressures.

- Learning and achievement are recognised in the widest possible sense. It is understood that learners will have all kinds of talents and skills, personal goals and interests. In the Rainforest these all have value.

As with any set of binary positions, the ideal might lie somewhere between. I suggested that perhaps a 'managed rainforest' represents a sensible midway position. I've had some positive feedback supporting that view from people who recognise the need for structure and control at certain stages. However, this feedback sits alongside other comments expressing disappointment that

I watered down the full rainforest ideal. As we will see in the *Fieldbook*, the response largely depends on where schools are in their journey.

At its core, Rainforest Thinking is about creating school cultures that allow teachers and students to thrive; to flourish; to excel; to explore the possibilities to the greatest extent. It's explicitly aspirational and hopefully serves as a reminder of the perils of excessive Plantation Thinking that stifles, inhibits and limits our view of what might be possible. The *Fieldbook* is packed with schools where the culture is either already strong and wonderfully orientated towards Rainforest Thinking or is being nurtured very gently and carefully with that goal firmly in mind.

2. The three-part structure

The tree metaphor serves as a way of capturing the three sets of tasks that constitute great teaching. I've had lots of positive feedback from teachers and leaders who have found this useful:

Establishing the conditions:

- Fostering the attitudes and habits needed as a basis for students to achieve excellence: having high expectations, teaching with rigour whilst also inspiring awe and making the whole process joyful

- Establishing effective behaviour routines and developing relationships that support students' self-esteem, motivation and, crucially, their engagement with teacher feedback

- Designing a curriculum where the knowledge and skills are structured in a way that supports long-term retention, builds confidence and allows connections to be made

Building the knowledge structure:

- Using effective instruction methods to build students' knowledge explicitly and deliberately: explaining, modelling, questioning in various ways and developing routines for practice

- Using effective formative assessment and feedback methods that make teaching highly responsive and support students to improve continually

- Teaching for memory in an explicit fashion, using a range of methods for learning by heart, making this a positive and joyful part of the learning process

Exploring the possibilities:

- Providing some opportunities within the overall curriculum for hands-on, authentic learning experiences, group activities and project work, with open-ended outcomes

- Using online tools and other resources to support students as independent learners with occasional opportunities to lead learning based on their own knowledge

- Giving speech activities a high profile as experiences in the enacted curriculum and finally celebrating excellence in all its forms

The message I always give to people during my training is that, whilst we should rightly dream big about the possibilities for learning, we can't simply wish excellence into being. We need to create the right conditions with high challenge at the core of our ethos and then very deliberately build knowledge so that students have strong foundations from which true excellence can spring. It's not a neat linear sequence – all three elements can grow together – but knowledge building requires a degree of rigour and discipline, without which the canopy never fully flourishes. This is where the research and practice around effective instructional teaching become so important.

3. Mode A vs Mode B

MODE A	MODE B
You explain.	They explore, discover, investigate.
You model.	You provide hands-on experience.
They practise.	Teach explicitly to inspire some awe and wonder.
You check for understanding and give feedback.	You go off-piste.
You test their knowledge and test them again later.	They make things, do projects, engage in open-ended tasks, make choices.

In Part 1 of *The Learning Rainforest*, I plot my way around a range of key debates including the way people align along an axis of traditional-progressive values systems. This feeds into ideas about behaviour management, curriculum design and the way people engage with research evidence. The three-part tree metaphor is my attempt at finding a way to harness these tensions. In Part 2 of the book I translate this into action through a set of practical strategies, introducing the notion of Mode A and Mode B teaching. Probably above all else, I've had very positive feedback on this; it feels right to people, albeit that their percentages wouldn't be the same as mine.

This is how I introduced the ideas:

Mode A teaching: 80%?

In our metaphor, building the knowledge structure is at the core of the whole process of creating the rainforest. I have suggested that, in practice, the strategies involved here might dominate daily school life – especially at secondary schools in typical academic disciplines. A short-hand I like to use is 'Mode A' teaching – because this is what you do most of the time. I've suggested that 80% is a rough proportion – but that is just to give a perspective on the balance. It's not scientific by any means and you'll have your own view depending partly on which subject you teach.

The core elements of Mode A teaching are about effective teacher instruction: explaining concepts and procedures, imparting information and telling stories; modelling what is expected in terms of standards and thought processes; giving time to guided and independent practice; effective questioning to check for understanding across a whole class; immediate feedback that is responsive and moves students forward; assessment that is largely formative, focusing on specific areas of content.

Mode B teaching: 20%?

In the Learning Rainforest, Mode B teaching strategies will happen alongside and interwoven with the more direct instructional Mode A teaching. Although they might occupy less time, in my view they are still vital. Exploring the possibilities signifies that we're building on knowledge to see what might be possible; we're creating conditions where learning and knowledge can be expressed in different ways and can go down a range of paths. At the same time, it's important to stress that all of these activities are also ways of building knowledge in various forms and of reinforcing the positive learning mindsets and classroom climate that create the conditions necessary for further learning.

We want the enacted curriculum experience to be as rich, challenging, motivating and multifaceted as possible so that we have the best chance of truly developing 'the whole child' with the maximum level of knowledge and cultural capital. Sometimes we don't do something because it is necessarily the most effective, because 'it works'; we do it because we give it value for its own sake – we think it should form part of a student's learning experience. Many of the Mode B strategies fall into that category: 'hands-on', projects, groupwork, reciprocal teaching, flipped learning, debates, 'play detective'.

I have a strong aversion to some people's tendencies to demonise each of these modes of teaching, something I've explored in some detail in my chapter in *The researchED Guide to Education Myths* (John Catt Educational, edited by Craig Barton, 2019). The 'myth' I chose to explore is that teacher-led instruction and student-centredness are opposites. Plenty of people argue that they are – but really, they're not at all. Mode A + Mode B is just one way to see past this.

4. A model for professional learning: the 60 strategies.

Perhaps the thing that has surprised and delighted me the most has been to encounter schools that have used *The Learning Rainforest* directly as a resource to support professional learning. In the case study provided by Chace Community School in North London (p. 108), there's a vivid illustration of this. Teachers have explored each of the three Learning Rainforest elements in turn, during a year's cycle of professional learning, using the tree image as a reference point. I've been to other schools where teachers have presented their work implementing a strategy from Part 2 of the book that they had selected to focus on for the year. This might have been 'Awe and Wonder', 'Signal, Pause, Insist' or 'Silence is Golden'. It might have been 'Teach for Memory', 'Think Pair Share' or 'Close the Gap'.

In all honesty, this is what I quietly hoped for but didn't dare expect, so it really is wonderful to know that teachers have engaged with the Learning Rainforest at this very practical level. Several people told me that they skipped Part 1 but found Part 2 valuable, whereas other people have had the opposite preference. I'm happy with that.

In general terms, I think it is worthwhile for all teachers to ask themselves questions linked to the three elements:

- Could I do more to establish the conditions for successful learning? Setting and establishing higher expectations? Enacting a more challenging curriculum? Fostering better relationships? Teaching with more attention paid to the ideas of awe and wonder?

- Could I do more to build the knowledge structure? Developing a wider range of explanations for key concepts? Teaching more explicitly for memory? Asking questions more effectively? Developing more effective ways to give feedback that is then acted on?

- Could I be more bold exploring the possibilities? Do I include enough opportunities for debate or other structured speech activities, to engage in open-ended personal projects, to engage in deep-end learning? Do I allow myself to go off-piste when the opportunities arise?

The 60 strategies work as stand-alone suggestions for focused professional development whilst also representing an overall philosophy around blending learning of different forms to create a rich, diverse learning experience for students; knowledge-rich but varied and expansive.

Some schools in the *Fieldbook* are using these teaching ideas directly but most have had their own versions for some time, expressed in their own language. However, what I believe all the schools have in common is that the three elements apply to their philosophy for developing teachers. Reading through the *Fieldbook* case studies, it is clear to me that Learning Rainforest schools all:

- Establish excellent conditions for teachers to engage in high-quality professional learning.

- Deliberately build teachers' knowledge structure about effective teaching and designing a broad and deep curriculum.

- Explicitly communicate the ambition for teachers to explore the possibilities for what they can achieve.

Increasingly I find that I use the metaphor to apply to teachers as much as to students. In essence it describes a growth process so perhaps this isn't surprising: teachers have to grow and thrive both professionally and personally throughout their careers.

CHAPTER 2: FIELDNOTES FROM A CHANGING SYSTEM

Since completing *The Learning Rainforest* in 2017, there have been various shifts in thinking across the system in the UK that, in some ways, illustrate the themes explored in the book. There have been some interesting changes in emphasis both at the policy level and at the level of consensus amongst teachers, school leaders and commentators like me. It seems to me that there is a strong two-way influence at work – which is to be celebrated. In this section of the *Fieldbook*, I will provide a brief account of these issues. Here are my 'field notes':

The central importance of curriculum

Without doubt, the most significant development across the UK education system in the last two years has been the increased level of attention given to the curriculum. Schools everywhere are wrestling with that all-important question: what should we teach? Invariably this is linked to the bigger question: why should we teach what we teach? The current wave of interest is leading to root-and-branch reviews with school leaders and teachers paying attention to the details in a way many have never done before. One of my light-hearted tests for school leaders is for them to name the books their Year 8 students are reading in English or the periods of history they are studying. Very often, leaders who have previously prided themselves on 'knowing their schools' by citing outcome measures for every sub-group (to three significant figures) cannot answer this basic question about their own school.

Happily, that is beginning to change. It's my firm view that in order to know your school, you need to know what is being learned by your students. To a great extent, your curriculum defines your school. It IS your school.

I am convinced that the strongest ideas in this area remain the three arts of the Trivium 21c[1] – grammar, dialectic and rhetoric – as expressed by Martin Robinson in his superb 2013 book. His 2019 follow-up *Curriculum: Athena Versus The Machine*[2] is a wonderful development of the principles, placing human engagement with knowledge right at the core of our thinking. Similarly, Peter Hyman's 'Head, Hand and Heart' continues to provide a strong

framework that resonates with a lot of people. This comes through in the *Fieldbook* entry for School 21 (p. 164).

A very significant, much-quoted influencer in this area is Christine Counsell.[3] In her superb blog series for leaders of curriculum she suggests:

> Curriculum is fundamental to schools. It is also fiendishly complex. Necessarily directional and dependent on recognisable channels, it must nonetheless be vibrant and changing for such is the character of knowledge and our relationship to it. It is at once a thing of beauty and of utility, and both matter. More like the waterways of Venice than a set of roads or paths, it needs specialist maintenance or it won't take you where you want to go, nor make it a rewarding experience. Moreover, like Venice, its waters don't stand alone. If you don't understand the relationship of knowledge in the curriculum to the wider oceans and rains of knowledge that renew or trouble it, you're liable to flood or drought.
>
> Such a thing needs leadership.

Counsell has introduced a lot of people to the interplay between the concepts of the 'core and the hinterland':[4]

> This pair of powerful words has proved **the** most important thing to help me think about subject difference within curricula. The trick here is to handle paradox. Even though clearly, as the word suggests, 'hinterland' is just a supporter or feeder of a core, when it comes to curriculum, the hinterland is as ***important*** as what is deemed core.
>
> The core is like a residue – the things that stay, the things that can be captured as proposition. Often, such things need to be committed to memory. But if, in certain subjects, for the purposes of teaching, we reduce it to those propositions, we may make it harder to teach, and at worst, we kill it. The term 'hinterland' is as fertile in curricular thinking as its literal meaning. It's not clutter … It helps us distinguish between a vital property that makes curriculum work as narrative and merely 'engaging activities' which can distract and make pupils think about (and therefore remember) all the wrong things.

Whether we are discussing this historical context for scientific discoveries and texts in literature, or the personal life stories of authors and scientists, or the etymology of technical terms, or a current affairs issue related to key concepts in economics or geography, or parallel historical developments that took place in a country other than the one we are studying, hinterland is a hugely powerful and practical concept to help teachers give value to this essential layer of curriculum without worrying unduly that it has been somehow 'left out'.

Another influential voice is Mary Myatt through her regular conference output and her popular book *The Curriculum: From Gallimaufry to Coherence*. She provides a series of key concepts for teachers and leaders to think about when planning a curriculum, moving away from an ad hoc assembly of disparate topics with tenuous links between them and moving toward something much more integrated, connected and coherent:

> **All our children ought to be able to tell us what they are learning about and why it is important. If they can't, we haven't taught them properly … If we can see where this links to the wider picture, we can often make other connections which make sense and are often enjoyable … When the curriculum lacks coherence, it is both harder to teach and harder for children to locate and place their new knowledge.[5]**

Of course, it has to be acknowledged that, whilst many schools have been developing their curriculum thinking at a deep level for many years – examples in the *Fieldbook* include Turton (p. 24), Saffron Walden (p. 18) and School 21 (p. 164) – a shift in emphasis by the English schools inspectorate, Ofsted, has catalysed a lot more activity. They have built their framework around three pillars:

- Intent: the planned content of the curriculum
- Implementation: the enacted curriculum in the real lessons children experience
- Impact: what children ultimately end up learning

Wales and Scotland have had their own curriculum review agendas for some time (as discussed in *The Learning Rainforest*) and now these 'three Is' have

1. Robinson, M. (2013)   3. www.bit.ly/2ksz5Bo   5. Myatt, M. (2018)
2. Robinson, M (2019)   4. www.bit.ly/2KEr2eW

entered the discourse in England. As ever, there is some confusion as people fall into the vortex of reductive accountability-driven Plantation Thinking – and while I remain utterly sceptical that an inspectorate can evaluate a school curriculum on one two-day visit with any degree of validity or reliability, at least Ofsted has got people talking about curriculum away from the arena of examination outcomes and that has to be applauded.

My most recent contribution to work on curriculum (beyond the relevant chapter in *The Learning Rainforest*) has been promoting the idea of a knowledge-rich curriculum through a series of blog posts.[6] In a particularly popular one I suggested that 'knowledge-rich' has four components:

Knowledge provides a driving, underpinning philosophy. The *grammar* of each subject is given high status; the specifics of what we want students to learn matter and the traditions of subject disciplines are respected. Skills and understanding are seen as forms of knowledge and it is understood that there are no real generic skills that can be taught outside of specific knowledge domains. Acquiring powerful knowledge is seen as an end itself; there is a belief that we are all empowered through knowing things and that this cannot be left to chance. There is also a sense that the creative, 'rounded and grounded' citizens we all want to develop – with a host of strong character traits – will emerge through being immersed in a knowledge-rich curriculum.

The knowledge content is specified in detail. Units of work are supported by statements that detail the knowledge to be learned – something that can be written down. We do not merely want to 'do the Romans'; we want children to gain some specified knowledge of the Romans as well as a broad overview. We want children to know specific things about plants and about the Amazon rainforest, World War II, *Romeo and Juliet* and climate change. We want children to have more than a general sense of things through vaguely remembered *knowledge encounters*; in addition to a range

of experiences from which important tacit knowledge is gained, we want them to amass a specific body of declarative and procedural knowledge that is planned. This runs through every phase of school: units of work are not defined by headings but by details: for example, beyond 'environmental impact of fossil fuels', the specific impacts are detailed; beyond 'changes to transport in Victorian Britain', specific changes are listed.

Knowledge is taught to be remembered, not merely encountered.
A good knowledge-rich curriculum embraces learning from cognitive science about memory, forgetting and the power of retrieval practice. Our curriculum is not simply a set of encounters from which children form ad hoc memories; it is designed to be remembered in detail, to be stored in our students' long-term memories so that they can later build on it forming ever-wider and -deeper schema. In addition to memorable experiences, this requires approaches to curriculum planning and delivery that build in spaced retrieval practice, formative low-stakes testing and plenty of repeated practice for automaticity and fluency.

Knowledge is sequenced and mapped deliberately and coherently.
Beyond the knowledge specified for each unit, a knowledge-rich curriculum is planned vertically and horizontally giving thought to the optimum knowledge sequence for building secure schema – a kinetic model for materials; a timeline for historical events; a sense of the canon in literature; a sense of place; a framework for understanding cultural diversity and human development and evolution. Attention is also given to known misconceptions and there is an understanding of the instructional tools needed to move students from novice to expert in various subject domains.

Some people react against this on the basis that 'knowledge-rich' is reductive – it's all about rote-learning and 'regurgitating facts' – but, to me, that is a wilful misreading of the idea. Every commentator who promotes this idea is also promoting a much deeper, ambitious notion of knowledge – a curriculum that is rich in experience, 'human-scaled',[7] designed to foster rounded, humane, principled 'philosopher kids'[8] or 'Twenty-first century renaissance scholars'.[9] As Robinson says: 'A curriculum cannot be said to

be knowledge-rich if it doesn't help children to know, respond to and learn about their emotional selves, as well as learn to use their emotions and their will constructively to broaden and deepen their experience of life.'[10]

If we blend these ideas together – head, hand and heart; human-scaled, hinterland, coherence, knowledge-rich – avoiding the reductive outcomes-focused tendencies inherent in Martin Robinson's 'machine', it feels like a strong conceptual platform from which to construct an excellent curriculum. The challenge of making all the choices in the detail of each subject remains and no two schools make the same decisions. Several of the *Fieldbook* entries make reference to the journeys they have been on in this area.

My go-to sources of inspiration are the blogs by the following people:

- Summer Turner – 'Pub quiz or published? What are the aims of a knowledge-rich curriculum?' – www.bit.ly/2IOgRdC
- Peter Hyman – 'What is a big education? Building a curriculum of head, heart and hand' – www.bit.ly/2IKAtPU
- Jon Brunskill – 'I'm bringing knowledge back' – www.bit.ly/2kGtKGq – worth reading along with his school's website info on curriculum – www.bit.ly/2IGK4at
- Rosalind Walker – 'My #rEDBrum talk: The Nature of School Science Knowledge' – www.bit.ly/2maKRRh
- Mark Enser – 'Knowledge in the classroom' – www.bit.ly/2kH1eoj
- Adam Boxer – 'Thinking curriculum: the one-stop shop' – www.bit.ly/2mbGMfH
- Rebecca Foster and Claire Hill – 'On our #rEDDurrington presentation: Practical approaches to bringing research-informed practice to the classroom, the department and whole school' – www.bit.ly/2kbHbOW
- Michael Fordham – 'Knowledge and curriculum' – www.bit.ly/2IJJSqY
- Clare Sealy – 'Memory not memories – teaching for long term learning' – www.bit.ly/2IHSZIT

6. www.bit.ly/2INHuja
7. Robinson, M. (2019)
8. Robinson, M. (2013)
9. Massey, R. (2019)
10. Robinson, M. (2019)

Assessment culture is shifting

In parallel with the discourse on curriculum, there has been a slow but definite shift in thinking about assessment in the schools that I have engaged with. The 'paradigm shift' that I allude to in *The Learning Rainforest* is definitely beginning to happen with more schools recognising the importance of authentic formative assessment, at the scale and frequency that supports the teaching and learning process, relative to the less important role of formal summative assessment and data tracking. There is still a long way to go but I'm sure that progress is being made in the right direction. *Fieldbook* case studies such as those from The Rise (p. 118) and London Academy (p. 124) provide details of how assessment thinking is moving forward.

Once again the inspectorate has been helpful in this area, downplaying the value of internal assessment data as a means of judging relative standards – given all the variables at play between subjects and between schools. Increasingly schools are reducing the number of occasions in a school year when teachers are required to log assessment information on centralised tracking systems. There seems to be a growing – and very healthy – scepticism around the use of elaborate flight-path systems and statement bank trackers (although far too many are in use for my liking!).

Not much has changed – or is likely to change – regarding the national frameworks for assessment and schools which are still very much geared towards maximising final outcome measures with some perverse outcomes. In England, this has had negative consequences for the take-up of arts subjects, for example, and the study of languages is similarly in decline.

One of my favourite insights in the last two years has been around the approach needed when sub-groups of a cohort are seen to be underachieving relative to the rest. Inspired by an idea from blogger and physics teacher Ruth Walker,[11] I have come to the firm conclusion that where, say, 'White boys on free school meals' or 'Bangladeshi girls' appear to be under-performing, this will not be due to some

niche characteristics of those students; it will be due to some underlying weakness in the general teaching that they are experiencing and, perhaps, being more strongly affected by. The solution to meeting their needs is not to tailor teaching more to meet their specific needs – as if they are different to everyone else's; the solution is to try to address the general weaknesses, to improve the quality of general teaching so that everyone is learning more effectively. 'Everyone' means 'everyone' – including the sub-groups. Trying to teach everyone better is just a far better bet than endlessly chasing niche needs which, even if they exist, are very hard to identify and will vary from one student to another.

Evidence-informed teaching is on the rise

One of the trends I continue to see across the system, in the UK and in international schools, is the growing interest amongst teachers in the research evidence for effective teaching. The researchED movement continues to grow; the Chartered College of Teaching is now publishing a regular *Impact* magazine highlighting current research; and, via social media, it seems that there is more discourse between academics and teachers than ever.

At the same time, I am continually fascinated to find pockets of teachers who have never read any of the research – at least not since their training many years ago. Of course, many teachers function quite happily without directly consuming research findings; it's not a prerequisite for being an effective practitioner. But, with that said, in my consultancy work I regularly encounter students who are struggling with learning where, without any question, their teachers would do well to engage more with some of the elements of what I'd call 'evidence-informed teaching'.

'Evidence-informed wisdom' in the spirit of the Learning Rainforest is not a free-for-all. It's firmly my view, more than ever, that we'd be a much more highly performing profession if teachers in general were more deeply engaged with research and acted on it. Too many teachers still do things that, quite simply, are not effective enough to justify, whilst others could be much more effective by focusing more tightly on instructional methods that are better bets in terms of securing learning, rather than merely giving the teacher the feeling of having 'covered' the material or of having created short-term engagement.

My most-read blog post in the last two years has been 'The five forms of feedback I give to teachers most often'. Very briefly, the five areas can be summarised as follows:

- Behaviour: Be more assertive; establish what you want to establish – following the work of Bill Rogers.

- Questioning: Ask more students more questions; involve everyone – invoking the ideas of Barak Rosenshine.

- Marking and Feedback: Make all marking an instruction for action – avoiding the pitfall of thinking 'marking' automatically provides feedback that students both understand and respond to and seeking to make the process more work for the student than the teacher.

- Knowledge and Recall: Specify what students should know; check that they do; give time for practice. Again these are key elements of Rosenshine's principles of instruction.

- Setting the standards: Define excellence for any task – following ideas from Ron Berger[12] or Daisy Christodoulou.[13] The need to exemplify the target standards for any learning process is supremely important.

Research new and old

Rosenshine's Principles of Instruction

In *The Learning Rainforest* I tried to capture a massive array of educational research into a single chapter. Of course, this was little more than a selective round-up of the key ideas that I had found useful at that point in time. Since then, as many readers will be aware, I have been an enthusiastic champion of the work of Barak Rosenshine and his popular 'Principles of Instruction',[14] leading to the publication of my short booklet *Rosenshine's Principles in Action*.[15] This has proved to be something of a hit with several schools buying a copy for every member of staff.

The reason for my enthusiasm (and the booklet's popularity) is that Rosenshine's principles provided a strong evidence-informed framework for improving the quality of instruction in a format that teachers can relate to;

11. Walker, R. www.bit.ly/2kbyrYF   13. Christodoulou, D. (2017)
12. Berger, R. (2003)

it cuts through any of the defences and walls of inertia that typically impede the flow of ideas from research to the classroom.

Rosenshine concludes his paper by discussing the research process, combining a range of sources of evidence. He suggests:

> Even though these principles come from ... different sources ... ideas from each of the sources overlap and add to each other. This overlap gives us faith that we are developing a valid and research-based understanding of the art of teaching.

In my presentation of the principles, I have found it useful to explore the ten ideas via four overlapping strands. This seems to make it even easier for teachers to engage with the concepts. The 10 principles are grouped as follows:

Sequencing concepts and modelling

2. Present new material using small steps.
4. Provide models.
8. Provide scaffolds for difficult tasks.

Questioning

3. Ask questions.
6. Check for student understanding.

Reviewing material

1. Daily review.
10. Weekly and monthly review.

Stages of practice

5. Guide student practice.
7. Obtain a high success rate.
9. Independent practice.

It has certainly been my experience that these principles address many of the issues that I identify in my work with teachers – all except issues around

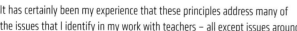

14. Rosenshine, B. (2012)
15. Sherrington, T. (2019)
16. Shimamura, A. (2018)
17. Willingham, D. (2009)

behaviour management and giving feedback – so I'm not surprised that so many schools are opting to base a lot of their professional development work around Rosenshine's research summary and recommendations for teacher actions. The thing that amuses me – and frustrates me just a little – is when some teachers protest that the principles are 'nothing new' or dismiss them as merely 'common sense'. This is absolutely inevitable given that the principles' origin lies in observations of what effective teachers typically do. To an effective teacher, they will seem obvious – obviously enough! And why good ideas need to be 'new' in order to justify being promoted with enthusiasm is beyond me. The best ideas stand the test of time, and given how long humans have been teaching each other, it would be surprising if the elements of effective instruction were actually 'new'!

Shimamura's *MARGE*

My favourite text from the last two years is a short, free e-book[16] published by Arthur Shimamura, a professor of psychology specialising in memory and cognition. It's written from a university lecturer's perspective but it has a great deal to offer classroom teachers in schools. The ideas are expressed through the neat acronym MARGE, a jokey reference to Marge Simpson. I found it a fascinating read, combining some interesting background neuroscience with the more practical cognitive science, and I find I refer to it in much of my work.

MARGE means: Motivate, Attend, Relate, Generate, Evaluate. Each element provides something useful for teachers and students to consider. As a whole it represents a model for how our brain works as we learn.

Motivate: We need to use energy to keep focused on the learning process and so our brains need to be motivated to do so. Motivation here can come from the learning itself. For example, by framing learning as a big question, we generate curiosity; we want to find out what happens or why things happened. We need to keep the big picture framework of what we're learning very prominent so students can organise their thoughts efficiently in a schema that facilitates further learning and retrieval.

Shimamura suggests that the 'aesthetic question' is powerful for motivating learning; 'What do you think? How does it make you feel? Why is it good?' As he explains: 'The aesthetic question engages emotional brain circuits and forces us to attend to and organize our knowledge.'

Shimamura also promotes the use of story-telling, much as Willingham does.[17] Stories have a range of motivational elements built in; they keep us hooked and they help us remember.

Attend: Academic learning is what Shimamura calls a 'top-down' activity whereby we have to consciously *attend* to the information needed to build our schema from all the stimuli we're exposed to. Ideally students will consciously attend to the learning goals at hand and will consciously make connections – but it's all too easy for minds to wander.

The suggestions here are to capture attention very early on, then to break up learning episodes and to deliberately refocus attention at various key points. He introduces the idea of the three Cs – categorize, compare

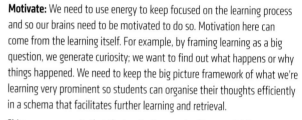

M

A

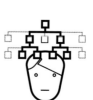

R

G

THINK IT SAY IT TEACH IT

E

and contrast – within the context of a big-picture question to help students sustain their attention on their learning goals. I like the idea that sometimes an instructor needs to act as their students' prefrontal cortex, conducting their thinking, encouraging their top-down processing.

Relate: This section is packed with ideas supported by biological insights about how we store and connect information through *memory consolidation*. The practical strategies include deploying elaborative-interrogative questioning – asking how and why – using mental images, analogies, constructing concept maps as schematic representations of sets of connected ideas and training students to make notes organised in hierarchical structures.

Generate: I found this section a superb addition to my understanding of retrieval practice. Shimamura suggests: 'Think it, say it, teach it! These are the simplest things to do to improve your memory.' He details multiple ways in which our memories are strengthened when we generate information from our memory. If we tell someone what we've learned we can improve our memory by 30–50%. This is all explained in terms of various brain functions and reinforces the widely known retrieval practice concept. However, Shimamura suggests it's important not to just restate information you've learned; you need to say it in your own words. This is the active self-generate effect. In common with others, he emphasises the implications for effective revision: 'For the most part, '"study" time should mostly be "test" (i.e., retrieval practice) time.'

Evaluate: The final element of MARGE is that we need to monitor our learning as it happens. There's an excellent exploration of the problem of the illusion of knowing when we are familiar with information even when we cannot fully recollect it. We can stop trying to learn more if we kid ourselves into thinking we already know it. This has implications for how students should be taught to check their understanding – using spaced, interleaved retrieval practice, with a gap after the initial learning, using any number of

self-testing techniques and (linking back to Generate) generating information by explaining our learning to others as a form of self-test.

Metacognition over mindsets

One of the areas that has seen a significant degree of exploration and re-thinking in the last two years has been in the territory of student motivation and the process of developing students' capacity for independent learning. I would characterise the current trend by suggesting that confidence in the fixed/growth mindset concept is waning whereas ideas about metacognition and self-regulation are on the rise. In part this is based on the findings from implementation studies such as those conducted by the Education Endowment Foundation.

The 2019 EEF report *Changing Mindsets*,[18] an effectiveness report on an extensive study into growth mindset training involving students and teachers in separate trials, found no significant impact – albeit with some positive effects that fell below the threshold for significance. This supports the view that the growth mindset concept, whilst plausibly evidenced in a controlled-study environment, is difficult to transfer into a school context where there are so many variables at play. I've heard Dylan Wiliam argue that, whilst effects are low, the costs of interventions are also very low so there is some value in them. But it seems that faith in transforming learner outcomes via grown mindset training is largely misplaced.

By contrast, the EEF's 2018 guidance report on metacognition and self-awareness,[19] based on a wide review of the literature and research, suggests that the potential impact is much stronger, with interventions yielding very significant gains. The report makes seven key recommendations:

Teachers should:

1. Acquire the professional understanding and skills to develop their pupils' metacognitive knowledge.
2. Explicitly teach pupils metacognitive strategies, including how to plan, monitor, and evaluate their learning.
3. Model their own thinking to help pupils develop their metacognitive and cognitive skills.

4. Set an appropriate level of challenge to develop pupils' self-regulation and metacognition.
5. Promote and develop metacognitive talk in the classroom.
6. Explicitly teach pupils how to organise, and effectively manage, their learning independently.

Schools should:

7. Support teachers to develop their knowledge of these approaches and expect them to be applied appropriately.

One reason I believe that metacognition is a better bet is that the suggested interventions are more obviously located in the curriculum, whereas growth mindset strategies are often delivered in a generic fashion away from the subject contexts where students actually experience the learning challenges. Too often, mindset interventions focus more on feeling better about failing than on engineering success – precisely the pitfall Carol Dweck was keen to avoid. There is something of a lag between school-level behaviours and the research but I'm sure we'll see a lot more focus on metacognition in the next few years.

Conclusion

It is apparent from these fieldnotes that within the two years since *The Learning Rainforest* was published, a great deal has emerged to report on! Ideas about curriculum, assessment and evidence-informed teaching are continually evolving. There is always more research and new ways of communicating old research. Attitudes shift; the consensus shifts as important debates rage on. This is life in the Learning Rainforest. It's dynamic! This is the context that all the case-study schools work in. Some are in a position to be more on the front foot, leading the change and providing models or what is possible; others have to be more responsive, given their circumstances, doing their best to adapt as the environment shifts around them.

I'm now handing over the *Fieldbook* to the schools to tell their own stories from their corners of the Learning Rainforest. I hope you find them as interesting, useful and inspiring as I do.

THE 30 FIELDBOOK SCHOOLS: MAP AND PAGE GUIDE

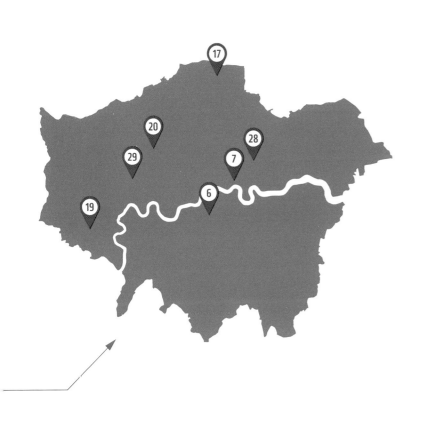

SAFFRON WALDEN COUNTY HIGH SCHOOL, ESSEX

INTRODUCTION

I decided early on that Saffron Walden County High School should go first in the *Fieldbook* to acknowledge that it was Executive Head, Caroline Derbyshire's original idea to produce a book of Learning Rainforest case-studies. Having read the book, Caroline invited me to her school to meet her team and I had the privilege of spending a day there, observing lessons and talking to staff. I think I saw 20 lessons that day and they were all superb. I wrote a blog post[1] about it: 'Saffron Walden County High School: An exemplary school. The Learning Rainforest made real.' This is what I wrote in the concluding paragraph:

> I hope the details shared here go some way to illustrate the Learning Rainforest: superb conditions, deep knowledge, exciting possibilities. Culture and systems. Rigour. Teaching to the top. Teaching for memory and recall. And Joy, Awe and Wonder in plentiful supply. SWCHS is a truly wonderful school that many could learn from.

However, this wasn't the first time that SWCHS had inspired a blog post. One of my very early posts, Making Feedback Count: 'Close the Gap'[2] back in 2012, was inspired by a visit I made when I was Head of another Essex school, King Edward VI Grammar School (KEGS) in Chelmsford. I had the opportunity to observe a staff training session after school that focused on a school-wide feedback process called 'close the gap' marking. I was immediately struck by the way a common idea – about structuring feedback so that students could take concrete improvement steps – could be developed and interpreted in so many ways In different subject areas. This wasn't a school where ideas were imposed on teachers in a rigid manner. This was

1. www.bit.ly/2kiPTuw
2. www.bit.ly/2m62xxg

'rainforest' thinking – introducing evidence-informed ideas but allowing them to take form in organic ways.

The person running that session was Polly Lankester who is now Associate Headteacher working alongside Caroline. As you will see from this case-study, SWCHS has developed into a superb, self-confident school. It wasn't always quite as successful or as confident as it is now but through relentlessly pushing their ambitious agenda for professional learning and commitment to curriculum breadth, they've reached a fabulous position where anything seems possible. That's where I wanted to start in this book – with a school that embodies a sense of what is possible in a school, providing a fabulous education for students and serving the wider community in a significant way.

How very fortunate Saffron Walden is to have such a wonderful school at its heart.
PARENT 2019

PROFILE

Location: Saffron Walden, Essex, UK

Type of Institution: Mixed Comprehensive and Academy

Roll/Age Range: 2200, aged 11–18

Year Founded: 1955 Opened by RA Butler

Motto: 'A Local School of Exceptional Quality'

Recent/Current School Production: *The Wizard of Oz, The 39 Steps, A Midsummer Night's Dream, The Glass Knight (Opera)*

Recent significant sports event/triumph: Boys won the 'Natwest' National Bowl for U15 rugby 2018.
U16 Essex cup rugby finalist 2019
U14 Essex Cup finalist 2018
Jack Stanton Stock is number 1 ranked in GB for U21 Triathlon
This year (2018/19) the U18 girls won the East Finals for Hockey to become Regional Champions
U14 girls came seventh at the National Finals in Netball in 2017 and an individual, Scarlett Hughes, who managed to get to the Futures Cup Team (England) for hockey and who plays for Loughborough Lightning for cricket & Essex Ladies.

Notable quirks/alumni: Saffron Hall – an international Concert Hall that doubles as the school hall
Saffron Screen – a cinema that shares the site
A school farm
A Sixth Form of 650
Platinum Artsmark
Coach Mark Gold
Ben Maher – Olympic Showjumper
Ailie Macadam – Engineer – 'Is this Britain's most successful female engineer?' (*Telegraph* 2017)
Joanna Nadin – Novelist (including some best sellers for children)
George Peasgood – Paralympic triathlete
Anna Greenland – Horticulturalist
Hannah Walker – Poet and playwright
James Gant – Actor (A great singer: performances in West End musicals such as *Les Misérables*)
Konrad Feldman – CEO

PROFILE

Caroline Derbyshire
Executive Headteacher and CEO
With contributions from Polly Lankester, Associate Headteacher, and Catherine Davis, Deputy Headteacher.

Saffron Walden County High – a large Learning Rainforest, buzzing with life

Saffron Walden County High School is a large, influential and oversubscribed 11–18 comprehensive in the north of Essex. There are 650 students in its Sixth Form. Its mission, which has not changed in three decades, is to be 'a local school of exceptional quality' and Ofsted, The Good Schools Guide and parents in the town recognise this to be the case. Its objective is to provide children with the academic and cultural capital that enables them to compete at the highest level with students from selective or independent schools. In the language of rainforests it is like the Amazon, providing the lungs for the argument that state schools can and should be first-rate. At Saffron Walden County High the conditions for learning (the roots of the trees in the rainforest) are really quite formal ones. Students wear a formal uniform and the school maintains the highest expectations of student behaviour. There are equally high expectations regarding the professional behaviours of staff including a requirement that colleagues are research-engaged and take responsibility for their own professional learning. Three senior leaders at the school are Fellows of the Chartered College of Teaching, many are SLEs for example. Academic rigour, at a subject level, is fostered and encouraged through strong subject area identities

and staff are actively encouraged to share their passion for their subject through collaborative pedagogical and scheme of work development. Subject teams all have their own workrooms with administrative support to further reinforce the significance of their distinct domains.

The trunk and branches of the SWCHS experience is the richness and specific nature of subject delivery. Our middle leaders lead the developments in their own curriculum areas. Our emphasis is not only on the acquisition of knowledge, although that is important to teachers, it is about a student's relationship to their subject and the skills of critical analysis and imaginative application that can be acquired when knowledge is rich. It would be unhelpful to characterise SWCHS as either a traditional or progressive school. It does not conform to these stereotypes.

This respect for subject domain is best illustrated by our system of assessment which evolved out of discussions around best practice in different subject areas.[3]

The canopy of the school is how it explores ideas in education. SWCHS is deeply committed to educational research and understanding what works, by partnering with the Institute of Education in London and The Faculty of Education in Cambridge. Themes for subject-based CPD in the school, like metacognition, are explored in the way it makes sense for each subject team. The school shares its practice at a MAT level, a leadership level and through its Teaching School Alliance.

We see children flourish and teachers grow and develop. They are not stifled by unhelpful structures or limited exam-driven ambitions nor left to flounder without them.

---

3. Tom Sherrington has already written an excellent blog post on this subject, www.bit.ly/2kHxfNO

STUDENT: TIMOTHY LANE

Age and Year Group: 15, Year 11

Most recent:

School Trip: China Tour – Shanghai, Xi'an and Beijing

Extra-curricular activity: Performance of a solo and ensemble Classical Guitar piece in our Music Festival in Saffron Hall, with a professional Classical Guitarist giving personalised feedback on performances.

Science experiment: An experiment to judge which of the alcohol homologous group have the most energy in per gram, by judging the masses burnt of four different alcohols to heat $100cm^3$ of water by 20 degrees.

Book/Play studied in English: *Frankenstein* (1818 Edition) by Mary Shelley

Learning:

Subjects Studied: Triple Science, Maths, Further Maths, English, Religious Philosophy and Ethics, Geography, Music, Computer Science and German

Recent learning highlight: Recently in Geography, we had a lesson where we investigated the investment into transport infrastructure in the UK. It was fascinating discovering the supposed benefits these planned multi-billion-pound projects would bring to the UK, alongside the downsides. Subsequently we had a debate, asking whether they were worth the money or if it was better spent elsewhere.

The most stand-out/interesting/challenging topic you've studied at school: For me personally, the stand-out topic in my time at school was the motion and forces topic in Physics. I took enjoyment and interest in this as it was a real click moment where things in the world just made sense. Natural phenomenon turned from 'that just happens,' to an understanding of why. This blew me away.

One of my favourite teachers: I enjoy lessons with Miss Routledge who teaches me Maths because she has the ability to engage all in the class in whatever we do, often branching out teaching so it's as personalised as possible, giving an alternate way to face a problem. This is often achieved by allowing us to figure things out first, in our own way or as a class, rather than just being talked at for an hour. Crucially however, we all have a good laugh and I think that's the most important quality a teacher can have. A teacher who engages with and respects their pupils as young adults will be treated with respect back and be engaged with equally. These interpersonal skills are what set apart the best teachers and I am proud to say this is a common trait in many of my teachers.

A favourite feature of the school: My favourite feature of the County High is the community of committed and inspiring teachers, aspirational and diligent students, alongside the team of support staff who all work together to help and benefit one another. Aiding academic achievement but arguably more importantly creating and inspiring the future generations of young adults. After all, a school without the people within is merely bricks and mortar.

STUDENT: FLORENCE WOLTER

Age and Year Group: 15, Year 10

Most recent:

School Trip: China Trip 2018
Extra-curricular activity: Bar Mock Trial national finals
Science experiment: Testing the pH of solutions with a variety of indicators.
Book/Play studied in English: *Macbeth,* William Shakespeare
History Topic: Conflict and Tension 1945–1972 (Cold War)

Learning:

Subjects Studied: History, Geography, French, PE
Recent learning highlight: Half-life and radioactive decay being a complicated concept to grasp, my Physics teacher recently modelled it for us with the use of Jaffa cakes which we repeatedly ate half of between time periods each half as long as the previous. Exponential decay of unstable atoms? Easy – Jaffa cakes!
The most stand-out/interesting/challenging topic you've studied at school: My last history topic was democracy and dictatorship in Germany 1890–1945. This fascinated me because I had never really appreciated how fragile and potentially transient democracy and peace can be. Studying the decline of an initially progressive, liberal society in to dictatorship and war gave me a new perspective on society and an appreciation for what I have, for which I am grateful.
One of my favourite teachers: One of my favourite teachers is Miss Bunting who teaches me English because I walk into her classroom excited. Lessons with her always push me further than I thought I could go, make me think in new ways. She is a good teacher because we learn the subject. She is a great teacher because we love it.
A favourite feature of the school: Something I love about SWCHS is the array of opportunities to get involved in. Whether developing a newfound interest in law through the Bar Mock Trial team, confronting apprehension in the English Speaking Union, or realising passion in one of the many sports or music clubs, there is always another experience to find and embrace. There is always more.

It was really rewarding to study something that was so current and have our lessons reflect the evolving landscape of the real world, not just that of the textbook.

OLIVER (OLLIE) ROWLEY

Lessons with her always push me further than I thought I could go, make me think in new ways.

FLORENCE WOLTER

It was a real click moment where things in the world just made sense.

TIMOTHY LANE

STUDENT: OLIVER (OLLIE) ROWLEY

Age and Year Group: 18, Year 13

Most recent:

School Trip: Berlin Trip/ Chicago exchange
Extra-curricular activity: Bar Mock Trial
Science experiment: Methane bubbles (Year 11)
Book/Play studied in English: *The Bloody Chamber* & *Twelfth Night*
History Topic: Tsarist and Communist Russia

Learning:

Subjects Studied: History, English Literature, Government & Politics, and German
Recent learning highlight: As part of our politics course, we did a case study on the 2018 Congressional midterms, which had happened only a few days before. It was really rewarding to study something that was so current and have our lessons reflect the evolving landscape of the real world, not just that of the textbook, encouraging us to conduct our own research into similar midterms and elections.
The most stand-out/interesting/challenging topic you've studied at school: I enjoyed studying German culture and festivals as part of the German course because it emphasised the language department's insistence on learning about the culture of the languages we study as well as just the language itself. In learning about German festivals, food, music, and so on, the German teachers have encouraged me and others to explore the potential of studying, working, or even living abroad post-education.
One of my favourite teachers: I enjoy lessons with Mrs Smith, who teaches me English literature, because she has been the most formative teacher in my development since I started at the Sixth Form. She's the most enthusiastic teacher that I've been taught by, and she knows her students on a personal level as well, making sure that if someone in a lesson is struggling or doesn't seem as engaged as usual, she does everything she can to help.
A favourite feature of the school: The school, and especially the teachers, encourage everyone to join extra-curricular activities, whether they be sporting or intellectual ones. These usually bring together the different year groups, with the most senior students in the school helping the younger years with the more developed and challenging tasks and work.

CASE STUDY: SUBJECT PASSION, INSPIRING OPPORTUNITIES AND TRUSTED SUBJECT LEADERSHIP

General Area: Curriculum
Authors: Caroline Derbyshire and **Polly Lankester**

At the heart of the SWCHS experience (the trunk and branches of our part of the rainforest) is the richness and specific nature of curriculum delivery. The school employs highly qualified graduate teachers with a passion for their subject who can share that passion through excellent subject teaching, and engage and inspire their students through their wealth of knowledge. A powerful and impactful curriculum depends on excellent subject specialist teachers, more than any other factor, and so we place emphasis on the recruitment, training, well-being, and retention of staff.

Vital to the quality of our curriculum planning and delivery is the deep trust shown to subject experts. Our whole school policies for teaching and learning establish principles but give departments the autonomy and flexibility to operate in ways that work best for them, respecting what Christine Counsell calls, the 'grammar of their subject'. Our middle leaders direct the developments in their own curriculum areas both in terms of the curriculum itself and how it ensures progression but also in terms of the subject specific pedagogy.

The school's curriculum offer is broad (four languages choices are available and Latin is one of them) and shows the value placed on all areas of learning. The curriculum decisions and the quality of provision at Key Stage 3 is reflected in students' option choices as they move up to GCSE. We offer Triple Science as a core subject and four options at GCSE, with ten or eleven subjects studied in total. This allows students to keep a rich and balanced curriculum throughout their Key Stage 4. The impact of this is that, whilst all EBACC subjects have high rates of entry, so do Art, Music, Drama, Dance, PE, Graphics, Textiles, Product Design, Business, Health and Social Care, and ICT. All areas of learning thrive and are valued. This is a school where over 90% choose at least

one Humanities subject and over 70% one or more Languages, without compulsion, but also one where GCSE Music can still run multiple groups in each year. We believe choice supports engagement and success, as long as this choice is underpinned by excellent information and CEIAG for both parents and students so that all involved are supported to understand the importance and impact of their choices.

This rich curriculum offer continues post-16. There is an impressive list of 45 subject choices at A Level and we are able to support minority subjects like Latin, Philosophy, Photography and Environmental Science alongside the very large numbers following facilitating subjects such as Maths, Physics, and English Literature.

Students make excellent progress and achieve exam success at SWCHS, but we do not see the curriculum as being synonymous with syllabuses; subject enrichment is built into the offer to students...teachers teach beyond the syllabus and teach to the top.

Our extra-curricular offer is also broad and the school makes no excuses for exposing young people to the very best creations that Western culture has produced. Saffron Hall is a living symbol of how this philosophy sits at the heart of the school. Built five years ago, this now internationally renowned concert hall is also the school hall. All students in the school get the opportunity to work with professional dancers, classical and jazz musicians and to attend concerts featuring the likes of Courtney Pine, Nicola Benedetti, and The London Symphony Orchestra. The school believes in building the cultural capital of all of its learners. This is exemplified by a recent visit of the Brooklyn-based group So Percussion who performed two excellent and challenging concerts to all of our Year 9 students, introducing them to a range of styles and composers. So Percussion then worked with a smaller group to compose a new piece of music that the students helped to perform in a public concert. Another example of

the quality of our extra-curricular provision would be the collaboration between the school and Saffron Hall on a newly commissioned opera *The Glass Knight*. Students performed on stage and playing in the pit, taking leading roles, alongside professionals. These kinds of projects led to our Platinum Artsmark status. However, it is not just the arts that have these rich opportunities: our staff lead fantastic extra-curricular opportunities for students in all subject areas as well as running the Duke of Edinburgh Award scheme. We want our extra-curricular provision to be open to all, as well as nurturing particular talents; our recent dance show saw over 200 students performing, whereas a Brass instrument Masterclass was for a select group of our top instrumentalists.

Our trips and visits programme is also ambitious and broad. There is a rich offer of trips within Europe as well as opportunities to travel further afield, including an exchange visit to China and a field trip to Zanzibar. We raise funds to try to ensure that the cost of these visits is not a barrier to participation.

We want joy, awe and wonder and exciting possibilities for all our students both in and outside of the classroom.

Link to Learning Rainforest:

- Self-sustaining through growing and nurturing leadership
- Respecting diversity of subject specific approaches and academic thinking
- Assessment that springs organically from the subject
- High Expectations
- Strong and trusted, autonomous Middle and Senior leadership
- Rich cultural breadth and depth

The school makes no excuses for exposing young people to the very best creations that Western culture has produced.

CAROLINE DERBYSHIRE AND POLLY LANKESTER

CASE STUDY: GROWING A CULTURE OF TEACHING AND LEARNING

General Area: Teaching and Learning
Author: Catherine Davis

In order for a tree to flourish, it relies on the vast network of conduits within itself to transport water and nutrients from the roots to the leaves. A school must also have strong networks to ensure the 'nutrients' needed to help teaching and learning flourish are successfully conducted through every aspect of the organisation.

At Saffron Walden County High School, the first of those networks is our 'Teaching and Learning Excellence' programme. Established 10 years ago as a way of articulating a shared vision of excellence, and, as the name for a whole-school CPD programme, 'TLE' has, like an organic structure, grown and evolved over the years. We have created shared principles around what great teaching and learning looks like. We have then used different models (such as lesson study) to explore those principles in the classroom. Some years we have worked in cross-subject teams; in others, we have allowed subject teams to personalise the CPD they want to explore. When the need has arisen, there have been years when we have coalesced around a specific theme – for instance, assessment for learning. In other years, we have allowed teachers the freedom to be responsive to the learners in front of them and use this to determine what they want to explore. This year, our theme is metacognition and the science of learning and we are working in subject teams to encourage staff to consider this theme through a subject-specific lens, thus strengthening teachers' knowledge of the 'grammar' of their subject.

Although our vision for Teaching and Learning Excellence has remained the same, we have also adapted to the changing educational landscape around us, particularly in seeking to make our staff more research-informed. Long gone are the days of our 'Research and Development Group' – a small, keen band of teachers cloistered in a classroom, working in isolation. Now, all teachers are required to be outward-facing, drawing on evidence-informed practice, engaging with the wider educational world and approaching their own CPD in a more robust and rigorous way. Our job as a school has been to make this shift happen. A couple of years ago, we commissioned the Institute of Education, University College London, to work alongside twenty 'CPD Champions' in the school to provide them with high-quality training on how to lead evidence-informed CPD to others. Alongside this, we commissioned a second project with the IOE called 'How do we know it works?' designed to support our middle leaders in ensuring the systems and strategies they implement in school are rooted in evidence and robustly evaluated. Alongside projects such as these, our teachers have worked with universities such as Cambridge and Oslo and even been published in the Chartered College of Teaching *Impact* journal.

Our approach to CPD is also personalised. Our 'Pick and Mix' programme gives staff the time they need to tailor their own professional development – whether that be in pursuing a further professional qualification such as a Masters, attending subject-specific training courses or networks, becoming an examiner, or taking part in CPD to support wellbeing. One aspect of this personalised programme is coaching. Awarded Coachmark Gold in 2017 we are proud to have established a school culture where coaching is something open to all staff in the school – from teachers, leaders, to support and administration staff. All NQTs, RQTs and new TLR holders are offered bespoke coaching as part of their entitlement. Coaching is offered to any colleague in the school both as part of or outside of appraisal conversations. We are currently introducing coaching into the other Trust schools in order to share best practice and help colleagues across schools grow together.

Finally, it is crucial to us that we nurture teachers who are new to the profession in order to retain them. As such, we have designed a comprehensive CPD programme for our newest teachers, which both supports and enriches them as they master the craft of the classroom and consider career development. Not only do they have access to high-quality subject-rich CPD but also opportunities to use CPD to shape their own career pathways. Our 'Aspiring Middle Leaders' programme is one such example, where leadership theory is placed alongside practical, on-the-job learning. In this way, we seek to give colleagues a high level of autonomy in forging the direction of their own CPD.

Like a rainforest, our school's CPD programme has adapted and evolved to ensure it remains strong and successful.

A school must also have strong networks to ensure the 'nutrients' needed to help teaching and learning flourish.

CATHERINE DAVIS

CASE STUDY: GROWING A CULTURE OF TEACHING AND LEARNING

Completing your training NQT (Year 1)

Core CPD entitlement

- 90% timetable
- Mentor period once every two weeks
- Personalised coaching (minimum of 6 periods)
- Induction programme and new staff training (term 1)
- Regular meetings with NQT Coordinator
- Termly report giving personalised targets and support
- NQT awarding body of Essex to quality assure mentoring CPD Support
- High quality Subject CPD in departments and across the school
- CTSN Research and Development Conference

Optional CPD

- A chance to join the CTSN 'Journal' club
- Pastoral development training
- Mindfulness courses
- Extra-curricular activities such as D of E
- Join subject networks

Mastering your classroom craft RQT (Year 2)

Core CPD entitlement

- Personalised coaching to continue development from the NQT year (minimum of 3 sessions to build on transitional targets) - (Term 1)
- RQT Conference, including SEND training and an introduction to career pathways - (Term 2)
- High quality Subject CPD in departments and across the school
- CTSN Research and Development Conference

Optional CPD

- Support to undertake research to develop teaching
- A chance to join the CTSN 'Journal' club
- Mindfulness courses
- Extra-curricular activities such as D of E
- Join subject networks

Career Pathways Year 3

Core CPD entitlement

- Personalised coaching
- Year 3 teachers conference
- Coaching skills training
- Buddying an NQT
- A place on the Institute of Education course *'How do we know it works?'*
- High quality Subject CPD in departments and across the school
- CTSN Research and Development Conference
- Place on the CTSN *'Developing Outstanding Teaching'* programme

Optional CPD

- Option to apply for a place on the *'Aspiring Middle leader'* programme which includes shadowing of pastoral and curricular roles in school and undertaking a whole-school development project
- Option to join the 'Middle Leaders Group'
- Mentoring training
- Support to undertake research to develop teaching
- A chance to join the CTSN 'Journal' club
- Mindfulness courses

Growing leaders in education Year 4 and beyond

Core CPD entitlement

- Personalised coaching
- High quality Subject CPD in departments and across the school
- CTSN Research and Development Conference

Optional CPD

- Non TLR holders - option to apply for a place on the 'Aspiring Middle Leader' programme which includes shadowing of pastoral and curriculum roles in school and undertaking a whole-school development project
- TLR holders - option to apply for a place on the CTSN *'Developing Middle Leaders'* programme
- Option to join the 'Middle Leaders' group - open access to anyone interested in leadership
- Option to apply to become an specialist Leader in Education to carry out outreach work with other schools
- Apply to undertake an SLT secondment, including shadowing SLT and career coaching
- Access to personalised leadership coaching
- A place on the Institute of Education/CTSN course *'How do we know it works?'*
- Mentoring training
- Support to undertake research to develop teaching
- A chance to join the CTSN 'Journal' club
- Mindfulness course

Link to Learning Rainforest:

- Strong learning networks
- Organic growth
- Adapting to the environment
- Diversity of approaches
- Self-sustaining

23

TURTON SCHOOL, BOLTON

INTRODUCTION

Turton School exemplifies so many aspects of the Learning Rainforest. I first encountered Sam Gorse when she and I wrote chapters for Martin Robinson's follow-up to *Trivium 21c*[1] – putting ideas about the Trivium into practice in our schools, much as this book hopes to do. I then delivered some CPD input for Turton staff and currently I work as their official school improvement partner, offering external advice as part of their process of review and development. I can safely say that Sam is one of the most inspirational school leaders I've ever met. She's deeply principled, very thoughtful about every aspect of school life and has created the most wonderful professional culture in her school. Her staff rave about her, spontaneously and often, whenever I visit.

At the heart of Sam's philosophy are a few very clear and powerful ideas that I explore in my blog post Principles over Patch-ups.[2] One is that the curriculum should drive the school. She's passionate about the Trivium and it's massively impressive to hear her staff talk fluently about grammar, dialectic and rhetoric. Martin Robinson's work with the school has become deeply embedded in their thinking and practice. They also have superb ideas about changing the behaviour culture through emphasising strong coherent messaging rather than the system of disciplinary consequences. This is communicated by what they call the Hive Switch after the work of Jonathan Haidt.

Finally, as featured in the Turton case-studies, is their commitment to professional learning, driven through the structure of triads where teachers work collaboratively in threes to develop and review their practice. I think it's magnificent as an expression of a school's philosophy and confidence that, when

asked, Sam's instinct was to represent Turton in the *Fieldbook* by letting her newly qualified teachers (NQTs) tell their stories. Each of the case-studies highlights an aspect of teaching practice that the NQTs have worked on. Such was her trust in them, she didn't even want to check what they'd written. The level of thought they've given their practice at such an early stage in their careers is inspiring.

1. Robinson, M. (2016) Trivium in Practice
2. www.bit.ly/2m62X60

You always learn from watching other people teach – no matter what subject.

JEANETTE BIMPSON
DRAMA TEACHER

PROFILE

Location: Bolton, Lancashire, UK

Type of Institution: Mixed comprehensive

Roll/Age Range: 1600, aged 11–18

Year Founded: 1954

Motto: 'Building on the knowledge of the past to help the children of today meet the challenges of tomorrow.'

Recent/Current School Production: *Mary Poppins*

Recent significant sports event/triumph: Year 10 football team won the town cup.

Notable quirks/alumni:

1) A student that left us last year to go on to study medicine, suffered paralysis in both legs after a climbing accident. As well as returning to his studies in medicine, he has also returned to climbing.

2) We train upwards of 40 trainee teachers/year, bringing good quality people into the teaching profession for the North-West region.

Sam Gorse
Head Teacher

Turton is a strongly values-led community school, with a clear ambition to provide the best possible education for our students. Our values are expressed through the Turton Touchstones. With the advancement of our work with students, the expression of our values and ethos has transmuted. Our original 6 touchstones have recently morphed into a deeper expression of who we are and what we are about, leading to 6 new touchstones:

PROFILE

wisdom: Florence Nightingale – mathematician, nursing reform;

courage: Rita Levi-Montalcini – Jewish refugee, Nobel Prize for medicine;

social justice: Claudia Ruggerini – partisan, freedom fighter;

humanity: Maya Angelou – writer and human rights activist;

temperance: Rachel Carson – ecologist and conservationist;

transcendence: Maria Mitchell – astronomer and advocate for girl's education.

Each Touchstone is represented through the great works of female figures. Female figures are chosen as a counter-balance to the fact that much of the best that has been thought and said across the limitations of subject curriculums is predominantly male.

Our focus is academic, and through a deep consideration of the best that has been thought and said, we provide a curriculum that is knowledge based, ensures progression and has the effect of developing scholarship and good character in our students.

Students are with us for five or seven years, and as well as good exam results, we aim for them to leave us with an education that is even better, going way beyond the confines of the GCSE. We view GCSEs as an important set of exams to be taken at the end of five years of study, as a recognition of a student's hard work, but more importantly students will take with them a deep knowledge of a broad range of subjects. Along the way they develop a desire to pursue understanding, develop virtue and morality; inward enrichment; character and intelligence, and develop discipline, focus and hard work on the path to wisdom and a good life.

In short, we want students to leave us with a 'well-educated mind' (Susan Wise Bauer).

STUDENT: ELA HODZIC

Age and Year Group: 15, Year 10

Most recent:

School Trip: A play in Blackpool called *Blood Brothers*

Extra-curricular activity: Drama outside of school

Science experiment: Investigating Specific Heat Capacity. We measured the temperature and mass of water and used the formula to work out energy transferred.

Book/Play studied in English: *A Christmas Carol*

History topic: 1920s America

Learning:

Subjects Studied: The options I have taken are Drama, History and French

Recent learning highlight: In English, we discussed various different techniques used in poetry and I was able to properly understand the use of enjambment and caesura. They are usually used to highlight certain thoughts and meanings within a poem that develop the purpose of the text.

The most stand-out/interesting/challenging topic you've studied at school: I enjoyed learning about WW2 in History, though it was also quite challenging since it is known to be quite a sensitive subject. Learning about the build up to WW2 was also compelling as it was interesting to find out why there was another war after the tragedy of the first one.

One of my favourite teachers: I enjoy lessons with Miss Murphy who teaches Faith and Ethics because I like to understand various different people's points of views on serious and relative topics.

A favourite feature of the school: One of my favourite features of my school is the Touchstones, creativity was one of the original set. Turton offers plenty of learning points and never stops expanding when it comes to creative subjects such as drama and dance. This helps us to be constantly be developing our innovative skills and focus on the things we are passionate about.

STUDENT: EMILY LAVERICK

Age and Year Group: 12, Year 7

Most recent:

School Trip: London – Victoria and Albert Museum

Extra-curricular activity: Netball, hockey, swimming, rounders, athletics, dancing (jazz, tap)

Science experiment: Friction – pulling a shoe along with a newton meter

Book/Play studied in English: *The Hobbit*

History topic: The reformation

Art topic: Pattern

Learning:

Recent learning highlight: In drama I have really enjoyed doing spy school and creating my own secret identity. I have also enjoyed learning about Constantine Stanislavski and naturalism in drama as I felt I learned, understood and enjoyed it a lot.

The most stand-out/interesting/challenging topic you've studied at school: I enjoyed studying/learning about Saint Thomas Aquinas in Faith and Ethics because the contrast of God and the big bang makes me think hard and it encourages me to put my hand up in class. In addition to that I also really enjoy Faith and Ethics, especially this topic.

One of my favourite teachers: I enjoy lessons with Miss Murphy and Mr Grogan who teach me in form and History because they make lessons enjoyable and fun but also educational. They also make things very clear and understandable and make everything interesting.

A favourite feature of the school: One of my favourite features about school is all the different after school activities as there are opportunities for everyone including PE and other subjects. Doing after-school activities can also give you the opportunity to learn something new that you might not do otherwise.

STUDENT: HARRY BAXTER

Age and Year Group: 14, Year 9
Most recent:

School Trip: Paris
Extra-curricular activity: Water polo, swimming
Science experiment: Showing the spread of STIs
Book/Play studied in English: War poetry and propaganda
History topic: World War II
Art topic: Portraits
Learning:

Subjects Studied: Computer Science, Geography
Recent learning highlight: One project I did recently was the dice game project we all did in Computer Science. The reason I enjoyed this project was the fact we were more or less free to do whatever we wanted with the game. We spent multiple lessons programming the game and at the end of it I was extremely satisfied with the result.
The most stand-out/interesting/challenging topic you've studied at school: I enjoyed learning about the World Wars in history because I find it extremely interesting to be able to look back on the past and seeing how both our technology and ideas have changed in around 100 years ago.
One of my favourite teachers: I enjoy the lessons with Miss Murphy who teaches me both History and Faith and Ethics because of the way she makes all her lessons interactive and interesting. During such lessons, the class will be able to get involved and put forth their ideas on the matter. By getting involved in the lesson we are able to go on small (but relevant) tangents, but afterwards we are able to continue on with the lesson knowing more about the subject.
A favourite feature of the school: One of the best things about Turton is the amount of opportunities which are available for all students. For example, in Year 8 we were able to go on a geography trip to Ambleside where we were able to see a real life example of all the changes a glacier can do the land.

CASE STUDY: WEEKLY REVIEW TECHNIQUES

General Area: Memory
Authors: Lily Murphy & April Paa, NQT Religious Education Teachers

A significant aspect of education practice is developing memory; how can we get pupils to remember a range of knowledge throughout their time at school? One of our aims as teachers is to transfer what is said in the lesson to the long-term memory. A substantial amount of research in psychology and in education has been carried out to try to investigate the best ways for pupils to learn and cope with the demands of exams.

For Key Stage 3, 4 and 5 there are several approaches that can be used to maximise long-term memory retention and we have used these to form our practice in the classroom. In *The Learning Rainforest*, it states that retrieval practice in the form of repeated low-stakes testing should be conducted and the practice of retrieval should be done as daily, weekly and monthly reviews as Rosenshine[3] calls it.

As NQTs we have been using the weekly review techniques to develop our practice and the memory of our pupils.

Key Stage 3

The reviews for KS3 come in the form of simple grammar tests at the start of lessons to recap what has previously been covered. Pupils should not be extending their knowledge until they have a strong foundation of what has come before. Using low-stakes review tests allows pupils the opportunity to practise retrieving the knowledge whilst being given the opportunity to address any misconceptions they might have previously encountered.

We have been conducting these low-stakes recall tests in the dual forms of simple multiple choice questions or questions that require one word or a simple sentence as the answer. Conducting these weekly reviews allow a routine to be established within the classroom to promote a positive working environment. These reviews allow pupils to practise recalling their already established knowledge and provides us as teachers with an opportunity to challenge any misconceptions that might have occurred.

The weekly reviews have allowed lessons to become a well-oiled machine with pupils expecting the review questions to be on the board ready for them to go.

Key Stage 4

Following the Trivium model, the knowledge that pupils need at KS4 has to be focussed on rhetoric (where they communicate their understanding more extensively) instead of basic grammar (simple knowledge recall). The idea behind the weekly reviews is that they are quick and snappy, to establish a routine at the beginning of a lesson and to ensure the foundations of knowledge placed in the lesson have been firmly set before extending the knowledge. So, in addition to the pupils answering grammar based questions, we have also provided pupils with the opportunity to recall how they would answer a 'rhetoric style' question. Due to the format of the weekly reviews we are unable to ask pupils for an extended essay response but a simple multiple choice question allows them to recall the knowledge needed for the rhetoric questions for example 'which of the following is not a cause of war: greed, self-defence, retaliation or reconciliation?'

Key Stage 5

Since the introduction of Linear A level courses, reviews have become an essential part of the learning process. The weekly reviews allocate time to reflect on learnt information and prevent

---

3. Rosenshine, B. (2012)

CASE STUDY: WEEKLY REVIEW...

a cognitive overload which can often result in retrieval failure. A way in which we implemented this review is by providing an audit which has a column for the modules we covered in the week. On its right are the indicators of how confident they are in those modules; examples include 'ready for an exam question!', 'I know it, but I need to revise a little bit more', 'I recognise it, I definitely need to revise!' and lastly 'Ah Miss, I need your help!'. To complete this audit, they must also flick through their notes to see if they feel confident about key theories and concepts. This is an important factor because it gives the students cues as well as categories for their knowledge. The students have responded to the reviews positively as they can instantly see the modules that require more revision, as well as the ones they require more assistance with. We also collect these reviews to find any patterns of concerns for any modules that I might need to go over again for the whole class.

Not only is it a good way to monitor the student's progress, they are also able to identify key topics for revision. From this activity, about 75% of the students found that the time to reflect on their progress has helped them in highlighting areas in which they need extra support.

Link to Learning Rainforest:

- Building knowledge.
- Retrieval Practice
- Think – Pair – Share

They can instantly see the modules that require more revision.

LILY MURPHY & APRIL PAA
NQT RELIGIOUS EDUCATION TEACHERS

CASE STUDY: THINK – PAIR – SHARE

General Area: Questioning
Authors: **Freya Ross**, NQT Chemistry & **Clare Tonge**, NQT – Design Technology

After reading that one of the most common recommendations Tom Sherrington gives after observing lessons is to utilise Think, Pair, Share, we thought it would be a good idea to focus on this simple strategy, to see if, by using it every day in every lesson, it could transform our teaching and help establish the conditions in our classrooms. As NQTs, it was not something that we utilised in every lesson due to concerns of behaviour management and getting an overwhelming number of answers. However, having introduced the strategy more regularly into lessons we have found it to be successful in improving questioning and exploring possibilities.

However, it wasn't always easy...

- **All that noise** – It can be hard to tell that all students are remaining on task with everyone talking.
- **Too much freedom** – Allowing student-led learning can encourage some students to take this as an opportunity to mess around as you circulate the room to hear the ideas rather than monitoring behaviour.
- **Friendship issues** – if groupings are not carefully thought out and conversations are not modelled, sometimes students can feel left out.
- **Timetable obstacles** – In DT, the frequency I see classes in lower school and the practical work involved in my subject makes me wary of giving so much time to a single question.

Nevertheless, not all is lost...

- **Confidence boost** – It gives confidence to those who do not normally voice their opinion and focusses discussions when a time frame is given. For example, in science, I spoke to a shy student during the 'pair' portion of the activity and by giving a positive response to her answer, she then felt confident enough to put her hand up to share to the whole class – despite going red, later on she put her hand up again!
- **Asking the right questions** – Having utilised the technique we discovered the importance of asking the right questions and modelling a response. Addressing misconceptions before the activity is vital so students are discussing the right content. Visual clues on the board can help with this.
- **Wake-up their brains** – By making the students interleave their knowledge from previous topics to answer the question, students must think for themselves. We found it also allows opportunity to break

up the lesson by having a quick discussion. However, it is important to keep a short time frame and tell students you will be picking people to feedback (rather than asking for hands up) so they stay on task and to ensure all students have prepared something to say.

- **Getting the flow** (Burns, 2012) – Pitching to the right level allows flow. Too high creates anxiety but too low and the learners will become disengaged. Discovering new information allows a level of excitement to work collaboratively to find the right answer and upon entering the room you can hear the learning. We found even the more disengaged students were working hard to find an answer if the correct question was selected due to an intrinsic motivation.
- **Differentiation** – A good seating plan allows mixed ability students to interact and share ideas. It encourages students to work with others that they may not usually interact with and encourages peer support.
- **Enquiry based learning** – As science and DT include practical aspects, we have found Think, Pair, Share great at helping students to make predictions and understand new concepts. We have used etymology and interleaving at the beginning of lessons to Think, Pair, Share our way to guess what the lesson is about, for example, the etymology of electrolysis; using concepts from science and DT to establish why bread rises; and linking unicellular vs multicellular organisms to other similar words to establish the difference between the two.

Think, Pair, Share has improved engagement in our lessons, allowing more student-led work to take place.

Bibliography

Burns, A. G. a. M., 2012. *Outstanding Teaching: Engaging Learners.* Carmarthen: Crown House Publishing.

CASE STUDY: DEVELOPING AN ORACY-BASED REVIEW PROCESS

Author: Sophie Cox, NQT English

The delivery of subject knowledge runs throughout the Key Stage 3 curriculum in a linear historical context, allowing pupils to purvey the chronological development of language through literature. Therefore, although teaching and learning follows a structure as detailed by Martin Robinson in Trivium 21c[4], the elements overlap, allowing pupils to build on knowledge and review understanding to ensure it is embedded.

Our current focus is to review learning more effectively throughout lessons so as to enable pupils to embed the knowledge to build upon. David Didau[5] suggests that through the use of review and the practice of procedural knowledge, pupils are able to free up working memory allowing for automatization. By reviewing and recapping knowledge regularly, we allow storage to take place in our long-term memory, thus giving our working memory the opportunity to gain new information.

Through the use of assessment for learning within the classroom, pupils should be able to receive instant feedback and a chance to reorganise their thoughts coherently. Many pupils feel intimidated by putting pen to paper and do not feel confident to do so. By allowing pupils to verbally summarise their own learning, having their peers support and by scaffolding their responses, more pupils are able to develop oracy skills which enable them to transfer knowledge to their long-term memory.

During our Triad Research Groups at Turton we are looking at developing the review process to ensure that it is an effective part of curriculum design and an operative assessment tool to gauge

and aid progression for all pupils. I have trialled various methods of review, which allowed pupils to embed knowledge/grammar of the topics they were studying. By allowing the repetitive, quick quizzes to become part of a routine, pupils were able to retrieve knowledge that had been embedded into their memory.

Across three mixed ability Year 8 classes studying Shakespeare and the Renaissance, I offered the same set of questions to pupils but at a different rate. These were based on contextual knowledge, quotations from a Shakespeare play and applied grammar skills. Class X were questioned every two weeks, class Y weekly and class Z every lesson. The repetitive responding to questions, for class Z, clearly had an impact as in the end of term tests they outdid their counterparts with higher grades. This revise, repeat, review clearly had a positive effect on the learning of knowledge and facts necessary to build upon.

Nevertheless, this was not allowing pupils to expand upon their knowledge. This area is covered – especially in English lessons – through written application. However, this is not something that can be assessed easily in a timely manner for formative assessment during class time. Pupils needed to engage directly to embellish upon answers and show their reasoning and understanding. Simply put, they needed to offer quick responses. This was easy enough to receive an eager response from those pupils who were 100% confident whether in personality or knowledge. But many pupils were not happy to engage. Within the classroom environment, many pupils are happy to take a back seat and not respond, knowing that someone else will offer an answer. I questioned as to whether the focus was on ability to

answer the question, or an uncertainty about standing out in the crowd. I put several methods into practice, which I then supported learners through the use of Socratic questioning.

It was through this encouragement of receiving verbal answers from pupils and helping them to reason through their argument with guidance and support, where I started to see a noticeable difference in their written work. It appeared through developing their oracy skills and working through an aural structure, pupils were being able to apply their knowledge more effectively. In some cases, this was evident in the language choices being presented and/or the order and depth of explanation. Other times, it simply offered confidence to apply pen to paper.

Although this is still a work in progress, it is demonstrating an impact on higher-level learners. Through application of oracy in my lessons, I was able to discuss knowledge with learners and then encourage them to present information to the class in the form of mini starters. Hence, allowing pupils to engage in dialectic: expressing opinions. Pupils were encouraged to do their own greater depth research in order to present knowledge to the class. Although they were able to use PowerPoint or handouts, the focus was on their oracy skills to present. Not only did this give a different style of teaching/learning for pupils to engage (through which they asked questions that they may not have asked me), but it also enables the speaker to create a greater understanding of the subject and a higher knowledge.

Thus, the process of development for research was the use of oracy based review.

This revise, repeat, review clearly had a positive effect.

SOPHIE COX
NQT ENGLISH

Think, Pair, Share has improved engagement in our lessons, allowing more student-led work to take place.

FREYA ROSS NQT CHEMISTRY & CLARE TONGE NQT – DESIGN TECHNOLOGY

4. Robinson, M. (2013)

5. Didau, D (2016)

CASE STUDY: DEVELOPING THE UNDERSTANDING OF SUBJECT LANGUAGE

Author: Tony Grogan, NQT History

Turton School is developing a 'Scholars' Pathway' for their most highly attaining students. From their entry into Turton School at Year 7 these students follow a slightly different curriculum which pushes them further in terms of their academic achievement and wider development. Whilst in its first year at Turton, I have been fortunate enough to have this group as my form class and Year 7 History during my NQT year and this has allowed me to really push both the students and me in how to enable learning within such an environment. Very early in my NQT year (October) I was fortunate to have Tom visit my class and observe the lesson for a period. Tom's input and support further informed my teaching not only with this class but across my other year groups. The creation of the Scholars' Pathway is having a positive impact on my teaching of students no matter what their academic ability or class.

Tom makes several interesting observations with regards to the debate about curriculum and I was keen to avoid almost starting to 'train' my students for GCSE questions early. I wanted my class to develop a love for history, for learning and the language of history. By following this direction there would inevitably be later benefits when they approached their GCSEs but that was not my principal aim. I sought to push my students on their use of and understanding of language and explore the possibilities to do that.

The lessons I want to discuss here are from a medieval scheme of work in which the class considered the role of the church in this period, and the relationship between Henry II and Thomas Becket in detail. I wanted to look at this event through several sources and interpretations, allowing the students to consider how the

language has changed over time. We used a basic account from a standard KS3 textbook, an account written in the style of a modern newspaper, an account from a KS4 textbook and the original medieval account written by Edward Grim. We considered the words used and really spent time taking apart each account, using dictionaries to truly understand the words and annotating the accounts with our own descriptions and notes.

By developing the understanding of language and our own comfort in using it we established a foundation which we will then be able to use throughout the time at Turton and beyond (many of the students already aspire to places at some of the best universities). This is very much in keeping with ideas promoted by Tom and the work of Martin Robinson with his Trivium of Grammar, Dialectic and Rhetoric. The students felt like they were taking ownership of the lessons whilst probing the information and the development of language built on their knowledge. It reached the point where the students were taking pride in their own success and the high level of rigour which is key for real progress was now being managed and driven by the students themselves.

Working with my NQT mentor, Charleigh Eccles, I then wanted the students to explore the application of this language today, not only in their written work but as academics in their speaking. Oracy is a skill which Turton values with whole school initiatives and weeks where oracy is pushed harder than normal. We looked at how the death of Thomas Becket is described by others in their speaking. From accounts clearly aimed at children through to accounts given by university academics both on mainstream TV through to more specialist channels and videos, we considered not only what the presenters said but how they said it. What words did they use, what did they do with their body, how did

they stand and view their audience? All factors in good oracy. Questions such as 'Why did one person appear more credible than another' and 'why did we value one account more than another' came to the fore and time was spent debating and considering these questions as a class, taking the point from one student with others developing it, challenging it and ultimately enhancing the understanding of the whole class.

By the end of the lessons I had a class of 35 students who not only could describe the death of Thomas Becket but they could explain how language has changed over time, how to develop ideas through classroom discussion and debate and a build on a growing understanding as to what makes a good speaker and how to present a convincing argument.

So where does this leave me now? The real desire to look at ways to examine sources and interpretations has become something which is informing my teaching across all year groups. An example of this is how I am working on several lessons for my mixed ability Year 9 students who will examine conscientious objectors during WW1 and how views of such actions have changed over time. Links to people who stood up for what they believed in at that time through to those who do the same now and how we challenge those ideas are themes I want to explore.

The students were taking pride in their own success and the high level of rigour which is key for real progress was now being managed and driven by the students themselves.

TONY GROGAN
NQT HISTORY

OLDHAM COLLEGE, OLDHAM

INTRODUCTION

I'm delighted that the Further Education sector is represented in this book by Oldham College. It's one of the most inclusive educational establishments I've ever worked in with a wonderful spirit about it, offering a very wide range of technical and professional courses. A walk around the college takes you from the bricklaying polytunnels, to plumbing, construction and motor vehicle workshops, hair-dressing and beauty therapy salons, digital and creative art and performing arts studios, computer labs, huge study spaces, specialist areas for young adults with complex learning needs and a whole range of classrooms where the learners study law, business, child care, maths, English, science, sport, travel and tourism, uniform services. It's a busy, dynamic place where the tutors are often experts in their respective professional fields, coming into teaching as a second profession.

I've been working with the college for the last two years developing a comprehensive teacher development programme that we call 'Teaching for Distinction'. The process has taught me a great deal about the complexity of teacher development as well as highlighting how universal some core ideas about teaching and learning are.

When Principal Alun Francis contacted me to discuss his ideas about how I might support them, he was adamant that he wanted his staff to develop their professional knowledge, to empower them with an understanding of what educational research has to offer, not simply give them a set of tools to deploy. He also wanted the programme to fuel greater aspirations for what learners could achieve – aiming for Distinction grades, not merely to gain a Pass. The Teaching for Distinction title captures this double meaning: it applies to teachers and to their learners. From the beginning, Alun knew this would be a long-term process where we rolled out the programme in stages with a launch and numerous waves of follow-up embedded in the college systems. It takes time for teachers to

adopt new habits but because of the approach we've taken, where each faculty takes ownership of the programme themes on its own terms, Rainforest style, we've seen some major steps forward right across the college.

One of the key elements of the programme has been the appointment of some Advanced Practitioners to act as Teaching for Distinction coaches and champions. Chris Jones who has written the case studies in this chapter is one of the APs. He and his colleagues, Sinead, Eve, Wendy, Joe and Sally and their manager Gill – work closely with middle leaders in the college to support tutors in all various professions to hone their teaching skills. Across the college we hear tutors talking about knowledge, modelling, retrieval practice, Austin's butterfly, feedback, practice, cold call questioning – all elements that are explored in *The Learning Rainforest*.

We all recognise that we're just at the start of an ongoing process but already there's a common language, a strong culture and great systems so we're also all very optimistic about the progress the college will make as Teaching for Distinction becomes more deeply embedded.

In August 2019, Oldham College was awarded the prestigious Princess Royal Training Award in recognition of the quality of the Teaching for Distinction programme – a wonderful accolade for all concerned.

PRINCESS ROYAL
TRAINING AWARD
2019

Success stories like yours really help us in our work to raise standards and attainments across the board in our education offer. It also inspires us, as leaders, to continue working hard to make this borough a place where the talented people that you teach and employ will want to live and work in the future.

CLLR SEAN FIELDING
LEADER OF OLDHAM COUNCIL

My daughter has attended college since September (school leaver) and in my opinion the college is outstanding. The ethos of the college is about so much more than just obtaining the qualifications. We see a much more confident happy girl every day.

PARENT COMMENT
OLDHAM COLLEGE FACEBOOK PAGE

Alun Francis
Principal

The college specialises in technical and professional education and training (which used to be called vocational learning). This differs from general academic education in numerous ways. It is focused on practical skills and knowledge needed in the real workplace. There is a wide range of choice for learners of all ages and abilities. No matter whether a learner arrives with good qualifications or none, programmes are tailored to the needs of individuals, from entry to degree level.

PROFILE

Learners also have a choice of pathways which are designed specifically for the industry or sector they wish to work in.

For some this is a mainly classroom based route, but most will have a considerable work-based element, and many (apprenticeships) are fully work-based.

All of the College provision is delivered in partnership with employers. It is the link between the educational setting and the workplace which makes technical and professional education and training unique and different.

Teaching for Distinction builds on Michael Young's concept of 'powerful knowledge'[1] which sees learning as cumulative, disciplined and systematic, and passed on from generation to generation. It is 'powerful' because it forms the basis of new developments in the field. We have applied the concept to technical and professional disciplines, which work in similar but not identical ways to academic subjects. It embraces practical skills and know-how alongside theory, linking the workplace and the classroom, but has the same emphasis on retained learning as the stepping stone to further development. Hence we adapt Matthew Arnold: it is 'The best that has been thought and said... and done', which is the foundation of expertise and the basis of a good society.

College ethos and where it is on its journey:

Oldham College caters for some of the most deprived learners, in one of the most deprived towns, in one of the most deprived regions of the country. For English and maths, the qualifications learners arrive with puts them in the lowest percentiles for performance tables and comparisons. Added to this was a suggestion that the college 'required' improvement... twice!

1. Ref for Michael Young

But really it needed a change. It needed a change to help learners become more resilient and focused. It needed a change that could better demonstrate the hard work and passion our teachers have for vocational education.

Around 18 months ago, the college began work and introduced an ongoing CPD programme that has come to be known as 'Teaching for Distinction'. Its basis is a knowledge-rich curriculum which, considering the college is primarily a post-16 technical and vocational college, was all quite new. The focus is on excellence in teaching, on learners focusing on remembering key information and then being able to apply it – often in the context of the workplace.

Tom was a key driver in establishing the principles of the CPD programme at the college, introducing the brushstrokes of Barak Rosenshine, Ron Berger, Eduardo Briceno, Dylan Wiliam, Daisy Christodoulou (and many others), as well as reintroducing Doug Lemov's *Teach Like a Champion* philosophy, to our teaching palettes.

The programme has 6 key principles, 'modules', that have helped to: strengthen the structure of lessons; defined behaviour, routines and expectations; and shifted focus to excellence through rehearsal and redrafting.

It's no longer suggested that we '*require improvement*', now we are '*Good*' and the CPD programme that has been established, whilst still developing, makes Oldham College an exciting place to work. What we are doing is '*Good*', and the impact is seen every day in the lessons delivered to the learners and the outcomes that are being achieved. Our goal now is to be a 'great place to learn... a great place to work', our embracement of a knowledge-rich curriculum has shown us a way to get there.

> It brings lessons to life and makes me want to work in the same industry.

IQBAL AHMED

> There is a strong bond between students and teachers – we are like a family!

YORAINA RODRIGUES

> So many features that allow students to prosper and achieve their full potential.

ALI RAZA

> Constantly challenged to reach my full potential.

KASHAF KARAMAT

STUDENT: KASHAF KARAMAT

Age and Year Group: 16, first year college learner
House: Caring Professions.

Most recent:

School Trip: Othello, Oldham Coliseum Theatre
Extra-curricular activity: Library assistant
Science experiment: Growing bacteria in agar plates
Book studied in English: *The curious incident of the dog in the night-tim*e by Mark Haddon

Learning:

Subjects Studied: GCSE Study Programme: English, Maths, Biology, Chemistry
Recent learning highlight: In English, I learned how nothing is definite or absolute – there is always room for improvement and you can never be certain of perfection. (Kashaf gained a Grade 7 in her GCSE English resit!)
The most stand-out/interesting/challenging topic you've studied at school: I enjoyed studying/learning about mental health, through reading *Curious Incident* because it is less talked about and sometimes considered taboo. It gave me exposure to different human behaviours and a chance for me to self-reflect.
One of my favourite teachers: I enjoy lessons with CHRIS who teaches me ENGLISH because...he understands me as a student. He is constantly challenging me and makes me reach my full potential. He is also *very* funny!
A favourite feature of the school: The college is very student oriented and adapts to the needs of the students. The faculties are very accepting and aid the students in improving. There is a very diverse culture at the college, with lots of opportunities for enrichment.

STUDENT: ALI RAZA

Age and Year Group: 19, third year college learner
House: CUEN

Most recent:

School Trip: *Othello*, Oldham Coliseum Theatre
Book studied in English: *The curious incident of the dog in the night-time* by Mark Haddon

Learning:

Subjects Studied: Currently studying GCSE Study Programme: English, Maths. Previously achieved: BTEC First Certificate in Business (Level 2).

Recent learning highlight: In English we looked at an extract about a frustrated teacher. I was really intrigued by this story and enjoyed learning how the writer had used multiple metaphors and personification to enhance her story, creating an enchanting atmosphere.

The most stand-out/interesting/challenging topic you've studied at school: I enjoyed learning about *Romeo and Juliet*, because I was captured by the different characters and their importance in the play. Also, the multiple occasions where the writer foreshadows and creates a sinister atmosphere within a hint of romance.

One of my favourite teachers: I enjoy lessons with PAUL who teaches me MATHS because … although I feel maths is my strong point, the topics covered link with my future job goals. I enjoyed learning about compound interest and compound measure, learning quicker and more efficient ways to answer questions.

A favourite feature of the school: I love the fact that Oldham College has so many features that allow students to prosper and achieve their full potential. There are lots of staff and organisations, whether internal or external, that play a very big part in ensuring the college runs smoothly.

STUDENT: YORAINA RODRIGUES

Age and Year Group: 19, third year college learner
Faculty: Sport and Travel

Most recent:

School Trip: Eurocamp Park Host shadowing experience, Amsterdam
Extra-curricular activity: Dancing and trampolining

Learning:

Subjects Studied: Extended Diploma Travel & Tourism (Level 3) GCSE English

Recent learning highlight: We did many role plays in Travel, they helped me to gain experience for future jobs. I also liked using Quizlet for English revision to learn different words and definitions.

The most stand-out/interesting/challenging topic you've studied at school: I enjoyed studying/learning about how to be a member of cabin crew. It gave me knowledge that I will need when I apply for employment.

One of my favourite teachers: I enjoy lessons with SUE and JULIE who teach me TRAVEL because … there is a strong bond between students and teachers – we are like a family!

I also enjoy lessons with CHRIS as he always helps me to improve my grammar, and pushes me to do better with extra work.

A favourite feature of the school: I like Oldham College because they treat everybody equally, and the staff always try to make the college a better place. I enjoy learning in the classrooms and the way teachers teach. The college feels like home as the staff are there for us and support us. I know I feel safe in college, staff listen to us and take action to listen to our views.

STUDENT: IQBAL AHMED

Age and Year Group: 19, fourth year college learner
Faculty: Sport and Travel

Most recent:

School Trip: Eurocamp Park Host shadowing experience, Amsterdam
Extra-curricular activity: Integrated Student Support Officer, Student Union Officer, and Voluntary Marshal, Oldham Half Marathon

Learning:

Subjects Studied: Currently studying: Extended Diploma Travel & Tourism (Level 3), Functional Skills Maths (Level 2). Previously achieved: NCFE Aviation Operations & Cabin Crew (Level 2), BTEC Award in Travel & Tourism (Level 1)

Recent learning highlight: Recently, we completed a unit on 'ski chalet hosts'. Part of this unit was to plan, buy, prepare and serve a three-course meal to some clients. The meal had to include a balanced diet taking into account specific dietary needs, as well as offer a vegetarian option. It was different from our normal type of written, or presenting style, of submission. It involved teamwork, communication, and planning; it was great to get feedback from staff that don't normally teach us!

The most stand-out/interesting/challenging topic you've studied at school: I enjoyed studying/learning about package holidays, because it involved thinking about the needs of customers and how these are met by travel agents and tour operators. This was particularly interesting to me, as in the future I hope to work in a travel agency. As part of this role I would be expected to plan and research clients' holidays – ensuring they get what they want from their holiday.

One of my favourite teachers: I enjoy lessons with SUE who teaches me TRAVEL because…she is always friendly and approachable whenever I am in her lesson. When I am unsure about something, Sue is always there to explain clearly what I have to do. It helps me to feel that I understand.

A favourite feature of the school: Tutors have previously worked in industry, this really helps, as they can talk about past experiences. It brings lessons to life and makes me want to work in the same industry. Guest speakers to come in and talk about their roles. This year, we have an opportunity to on an overseas trip to Holland. The college itself has lots of friendly and helpful staff and everyone is approachable.

CASE STUDY: HOW A KNOWLEDGE-RICH CURRICULUM LEADS OUR LEARNERS TO EXCELLENCE

General Area: Teaching and Learning

Author: Chris Jones. Advanced Practitioner, Programme Tutor – English

At Oldham College we introduced an ongoing CPD programme called 'Teaching for Distinction'. The aim is to have a knowledge-rich curriculum, of effective evidence-informed teaching and pedagogical approaches, to lead learners towards excellence. We want to improve teaching and learning; we want to develop staff, share good practice, and encourage a confidence to try new things, learn from each other, and own our CPD.

The programme is comprised of six 'modules', each required viewing and reading for all tutors and managers at the college. The goal is for a secure knowledge of the material to be evidenced in lessons across the college.

1	**Theories of Learning**	Memory and practice; novices and experts. Core Knowledge. An Ethic of Excellence: Austin's Butterfly. Growth Mindset. Carol Dweck; Pygmalion Effect.
2	**Curriculum Design for Distinction**	Curriculum Planning, Industry/workforce context. Industry expectations and working practices. Engagement and Retention: Relevence; relationships; success, Specifying the knowledge and skills: knowledge organisers.
3	**Principles of Instruction**	Barak Rosenshine; Modelling, Explaining, Metacognition Questioning Retrieval Practice: Daily review
4	**Assessment & Feedback**	Setting expectations and standards: 'Defining the butterfly' Responsive Teaching: Dylan Wiliam. Feedback and improvement strategies. The role and nature of summative assessment: Daisy Christodoulou.
5	**Securing Excellence**	The ladder to success. Exemplars and scaffolding within the terms of the course specification. Goal-setting: Using data and descriptors intelligently. 'Redrafting' and what this looks like in context Using oracy as a tool to secure deeper learning. How does tracking secure Improvement and excellence?
6	**Behaviour, Routines and Expectations**	College Behaviour Code. Routines for learning; disciplined engagement with the programme. Choices and Consequences within a 'not more school' context. Managing challenging situations and low-level disruption.

The 'TfD' approach informs everything we do at Oldham College. How we plan lessons, how we assess learners in the classroom, how we set the bar for behaviour/entering the classroom/being ready to learn. It is a holistic view of what we want our learners to be doing. It isn't complete or perfect, it's probably too large to ever be 'done'. However it is what we are striving towards day-in, day-out, in classrooms and workshops and poly-tunnels. It provides us all with a structure, signposting how we achieve excellent teaching, consistently, week after week, term after term. We've found that the more embedded the pedagogy, the more consistently the techniques are used, the more successful the outcomes are. Learners engage with sessions even more – they know what is coming and, perhaps more importantly, they know what isn't. There's no surprise test, or secret grading attached to a piece of work – not in the Learning Zone. Mistakes are encouraged, redrafting is a given, improvement is natural. It doesn't matter whether a learner is doing plumbing, maths, or drama. The learning process is the same.

There are a lot of pieces to 'TfD', some departments are stronger in one area than others – but that's fine. They've used the evidence to better inform their practice and to help their learners improve. We know there is still a lot to do due to the nature of the programme.

For a flavour of what we've introduced, below are two typical examples of lessons that really reflect the links between the theory of teaching and the subjects they are applied to.

Example of Teaching for Distinction, embedded into a Performing Arts dance lesson:

Timing	Task	Rationale
5 mins	Physical warm-up	**Guided Practice** demonstrated and linked to specific technique/performer. Tutor closely supervises physical warm-up routine, spotting errors in posture early and giving corrective guidance. Learners are able to master simple skills through regular repeated practice drills. Whilst this is a tutor-led activity, there are opportunities for a learner (or multiple learners) to lead all, or part, of the activity. This would provide another opportunity to assess retrieval practice, as well as *aiming for excellence* and giving tutor and/or peers opportunities to *feedback* on the effectiveness of the routine.
10 mins	Daily retrieval	**Retrieval Practice**. Prior learning/positioning of choreography material is reviewed through demonstrations of the procedural routines they are linked to. Feedback is given to learners on positioning and they are given time to action/demonstrate progress. There are also opportunities here to *check for understanding*, prior to demonstrations, to assess if learners are confident in being able to either recall or explain the movement to others.
5 mins	Prior learning	**Modelling** is used to recap choreographic material from the previous session via a tutor, or high ability learner, demonstration – there is questioning to recap specific artists/techniques. There is an opportunity to use **Cold Calling** and/or **Probing** questioning throughout this point, to gain a greater understanding of how many learners knew, or even could demonstrate, a part of movement – and how secure that understanding or recall is.
5 mins	Modelling	**Modelling** is used once more to demonstrate **expectations**. Learners are pushed to produce high quality, efficient performances that meet expected time cues.

CASE STUDY: HOW A KNOWLEDGE-RICH CURRICULUM LEADS OUR LEARNERS TO EXCELLENCE

Timing	Task	Rationale
25 mins	Recap choreography	Group work and **Austin's Butterfly** is used highly effectively. Excellent work is regularly referenced and all learners knew what **excellence** looks like through **modelling** by the tutor and their peers. Learners are given ample opportunities, and time, to practise, rehearse and make mistakes in this **Learning Zone**; though there is a clear sense of **urgency**, to perfect routines. Performances are recapped and critiqued, with the **language of Distinction** very prominent and a **focus on excellence** in all aspects of work. **Behaviour of the learners** is expected to be flawless, with 100% focus on the tasks at hand – even during transitional periods. Frequent **checking of understanding** is demonstrated through 'show me', rather than relying on oral questioning. Some questioning of how movements link to specific techniques is embedded for some learners to scaffold or confirm deeper understanding.

Exemplar of an English lesson, putting the Rainforest into action:

Timing	Task	Rationale
10 mins	Strong Start w/recap	Students are expected to know – and be able to quickly and efficiently recall – key definitions for language terms that are needed to access the content of the session. The starter activity is used as **Retrieval Practice**, happening each lesson to consistently review and strengthen the terms that have been taught previously. The terms and definitions are detailed on the students' **Knowledge Organisers**, this supports retrieval practice as students know they will be quizzed on them each lesson and know they are meant to learn this information by heart. The starter, therefore, gets the students into the mindset of the session from the outset, promoting learning and high expectations from the very beginning.

Timing	Task	Rationale
10 mins	Guided Reading	Each lesson explores a new text, or a different part of a previous text. **Guided Reading** is used to promote **Oracy**, modelling fluid reading and explore pronunciation of ambitious vocabulary. A series of **Questioning Techniques** is used during, and after, reading to check understanding and **Probe** key parts of the extract, highlighting their importance and linking them to the key terms and definitions covered in the Strong Start. **Cold Calling** is used as a default for this activity, however the questions are scaffolded and differentiated based on ability.
30 mins	Modelled response	Using the Knowledge Organisers as a scaffold to learning (they contain key sentence starters for each question), **Cold Calling** and **Probing** questioning is used to produce an exemplar answer together on the whiteboard. The focus is always on **Aiming for Excellence**, as the aim is to produce a full mark (or at least Band 4) response. In this session, the aim was for 8/8 marks – Band 4. The language of distinction is key here, as ambitious vocabulary is necessary. Using the whiteboard, we use the concept of **Austin's Butterfly** to frequently rub out/change/adapt words or sentences that become weak based on the evolving answer. The goal of this is to consistently demonstrate the mindset needed to achieve a high mark – being critical of what you have written, and accepting that it may need to be re-written and/or re-drafted. **Probing Questions** have a core role during this activity as I **Cold Call** learners as to *'how could this part be phrased better?', 'are you happy with this word?', 'we have repeated the word 'makes' here and here...which needs changing? To what? Why?'* This tasks helps to show learners how a top answer is crafted, and also, how my mind works as an examiner reviewing it. **Checking Understanding** is used to drill down why a sentence deserves marks, *'what has been written here to take it out of Band 2? Why is that part better?'*

CASE STUDY: HOW A KNOWLEDGE-RICH CURRICULUM LEADS OUR LEARNERS TO EXCELLENCE

Timing	Task	Rationale
20 mins	Individual response	At this point in the session, scaffolds for learning are removed (partially, they can still refer to their *Knowledge Organiser* and have the model answer as a reference point) and they are expected to produce a response of their own in a time recommended for completing that question in the exam – 20 minutes. **Aiming for Excellence**, **Guided Practice** and **Expectations** are key elements of this task, as I deliberately circulate the room to review the work being produced. I am tracking, not observing, to push students to extend certain phrases/sentences, *ensuring efficiency*; remind learners of *time cues* and what is expected to be produced so far; *supervise work* to *spot errors early* and *give corrective guidance* and to **Feedback** what learners are doing well/need to adapt to improve. The **Expectation** is reinforced consistently – focused, quiet work to produce a clear written answer that is at least the top of Band 3 (6/8).
15 mins	Feedback www/ebi	Students completed responses are shown under the visualiser, with a focus on **Feedback www/***ebi***. The **Language of Distinction** is again focused on and **Cold Call** with **Probing Questions** is used to ask either the writer *'Why did you include this phrase? What were you trying to explain? How could this part be adapted to be clearer?'* or other members of the group *'What mark band would this be in? Why? What do we like here that gets us marks? How could this part be changed to get into the next band? What is missing?'* This element links back to **Austin's Butterfly** used in the model answer section of the session, as are expected to know what excellence looks like in any piece of work and are expected to be able to discuss ways to improve mirroring the language of the exam and the mark scheme.

Timing	Task	Rationale
5 mins	Homework overview	The session is recapped at this point: reinforcing the thread between the starter activity of knowing the meanings of language techniques, knowing that this feeds into being able to spot them in an extract and then being able to discuss and write about the importance of words and phrases in the modelling/individual response sections. Students are then directed to their homework booklet. The **expectation** is to complete another independent language response, this time to a new extract, ready for the next session. This pulls all parts of the session together and allows **Course Tracking**. Learners can review their progress of being able to complete the task independently, based on the learning of the session. The task is walked through under the visualiser, reinforcing the **expectation** and **checking understanding** with a range of students to ensure there is no miscommunication in the instructions.

Link to Learning Rainforest:

The Teaching for Distinction programme ties closely with many of the Learning Rainforest ideas, particularly 'Establishing the Conditions'. As seen in the example lessons above, many of the strategies in the Rainforest are core and reflected in the CPD principles. We create habits for excellence; there is specified knowledge in each subject, department, faculty; students use scaffolds for learning, such as sentence starters/phrases; we use regular skills and drills to rehearse, practise and perfect; checking for understanding is a constant, and in a variety of different ways; tutors model, guide and show literal examples of distinction and top band material; and we teach for memory, there is an expectation of recall. The Rainforest is intertwined with the principles of TfD and they support each other.

We want to improve T&L; to develop staff, share good practice, encourage confidence, learn from each other, and own CPD.

CHRIS JONES

KENTS HILL PARK SCHOOL, MILTON KEYNES

INTRODUCTION

I first met James Pilgrim, Headteacher at Kents Hill Park, when I delivered some training for his previous school where he was Deputy. I was thrilled when he then contacted me to tell me the great news that he'd landed a job as the Head of a brand new school in Milton Keynes, opening with a Year 3 and a Year 7 in 2018, growing into a full through-school over the next five years. Later, I was honoured to be invited to provide some input for James' staff development and to give him an outside perspective on the standards they were setting early on.

I will always remember visiting the new school building in the summer before the school opened – fully finished but empty, except for James! At that stage it felt like anything was possible – the school buildings symbolising the blank slate. It's both incredibly exciting and daunting as I know from my own involvement with setting up a new school in 1999.

From the beginning, James was committed to the idea of a knowledge-rich curriculum and early on established the school motto: Confident, Independent, Forward-thinking. I passed him a copy of *The Learning Rainforest* because I felt it might chime with some of his thinking – and as the case studies show, I think there is a strong resonance.

Whilst setting out with ambitious goals, James isn't someone to impose his ideas rigidly from on high and was determined that the first year was one of team-building, giving the first teacher recruits time to bond and to make their mark by designing their own areas of the curriculum. This has been a superb process to see in action; Katy, Susanne, Mark and Emily capture the spirit of it very well. Their willingness to reflect, learn adapt and change at this crucial early stage has been impressive. There are multiple references to assessment issues and Rosenshine's principles and it's attending to these details alongside the collective desire to

set-up a strong, rich curriculum with multiple experiences that has been so interesting.

I was curious to learn that the school's logo was designed by two members of their Academy Trust based on a locally famous sculpture of a boy and girl by Robert Koenig. The lines now also represent threads in the curriculum.

The first Year 3s and Year 7s have had a wonderful first year, blazing the trail, and it will be fascinating to see how the school grows.

It genuinely is a pleasure to come to work each day and help create something that will be here long after the first set of pupils and staff have passed through our doors. If someone had said to me that I would get the opportunity to set up my own school and shape it with the very best educational thought, I wouldn't have believed them. It is hugely rewarding, but made great fun by the team I have with me.

JAMES PILGRIM
HEADTEACHER

PROFILE

Location: Milton Keynes, UK

Type of Institution: All-through mixed comprehensive

Age Range: Eventually 2–18, presently Year 7 & Year 3

Year Founded: 2018

Motto: 'Confident, Independent, Forward-thinking'

Recent significant sports event/triumph: Our first ever trophy won by the Y7 boys football team

Notable quirks/alumni: No-one has ever said 'that's the way we've always done it'!

James Pilgrim
Headteacher

We are very much at the plantation stage, but taking the very best bits of the rainforest to grow and develop an exceptional environment for learning.

We are fortunate that we can grow from the ground up, taking only one secondary and one primary year group each year until we are full. This gives us the luxury of time and the opportunity to plan whole-scale and long term.

Whilst keeping a view of ultimate outcomes, we have focused entirely on KS3 and built our CPD around the curriculum plans.

Using Christine Counsell's ideas around core and hinterland knowledge, we have mapped in detail, down to the week, exactly what we expect every pupil to know at every stage of KS3. We have looked at how these topics and knowledge content flow throughout the years and forms to give a coherent, structured approach to the knowledge required for the curriculum.

PROFILE

We have also looked at which key figures, books, art, music, literature, visits etc. we are teaching so that we can be precise in our rationale and thinking around our curriculum.

All of this has required considerable time and has been mapped in our CPD programme. We run short, regular CPD sessions and a good proportion of this time has been given to staff to work collaboratively across the subjects and curriculum. This has seen some superb and intelligent conversations around our curriculum intent, and some robust discussion. It has taught us as much about each other as it has about curriculum, and made us an even tighter group of staff, clear in our purpose.

Knowledge organisers and topic booklets to further support the pupils; we have trialled lead lessons to the whole year group, and DEAR time is now a fully embedded part of our routine. We have seen clear impact on the quality of discussion and the level of work produced, and the pupils' vocabulary is developing well as they are focused with more challenging texts and higher expectations.

As a new school, the ethos, expectations and attitudes embedded within the school have been a key aspect of our work. Although the curriculum is very much part of our long term strategic direction, our behaviour and expectations are key to being successful now and setting clear boundaries for how we perform in the future. Centralising as much of this as possible has been an important driver, and ensuring a collective responsibility for behaviour and ethos has been incredibly important to allow staff to get on with what they do best without distraction.

In planning for future years we are looking at how we can further synchronise our primary and secondary phases. We very much feel as though we are one school, but there is more to be done around the curriculum, timetabling and developing staff skills through all phases.

Our pedagogy at every stage is based on Rosenshine's Principles of Instruction, but we also refer greatly to Tharby and Allison's 'Making Every Lesson Count'[1]. These are reflected in our routines and evaluations of the quality and impact of teaching, and woven through our curriculum plans.

As we write this we are also consulting with stakeholders around extending the school day to include a 'prep' session at the end of the day. In this time homework would be completed and support and intervention groups would run. We think that it would have a significant positive impact on all pupils, but particularly at the low and high ability range.

The school that will be here in five years' time will, I imagine be very different from the one that we have just started. What won't be different, however, will be the ethos and vision of excellence that we have created and the positive impact we are already having on our community.

1. Allison, S and Tharby, A. 2015.

STUDENT: SARAN

Age and Year Group: 12, Year 7

Most recent:

School Trip: Big Bang Fair, Birmingham
Extra-curricular activity: Football 1st Team
Science experiment: Energy/Forces – series of mini experiments
Book studied in English: *The Invisible Man*, HG Wells
History topic: The Tudors
Arts project: Replicating van Gogh

Learning:

Subjects Studied: All KS3 subjects

Recent learning highlight: In English I learnt about structure. We used the image of a building to think about the different layers and structures to help consolidate our understanding. It really stuck.

The most stand-out/interesting/challenging topic you've studied at school: I enjoyed studying/learning about science because it always keeps me engaged and I love the experiments. They really bring our knowledge and learning to life.

One of my favourite teachers: I enjoy lessons with Mrs Sewell who teaches me Science because there are so many cool facts in science about the world that we live in.

A favourite feature of the school: Here at Kents Hill Park, I believe the staff have really been able to motivate the students and help them through this first year. I have been able to learn in an amazing environment and with this knowledge rich curriculum I think that students will really be able to do very well in the future exams and the real world.

STUDENT: KAI

Age and Year Group: 12, Year 7

Most recent:

School Trip: Body Works exhibition in London
Extra-curricular activity: Cricket
Science experiment: Forces
Book studied in English: *The Invisible Man*
History topic: The Tudors
Arts project: African Masks

Learning:

Subjects Studied: All KS3 subjects

Recent learning highlight: The Big Bang Fair in Birmingham was amazing. It was such a good way to get involved in Science and how it relates to our world around us. It was so inspiring.

The most stand-out/interesting/challenging topic you've studied at school: I enjoyed studying/learning about forces in Science because it's really challenging and interesting. In fact, it's mind-blowing to know all these things are going on around us and we can't even see them.

One of my favourite teachers: I enjoy lessons with Miss Riley who teaches me English because she makes the lessons really interesting and challenging, but in a fun way, and we get to look at literature that we wouldn't normally do. I love reading, so DEAR time is also really fascinating.

A favourite feature of the school: Our knowledge-rich curriculum is absolutely great in helping me remember my key knowledge. The knowledge organisers are also really helpful and regular quick-fire quizzes help us to remember the important subject knowledge. It is a great way to challenge our thinking and help us to identify what we still need to work on.

STUDENT: ALINA

Age and Year Group: 12, Year 7

Most recent:

School Trip: The Big Bang Fair

Extra-curricular activity: Art Club, Code Club, Tennis Club

Science experiment: Setting methane bubbles alight

Book studied in English: *The Invisible Man, Wonder*

History topic: The Tudors

Arts project: Whole school art project (style of Jackson Pollock)

Learning:

Subjects Studied: All KS3 subjects

Recent learning highlight: I liked the lead history lesson to the whole year group in the hall as it was interactive and prepared us for similar lectures in the future.

The most stand-out/interesting/challenging topic you've studied at school: I enjoyed learning about the book 'Wonder' because it was extremely interesting and well written.

One of my favourite teachers: Senora Holland – Spanish – because she makes me smile.

A favourite feature of the school: My favourite place is the library because it is well equipped and a place where you can relax and escape into other worlds through a wide range of books. I love reading and we get the opportunity to read far more than I have experienced before. It's brilliant.

A place where you can relax and escape into other worlds.

ALINA

It is a great way to challenge our thinking and help us to identify what we still need to work on.

KAI

I have been able to learn in an amazing environment.

SARAN

CASE STUDY: HOW WE HAVE DEVELOPED KNOWLEDGE IN THE PRIMARY SETTING

General Area: Curriculum Design

Author: Katy Tough, Assistant Headteacher, Primary Lead

Having the opportunity to create a unique knowledge-rich primary curriculum that suits the needs of our brand new, ever-evolving community, has been extremely fulfilling.

The structure of our planning has been influenced by Christine Counsell's 'Core and Hinterland' model, mirroring that of the Secondary School. Rather than planning lessons by thinking of activities first, 'core knowledge' and the 'hinterland' are now carefully considered, identifying what the children need to know and what will support them to learn it. This is a significant change to how I planned previously and has made the planning process more rigorous, structured and gives greater clarity for expected outcomes. Knowledge organisers have further supported my change in planning style. They have been gradually introduced through the year in History and Geography and are having a positive impact on the children's knowledge retention and recall. I have found the organisers to act as a scaffold for all abilities, enabling those who are developing their long-term memory retention to recall facts with improved confidence as well as acting as a platform to challenge the more able pupils through deeper questioning.

A high quality text lies at the heart of every topic and creates the framework in which purposely chosen core knowledge sits. A wide range of texts, both fiction and non-fiction, have been chosen to widen the children's experience of literature, provoking questions and inspiring thinking and creativity. As the children progress through each topic, and the academic year, intentional links are made between lessons and topics to enable schema to develop and embed.

Taught lessons are, of course, essential but so is knowledge delivered by those who have experienced events first hand. From mountaineers to World War Two evacuees, visitors provide the children with vital hinterland knowledge to ever strengthen schemata.

Barak Rosenshine's 'Principles of Instruction' lay at the centre of our teaching approach. Repetition, practice and daily review are threaded into our daily routines to create ever-connecting schemata and embed key information into pupils' long-term memories. I have begun to use a larger proportion of lesson time 'lecturing, demonstrating and asking questions' rather than giving a longer time for task completion. This has led to increasingly in-depth discussions between the class as a whole, developing the children's concentration and conversation skills. Furthermore, we have largely focused on 'asking and answering questions like a scholar' whereby we expect the children to speak in full sentences, using key terminology with accuracy. After the use of heavy modelling and scaffolds, such as sentence starters to link ideas and generate questions, the children are now far more confident to respond to their teachers as well as their peers.

CASE STUDY: HOW INTRODUCING DEAR TIME HAS SUPPORTED LEARNING

General Area: Teaching and Learning/Curriculum Design

Author: Susanne Riley, Head of English

We ask our pupils to retain and retrieve vast amounts of knowledge daily; DEAR time (Drop Everything and Read) further aids with this process and the rate of pupil progress. Across all curriculum areas, we are keen to develop the pupils' use of vocabulary moving from tier one to tier two; increasing their use and understanding of high frequency vocabulary. Pupils find an increased need to use not only tier two vocabulary, but to delve into the use of tier three vocabulary when accessing particular topics and subjects. DEAR time will make a huge difference in normalising the type of vocabulary we aspire for our pupils to use with ease.

The decision to implement DEAR time at Kents Hill Park School came following a visit to Bedford Free School. DEAR time is used to encourage pupils to dedicate time to reading for pleasure, whilst developing an ability to read challenging texts; something that as teachers we strive to instil in our classes. Through the scheme, pupils are exposed to texts they may never have otherwise been able to access. DEAR time develops confidence in our pupils, encourages independence in their reading and asks them to be forward-thinking; keeping up with the book and thinking about what may happen next.

Our pupils have all had to buy in to DEAR time and it has become embedded in their daily routine. Pupils, as a class, read a text, out loud and together during DEAR time; three times a week. These texts vary in genre and also complexity of language. The selection of texts covers the 'classics', whilst also including some modern novels that have sparked the interest of the pupils. Our text choices, create links to the PSHE curriculum, providing contextual information on historical and current issues/problems we as a society face today.

Staff are undoubtedly playing a vital role in its delivery and impact. Staff facilitate the sessions and help provide an environment in which pupils feel they are able to read with confidence. Modelling, by staff, of how reading should be done, begins each DEAR session; followed by the reading from the pupils. Individuals are selected to read out loud to the rest of the class. There is a driving focus on the pupils tracking the text as it is read, ensuring they can 'take over' when it is their turn. Delivery of the text, when read, is another element that requires focus when DEAR is being delivered. Mistakes in pronunciation and delivery are corrected and repeated by the pupils before they read on, creating a supportive nature in the lessons and between peers. When taking part in DEAR time, pupils are working on the fluency of their reading, as well as understanding how to use pace and expression to bring the text to life. DEAR happens in all subjects, from English through to PE. Reading has quickly become part of our ethos.

At this relatively early stage, pupils have engaged well with the implementation of DEAR time. It has seen all pupils engaged in compulsory reading for one hour a week. Confidence in those who would never volunteer to read out loud has increased, with some of our most reluctant pupils volunteering to read first. This has only been further highlighted through the success of our 'Pop-up Reading Café', which was implemented as part of World Book Day. Pupils who initially were disengaged with reading are now far more engaged and we see them choosing reading in their own personal time.

CASE STUDY: THE USE OF KNOWLEDGE ORGANISERS

Title: The Use of Knowledge Organisers in Maths and Humanities

General Area: Curriculum Design/ Assessment

Authors: Emily Yates, Head of Maths, and Ellie Horton, Head of Humanities

Our knowledge organisers are given to pupils in each subject each half term. They provide facts, figures, vocabulary and content that will be covered that term. In skills subjects such as maths it includes more methods, rules and routines, showing examples of how to apply them.

Within the humanities subjects, pupils are expected to bring knowledge organisers to lessons as part of their equipment, as they are used as an extra resource to support their learning. As pupils progress through the course they are encouraged to acknowledge which part of the organiser they are working on and retrieve relevant information from it. Weekly homework is revision based on the knowledge organiser with pupils being given a specific section to revise which is then tested with small, in class topic tests. Pupils are expected to achieve a score of at least 70% as a minimum. As a result of this the expectation of pupils to have a deeper understanding of the content is higher than I would have previously had.

Within maths pupils are given the knowledge organisers at the end of a topic to summarise everything that has been learnt and give pupils simplified methods and routines to answer different question types. Examples are included to show how these can be applied, with some specifically chosen to highlight common misconceptions. The knowledge organisers can then be used by the pupils to revise for end of topic and end of term tests. In maths lessons where new skills are being introduced, there is a heavy focus on teaching the mathematical understanding; the knowledge organiser provides reminders of the rules once these have been understood.

Link to Learning Rainforest:

- Curriculum /knowledge
- Assessment
- Building the knowledge structure

CASE STUDY: HOW ASSESSMENT SUPPORTS THE KNOWLEDGE CURRICULUM

General Area: Curriculum Design/Assessment

Author: Mark McGarvie, Assistant Headteacher, Curriculum and Standards

Initially to measure attainment, we established a tier-based system. Teachers would derive a judgment on pupil attainment from class tests and classwork. This was then assessed against subject criteria and a tier judgement was then made for each pupil.

Teachers were also asked to make judgements on attitude towards learning, homework, behaviour and progress.

We realised that the assessment system we had established did not tell us the information we wanted about pupil progress. Attainment judgments were difficult to track as they were subjective and did not identify clear gaps in knowledge and understanding. Its intended audience, pupils, parents/carers and teachers found it difficult to understand the context of the data. Teacher judgements on attitude to learning, behaviour and homework were being made after the fact and action needed to be more proactive using live data. We redesigned the whole of our assessment strategy and how it linked to our knowledge rich curriculum. We researched other models and invited contributions from staff.

We identified our key principles:

- Ensure there is a clear reason for the data we collect.
- Ensure we use the data effectively to impact on pupil progress.
- Impact of data collection on staff workload and keep collection of data to a minimum.

We introduced an assessment system across all subjects focusing on two specific approaches which linked into our knowledge-based curriculum.

Short term recall – This focused on providing teachers and pupils with individual information to address gaps in knowledge and misconceptions at a classroom level. High frequency low stakes topic tests are used in class and for homework to identify gaps in knowledge and understanding.

Longer term retention of knowledge – Mid and end of year exams which are standardised across each subject area. These are used to report to parents.

Teachers enter one active assessment piece of data per pupil following an assessed piece of work/test. The data is a 'real' standardised score (%) not a subjective judgment. The assessment score will be compared electronically against the pupil's indicative outcome to determine progress at each point. Live information is being recorded using ICT systems which identify patterns and trends in pupil attitude towards learning, homework, behaviours, punctuality and attendance. All of this is centralised and auto-generated.

Whilst we still have much work to do, we now believe that we are in a strong position to identify gaps in pupil knowledge and support pupil progress. Linking the assessment of pupil attainment and progress to our knowledge-based curriculum provides real actionable data to support pupils in a proactive and effective manner.

We realised that the assessment system we had established did not tell us the information we wanted about pupil progress.

MARK MCGARVIE
ASSISTANT HEADTEACHER,
CURRICULUM AND STANDARDS

Rather than planning lessons by thinking of activities first, 'core knowledge' and the 'hinterland' are now carefully considered, identifying what the children need to know and what will support them to learn it.

KATY TOUGH
ASSISTANT HEADTEACHER,
PRIMARY LEAD

The Kents Hill Park School journey links to several core ideas in *The Learning Rainforest*:

- The plantation/rainforest analogy – our school culture.
- Curriculum/knowledge
- Assessment
- Establishing the conditions
- Building the knowledge structure
- Exploring possibilities

In maths lessons where new skills are being introduced, there is a heavy focus on teaching the mathematical understanding; the knowledge organiser provides reminders of the rules once these have been understood.

EMILY YATES
HEAD OF MATHS
AND
ELLIE HORTON
HEAD OF HUMANITIES

THE LEARNING RAINFOREST

THE PROGRESSIVE-TRADITIONAL DEBATE AND THE TRIVIUM

" HOWEVER WE DEFINE THE OPPOSING POLES OF TRADITIONAL AND PROGRESSIVE PEDAGOGY, THEY BOTH HAVE A VITAL ROLE IN A CHILD'S EDUCATION. I AM NOT SUGGESTING THAT THERE IS NO DISTINCTION.

" IT'S IMPORTANT TO UNDERSTAND THE TRADITIONAL Vs PROGRESSIVE DEBATE – BUT IT IS ALSO POSSIBLE TO AGREE WITH POSITIONS ON BOTH SIDES.

" IF YOU ASSUME CLAXTON'S 'BELOW THE LINE' THINKING GOES HAND IN HAND WITH A STRONG BEDROCK OF TRADITIONAL KNOWLEDGE-RICH CURRICULUM DESIGN, IT MAKES SENSE; EDUCATING 'THE WHOLE CHILD' TRANSCENDS THE PROG-TRAD DIVIDE.

" THERE ARE LOADED CRITIQUES FROM BOTH SIDES THAT I RECOIL FROM INCLUDING SIR KEN ROBINSON'S NOTION OF SCHOOLS 'STRIPMINING' CHILDREN'S MINDS OR THE IDEA THAT STUDENTS CANNOT MAKE CHOICES ABOUT THEIR LEARNING OR THAT ANY COLLABORATIVE LEARNING MUST BE WEAK.

" THERE'S ALWAYS A RISK IN DOWN PLAYING KNOWLEDGE; IN THE LEARNING TREE METAPHOR, KNOWLEDGE IS ALWAYS CORE.

" HYMAN'S 'HEAD, HAND AND HEART' AND THE IDEA OF A TRIVIUM FOR THE 21ST CENTURY – GRAMMAR, DIALECTIC AND RHETORIC – RESONATE WITH THE RAINFOREST METAPHOR.

" EACH SPECIMEN IS ONE OF THE 'PHILOSOPHER KIDS' OUT IN THE GLOBAL AGORA'.

THE CURRICULUM DEBATE

" WE WANT OUR CHILDREN TO HAVE IT ALL: KNOWLEDGE AND UNDERSTANDING ACROSS MULTIPLE DOMAINS' A RANGE OF PRACTICAL AND INTELLECTUAL SKILLS AND A RANGE OF CHARACTER TRAITS – RENAISSANCE PEOPLE.

" WHAT WE TEACH AND HOW WE TEACH ARE INTERLINKED IN THE ENACTED CURRICULUM.

" CURRICULUM IS SPECIFIED IN DIFFERENT WAYS BUT THERE IS ALWAYS SOME ROOM FOR TEACHER INPUT – OFTEN A LOT OF FREEDOM TO CHOOSE THE BOOKS AND HISTORICAL PERIODS THAT STUDENTS STUDY.

" THE CORE KNOWLEDGE DEBATE IS VITAL – WHAT KNOWLEDGE SHOULD ALL STUDENTS HAVE? ANY SELECTION HAS CULTURAL BIAS – SO WHAT DO WE INCLUDE AND EXCLUDE?

" CULTURAL CAPITAL NEEDS TO BE TAUGHT DELIBERATELY – AND SHOULD INCLUDE EXPERIENCES LIKE CONCERTS, PLAYS, WALKING IN MOUNTAINS, VISITING MUSEUMS AND ENGAGING IN CURRENT AFFAIRS.

" BEYOND TEACHING 'THE BEST THAT'S BEEN THOUGHT AND SAID' WE'RE TRYING TO GIVE STUDENTS THE KNOWLEDGE TO ENGAGE IN 'THE CONVERSATION OF MANKIND'.

BRUNE PARK SCHOOL, GOSPORT

INTRODUCTION

I have known Kirstie Andrew-Power and Ian Potter for a long time, personally and professionally, and I've been a great admirer of their work at Bay House School, a very successful, popular school in Gosport on England's south coast. I was, therefore, very excited to be asked to provide some additional 'capacity-building' support when, in 2017, rather bravely and boldly, they took on Brune Park School into their MAT when it was in a very challenging situation – as they describe below. I honestly don't think I've ever met a more resilient, more courageous group of school leaders – and it is certainly rare to meet people with such strong philosophical, principled views on school leadership, resolute in their determination to take the long-term path rather than the short-term fix, even when this feels counter-intuitive to outsiders.

Every term for the last two years I have visited Brune Park on a number of occasions, working closely with subject leaders in certain departments and their senior leader colleagues around aspects of teaching practice and curriculum design. It's fair to say the school has changed more than any other in the *Fieldbook* during that time. Every success has been hard won; the setbacks have often been significant but the pay-off is clear to see with every visit I make. The philosophy at Brune Park is about as far from 'plantation thinking' as you can get in leadership terms and their commitment to staff empowerment and to what I call 'rainforest thinking' is profound – although they don't use the term directly.

In many ways, the journey has just begun, but the culture shift I've already witnessed is palpable and I'm extremely proud to present this insight into that journey as told by David, Kirstie and Ian and their students Frances and Joseph.

PROFILE

Institution Name: Brune Park Community School Gosport and Fareham Multi Academy Trust
Location: Gosport, Hampshire, UK
Type of Institution: Mixed Comprehensive
Roll/Age Range: 1500, aged 11–16
Year Founded: 1965
Motto: 'Toujours Pret'
House Names: Gielgud, Lennon, Fontane, Hepburn
Quote: From a Year 11 student to a teacher:

'I can never put into words how thankful I am to have been one of your students in the last year. Thank you for teaching us to love English. Thank you for always giving me guidance when things got super tough; you have always taught me that anything is possible and even if I don't think I can get somewhere you've always told me to believe and never give up. You took me on feeling under-confident, fragile, not believing I could achieve. I finally feel that I can now move on and blossom into what I want and aim to do. I will never forget your humour and kindness and treating the whole class as individual people. If you remember only one thing about the 'class of 2019' I hope it is the lasting impact you made on me and on every individual in our class; you never once didn't believe in us and for a little old cohort like ours that from a teacher is something we'll never forget. Now I'm moving on I feel so much more confident in my academic ability across the subjects (even grown to love them!) but more importantly, I feel confident in myself as a person and you Sir have been a huge influence on that. Thank you for a year of laughter, tears and T3C[1].'

Our MAT Ethos: Brune Park is part of a local Multi-Academy Trust – Gosport and Fareham MAT or GFM (one of the first nationally) – focused on raising aspirations and outcomes for learners across the Town of Gosport; it comprises five schools working collectively locally to support each other on their improvement journey; not in competition but in co-operation for ambition for all young people in Gosport.

Kirstie Andrew-Power
Headteacher

Ian Potter
CEO GFM

---

1. T3C means 'Thesis, 3 supporting statements, conclusion' – a framework for writing essays.

CASE STUDY: CREATING AND SECURING THE CLIMATE, CONDITIONS AND COMMITMENT TO 'BETTERMENT FOR ALL'

General Area: Leadership

Authors: Kirstie Andrew-Power, Headteacher, and **Ian Potter**, CEO

Brune Park is a vibrant and energising place to be; a school community united by positivity and belief – in each other and in the potential of the school to be truly great.

We are also honest about where we are. The school has been 'in challenge' for 20 years (as the school's inspection history demonstrates – if that is a measure you draw from ...) We know we are making progress but it can still often feel very, very tough (we describe this as falling down seven times but still getting up eight times!) We are restless in wanting to hasten to where we want and need to be; we want everyone in the Brune Park community to be proud to be 'Brune Park' and that with that pride comes success – both academic and personal.

As a staff we are positive, motivated and driven; honest in our reflections, honest about the challenges we face and strive to embrace them head on. In an educational world where much is challenging, and much can be negative as a staff and school, we are resolute in being positive, having relentlessly high expectations of ourselves and each other, focusing on collective endeavour, and togetherness and we believe this is how we can transform the school for good (not just to get a 'Good' inspection rating.)

Our leadership focus has unashamedly been that the impact of anything we do as school leaders should be evaluated in terms of the young people's experience. And we know that the quality of provision they receive is mainly, if not perhaps wholly, facilitated by their teacher. It is the teacher who creates the climate for their learning; is excited by the agendas they chose to set; is thoroughly motivated by the content they impart because they have understood the difference it can make to the students; and thinks carefully about the method and design of a selected mode of delivery, presentation, activity or guided discovery. We contend what David has written exemplifies this espousal.

Obviously, the responsibility cannot be placed entirely with the teacher. Others have their responsibility, including the learner. For example, however hard an enabler enables, the impact of what they do is reduced if the disposition of the learner 'blocks' the efforts of the teacher. In much the same way, the endeavours of a manager are reduced if those being managed choose a negative attitude towards it. Whilst the approaches taken by a teacher or manager will support creating a positive response to their intentions, if someone's disposition is so poor it is an awful challenge. This is especially so when they are unprepared to listen, to reflect and be open to a different way of being. Therefore, if they reject the offer to be the best they can be, a leader needs to illuminate this to them.

It was this process of illumination that we took as leaders in a school that was in denial about its culture. We do not blame the school; it was the product of the way it had been treated by a system that was about blame and retribution. Thus, the leadership had to enable a different process of school improvement. It had to give permission for people to 'look-to-thyself' and evaluate their own disposition. Colleagues in the school had to feel safe enough to be honest with themselves and recognise cognitive dissonance when it happened. We, with positional leadership authority, needed to support staff build the confidence to entertain changing how they felt about themselves, and therefore each other, the school and, of course, the young people.

Hence, the reflective practitioner is absolutely at the heart of what we are about. An absolute priority for professional learning is continually signalled. Reflecting on what are the barriers to improvement and assessing the motivation levels to want to overcome them becomes the mantra. Choosing one's disposition and admitting that how each of us opted to behave influenced the culture of the whole school, making the decision to change oneself would have a positive benefit for all. It was a matter of realising that the locus-of-control rests with each of us rather than external to us. It was an active choice to contribute to the collective endeavour for the good.

There was a text we used as a 'go-to' to keep reminding us of the purpose for promoting this sort of discourse. We sought opportunities to share it. It is:

'I've come to a frightening conclusion that I am the decisive element in the school. It's my personal approach that creates the climate. It's my daily mood that makes the weather. As a teacher, I possess a tremendous power to make a child's life miserable or joyous. I can be a tool of torture or an instruction of inspiration. I can humiliate or heal. In all situations it is my response that decides whether a crisis will be escalated or de-escalated and a child humanized or dehumanised.'
Haim G. Ginott

Link to Learning Rainforest:

The rationale for this perspective on leadership is that 'top-down' reform is a less sustainable way to transform a school. We can always make ourselves feel good as managers and achieve quick wins that demonstrate 'impact'. Any gains are so often short term. It is understandable that, in a targets-driven environment, we can find ourselves behaving like this. It can incentivise competitive behaviours that lead to results in a shorter time frame being a more important outcome than longer term sustainability. The product should be organisational climates that grow people rather than the potentially toxic relationships and pressures that short termism can lead to. At worst, it results in 'good' people doing things they would not normally do, particularly if they are sensing a need to survive. Therefore, the leadership challenge is to enable those we lead to feel safe enough to be honest with themselves and have the skill set to do this in a way that does not compromise on a direction-of-travel of improvement and betterment. The young people we serve deserve the aspiration that they experience the best quality teaching that we can enable for them.

Our strategy for attempting to achieve this is illustrated in the messages we shared with colleagues at our first meeting together. As well as the slide shared in David's entry above, we shared the following:

The Plan:

- To support you to be the best you choose to be.
- It is a choice that reveals your disposition – we choose our attitude!

The Rationale

- It is less about 'top-down' initiatives; instead, it is to expect everyone to want to maximise their own performance.

It is a message we regularly revisit:

CASE STUDY: CREATING AND SECURING THE CLIMATE, CONDITIONS AND COMMITMENT TO 'BETTERMENT FOR ALL'

How can I reach him/her?
What else can I do?

I'm finding this hard. I'll ask my line manager for some ideas and support.

Someone else needs to deal with this student.

I'd be fine if other staff had the same high expectations as me.

If we all had the same expectations and stuck to them it would be much better.

Students in this school/ year group/Gosport just don't know how to behave.

- A large number of you are experienced teachers/staff who, given the trust, excel. Get on with excelling.

- Not all of you may trust yourselves, so please be honest and seek support. Ask and we will do what we can.

- Some may have lost confidence in what is now expected and what constitutes high performance. Therefore ask!

- Others are less experienced and will be keen to receive support. Great!

- If you are less motivated to excel or improve, then please talk to us.

Some of you may still be growing trust and confidence in yourself, and what constitutes high performance. Please keep being honest and seeking support.

You are curious, reflective, motivated to improve...You seek support to enable you to try new and different ways to meet challenges...and you are committed to making changes, practising doing things differently...

You have high expectations; you reinforce these; you seek support to help you assert these when you need to. You are firm and fair...students really value you.

Thank you for being motivated and driven!

I'm finding this hard. I'll ask my line manager for some ideas and support.

Someone else needs to deal with this student.

I'd be fine if other staff had the same high expectations as me.

There are now very few staff who are less motivated to excel or improve...

There are now very few staff who want to pass the buck or dodge their accountabilities...

But...there are moments of uncertainty...

There are moments of 'reverting' to old ways of doing things or old ways of thinking...

If we all had the same expectations and stuck to them it would be much easier.

Students in this school/year group/ Gosport just don't know how to behave.

Many of you are experienced teachers/staff who, having been given the trust, are excelling.

You are curious, reflective, motivated to improve...

You constantly seek new and different ways to meet challenges...

You have high expectations and support and enable students to meet these expectations. You are firm and fair...students really value you.

Thank you for getting on with excelling.

How can I reach him/her? What else can I do?

And it reflects, to a degree, a 'non-negotiable' in approach to believing in betterment for all: us as leaders, colleagues and students. It is an approach we suggest, takes time to process in conversation with colleagues, students and often parents and relies on creating opportunity for thoughtful, reflective dialogue.

- Our professional responsibility is to believe we ALL capable of excelling.

- It is to have faith in the learner, be they an adult or young person.

It requires challenging individuals to consider the role they play as individuals working in the collective; to challenge thinking and challenge ways of working, and then create opportunities so the climate for 'betterment' is one of professional support, at times inspiration, at times robust challenge.

The climate created for and with teachers can become the 'Teachers' Learning Rainforest' with professional learning opportunities being a so valued, and so productive for staff it is an entitlement for a school community, shared, co-constructed: a collective endeavour to support the collective endeavour – perhaps summed up by Fullan and Hargreaves:

'The power of collective capacity is that it enables ordinary people to accomplish extraordinary things – for two reasons. One is that knowledge about effective practice becomes more widely available and accessible on a daily basis. The second reason is more powerful still – working together generates commitment.'

The drive to secure lasting, embedded change with and for a community that has suffered from years of low confidence, low aspiration and poor standards is a moral drive. The approach we have chosen to take was not consciously in line with the Learning Rainforest metaphor. But it is: it is about creating and securing the climate, conditions and commitment to 'betterment for all', it is about building the professional capital and art of teaching and leadership, it is about there being endless possibilities being achievable. It is the climate and conditions to build collective capacity in order to secure lasting and embedded change. Time will determine whether the approach we have chosen to take will work, what we can be clear on is that the drive, the commitment and the desire is there – to complete the Fullan and Hargreaves quote: 'Moral purpose when it stares you in the face through students and your peers working together to make lives and society better, is palpable, indeed virtually irresistible.' Why wouldn't we?

STUDENT: FRANCES WESTON

Age and Year Group: 16, Year 11
House: Lennon

Most recent:

School Trip: Disneyland Paris, February 2019
Extra-curricular activity: Singing lessons, Student leadership activities
Book/Play studied in English Literature: *Macbeth*
History topic: Super power relations and the Cold War
Arts project: GCSE Music Coursework

Learning:

Subjects Studied: English Language; English Literature, Mathematics; Combined Science; History, Music, BTEC Business Studies, Certificate in Financial Education, GCSE Citizenship
Recent learning highlight: Over the past year, the course of Business Studies grasped me in ways I didn't think was imaginable. Learning the exam unit made me come to a realisation of how to work in the 'real world' and showed my strengths within the course.
The most stand-out/interesting/challenging topic you've studied at school: When going through my GCSEs, studying music hasn't always proved to be easy. I enjoyed learning all the set-works despite some setbacks when things got hard.
One of my favourite teachers: I enjoyed my lessons with Mr Andrew-Power in English the most during the last 10 months. He always assured we had the best experience within the subject and gave me the ability to reach grades I didn't think were achievable for someone like me. (I'm the student that wrote the letter quoted at the beginning of our case study!)
A favourite feature of the school: Whilst attending Brune Park one of my favourite things about the school was the culture. The community vibe you get from day one leaves you truly believing you are welcome anywhere and have the ability to speak up at anytime.

STUDENT: JOSEPH DAWSON

Age and Year Group: 16, Year 11
House: Gielgud

Most recent:

School Trip: UK Parliament
Extra-curricular activity: Student Leadership team and various student councils
Science experiment: Titrations
Book/Play studied in English Literature: *An Inspector Calls*

Learning:

Subjects Studied: BTEC Business Studies, BTEC Engineering, Geography, Separate Sciences, English Lit & Lang, Maths, Statistics, Certificate in Financial Education, Citizenship
Recent learning highlight: In Summer I'm taking part in a Model United Nations event. In English we were taught to look at texts through different conceptual lenses, so when we read a piece we look at it from many angles. I was reading the UN briefing, it mentioned they 'need new conceptual lenses' for managing global issues. And it showed how, although we're working towards an exam, the work we do in class ties into the real world. I emailed my teacher said: 'I'm reading documentation for a 'model UN' and it made me think of English and how the whole way I look at our pieces and my enjoyment from reading them changes with concepts and it showed that lenses also contain relevance to the UN. Effectively, I thought it was really cool what you were doing with us in class is also a thing the UN does. Thanks for being a fab teacher.'
The most stand-out/interesting/challenging topic you've studied at school: Engineering was, for me, the most interesting, learning the processes to make everyday items as well as the properties of different materials with a heavily coursework and practical based course kept the lessons constantly interesting as we moved through the units without having to focus on an exam deadline.
One of my favourite teachers: I enjoy lessons with Mrs Hillawi who teaches Chemistry because she makes sure we're challenged and adds real world context to everything we do (so we're not just trying to pass an exam).
A favourite feature of the school: One of my favourite features of Brune Park is the student voice, if we ever have a concern or wish our school allows us to directly query or act upon it, giving us ownership over Brune Park.

I thought it was really cool that what you were doing with us in class is also a thing the UN does. Thanks for being a fab teacher.

JOSEPH DAWSON

Now I'm moving on I feel so much more confident in my academic ability across the subjects (even grown to love them!) but more importantly, I feel confident in myself as a person and you Sir have been a huge influence on that.

FRANCES WESTON

CASE STUDY: TRANSFORMING A SCHOOL FOR GOOD

General Area: Teaching and Learning/CPD/Leadership

Author: David Higginbottom, Assistant Headteacher, GFM's Institute of Education

As leaders we joined a school that was under confident and in many ways 'in crisis,' there were lots of actions that we could have taken, things we could have done and advice from external evaluation audits and visits that we could have followed. We decided on the approach we would take and committed to it: not 'top-down' and 'you will do X, Y and Z,' or one of rolling out whole school policies hoping they might 'stick'. We recognised that these approaches had been taken in the school for many years and had not secured sustainable, positive change. We committed to a strategy and approach to enable all to change their behaviours, to want to change as part of an improvement of self and others.

Our approach focuses on co-constructed and co-owned strategies and a commitment to a shared understanding of each of our accountabilities to secure the school we all want it to be. This approach is different in style to more 'traditional' models of the leadership and management of change, it is unorthodox, we did not start from a point of believing we were 'right' but recognised we needed to do something different to the models that had been in the school, or bought into the school over the past twelve years by different leaders. It may be 'right' it may not be, but it is the approach that we have committed to – a collectively improved and 'owned' school will be a collectively successful school. Why? Because we believe collective endeavour changes culture and through changing the culture of the school we will enable higher expectations, higher aspirations and self-belief in a community that needs and deserves more. We will bring about sustainable changes that will be long lasting.

Example 1: subject driven behaviour management

We recognised that where teachers felt a sense of ownership of their classroom, set themselves and students high expectations, had robust follow up to support students modify their behaviour, working with parents and effective subject leads – classroom conduct and engagement was very positive. In these classrooms, teachers were embracing opportunities to further develop their teaching, were actively involved in reimagining the curriculum and approaches to assessment and were instrumental in creating positive shifts in thinking for themselves and across their teams. Many of these colleagues were not in formal leadership positions, yet their leadership of change was and is significant. To bring in a 'top down' whole school behaviour policy would undermine the messages Ian and Kirstie describe above.

The cries for a whole school behaviour policy continued from those who were finding some classes or individual students tricky, who wanted to teach 'without them in the class' who didn't feel it was their responsibility to deal with the complexity of challenge around inclusion. We were and are empathetic – as leaders our classes do not necessarily run smoothly, we have and are having to work very hard using everything in our 'toolboxes' to support some students change and modify their behaviours.

Our resolve has been tested, and continues to be tested. We actually have a clear, co-constructed policy but what some colleagues want is a set of sanctions that can be applied if a child does not do as expected that, ideally, the class teacher does not have to see through; a punitive approach so students know if they step out of line X or Y will happen. As has often been the case, we have had to hold our nerve. To have responded with a 'top down' policy would compromise and potentially undermine the cultural shift that is taking place across teams and classrooms in the

school. It does not secure or embed changes in the climate where staff choose to attend professional learning or seek support and ideas from others to try in their own classrooms. It does not provide the staff most in need of support the opportunity to step out of their comfort zone, to try something new, to feel accountable and see the accountability through. It would not support staff who are learning how to work with students (and parents) in a positive way in order to secure changes in behaviour. It does not encourage or further build confidence in staff to self-reflect on their disposition as being a choice. To bring in a whole school policy would and will undermine the positive work of subject teams in 'owning' what high expectations of the classroom are, and how they can be achieved.

The focus has remained on creating frequent opportunities where colleagues come together to work on how to improve their teaching, sharing ways other manage the tricky class or individual, practising the 'tweaks' or new ideas, nurturing and growing the toolkit' of strategies.

And our greatest challenge, of course, is ensuring the positive progress continues and the improvement start to 'stick'. It is about being relentless in getting the 'wins' successes, positives and collective strategies to still be active and effective in two weeks, or four, six, even 10 weeks time.

Example 2: Supporting positive improvement through co-planning:

To provide a structure that enabled regular professional learning, frequent opportunity for high quality professional dialogue, revisits, opportunity for reflection practice etc., we made a decision early on to think carefully about how we deployed directed time. We wanted to ensure staff had high quality,

Establishing attitudes and habits for excellence and creating an ethos where professional learning, continued professional development and educational research is valued remains key to underpinning our school improvement ethos.

DAVID HIGGINBOTTOM
ASSISTANT HEADTEACHER,
GFM'S INSTITUTE OF EDUCATION

CASE STUDY: TRANSFORMING A SCHOOL FOR GOOD

structured, organised and learning focused time together minded of course, for the challenging time demands on all staff. We planned how directed time could be well used to focus on professional learning throughout the school year

In September 2018, following a review and supported by Tom Sherrington, we established four focus areas for improving the quality of teaching and learning across Brune Park:

1. Behaviour and expectations – assertive and consistent reinforcement of expectations coupled with warm, positive relationships. Dealing effectively with major disruptions and tackling low-level disruption at its onset

2. Focus on knowledge – placing more emphasis on direct teaching in knowledge heavy subjects, based on Rosenshine's Principles of Instruction. More direct modelling and explanation. Further development and use of knowledge organisers in classrooms

3. Questioning – eliciting responses from all and retrieval practice. Embedding 'Cold Calling' and 'Checking for Understanding' to engage more students in the discourse in lessons

4. Curriculum planning and resourcing – designing high quality 'standard' resources for standard topics, to provide a secure knowledge base and references for students

To enable colleagues to focus on these four areas we recognised the need to provide professional learning time for professional dialogue, inputs, reflection time, time to practise etc. We built 'co-planning' sessions into our directed time calendar – calling it co-planning rather than 'meetings.' Co-planning meetings were divided into; Subject Team Co-planning, Leadership Co-planning and Tutor Co-planning. The rationale behind this approach was that subject teams, year teams and middle leadership

colleagues would have dedicated time to work collaboratively on; co-constructed behaviour strategies (both subject-led and year team-led), curriculum planning and resourcing – with a clearer focus on direct teaching for knowledge and on developing questioning strategies. Thus the accountability for driving improvements in the quality of teaching became and continues to be shared – a collectively improving and 'owned' school we expect will have greater scope to become a collectively successful school. Co-planning sessions also provide the space and time for colleagues to meet regularly in teams to engage in professional dialogue about their practice. Therefore the notion of being a reflective practitioner, which has become the core of what we are about, flourishes and is nurtured.

Points of reflection

1. Awareness of assumptions. We have come to learn that we often make assumptions but we don't always know what we are assuming! For example; a co-planning session that is positive, energetic and energising, with everyone engaged and enthusiastic does not equate to changes in practice in the classroom that have been explored and discussed. X doesn't equal Y and we have needed to, and continue to have conversations where we focus on the desired outcome, and work back to see if we are making any assumptions along the way.

2. Taking actions and strategies to the point they are embedded or 'sticking'. People need motivation to 'get on board' and but morale can sometimes dip. As leaders we need to remain optimistic and positive and keep driving change while being resilient and not be put off ourselves by temporary dips before the benefits of change start to show green shoots. Driving some colleagues out of their comfort zone takes a

continued effort and we have needed to have patience with some in the early stages. 'Hurry up' traits can be damaging and however uncomfortable being in an 'unfrozen state' feels, we have needed to help people move away from keeping old strategies working whilst we have created new ones.

3. Feedback to colleagues leads to changes in classroom practices/improvements in the quality of teaching – we have learned again and again that we need in our 'toolbox' wide ranging strategies to deploy in order to feedback to colleagues about their teaching in ways that prompt reflection, thought and a desire or will to want to make changes. We are continuing to learn the need for us to do things differently to bring about changes in behaviour so that changes in teaching become habitual. Striking a balance is hard; open and honest conversations need to happen in order to bring about change but how do you achieve this without crushing staff confidence, particularly when staff are working really hard, are really committed to change but perhaps don't know how to change.

4. Schools are busy places. This makes it difficult at times to say 'we are not accepting second best'. We have to be relentless in our drive for continued improvements in the quality of teaching across the school and this can be exhausting at times. We have to rely on the leadership team to be together and supportively together as 'relentless.'

It is about creating and securing the climate, conditions and commitment to 'betterment for all', it is about building the professional capital and art of teaching and leadership, it is about there being endless possibilities being achievable. It is the climate and conditions to build collective capacity in order to secure lasting and embedded change.

KIRSTIE ANDREW-POWER
HEADTEACHER
AND
IAN POTTER
CEO

ARCHBISHOP TENISON CE SCHOOL, LAMBETH

INTRODUCTION

Archbishop Tenison's School is a gem of a school; a bona fide inner-city school where the library windows look right over into London's Oval cricket ground between the stands. Housed in Victorian buildings that bear all the signs of tradition, its long history and Christian ethos, the school is occupied by students, teachers and leaders with a thoroughly contemporary outlook. From the moment students enter the front doors each morning, there is a strong feeling of belonging with lovely peer-to-peer camaraderie and teacher-student interactions that communicate love, care and no-nonsense high expectations. It's fascinating how quickly a school's spirit can come across.

The great ATS cheerleader is Natasha Fox, Assistant Head, who spends every minute engaging busily with students and staff on all manner of day-to-day issues as well as leading on teaching and learning and the whole curriculum review process described below. Such energy and enthusiasm is wonderful to behold. Natasha (Tash) raves about Jim – interim Headteacher for two crucial years – and a source of huge experience, wisdom and calm strategic know-how. It's been a real joy to work with them both on the ATS curriculum. Jim's account of the history of curriculum bolt-ons over the last 30 years is superb, capturing the situation that many schools find themselves in now. Similarly, his critique of assessment and feedback practice is spot on. Jim and Tash's commitment to changing their school culture is impressive and they've done a superb job bringing staff with them.

I'll retain fond memories of all my small-group and one-to-one discussions with the ATS subject leaders, exploring their curriculum models, the choices they made, the things they were determined to keep or had to leave out, the way they tried to reflect the make-up of the school community. I was impressed with their earnest engagement in the process – a willingness to adapt and change, to find interesting links across subject disciplines. When we put it all together, the curriculum overview seemed hugely impressive to me – culturally diverse, expansive in terms of global case-studies, conceptually well sequenced, blending contemporary and traditional genres and weaving in enriching projects and experiences beyond the classroom. Jim is leaving a school in great shape – and in capable hands!

Let your light shine before others.

MATTHEW 5:16

PROFILE

Location: Kennington, Lambeth, South London

Type of Institution: Co-ed Church of England academy

Roll/Age Range: 400, aged 11–16

Year Founded: 1685

Motto: 'Educating Mind, Body and Spirit since 1685'

House Names: Canterbury, Durham, Winchester, York

Recent significant sports event/triumph: Ten of our students were given tickets to see Michelle Obama at Southbank in December 2018. This was a really inspiring event and one of our Year 10 girls talked to a large audience at school about how it had inspired her as a young black woman.

Notable quirks/alumni: The England cricket team uses our playground as a car park when there is a Test match at The Oval.

Jim Henderson
Headteacher

Natasha Fox
Assistant Headteacher

Archbishop Tenison's School (ATS) was founded in 1685 in the crypt of St Martin-in-the-Fields church by Thomas Tenison who went on to become Archbishop of Canterbury. Its founding principle was to provide an excellent, free education for the boys

PROFILE

STUDENT: ADAMATU BANGURA

of the parishes of St James', Piccadilly and St Martin-in-the-Fields. The school expanded and moved over the centuries until it settled in its current building in 1927 opposite the Oval cricket ground in South London. It had always been a boys' school and it was a grammar school up until the 1970s. It then became a comprehensive school. In 2015 it went co-ed in Year 7 and is now a co-ed school all the way through to Year 11. As a small school and with funding changes to post-16 places and many large post-16 providers close by, the small sixth-form was always vulnerable. And in 2016 the decision was made to close it. The last cohort graduated in summer 2019.

The school went into Special Measures in October 2016 and, after a short period with an interim headteacher, Jim Henderson was brought in in September 2017 as Consultant Headteacher for two years. He discovered a school with lots of distinct strengths and areas of excellence but without a galvanising philosophy. He also recognised the traumatic impact that the 2016 Ofsted judgment had had on a team of dedicated, hard-working professionals who were utterly committed to the wellbeing and success of the students at the school. In his words, on his first day, his job was to help the school, staff and students to 'get your mojo back'.

A key driver of the improvement strategy was to encourage professional reading and reflection to rebuild professional self-belief and self-confidence amongst teachers and, through this prism, to re-examine all practices at the school in a context of best practice research and a need to look after the wellbeing of staff and students. Tom Sherrington's blog and *The Learning Rainforest* were two of the most highly recommended reads that staff shared with each other. The principles have helped to shape a coherent framework for discussion about teaching and learning, assessment, curriculum, classroom ethos.

What you see today is a school where excellent relationships, happiness, real focus in classrooms, confidence to take risks (both staff and students), pride and high expectations define the culture. The school exam results improved significantly in summer 2018 and were radically transformed and strong across the whole curriculum in summer 2019.

The school became an academy on 1st January 2019 within the Southwark Diocesan Board of Education (SDBE). It has been providing education for young people in London for 334 years and now looks forward to another 334 years of successes, holding onto its strong traditions and history, whilst adapting the way it educates its students in mind, body and spirit to develop happy, active, successful and engaged citizens.

Age and Year Group: 14, Year 9

House: Winchester

Most recent:

School Trip: As part of the school's Girlhood to Womanhood programme I went to see 'Motown, The Musical' at the Shaftesbury Theatre. The programme is about building self-confidence and I saw this portrayed on stage.

Extra-curricular activity: I love drama and have been in three school plays: *Christmas Carol* (as an angel); a school-written version of *Romeo and Juliet* (as Juliet) and *Back to the Future*. In this one I mainly played Marty's dad but had a few character and gender changes. I am passionate about acting. It is something I love to do.

Science experiment: We investigated the thermal insulation properties of materials by wrapping a beaker of hot water in different materials and recording the temperature change. The best insulator was giant bubble wrap.

Book/Play studied in English Literature: We have been studying one of the GCSE texts, Shakespeare's *Romeo and Juliet*. It is interesting to learn to interpret Shakespeare's language and we are now analysing and interpreting different themes in the text.

History topic: We study the history of medicine from the Middle Ages to the present day. We are currently learning about the significant impact on lives of the development of anaesthetics and Penicillin.

Arts project: We are currently studying Pop Art. We have been using the box method for our drawings. I am learning how to follow the steps accurately.

Learning:

Subjects Studied: English, Maths, Geography, History, French, Art, Music, D&T, Computing, Science, Religious Studies and PE.

Recent learning highlight: I really enjoyed learning in PE from Mr Thomas about the components of fitness. I enjoyed seeing how many components are important in sport and in a generally healthy lifestyle. It has helped me to analyse how different sports and fitness activities develop different components.

The most stand-out/interesting/challenging topic you've studied at school: For ages I have struggled with the concept of Compound Interest in Maths. I would always leave it out in tests. However, Mr Guenkou has been really patient and helpful in explaining it to me and now I know and can apply it.

One of my favourite teachers: Miss Lynch was my form tutor and has always been there for me. Recently I was upset by a sensitive issue and was crying. She helped me to feel better and take control. She is like a mother as well as a teacher. She is unique.

A favourite feature of the school: I love the small size of the school. It means that everyone knows each other and is happy to talk. This brings our community really close together. Being in houses helps younger and older students make connections too.

If you don't believe you can do it, how can it be done?

ADAMATU BANGURA

STUDENT: DANIEL BENNETT

Age and Year Group: 14, Year 9
House: Durham

Most recent:

School Trip: We went on a science trip to the National Theatre. We were shown the science and technology used backstage to help the production such as lighting, sound and special effects. I am really interested in music so I really liked seeing their sound system.

Extra-curricular activity: I have been learning piano here since Year 8. I did my first public performance at an inter-school concert in Southwark Cathedral in the summer.

Science experiment: We created methane bubbles by pumping gas through water with washing-up liquid. When we held the bubbles and ignited them there was a huge ball of flame.

Book/Play studied in English Literature: We studied *Macbeth* in Year 8 and are now studying *Romeo and Juliet*. I prefer *Macbeth* as there is more action and less romance. I enjoy studying the characters' motives.

History topic: We learnt about life in the trenches on the Western Front. We did this using official reports and also the writings and poems of soldiers. The conditions sounded awful.

Arts project: I composed a piece of music in a reggae style using the school's music technology equipment. We had listened to Bob Marley and analysed his music to help me with my composition.

Learning:

Subjects Studied: English, Maths, Science, Religious Studies, Music, French, D&T, Art, History, Geography, PE.

Recent learning highlight: We watched the Baz Luhrmann film of *Romeo and Juliet*. This helped me to understand the play. It was interesting to see how he changed the setting but kept the underlying concepts the same.

The most stand-out/interesting/challenging topic you've studied at school: Learning trigonometry in Maths was a real challenge but I enjoyed making the effort to understand it and can now use sine, cosine and tangent applications to solve triangle problems.

One of my favourite teachers: Ms Lynch enhances her English lessons through the use of drama. It really helps to get some of the concepts across.

A favourite feature of the school: I like being able to have access to the music room at break and lunchtime to practise my piano playing. I am currently practising a grade 5 piece called Film Noir.

An investment in knowledge pays the best interest.
BENJAMIN FRANKLIN

As a man thinks in his heart, so is he.
PROVERBS 23:7

STUDENT: ELLA CLARKE

Age and Year Group: 15, Year 10
House: Canterbury

Most recent:

School Trip: We visited St Martin's School for a sixth form taster day. I was involved in A-level sessions on Psychology, Sociology and Drama. It has reinforced my excitement to study these subjects in the sixth-form

Extra-curricular activity: We run a physical literacy programme called STEP to help our Year 7 students with their concentration, motor skills and literacy. I am a programme supervisor and take the children through their exercises.

Science experiment: We made an insoluble salt. We learnt the need for precision and safety and saw how our laboratory process could scale up into an industrial context.

Book/Play studied in English Literature: I enjoyed studying *An Inspector Calls* because it highlights the class structure of this country. It introduced me to the concepts of socialism and capitalism.

Geography topic: As part of Human Geography we studied the urbanisation of Mumbai. We learnt about the huge economic divide between rich and poor and how the poor are pushing bottom-up strategies to improve their lives.

Arts project: In PE we were taught how to draw human anatomy. I enjoyed learning how to draw scientifically accurate diagrams.

Learning:

Subjects Studied: English, Maths, Science, Religious Studies, Business Studies, French, GCSE PE.

Recent learning highlight: In Religious Studies we learnt about the prison system. In particular we looked at the role of chaplains and other religious workers in prisons and how they fit into the judicial system.

The most stand-out/interesting/challenging topic you've studied at school: Our Religious Studies teachers are keen to stretch our thinking. Recently we studied the A-level topic of the inconsistent triad. This considers evil in the world and asks why, despite God being omnipotent and omnibenevolent, evil exists.

One of my favourite teachers: Ms Joyce is a great teacher of Geography. She explains things very clearly and thoroughly and is always happy to help me outside lessons if I need it.

A favourite feature of the school: The constant feeling of community support. In a small school we all feel well-known to each other, known and understood.

CASE STUDY: CHOOSING THE NUTRIENTS OF THE RAINFOREST FLOOR – A REIMAGINING OF KS3 CURRICULUM

General Area: Key Stage 3 curriculum development

Author: Jim Henderson, Headteacher

Introduction, background and context (Jim Henderson)

The documentation of curriculum in schools is often one of those creative works of invention which we are only too good at in the education world. It is one of many areas of school activity that has been turbo-boosted by the growing accountability framework since the 1990s. When I started teaching in 1984 at Eastfields School in Mitcham, the head of science, Bob Hamblin, gave me a copy of the textbook for each year group, a key for the banda masters room (even older readers of this book are more likely to have known banda worksheets from their intoxicating impact as a student rather than through deploying them for learning purposes!) and told me to get on with it. As long as I had covered all the chapters by the time of the end of year exam, I could teach in any sequence I wanted and how I wanted. And if I wanted the students to do something more than copy out key information or answer textbook questions, I could look through the banda masters to find a worksheet that might fit what I was teaching. Fortunately, I also had Dave Clark in my department who let me watch his lessons and talked to me about effective pedagogy in science teaching.

Then, in 1989, the National Curriculum came into being. This now became the framework for what should be taught and publishers quickly redesigned textbooks to be NC compliant.

Finally, in 1992, Ofsted came along to check up on us all and the bush telegraph suggested that they would expect all curriculum programmes to be fully documented with long-term plans, medium plans and lesson plans. This kick-started a frantic writing programme in many schools often responding to the urban myths

of what inspectors were demanding to see rather than what was actually wanted. And it was amazing how quickly these urban myths circulated and became school lore even before the internet.

The National Curriculum has been revised many times over the last 27 years. And many over-arching cross-curricular themes have subsequently been highlighted as needing signposting in documentation. Numeracy, literacy, ICT, global citizenship, vocational relevance, oracy, British values have all been granted their own column in many schemes of work templates – as have the now discredited learning styles. In addition, a perceived need to be formally evidenced to be taking differentiation seriously often led to a proliferation of all/most/some type lesson objectives which took up further columns.

Such a huge investment of effort and energy, not just at ATS but at schools across the land, along with a lack of time for a coherent and comprehensive review, has often meant that the documentation of KS3 curriculum is seriously out-of-date. It does not build on modern KS2 curriculum experiences and does not provide the right establishing conditions or knowledge base for the new GCSE specifications so recently introduced.

So often, all the original authors of the schemes of work have long moved on. Thus, the documented (intended) curriculum will be unowned and out-of-date with bolt-ons added by subsequent heads of department when they have been required to capture the prevailing zeitgeist priorities in anticipation of an inspection. The enacted curriculum will probably bear little relationship to the written document anyway. Departmental communality in structure and sequencing of programmes of study these days is much more likely to be established by a range of Powerpoint files than any overarching document.

At ATS, as in any school in special measures and under scrutiny, there was initially an urgent need to improve outcomes at GCSE and this had to be done in the form of pragmatic, interventionist strategies which are very time-consuming and not sustainable in the longer term. They are also about getting students across the line rather than securely establishing the conditions for more secure learning at that late stage. This certainly dominated much of our focus during 2017/18 at ATS.

However, alongside this, we also established a staff library with the purpose of embedding a culture of educational reading and discussion. We asked staff to write short reviews of books, articles and blogs that they had read and to recommend new books for our professional library. In addition, staff were encouraged to attend generic and subject-specific courses and conferences and we hosted sessions by some of the book and blog authors in our INSET programme. This newly emerging institutional culture of research-informed debate and practice quickly began to create an appetite for us to undertake a major review of three foundations of our practice: our teaching and learning policy; our feedback and assessment strategies; our curriculum.

We will give a flavour of the first two as the development of these helped us to create a model for how to effect deep change and because many of the rich discussions that were central to achieving change in these areas also helped to anticipate many of the key considerations when we began to look at our KS3 curriculum afresh.

Teaching and Learning Policy (Natasha Fox)

We wanted to distil all of the new ideas that had come into our collective awareness through our reading and attendance at courses and conferences into something at ATS which was a

You can't fully separate what you teach from how you teach it.
(*LEARNING RAINFOREST*, P. 72)

CASE STUDY: CHOOSING THE NUTRIENTS OF THE RAINFOREST FLOOR – A REIMAGINING OF KS3 CURRICULUM

coherent approach, which was well-rooted in pedagogic research and which we all bought into. I encouraged teachers to take ideas and approaches drawn from their reading and courses, to try them out in practice and to co-develop and establish this by working collaboratively with a colleague. We emphasised that we are all learning and I demonstrated this by opening my lessons to observation and taking critique and recommendations on improvements.

We encouraged an open door culture and encouraged teachers to visit other lessons for mutual learning, both discussing and critiquing what they saw and taking ideas back into their own classrooms. As a senior team we encouraged the concept that we would be happy to see an exciting and risk-taking initiative being attempted in a classroom, even if it didn't go well as long as there was good evidence to support its validity and a willingness to keep developing the approach until the teacher and students got familiar with it.

After a few months of this culture emerging, we gave the agenda of a training day over to developing a formal policy on our approach. I had conducted a survey with students asking which elements of their lessons contributed best to their learning and most to their self-confidence as learners and love of the subject. I then asked teachers to consider the elements of their own classroom practice that they felt had had most impact on learning and engagement.

Through the findings from this I developed the ATS8. These are eight elements that research and the empirical findings suggested were critical to effective teaching and learning. They are: **Mastery; Challenge; Modelling; Questioning; Engaged Learners; Pride; Eureka Moments; Stickability**.

Using the influential ideas described in *The Learning Rainforest* the policy emphasised the need for stretch and challenge, teaching to the top, mastery and the importance of knowledge-rich lessons to provide strong roots and trunk of learning.

These ideas were detailed and exemplified in the policy document and formative lesson observation documents were produced to allow commentary on how these key themes were enacted in the classroom and the @teachertoolkit five-minute lesson planning template was adapted to encourage teachers to reflect on how these elements might be incorporated into their lessons.

It has been really powerful to have a common vocabulary for what goes on in our classrooms. None of the ATS8 are described prescriptively. There is a clear understanding that the way these dimensions play out in different subjects and different age groups varies enormously. And there is a fundamental principle that the teacher will incorporate these elements into her/his teaching in line with her/his own professional judgment and practitioner confidence. But this just makes it all the more interesting when an experienced Art teacher and an NQT in Modern Languages (for example) have a discussion as to how, say, curiosity can be developed in their respective subjects.

Assessment and Feedback strategy (Jim Henderson)

Over the last few years, this area has been highly contentious in schools. The increasing perception of a need for macro summative data tracking, as Tom Sherrington calls it, to provide a proxy assurance to SLT or external visitors from MATs or Ofsted that students are following some beautiful flight path of progress has been utterly corrosive.

Firstly, the way the data is produced, analysed and reported is so far removed from the granular nuances of learning in any

classroom for any child that it generally is not able to tell us anything of any educational worth that a capable classroom teacher would not already know and be able to act on to much greater purpose.

Secondly, it has served to undermine the very proper conversation we need to have about how to reliably understand how learning has been constructed in the brain of each child and what next steps to take to secure and deepen that learning.

And thirdly, there has been so much emphasis on physical marking as a tool for assessment and feedback because this is the easiest proxy for a fleeting classroom visitor to use to decide whether teachers are doing their job that huge volumes of teachers' time have been sucked into the vortex of triple marking, dialogic marking and other strategies which, as Tom Sherrington says, have been much more to do with how marking looks than any useful purpose it serves. As he states on p. 116 of *The Learning Rainforest*, '[m]ost marking is wasted and yet is often the cause of major teacher overload'.

We therefore used the evidence from research to redevelop our approach. We liked Dylan Wiliam's renaming of 'assessment for learning' into 'responsive teaching'. This also found echo in the Mark, Plan, Teach approach of Ross Morrison McGill. We wanted our interactions with children's learning to provide a circle back to our teaching in the most efficient way possible. The new policy provided a philosophical and educationally robust underpinning for our new approach. It also allowed teachers to breathe more easily. Particularly popular has been Yellow Box marking which has supported focused marking and feedback with the opportunity for students to redraft and improve. This links to the Learning Rainforest concept of 'feedback for excellence' and the Austin's Butterfly illustration which we showed to staff.

We therefore used the evidence from research to redevelop our approach.
JIM HENDERSON

It has been really powerful to have a common vocabulary for what goes on in our classrooms.
NATASHA FOX

CASE STUDY: CHOOSING THE NUTRIENTS OF THE RAINFOREST FLOOR – A REIMAGINING OF KS3 CURRICULUM

By supporting 'assess smarter, not harder' approaches, their responsibility was to use some of the strategies in ways that served them in the classroom. Any external scrutiny of assessment would see that teachers were able to implement our policy. The question would then be whether we, as the senior team, had established a strategy that was effective. Knowing how our approach was supported by the research findings summarised by Sherrington, McGill, Wiliam, Hattie, Christodoulou and others gave us confidence that we had.

Reimagining the KS3 curriculum (Jim Henderson and Natasha Fox)

And so, by the start of September 2018, buoyed by a significant improvement in GCSE outcomes and beginning the new academic year with a common language for and approach to teaching, learning and assessment, we began to discuss how we might move the school from a position of up-against-it interventionist sticking plaster frenzy in Year 11 to investing our time in building strong foundations for future improvements that would be less manic and exhausting.

Our attention turned to our KS3 curriculum and how we might make it the engine-house of learning confidence, providing a knowledge base well-established into long-term memory and an environment richly supplied with the nutrient soil to help the trees in the Learning Rainforest to flourish. It would incorporate all of the principles we had developed in our discussions on teaching, learning and assessment and tie them into a coherent curriculum framework. It would emphasise the importance of subject disciplines and not only the core conceptual ideas that underpin deep understanding of the subject but also the big cultural capital ideas that we believed should be part of the knowledge foliage

of any well-educated person. And it would also use the cognitive science findings about learning to ensure that knowledge and ideas were returned to over time both in teaching and in low-stakes testing to build proper mastery which would sit in the long-term memory and provide the establishing conditions and construction of knowledge which could act as a secure starting point in KS4.

We agreed that it was better to teach less stuff profoundly than to try to teach enormous amounts in a very surface way. In a Physics context, we wanted every child moving into Year 10 to be securely able to construct a series and parallel circuit and explain the interplay of current, potential difference and resistance in these circuits even if that was at the expense of how an electric motor works. There would need to be hard decisions made with a realistic understanding of how much learning time might be needed for proper mastery.

Behind this lies the idea that a rapid gloss of too many ideas without time for students properly to incorporate them into their own conceptualisation is what is most likely to lead to dissatisfaction with the subject, displacement activity to mask the lack of understanding, a fixed mindset in which they tell themselves that this stuff is beyond them and a requirement for the Year 10 teacher to go right back to basics because no secure conceptual understanding can be assumed.

The final strand of this curriculum development is to allow us to get the balance between what Tom calls Mode A and Mode B teaching. We want our children to be able to explore the possibilities, to spend time on developing, refining and being playful and creative with the ideas they learn. But, like the clown on a tightrope, children (indeed all of us) can only be playful with ideas in the canopy once we are absolutely secure with the basic skills and knowledge base.

This curriculum development project has been a work in progress throughout the academic year 2018/19 with the intention that we will bring this new curriculum into Year 7 (and possibly retrofit for Year 8 and 9) in September 2019. Tom has helped to take the vision and priorities we have for this curriculum and turn it into a series of sessions he has led with our subject leaders. This has been made possible by the fact that our thinking has been so impacted already by Tom's writing and the work of others that he has pointed us towards that Tom and our subject leaders are operating with the same paradigms, vocabulary and exemplars.

It is very exciting to see all the strands of our work over the last two years coalescing in this work and to see the enthusiasm for subject and cross-disciplinary connections being enjoyed by our subject leaders in this work. *The Learning Rainforest* has been a critical text in this journey of improvement for our school, not just in its own content but in its generous signposting to other work by other education thinkers and writers. Not only has it nourished the school, it has nourished the professional enquiry and curiosity of all teachers and leaders in the school.

Not only has it nourished the school, it has nourished the professional enquiry and curiosity of all teachers and leaders in the school.

JIM HENDERSON AND NATASHA FOX

ST MATTHIAS PRIMARY, TOWER HAMLETS

INTRODUCTION

As soon as the *Fieldbook* concept sprang into life I knew I wanted to include Clare Sealy's fabulous school and I was delighted when she agreed to take part. Clare is one of the key voices of reason in the Twittersphere, telling fabulous stories about St Matthias via her blog *primarytimerydotcom*, a champion of a knowledge-rich primary curriculum but always with a rounded, holistic view of what education is for. Her talks at researchEd events are fabulous; great humour combined with fabulous insights into the learning process. Her 'Fibonacci Clock' is something of a conference classic, highlighting how powerful automaticity in recall can be.

Last summer, I had the pleasure of visiting Clare at St Matthias, tucked in just off Brick Lane in London's East End. She was coming to the end of her time there – 28 years, with 22 as Headteacher! – before heading off to lead on curriculum across Guernsey. To give that kind of service to a community over so many years is truly awe-inspiring.

On my visit I had the best time. When I arrived, Clare was about to take the daily assembly, promoting one of their core values 'awe and wonder'. To do this she had chosen to celebrate the 'awe and wonder' of the fact that all the materials in the universe, everything we see and touch, are made of only three things, arranged in different combinations.

A deeper layer was to show this in more detail with a model for electrons, protons and neutrons. I was invited to join in as Clare's assistant as we used giant Duplo blocks to show the children how first hydrogen, then helium, then lithium – and later on, carbon – are made by adding different numbers of electrons (yellow blocks), protons (red blocks) and neutrons (blue blocks). It's such a powerful idea – one that hopefully will feed into their future understanding of the world around them. Just getting them thinking about the idea that materials have hidden structure

was amazing; hearing them using the words felt like a great way to begin; electrons, protons, neutrons. Just words and patterns of simple things – nothing to fear – and all part of a carefully designed spiralling curriculum.

The insight into the St Matthias philosophy from my short visit was wonderful. The school website provides parents with details of the curriculum – it's well worth taking a look. Clare is a firm believer in the value of organising the curriculum in subject disciplines rather than teaching in artificial topics and its fascinating to explore the detailed planning. In the case study below, Clare sets out the school's approach to assessing progress in her wonderful reflective, evidence-informed style. And the contributions from Ahnaf and Kayla are a delight.

PROFILE

Location: Bethnal Green, Tower Hamlets, London, UK
Type of Institution: Church of England primary school
Roll/Age Range: 240, aged 3–11
Year Founded: 1844
Motto: 'Learning to live life in all its fullness'
Recent/Current School Production: *Nativity Play*
Recent significant sports event/triumph: Won the Tower Hamlets tennis tournament four years in a row.

Clare Sealy
Headteacher

St Matthias may be a small school, but it punches way above its weight in terms of its contribution to system wide school improvement. Over a hundred teachers visited this little school last year to learn about how we replaced marking with whole class feedback and how we are structuring our curriculum. That's on top of Clare tearing around the country delivering training.

We try, as far as possible, to be an evidenced informed school that does things because of research indicate they are more likely to work, rather than doing things because they are the educational orthodoxy. For example, we've been swimming against the tide with regards to the kind of data we collect about pupil achievement, having a much bigger place for small scale assessments about what children can and can't actually do right now. We don't think that progress can easily be measured so that's not something we waste time doing. Our pupil progress meetings focus on what are the bottlenecks to learning children

PROFILE

are facing and practical solutions to overcoming them. We do frequent low stakes, developmental lesson observations instead of termly high stakes 'showtimes.'

Teachers still work incredibly hard, but we've tried hard to eliminate meaningless tasks. Working on things you don't see the point of is exhausting whereas working on things you know will make a difference can be energising.

We have been working for the past three years on making our curriculum as coherent as possible, making sure key concepts within a subject are revisited over the years so that pupils encounter the same concept in a variety of different contexts. We believe this helps the children develop sophisticated schemas over time, as each time they encounter a concept afresh their understanding of it becomes more complex and more nuanced. We make sure children do retrieval practice of subject content not just while they are learning a topic but months later and at the end of the year. Otherwise we know they will forget it.

But what we are most proud of is the way in which we have created community cohesion, especially between the white working class population of Bethnal Green and the Bangladeshi Muslim community who form the majority of this Church of England school.

STUDENT: KAYLA ALBOROUGH

Age and Year Group: 6, Year 2

Most recent:

School Trip: Museum of London to learn about the Fire of London

Extra-curricular activity: Reading Gladiators, football club

Science experiment: Experimenting to see which materials were waterproof so we could know what material was the best for making a raincoat. Plastic was the best. Brick was also waterproof but that wouldn't be good for a coat because it's too heavy!

Book/Play studied in English Literature: *The 100 Mile an Hour Dog* by Jeremy Strong

History topic: Learning about nurses in the Victorian times who went to help soldiers in the Crimean War – Mary Seacole and Florence Nightingale

Arts project: Drawing faces with chalk pastels inspired by Sandra Silberzewig

Learning:

Subjects Studied: English, maths, science, RE, computing, history, geography, art, DT, music, PE, dance, fitness, French, PHSE.

Recent learning highlight: In dance we are making actions to show how different rainforest animals move.

The most stand-out/interesting/challenging topic you've studied at school: Learning about the problems Mary Seacole faced and how she overcame them such as finding a cure for cholera from plants. She went into the middle of a battlefield just to save people. People were mean to her about her skin colour but she didn't give up her dream to be a nurse and help sick people.

One of my favourite teachers: Mrs Crozier who is my class teacher because she makes things easy for us. At the beginning they are hard but in the end they are so easy.

A favourite feature of the school: The people are very friendly and everybody cares about each other – not just a couple of people but everybody cares.

STUDENT: AHNAF TAPADER

Age and Year Group: 10, Year 5

Most recent:

School Trip: I took part in a geography bee at a school in Newham so I had to learn all the countries and capitals in the world and where they are on a map.

Extra-curricular activity: I don't do any clubs in school but I do Arabic class after school 4 days a week.

Science experiment: We tested the effect of different surfaces on how far a toy car could travel. Smooth surfaces allow the car to travel the furthest because bumpy surfaces have more friction than smooth surfaces.

Book/Play studied in English Literature: *Room 13* – we are just up to the bit where they discover the door with the missing number.

History topic: Ancient Greeks – most of the city states had schools but girls weren't allowed to go. In Sparta when boys went to school they just learnt to fight so they could then join the army for their whole life. Sparta and Athens didn't like each other much. Athens lived for entertainment and fun but Sparta lived for war.

Arts project: Seascape paintings, so we looked at Turner. We experimented mixing paints with black and white to create different tones.

Learning:

Recent learning highlight: We have been learning how to do coding when we do computing. We are using Scratch and we managed to make our own chasing game using arrow keys instead of the mouse.

The most stand-out/interesting/challenging topic you've studied at school: My favourite topic was learning about space in science. I found out that some planets might only be dwarf planets and that asteroids also orbit the sun (not just planets). We went on a trip to the Greenwich Observatory to the planetarium and saw the different planets and learnt them. Did you know Jupiter and the other gas giants also have rings – but we just can't see them. It's not just Saturn!

One of my favourite teachers: Ms Morris because she helped us understand the difference between urban and rural areas went we went on our school trip to Gorsefield. She knows a lot about this because she lives in a rural area. We all live in an urban area. Both urban and rural places have disadvantages – urban places are noisy but rural places have lots of bugs! I think I will choose urban when I am a grown up!

A favourite feature of the school: All the teachers are kind and helpful.

CASE STUDY: THINKING ABOUT PROGRESS.

Title: Thinking about progress. How we introduced small scale assessments and pupil book talks instead of attempting to judge progress through work scrutiny or looking at aggregated data

General Area: Teaching and Learning/Leadership

Author: Clare Sealy, Headteacher

Being able to 'measure' or at the very least gauge progress is a bit of a Holy Grail in teaching. It's definitely a ritual senior leaders are expected to solemnly engage in, a sort of feast of obligation. I've become more and more disillusioned with this over the years and Professor Becky Allen's work was the final nail in the coffin. She said that the statistical noise surrounding test data is just too huge to make measurement of progress meaningful. We might like the illusion of rigour that colour coded excel tables give us, but the rigour is spurious and misleading. Daisy Christodoulou's book 'Making Good Progress' also suggested that doing little low stakes granular assessments on discrete elements of teaching was much more likely to be useful that big tests that tried to give some sort of overall judgement. So, over the last couple of years we have been looking carefully at all the assessments we do and deciding if they are actually worth doing. We know ask ourselves 'what do we want to find out and what will we do differently as the result of this assessment?' If we don't know, then we don't do it!

We decided what we did want to find out was if children remembered really crucial things such as their number bonds or to use full stops and capital letters in their writing. Or if they could remember key vocabulary from topics they had been studying. Not all learning objectives are born equal, probably about 20% of them do 80% of the heavy lifting. If a child can't do something from this precious 20%, that will form a bottleneck

in their learning preventing further progress, maybe not right now but over the year. If a child doesn't know their times table by the end of Year 4 for example, their maths learning in upper KS2 and beyond is going to be really dragged down by the omission.

So it is vital that we know what these gaps are and address them. This means we need assessments tailored to identify just that – not the normal kind of test that covers all sorts of things and gives an illusion that everything is fine because on average a child's grade is sort of OK. That's where granular micro assessments come in.

The first step was to decide what we thought were the 20% most crucial learning objectives. This has gone through various revisions over time, but now I think in writing at least we are happy with what we've got. We now closely track a massively slimmed down set of objectives in KS2 – basically we look at what children need to be able to do at the end of KS1 to achieve expected level and then continue to track that to make sure children continue (or in some cases start) to do these things independently and consistently in all their work. That might sound not aspirational enough but I am sure secondary school teachers would be delighted if the overwhelming majority of children transferred to Year 7 being able to use sentence punctuation consistently, get tenses to agree, write sentences that made sense, spell, write with legible handwriting and so on.

The crucial point is, this tracking highlights bottlenecks that the teachers then respond to. It is talking about these bottlenecks and what is going to be done to address them that forms the bulk of our pupil progress meetings now.

On top of that we want to check that the new stuff we are teaching them is also being applied independently. To check this,

teachers to a piece of 'cold' writing (i.e. completely independent with no prior teaching) on a genre they are about to teach. They then analysis this for 5 or 6 sentence structure or other grammatical features that they are planning to teach over the next few weeks. If they find that actually, almost everybody already knows how to use adjectives to describe, they then adjust their plan and teach less of that. They therefore spend the vast majority of their time teaching the things children can't do yet. Then at the end of the unit, children do another independent piece of writing and that is analysed again to see what progress has been made. When I say, 'what progress', I don't mean we get some sort of numerical score at the end. We can however simply see that at the beginning of the topic only a few children used paragraphs with topic sentence but by the end of the unit most of the class did. That's progress.

With subjects such as the humanities and science we introduced brief 10 question multiple choice quizzes which children do at various points when they are learning a new topic as well as at the end. But it's easy to remember things when you've just learnt them, the proof of the pudding is can you remember it two months later? So we do follow up quizzes at some remove from the original teaching and then at the end of the year, a 15 question 'super quiz' featuring questions from all their geography topics or whatever. This enables us to produce average scores for pupils and for subjects in each class. This is useful to us because it enables us to ask questions of ourselves. Why is science getting a lower average score than geography? This is useful feedback about our curriculum. Maybe the science isn't clear enough, or isn't being given enough time? Maybe certain key terms need really emphasizing as so many children confuse them? Why is this child who seems so capable in class doing badly when it comes to

Did you know Jupiter and the other gas giants also have rings – but we just can't see them. It's not just Saturn.

AHNAF TAPADER

Mrs Crozier makes things easy for us. At the beginning they are hard but in the end they are so easy.

KAYLA ALBOROUGH

CASE STUDY: THINKING ABOUT PROGRESS.

long term recall? And look at this child who seems to struggle yet remembers so much months later.

Book Talks

We've been doing all of this for a couple of years now, but in January we introduced something new that really compliments this approach. Alex Bedford introduced me to pupil book talks. What these involve is getting three children from a class to bring their books for a couple of subjects, and then asking them to find something in their book which they are really proud of or which they found really interesting. You then get them to explain what was so interesting, asking further follow on questions (in an interested, inquisitive way, not grilling them) for example, 'so who were these Anglo Saxons? Where did they come from? I wonder why they came to England? Were they the only people who came to England from elsewhere or do you know about others? (This does involve a little bit of boning up on what they have been learning beforehand!)

What happens is after a few hesitant minutes, the flood gates open and this torrent of knowledge comes tumbling out, the children animatedly adding to each other's contributions and telling you more about more than you would ever think could fit into a seven-year-old's head! Well that's what usually happens. Sometimes they dry up and really don't know much – looking at their book forlornly and wistfully turning over pages they half remember studying. We worked out what had happened when this happened. If the teacher had got children to research the content rather than teaching it and then getting children to elaborate upon it, then children did not remember very much. This should not have been a surprise as we already knew from cognitive science that if your working memory is focused on finding something out it is unlikely to also be focused on

remembering whatever it was you found out. It was a shock to see this actually happen though! The other thing that sometimes happened was that in science they remembered the experiment rather than the actual science – again entirely predictable from cognitive science but a salutary reminder to teach the science first and then do experiments to confirm, rather than discover afresh, the science.

Sometimes class teachers sit in on these book talks. It's great for them to see the progress children have made when they can speak eloquently about learning they did months ago. And on those rare occasions where children can't remember, this helps us all reflect on why this has happened and to do better next time.

In the next few weeks, we are going to do process with art and DT – probably involving walking around the building looking at displays rather than books, and then with children who have an education and health care plan. I find this process so much more informative than book scrutiny. I can see if children have internalised and remembered what they have t=been taught a while back and I can see their passion and excitement in telling me all about it. This beats some spurious excel spreadsheet any day.

People ask about governors and how do they hold us to account without data. Well it's a pretty strange holding to account if the data is highly dubious. We've explained to governors the pitfalls of our previous approach, haring articles that show we are not just making this up. We can't produce neat, easily understandable (but spurious) reports, we can only give a narrative. I haven't yet got a governor to join us for a pupil book talk but I intend to. We've had our school improvement partner sit in on one and she found it much more revealing than a table of numbers.

Link to Learning Rainforest:

Our approach exemplifies and builds on the approach to assessment outlined in *The Learning Rainforest*. Much of what really counts in not straightforwardly measurable and it is futile to try and pretend that it is. Quasi-scientific 'measurement' of progress is repudiated; absolute measurement of progress is not possible. There is no global standard for progress in some temperature controlled Parisian vault.

We know ask ourselves 'what do we want to find out and what will we do differently as the result of this assessment?' If we don't know, then we don't do it!

CLARE SEALY
HEADTEACHER

ST COLUMBA'S COLLEGE, DUBLIN

INTRODUCTION

My contact with St Columba's College began after a Twitter-mediated exchange with the account @ sccenglish. I had always associated the distinctive blue Shakespeare portrait avatar with a voice of polite, reasoned engagement and, now having met Julian Girdham in person, the man behind the profile, this makes total sense. Julian, Sub-Warden at St Columba's, publishes a superb e-newsletter – 'Fortnightly', a fortnightly take on reading, writing, teaching, thinking – a treasure trove of reviews and recommendations that I'm always pleased to see pop up in my inbox. When he invited me to Dublin to lead some training, I leapt at the chance.

St Columba's is a fabulously historic, traditional school in the most gorgeous grounds on the outskirts of Dublin – you can see the city in the distance from the windows. When I stayed in Julian's on-site house, there were deer in the garden outside his kitchen at breakfast; there's a short forested walk from the house to the school – it's really rather magical. The hat-stand in the staffroom draped in the black academic staff gowns is just one of many signs and symbols of a school that wears its traditions overtly – with a bit of panache.

I've found that it is a mistake to assume a traditional school would not be engaged in exploring contemporary ideas. In fact, under Julian's guidance, St Columba's will host the first ever researchED event in Ireland in October 2019 and it was clear from talking to staff that they are enthusiastic about exploring educational ideas. To some extent, this is helped by the support from cognitive science for traditional instructional methods. I was delighted when a soon-to-retire Latin master approached me after my training session to tell me it was 'the most marvellous training' he'd had in twenty years! Why? Because I was giving value to the instructional approaches he'd long found to be effective. And, without question, at Columba's there is also ample opportunity for 'exploring the possibilities'.

I love the selection of contrasting case-studies presented here – and the details of each student profile. It never occurred to me that the Learning Rainforest might find resonance in anything physical but, for sure, the labs at St Columba's are probably the best classrooms for teaching science I've ever seen; another aspect of ultra-modernity nicely juxtaposing the school's deep traditions. From reading the school motto to hearing that one of the alumni is U2's Adam Clayton (how fabulous is that?!) – there's no end to the charm and quirkiness of this fabulous school.

PROFILE

Location: South Dublin, Ireland

Type of Institution: Mixed, mostly boarding, fee-paying

Roll/Age Range: 340, aged 12–18

Year Founded: 1843

Motto: 'Simplices sicut Columbae, Prudentes sicut Serpentes' (Be gentle as doves, and wise as serpents'.)

House Names: Glen, Gwynn, Stackallan, Hollypark, Iona, Tibradden, Beresford

Recent/Current School Production: Gogol's *The Nose*, Rodgers and Hammerstein's *Oklahoma!*

Recent significant sports event/triumph: Sixth Year pupil Sophia Cole is on the Ireland under-18 hockey squad.

Notable quirks/alumni: We are the only school in Ireland where both teachers and pupils wear academic gowns. Alumni range from the great novelist and short story writer William Trevor to the bass player of U2, Adam Clayton.

Julian Girdham
Sub-Warden/Deputy Head

In 2018 our school had its 175th anniversary, an occasion for reflection about the journey we have made over several generations. On the surface we look very traditional: we all still wear gowns, we all still meet in our beautiful granite Chapel every morning before classes. But we are also now a multi-national, hyper-connected, outward-facing community, open to both the challenges and opportunities of a world very different to that of 1843.

Tom Sherrington writes of the ways schools have to 'navigate' many 'contradictions and tensions', and this is very much our task too: how do we hold onto the best of what has been, while simultaneously making sure that we are not complacent? How do we change in sensible, fruitful, incremental ways?

The two case studies which follow embody this dilemma. Like other schools, we are trying to deal with a generation of 'screenagers' who are always connected and possibly easily distracted. Evan Jameson writes about our determination to encourage that most foundational deep activity, the reading of books. Then Mary Singleton and Humphrey Jones describe the stunning renovation of our Science Building. Certainly it is kitted out with all the latest technology, and is a thrilling environment for them and their fellow Science teachers, but to 'establish the conditions' they had to think deeply about their teaching principles. In real classrooms, great teaching doesn't depend on the latest touch-screen monitor.

We have 240 boarders on campus throughout term, with 100 day boys and girls joining them every morning, six days a week. We pack in sports, drama, music and a bewildering blizzard of other extracurricular activities. This is a way of life, and a particularly intense one at that. It can seem relentless. However, it is also, truly, a joy.

STUDENT: SHANNON DENT

Age and Year Group: 17, Sixth Year
House: Beresford

Most recent:

School Trip: My Physics class recently went to a lecture about waves (a topic we are about to cover in class) at University College Dublin.

Extra-curricular activity: CanSat is a team project I have been working on since the start of the year. It involves making a small satellite the size of a can and designing it to record things like atmospheric pressure and temperature. I work on the programming aspect of the project.

Science experiment: In our most recent Physics experiment we had to find the heat capacity of water. My team and I weren't able to use one of the machines for calculating energy, so we had to use a longer and more tedious method. This taught us that there are always ways around problems in Physics.

Book/Play studied in English Literature: This year we studied *Hamlet* in our English class. It is such an interesting text to study as it brings up so many questions about people and our own lives. How much of our lives do we really control?

Learning:

Subjects Studied: Physics, Applied Maths, Chemistry, Geology, Geography, Spanish, English (compulsory), Maths (compulsory)

Recent learning highlight: In our English class we chose a prompt to write a composition. I wrote a descriptive piece about a character walking in the woods, when suddenly he sees something moving on a faraway hill. It was a pleasure to write this piece as it helped me exercise my imagination. I like coming up with short stories and describing the imaginary places I think of often.

The most stand-out/interesting/challenging topic you've studied at school: Applied Maths is a subject I study and although very enjoyable it is also very challenging. It's so different to regular Maths. Applied Maths is all about thinking of a clever way to approach a problem instead of following a specific set of steps. You can spend ages on a single problem and not realise how much time you've spent on it!

One of my favourite teachers: I enjoy lessons with Mr Higgins who teaches me Maths. He knows how to run a classroom really well and answers all of our questions.

A favourite feature of the school: We're lucky to be right on the edge of the mountains. We do a lot of hikes on the weekends with a couple of our teachers. One specific hike remains glued in my brain. At the end my teacher took us to have ice cream: as I sat there enjoying my frozen delight I knew this would be a memory to treasure!

STUDENT: SAM LAWRENCE

Age and Year Group: 17, Sixth Year
House: Stackallan

Most recent:

School Trip: Over half-term a group of 20 pupils and teachers went on a service trip to our Warden's former school in South Africa. We helped in soup kitchens and a disabled centre near the school.

Extra-curricular activity: A few pupils from my year, myself included, gave informal talks to our peers in the style of a TED talk. Mine was 'Bringing the past back to life – cloning extinct species.'

Science experiment: In Chemistry class we have been performing titrations where we neutralise acids and bases.

Book/Play studied in English Literature: *Hamlet* and *The Playboy of the Western World*.

Learning:

Subjects Studied: Irish, Spanish, Chemistry, Physics, Latin, Geology, English (Compulsory), Maths (Compulsory)

Recent learning highlight: I enjoyed The Playboy of the Western World in English recently not only because the story is interesting in itself, but because I learned about the ways in which the play is written, and also about the shapes of stories in general.

The most stand-out/interesting/challenging topic you've studied at school: The most intriguing topics I have studied in school are in Physics class. It's very interesting to learn about the laws of the universe and the ways things work. The calculations and experiments are always challenging.

One of my favourite teachers: I enjoy Latin class with Mr Brett because the material is always intriguing and his style of teaching is quite casual. Learning about the ancient world is fascinating because so many links can be drawn between now and then. The language aspect of Latin is also a challenge, and it keeps me absorbed.

A favourite feature of the school: My favourite feature of the school has to be the balance between lessons and sports. We have compulsory sport six days a week, which is great for fitness and also for mental health. I was once off sport for two weeks and I felt groggy and tired all the time: this made me appreciate how good it is to be able to play hockey or rugby with your friends after classes.

Learning about the ancient world is fascinating.

SAM LAWRENCE

There are always ways around problems.

SHANNON DENT

A school is far more than its academic or sporting results and all that we do here is within a context that encourages and nurtures the spiritual development of all our children.

MARK BOOBBYER
WARDEN

CASE STUDY: DEVELOPING READERS IN THE SCREEN AGE

General Area: English

Author: Evan Jameson, English teacher

My approach to teaching English changed quite radically last year, after I became involved in the WellRead initiative, a scheme in Ireland to promote reading in schools and in the wider community. The goal of WellRead is to create a reading culture in schools, in other words to make books more visible, to make school a place where people talk about books, share books. Thus the school's book club has been joined by an annual book week and a strenuous effort has been made to make the library a friendlier and more attractive place. Coupled with what I learned from Kenny Pieper's book *Reading for Pleasure – a passport to everywhere*, WellRead made me re-think my role as an English teacher and also re-examine my relationship with my pupils. One year on, I can say it has made my job at once more interesting and more challenging.

After reading Pieper's book, I asked all of my junior pupils to bring in whatever book they were reading and began to devote the first ten minutes of every lesson to reading. Of course, many of them weren't reading anything so I allowed them to go to the school's library or to choose a book from the bookcase in my classroom, almost all of which I got at knockdown prices from charity shops. After a week of this, I gave each pupil a slimline exercise copy which included a table at the back with spaces into which they would write the titles of books they had read over the course of the year. At the front of this reading response journal I wrote them a letter, asking them about the book they were currently reading. Over the week, in their own time, they wrote a reply. Every Saturday, I collected the journals and then wrote a reply which contained some more questions about the book they were reading. My questions were lower order for the most part – What

has happened since you last wrote here? Has anything surprised you about the book? Do you have anything in common with the main character? I didn't 'mark' their responses for grammar or spelling.

The aim was to give them a place where they could comment on their independent reading and give some recognition to this quiet but important activity. And for the most part it was a success. Most of the pupils quickly got into the habit of reading from the moment they sat down in class. Most of them liked the journals and the idea of filling in the table at the back. Many said they found it a relaxing way to start the lesson. I got to see the books they were reading and to see how quickly or slowly they read. I was able to talk to them about their books and recommend other ones (with mixed results, naturally). At the end of term, I was able to commend them on achievements in independent reading and mention their progress as readers in their report.

One major change the reading strategy has made to my teaching is that it has altered my view of success, which I now link to the number and quality of books they read over the course of a term. What I like best about the strategy is that I am less fatalistic about the pupils. Previously I would have simply shrugged my shoulders and written some of them off as reluctant readers, whereas now I can at least say that they have read one or two books outside of the course. I also like being able to correspond with pupils on different levels. At one end of the group, I can congratulate someone on reading *Diary of a Wimpy Kid*, while at the other end I can ask a pupil high-order questions about *To Kill a Mockingbird* and encourage them to read similarly sophisticated books. From reading their responses and seeing which books are popular, I've also become better at recommending Young Adult and children's novels.

Caveats? It is an inevitably quiet, low-energy and repetitive way to start a lesson. This suits some groups but not others. The other problem has been finding a book that suits certain reluctant readers. A small minority of pupils have been very vocal in their insistence that they don't like any of the books I or the librarian or their peers recommend. In a few cases, there has been real resistance to reading and my gentle coaxing has had little impact. I have suggested non-fiction titles, sports autobiographies, books of facts, newspapers and comics but the idea of reading for pleasure just doesn't seem to be part of their culture.

Most studies claim that the best way to get young people to read is through peer influence and as part of book week (and occasionally in my own lessons) we do sessions of book speed dating. Also, we are trying to get pupils to write recommendations that we will display on the shelves of the library. I am a strong believer in the power of chat – I've always thought that much of the popularity of sport is that it gives people something to talk about rather than watch – and the more pupils share their reading experiences with one another, the better.

Link to Learning Rainforest:

Reading is central to education, not just to English. So much of our pupils' knowledge comes from reading, and we have to go out of our way explicitly to create the conditions for periods of sustained reading. Without this, their knowledge base is thin. With it, their ability to express themselves and read critically is enhanced. We certainly can't *assume* they will read: we have to nourish those roots.

We wanted to create spaces for joy, wonder and awe.

MARY SINGLETON
HEAD OF SCIENCE
AND
HUMPHREY JONES
HEAD OF BIOLOGY

The aim was to give pupils a place where they could comment on their independent reading and give some recognition to quiet but important activity.

EVAN JAMESON
ENGLISH TEACHER

CASE STUDY: DEVELOPING STEM INFRASTRUCTURE FOR THE 21ST CENTURY

General Area: Science teaching

Authors: Mary Singleton, (Head of Science), **Humphrey Jones,** (Head of Biology)

Our Science Building originally opened in 1971 and was designed by Miesian Irish architect Robin Walker, featuring a double-skin glass exterior. The building provided four laboratories and it remained relatively unchanged until 2016; the original wooden furniture and glass-fronted, glass-backed display cases (attached to the windows) stood the test of time.

However, while the design was architecturally lauded, the building itself was beginning to lack functionality. The innovative heating system originally designed by Walker was unable to heat the building properly in winter (the thin glass allowing heat escape easily) while the science teachers and their charges sweltered in the summer sun. In 2015, the temperatures varied in the building between a low of 4oC (with the heating on full blast) and a high of 38 oC (with all the windows open). The layout of the laboratories was very traditional; long front-facing wooden benches, with an elevated desk for the teacher, designed for demonstrations rather than collaborative practical investigations. There was a charm to the building and the laboratories but science, and its instruction, had changed a lot since it was first built. So, when the decision to refurbish, update and future-proof the building was taken, we in the Science Department were offered a special opportunity to design our own learning environments.

We gratefully received the opportunity to sit with Coady Architects and have meaningful input into the design and layout of the laboratories (and prep room areas). However, what we had not expected was that the opportunity to re-design these spaces sparked a deeper debate. We began asking ourselves *'What do we value in science education?', 'What is our department philosophy?', 'What are our current strengths and weaknesses?'* and *'How do we maintain and build on our high standards?'*

We wanted to create classrooms that would inspire, that allowed for movement and collaboration and were habitats for excellence. We wanted to create spaces for joy, wonder and awe. Practically, we also wanted to create a space for teacher collaboration alongside equipment and chemical storage. Significantly, after our initial conversations with the architects, we also wanted to respect the integrity of Walker's design and ensure the character of the building was maintained, while embedding modern technology.

We decided to seek the advice and experiences of other local schools who had recently refitted their own laboratories. We were impressed by some of these, but after several visits realised that, while we could learn from each school, we needed to come up with a workable design ourselves that fitted our own unique building. We quickly agreed that a pod-based system would best suit the layout of our new laboratories, most closely matching our teaching philosophy, and would be best aligned to the principles of the new Junior Cycle Science specifications. We had come across such a system in Belfast's wonderful science museum W5 and, while the design wasn't perfect, we knew it best matched our aims. We agreed that six pods, each capable of seating four pupils (with two work stations in each) would be best. We played with the shape of the pods – square, octagonal, round, oval – but quickly agreed on 'bean-shaped'; this would allow us to have seating on the curved side and to position the electricity, gas and water opposite, thus minimising distraction when not carrying out practical activities. The bean-shape would best suit the size and shape of the rooms since the pods could be turned and positioned to maximise the space between them.

We built a series of full-sized models of the pods, playing with the curvature, length and width, to check that they would fit within the space and be able to accommodate the equipment. The shape of the pod altered slightly, introducing a straight edge for the water, gas and electricity. Excitement built as we neared the end of term in the summer of 2016. The building was cleared, equipment packed up and we even had a few surprises (including a visit from the Army Bomb Squad for the safe disposal of a vial of 2,4 diphenylhydrazine which we discovered at the back of a cupboard in the Chemistry lab).

The complete restoration of the building and the refit of the laboratories were completed in just three months over the summer of 2016. A fifth slightly smaller laboratory, constructed under the Physics lab, came on stream soon after. The architects had decided to give each lab its own colour; yellow (Chemistry), green (Biology), teal (General Science) and purple (Physics). Each room was fitted with a 72-inch Android interactive monitor and high speed wireless internet. Two mobile fume-cupboards replaced the fixed units in the previous labs. Some of the original features of the old labs were maintained including the wonderful 'Belfast sinks'. One of the best features of the new building was the creation of a shared preparation area and teacher space between the Biology and Chemistry labs. We agreed that one wall in this 'prep area' be dedicated to a tray-based storage solution, which has worked out extremely well. In truth, the creation of this space was transformational. As a department we now actively partake in joint planning, collaboration and methodology discussions, sharing best practice and exploring ideas.

Interestingly, the uptake of Science subjects at Senior level is at its highest levels in recent memory and, although it's impossible to prove causation, our results in 2018 were our best to date.

We were blessed to be given the opportunity to design what we felt were the ideal classrooms for science. While there were obvious limitations, we now feel our laboratories are hubs for learning, exploration, collaboration and wonder. Involving teachers in the design process not only ensured the new laboratories were fit for purpose, and reflected best practice, but, more significantly, they facilitated a discussion on what we valued as science educators and framed the direction of our department, in terms of teaching and learning, for the decade to come. Yes, we do now have fabulous, bright and welcoming learning environments, packed with modern technologies, up to date science equipment and functional furniture. However, more significantly, we now have a team of science teachers who have actively reflected on what they value most in science education and who are fully invested in those shared values.

Link to Learning Rainforest:

This project made us think deeply. We were involved in creating infrastructure that would be used by generations of pupils and teachers, and we had to get the foundations right. We based our decisions on evidence and research. In the words of *The Learning Rainforest*, 'there is huge power in having strong alignment across teachers around some core principles', and we have a strong sense of these now.

PORTLEDGE SCHOOL, LONG ISLAND

INTRODUCTION

When Principal, Simon Owen-Williams, a Welshman working on Long Island, expressed some interest in the Learning Rainforest via the Portledge Twitter profile, I looked up the address: Duck Pond Road, Locust Valley, New York. I'm not sure about the ecological coherence here, but I couldn't think of a more exotic-sounding destination for my book to have reached! My subsequent interactions with the staff at Portledge School have certainly been unique among the *Fieldbook* contributors: through the power of Zoom – the online video-conference platform. When a face-to-face visit couldn't work out we arranged a series of webinars, including some initial input from me, responding to questions about the book, and a follow-up discussion with faculty from each of the three schools: lower, middle and upper.

It was fascinating to see which elements of *The Learning Rainforest* resonated with staff working in a very different context to those I've experienced personally. Perhaps more explicitly than any other school in the *Fieldbook*, Portledge has been exploring its identity along the progressive-traditional axis. Teachers talk warmly and proudly of the progressive elements of the curriculum and teaching philosophy with an emphasis on student-centredness and commitment to project-based learning. However, they are also drawn to the possibility that research evidence might challenge some of their assumptions and dispositions, not least because the school also has numerous more traditional characteristics. It was pleasing to learn that the Learning Rainforest had helped by offering the possibility of blending progressive and traditional ideas into a coherent whole without forcing a neat resolution of competing ideas.

I thoroughly enjoyed our online exchanges and the case studies below provide a wonderful insight into the culture and thought-processes at work in the school. If you get a minute to check out the video link at the end of Jeff Suzda's case study, I recommend it. In what Jeff suggests could be a 'world first', the Portledge concert band performs First Circle by jazz guitarist Pat Metheny, posted on Youtube with a subheading, 'trust leads to rigor', referencing the Learning Rainforest.

Isn't it great how ideas about teaching can spread and take so many forms!

We live by the mantra of our four pillars (kindness, purpose, honor, respect). This combination of community and character, as well as our focus on academic excellence, makes Portledge a very attractive option for students that are looking for an education that is forward thinking and will serve to prepare them for college life and beyond.

SIMON OWEN-WILLIAMS
HEAD OF SCHOOL

PROFILE

Location: Locust Valley, New York, USA

Type of Institution: Co-educational Independent School

Roll/Age Range: 525, aged 2–18

Year Founded: 1965

Motto: 'Explore. Create. Excel.'

Recent/Current School Production: Middle School Musical – *You're a Good Man Charlie Brown*. Upper School Musical – *Drowsy Chaperone*. Lower School – *The Sound of Music*.

Recent significant sports event/triumph: Girls varsity soccer team won 5th consecutive league championship in fall of 2018. The 5th was hard fought and won after graduating eight seniors, most of whom played all four years of their high school career, and the new younger team started two middle school students.

Notable quirks/alumni: Taryn Simon graduated from Portledge in 1993, went on to Brown University, won a Guggenheim Fellowship to work on her first major exhibition, The Innocents, and continues as an innovative photographer and artist utilizing photography, text and performance in thoroughly researched works which are displayed at leading museums around the world.

PROFILE

Daniel Naftalis
Upper School teacher

Portledge seeks to balance a rigorous, traditional college preparatory program with the progressive techniques and principles that have been instrumental since the school's founding in 1965. At the heart of Portledge's educational philosophy and approach is the nurturing of individual relationships, particularly the relationship between teacher and student. As such, it has seen itself as largely a progressive school, with traditional aspirations for our students, who are virtually all college-bound.

All three Portledge divisions maintain their commitment to the importance of personalized learning and the many progressive teaching practices we, as a faculty, have adopted. Yet the lower, middle, and upper schools maintain distinctive identities and approaches. The lower school's methodology is rooted in Reggio Emilia, the middle school stresses project-based learning and the upper school is grounded in a student-centered philosophy influenced by the International Baccalaureate program. In some ways, this confederated approach may appear decentralized. However, it grants teachers the necessary autonomy to develop teaching practices that both play to their strengths and best serve their students. In this way, all three divisions are committed to being responsive to the educational and emotional needs of their learners.

Having moved beyond our awkward 'teenage years' as a school, our sense of who we are and who we wish to become has continued to evolve. The Learning Rainforest has served to help us in this regard, particularly as we seek to define our identity as either a traditional or progressive school. Examining what it takes to cultivate a 'managed rainforest' has freed us to fully embrace who we are. We can begin to see that the distinction between the traditional and progressive approaches may be irrelevant to our task, that being to meet the particular needs of each student at Portledge, no matter how those approaches may be defined.

STUDENT: CHARLIE

Age and Year Group: 10, Grade 4

Most recent:

School Trip: The Long Island Aquarium

Extra-curricular activity: Soccer, chess and basketball

Science experiment: We put Mentos in Coca Cola. The reaction is a giant explosion of Coke. We were learning about chemical reactions.

Book/Play studied in English Literature: *The Hunger Games, The Apaches*

Arts project: We performed the play *The Sound of Music*

Learning:

Recent learning highlight: I learned how to change a fraction that doesn't have a denominator of 10, 100 or 1000 into a decimal. I love math.

The most stand-out/interesting/challenging topic you've studied at school: I really liked studying/learning about the Native Americans in third grade because I really like history and I normally don't study about early, early history, and there are a lot of different traditions Things were way different.

One of my favourite teachers: I'm going to go with Ms. Scarcella because I had her for two years. She's really nice, but she's strict when she has to be.

A favourite feature of the school: I like Portledge because you're more independent. I also like that I'm able to go up and do more challenging math, and I don't have to do fourth grade math. I can do fifth grade math. And also the playground is really nice.

I like Portledge because you're more independent.
CHARLIE

STUDENT: TYLER

Age and Year Group: 17, Senior

Most recent:

School Trip: The DNA Learning Center
Extra-curricular activity: Theatre
Science experiment: Resource management for environmental science. It involved 'mining' and interacting with a fictional economy as we had to purchase equipment (toothpicks) for mining (extracting chocolate chips from a cookie) and managing our resources (chocolate chips).
Book/Play studied in English Literature: *Things Fall Apart*, Chinua Achebe
History topic: Authoritarian leaders: Fidel Castro
Arts project: A collaborative exercise where we had to plan, write, and stage an original piece with a 'message' for a selected audience (IB theatre).

Learning:

Subjects Studied: AP Statistics, Graffiti Art, IB Environmental Science, IB History, IB Spanish, IB English, IB Theatre
Recent learning highlight: Writing my extended essay. I've been thinking a lot about my personal philosophy and understanding of the world, but I had never read extensively on philosophy on a scholarly level. Studying Nietzsche was challenging and personally rewarding. It was good to be able to connect his ideas and the ideas of other academics to my own thinking.
The most stand-out/interesting/challenging topic you've studied at school: In English we read Heart of Darkness and explored the colonial view of Africa and followed up with Achebe's contrasting account of Africa from a native perspective. I knew almost nothing about African culture going in, so it was fascinating to learn about the culture of the Igbo people, and especially enlightening to see the world from their point of view. I learned much about the importance of perspective in storytelling.
One of my favourite teachers: Mr. Naftalis, my English teacher. We learn so much in his class and yet it is the kind of learning you obtain from having intellectual, respectful conversations. He is very knowledgeable but draws out our insights through questions and then we have multiple opportunities to reflect on what we know and what we have learned
A favourite feature of the school: It's smallness and warmth. It feels like a home. It is a warm, comforting atmosphere. After lessons, the rooms are often open for hanging out to either relax, study, or converse, which provides a nice change of pace from the rigorous coursework.

STUDENT: LEILA

Age and Year Group: 13, Grade 7

Most recent:

School Trip: The DNA Learning Center
Extra-curricular activity: Travel soccer, member of the Metropolitan Youth Orchestra
Science experiment: A physical and chemical changes lab. We mixed various substances and mixtures together and determined whether there was a physical or chemical change.
Book/Play studied in English Literature: *Much Ado About Nothing* – Shakespeare
History topic: The First Five Presidents
Arts project: A self-determined project where we got to decide how to use a sheet of paper. I was able to practise my drawing skills by studying sharks, which so intrigue me.

Learning:

Subjects Studied: American History, English, Physical Science, Algebra, Spanish, Digital Citizenship, Health, Chorus, Band, Art
Recent learning highlight: The periodic table. I learned how you can determine an element's valence electron and energy levels.
The most stand-out/interesting/challenging topic you've studied at school: Deciphering the meaning behind Shakespeare's language. Once you understand it, it makes the text much more meaningful and sometimes really funny!
One of my favourite teachers: Sra. Arrascue. We have a lot in common; I feel like she gets me and I get her. She speaks in Spanish most of the time. The class is always interactive, and we actually read books in Spanish!
A favourite feature of the school: The place is so welcoming; it's like a family. The people there make you feel at home, and there is always so much to learn.

Be yourself. Everyone else is taken.

LEILA'S FAVORITE QUOTE

I have been challenged, and when I have wanted to push the challenge or level of rigor, Portledge has always met my needs and encouraged me-- but ultimately the choice to push myself was something I had to self-motivate.

TYLER

CASE STUDY: ESTABLISHING CONDITIONS WITH TOOLS FROM BOTH THE TRADITIONAL AND PROGRESSIVE TOOLBOX

Title: Establishing Conditions with Tools from Both the Traditional and Progressive Toolbox; The best of both lead to risk taking and deeper learning!

General Area: Teaching and Learning

Authors: Andrea Scarcella, Third Grade teacher, **Nancy Aranda**, Third Grade teacher

From a traditional/progressive standpoint, the culture in my third-grade classroom is difficult to pigeonhole. On the one hand, it's a community and a family, characterized by acceptance and trust. We build trust over time, in small ways. I try to be consistent and compassionate in how I respond to them as people, and to be transparent and honest so they can trust my word. It is because of this, I believe, that my students take risks. They feel safe enough to question what they hear rather than accept things at face value.

On the other hand, I am the teacher, and I'm always in control, a hallmark of a traditional classroom. We are all safe, physically, emotionally and intellectually, because I make sure of it. So, in terms of 'establishing the conditions,' it's a rather mixed bag, where teacher-in-charge (traditional) and trust (progressive) are both vital elements of the learning environment.

Something remarkable happened one day, and I assert here that it happened in large part because of established conditions; my third graders felt safe enough to wonder aloud.

In February 2018, we were studying Black history, and the essential question was, 'How did these Americans show moral courage?' The reading materials were intentionally selected, but through a series of lessons and guided discussions, I put it on THEM to 'discover' the connections between who they were reading about, and WHY, with the hope that they would be able to address the essential question. While each text was carefully selected with this theme in mind, it was my intent to only guide them to reasonable conclusions about the connections between black history and moral courage. Despite the carefully plotted course of this unit and the methodically collected teaching materials, I decided to merely facilitate their discovery, to be their 'guide on the side.'

It was after a reading of *The Story of Ruby Bridges*, by Robert Coles, that 9-year-old Abby asked 'why?' She referred to a part in the book about Ruby's father being a janitor. It was clear in the story that they struggled financially.

'Wait,' she said. 'If Ruby's father was a janitor, he probably didn't make a lot of money, and he probably didn't go to college.'

I probed with the question 'Why are you wondering about Ruby's father going to college? How would that have changed things for Ruby?'

As the lesson took this student-driven turn, an intense discussion ensued, and with guidance, many began to connect some theoretical dots. If schools were segregated based on race, and the schools for the white children had more resources, then black children weren't afforded the same quality education as white children. Their conclusions were that if children of color didn't get a good education, they couldn't get a good job, make enough money and have the same choices as white children. The consequences were grave, they understood, as they realized that Ruby's father had been trapped by an inequitable system, and that Ruby would inevitably be trapped as well.

Henry tilted his head to the side and wondered aloud 'How did this happen? Why isn't the government making sure everything is fair?'

There were two things I could have done. The more traditional approach would have been to instruct; to tell them about Brown vs BOE, and some of the legal history of the Civil Rights Movement. I chose the more progressive path; I displayed on our Mondopad an image of the Supreme Court justices during that period and turned to the class with no comment.

Abby saw it first. 'They're all white.'

At this moment, they came to understand that on a very basic level, perhaps no one was looking out for black people because there were no black people on the Supreme Court.

When we finished the book, we returned to the question of why we selected Ruby Bridges as a focus of our study in this unit. With the essential question in mind, I led the group to see the connection between their observations about government sanctioned inequity, and the moral courage it took for Ruby to participate in desegregation. Their understanding of this connection was made deeper, I believe, through the 'progressive' approach I choose at that juncture.

Link to Learning Rainforest:

Elements of **both** a progressive and traditional approach were critical to 'establishing the conditions;' children felt trusted and emotionally cared for, AND they knew that the teacher in charge would give them the structure and information they needed to take the academic risks conducive to deeper learning.

There were two things I could have done. The more traditional approach would have been to instruct; to tell them about Brown vs BOE, and some of the legal history of the Civil Rights Movement. I chose the more progressive path; I pulled from the internet an image of the Supreme Court justices during that period and turned to the class with no comment.

ANDREA SCARCELLA
THIRD GRADE TEACHER
AND
NANCY ARANDA
THIRD GRADE TEACHER

CASE STUDY: HOW TO MAKE THE MOCKINGBIRD FLY

Title: How to make the mockingbird fly – a case study on the progressive/traditional debate.

General Area: Teaching and Learning

Author: Janice Groden, Middle School English Teacher

One of my most memorable experiences occurred with my 8th grade advanced English class. It was my first time teaching *To Kill a Mockingbird*, and I was a bit overwhelmed. I chose to explore the text as a commentary on society and to focus on three specific topics: education, race, and gender. Following my traditional teacher's training, I did all the necessary things to prepare my students for the debate. I required copious annotations, historical research, and comparison charts. Students had to make claims surrounding these topics and support them with textually cited evidence.

It should be noted that this unit occurred during a somewhat tumultuous time in the United States, right after the presidential election. Faculty had been trying to come to grips with our differing political views, and these eighth graders were divided as well.

One day, we were exploring gender and the high demands that Aunt Alexandra expects from Scout as a woman. The students had read the chapter, had annotated, and were prepared to debate. I opened the class discussion with a question: Based on everything we have studied about this period in time, and what you know of the characters, do you believe that Aunt Alexandra is doing the right thing?

Having taught this group of students for the past two years, combined with the current post-election climate in general, I was ready and waiting for the great class debate. Those who had strong opinions would voice them, and those who love to play

devil's advocate would stir the pot. One of my more assertive female students raised her hand and meekly said, 'Not that I'm a feminist, but I think Scout should be able to act and dress however she likes.'

When she said the word 'feminist,' she made a face to show how scandalous that word is and lowered her voice as she said it.

I was completely taken off guard. As a feminist myself, I felt obligated to do something about her apologetic demeanor. I asked the students what the word feminist meant. Students started talking about female presidential candidates. All participants defined feminists as militant anti-men activists. All the post-election debates reignited. Students were angry and divided.

After giving them the dictionary definition of feminist, one who believes that men and women should be treated equally, I asked my class, 'Now that you know the definition, who in this room considers himself/herself to be a feminist?' Every kid raised his/her hand. In that moment, taking a more progressive approach, I decided to scrap my whole plan for teaching the book. This involved more 'flying by the seat of my pants' than I would ever feel comfortable with. I decided that the most beneficial way to teach it was to actively tie it into all the issues they had been debating about since the election.

I had always been told that students learn best when the literature we teach becomes personal. As Sherrington says, 'This changes the dynamics significantly; all of a sudden the outcomes become more meaningful and students raise their game to meet the challenge.' It was the perfect marriage of traditional and progressive approaches that not only prepared students for the debate but made it come to life.

Link to Learning Rainforest:

'Debating comes into play when students have the knowledge required and where the question in hand is genuinely worthy of debate, with legitimate opposing views that students can engage with from a position of some authority.'

(*The Learning Rainforest*, p. 264).

This quote from *The Learning Rainforest* strongly resonated with me. As an English teacher, I often choose to explore topics through debate.

I had always been told that students learn best when the literature we teach becomes personal ... It was the perfect marriage of traditional and progressive approaches that not only prepared students for the debate but made it come to life.

JANICE GRODEN
MIDDLE SCHOOL ENGLISH TEACHER

CASE STUDY: PROGRESSIVE-TRADITIONAL BLEND LEADS TO SUCCESS ON STAGE

General Area: Teaching and Learning

Author: Jeff Suzda, Band Teacher, Music Department Chair

When one thinks about a band teacher, the idea of progressive teaching doesn't usually come to mind. There are sometimes over one hundred students (with instruments!) ready to make sound. In order to keep rehearsals organized, there are certain 'Traditional – Teacher Centered' aspects that are utilized and dictated by the very nature of the position:

1) teacher at the front of the classroom in a position of 'power and control'

2) students have assigned seats -in rows – where they remain for the entire year

3) silence (obedience/compliance) is needed at all times when students are not playing

4) direct instruction must be given

5) teacher is the expert who delivers knowledge

Looking only at these aspects, it might seem that every rehearsal is very rigid, however, I have found that I am able to achieve a higher level of rigor, and also achievement, by blending these needed and necessary Traditional aspects with more Progressive – Student Centered ideas.

I am in a fortunate position at the Portledge School, as our schedule allows for regular band rehearsals as well as individual lessons during the school day. These lessons are an ideal place to help and tutor students on individual musical passages, but, more importantly, they allow time to connect and build a strong student-teacher relationship. I dedicate part of each lesson to simply talking about their lives before diving into notes and

rhythms. In doing this, we forge the most important aspect of my teaching – the trust that comes from a strong student-teacher relationship.

After reading *The Learning Rainforest* in the summer of 2018, I selected a piece for my oldest band that 'pitched the material very high' (page 157/158) and one that would only work if I had the trust of my students. I researched the composition to try to find another high school concert band that had recorded or performed the piece, and I could not. After re-writing all the original jazz band parts to fit our instrumentation, I handed out the music and was met with blank stares; the piece was well beyond their ability at the time – they knew it, and I knew it. Every musician in the room, even a college-bound senior who would be attending a prestigious music conservatory, was going to have to work tirelessly at this piece. The only thing that I had was their trust and their belief that I was not going to let them fail.

I ensured success by blending in Progressive techniques:

1) trust and openness – I let them know that this piece was also a stretch for me as a conductor; we were working toward success together.

2) personalization – I rewrote parts for individual students based on their abilities.

3) 'teacherless' group work – I gave the older students the power to lead sectional rehearsals without a teacher.

4) 21st-century technology – I video recorded all of the individual parts and posted them online so that the students were able to have a teacher with them when they needed, and could hear what mastery sounds like.

I knew that I was reaching my students when I looked at empty shelves in my classroom over the weekends. Normally, due to busy external schedules and academic homework loads, most of the students left their instruments at school and practiced sporadically. This piece proved different however, because they *wanted* to practice; I presented them with a piece that they had to work to master, and more importantly, they *had an intrinsic desire* to practice because it was a stretch and they yearned to master the complex.

Video link at https://youtu.be/K-e8aVKidZE

Link to Learning Rainforest:

Demanding rigor and pitching the material very high led to intrinsic motivation in my students.

I let them know that this piece was also a stretch for me as a conductor; we were working toward success together.

JEFF SUZDA
BAND TEACHER, MUSIC
DEPARTMENT CHAIR

NISHKAM HIGH SCHOOL, BIRMINGHAM

INTRODUCTION

I was invited by Principal, Damien Kearns, to support the Nishkam science team in developing their A level teaching, visiting the school almost weekly for a term. I didn't really know what to expect from a Sikh-based multi-faith free school; what I found was a school with a lovely friendly atmosphere – with values and virtues projected very strongly every day – mixed with very explicit ambitions for academic excellence. All around the school you find a graphic reminding students of the school's 50 virtues – almost an A-Z from Awe, Courage, Discernment through to Tact, Tolerance, Trust and Wisdom. This is amplified at various key points in the week: daily multi-faith reflections that take place in the magnificent carpeted atrium at the heart of the school building; daily reflections before the communal lunch sittings and at weekly end-of-day faith-group sessions – where students with common faiths (including no faith) gather together.

As a visiting consultant, it was lovely to get to know a team of effective, committed science teachers, earnestly seeking to improve further still. I met one of the best NQTs I've come across in years – amazing to have such confidence and drive – and I had the chance to discuss some of my favourite topics including the joy of making motors! Most significantly, I learned a lot about the process of supporting a teacher to improve their practice. You need to focus on very specific ideas that can be tried out and deliberately practised – otherwise change doesn't really happen or stick. It was great to see tangible shifts amongst the Nishkam teachers I worked with as they explored aspects of questioning and checking for understanding. It was also interesting to note just how important curriculum knowledge is. Whilst general questioning techniques can be very powerful, a lot of the time where students have difficulty, solutions lie in knowing how to unlock the specific misconceptions – not in some general

pedagogical approach – and this was interesting to explore with the team.

With that in mind, it was really interesting to read Andy Brown's case study about the development of their approach to professional learning which reinforces these ideas.

Nishkam is a different school. It helps my child to appreciate every day human values and, at the same time, supports him to reach for academic excellence. Not every school has such a balanced approach.

PARENT

Nishkam is a family, a community.

STUDENT

PROFILE

Location: Birmingham, UK

Type of Institution: Free School – Sikh based multi-faith secondary school

Roll/Age Range: 700, aged 11–18

Year Founded: 2012

Motto: 'To be humble, to be wise'

House Names: Compassion, Contentment, Humility, Love and Truth

Recent/Current School Production: *Mary Poppins*

Recent significant sports event/triumph: Birmingham, Girls' Futsal Champions – U16s

Notable quirks/alumni: The school was originally built by Sikh volunteers, all of whom invested their own time freely as part of 'Seva', the selfless service of others with no sense of wanting reward.

Andy Brown
Assistant Principal

Nishkam translates to 'selfless service' and our motto is 'to be wise; to be humble'. This is the starting point for all that we do. Nishkam High School is part of a multi-faith trust that uses a virtues-led approach to education; in the Learning Rainforest, these virtues provide the spiritual equivalent of 'photosynthesis' in that they nurture children with values, enable them to grow academically and spiritually and, from there, serve humanity well.

The result is an interwoven curriculum that examines, for example, contentment within Shakespeare, accountability within genetic engineering or the place of humility in profit making

Nishkam High School uses a virtues led approach to education. It is the lens through which all matters are viewed. We believe passionately that 'all children can, and will, achieve.' We adopt an approach of 'excellence for all' and scaffold up to that where necessary. Humility is central to all that we do; leading our school is rather like standing in the rainforest, my first responses are wonder, awe, gratitude and respect. At Nishkam, we are engaged in sowing the seeds for trees that we will not necessarily see.

PRINCIPAL

PROFILE

STUDENT: LUVPREET TOOR

STUDENT: SAFFRON KULAR

organisations. When done well, the virtues support and interact with learning in the way that plants and animals co-exist and support each other in the rainforest. The virtues are our anchor point for students' standards of behaviour; they provide the moral compass to guide them in difficult terrain and always point 'north' towards the correct path.

These virtues are modelled by our teachers and are embedded in their language and actions around the school. Our 'language of values' programme is every bit as developed as our 'language of learning'. This is further illustrated within our Monday morning 'staff reflection' when a member of staff chooses to share a story, a memory, a poem, a photograph or some other personal reflection that mirrors our virtues. This reflection allows us to return to the fundamental virtues at the beginning of each new week.

The school's focus on our virtues-led approach to education provides an environment where staff can pursue excellence; that is, nurturing our children to be good human beings and the best that they can be, as well as achieving excellent academic outcomes.

TEACHER

Age and Year Group: 12, Year 7
House: Compassion

Most recent:

Extra-curricular activity: Holi Celebration
Science experiment: Metal and acid reactions
Book/Play studied in English Literature: *The Tempest*
History topic: The British Empire
Arts project: Portraits through Picasso and Warhol

Learning:

Subjects Studied: English, Maths, Science, French, Punjabi, Drama, PE, RE, Computer Science, Food Technology, VFPD (Values, Faith and Personal-Development)

Recent learning highlight: In French, we have moved onto learning phrases such as, 'On porte une chemise blanche, un pantalon gris et des chaussettes blanches'. I love the chance to learn a new language.

The most stand-out/interesting/challenging topic you've studied at school: The most challenging topic was gradients in Maths. I really struggled with Maths at the start of the year; however, thanks to my teacher, I am more confident in Maths and especially, gradient questions.

One of my favourite teachers: I don't have one favourite teacher as I like all my teachers because they share the same values. They strive for excellence in me and my peers.

A favourite feature of the school: My favourite thing is how teachers put an interesting twist on all the lessons using our virtues, their knowledge or their sense of humour. There hasn't been one lesson where a teacher hasn't made me laugh and enjoy the learning (apart from tests!).

Age and Year Group: 16, Year 11
House: Contentment

Most recent:

School Trip: David Starkey History Conference
Extra-curricular activity: Supported 'Open Day' for prospective new students
Science experiment: Flame Tests
Book/Play studied in English Literature: *An Inspector Calls/ Macbeth/Jekyll and Hyde*
History topic: Health and the People/Conflict and tension/ America 1920–1973/Elizabeth I

Learning:

Subjects Studied: English, Maths, Biology, Chemistry, Physics, Punjabi, PE, RE, Health and Social Care, VFPD

Recent learning highlight: A lesson in History, where we had to rank the importance of key individuals in the medical course.

The most stand-out/interesting/challenging topic you've studied at school: I have enjoyed studying America in History because I was intrigued by the developments of America from 1920 to 1970. I loved the opportunity to learn more about a country's past.

One of my favourite teachers: I really enjoy lessons with Mr Nandra because he equally supports all the students to ensure that everyone receives the support that they need to reach their potential.

A favourite feature of the school: My favourite aspect of the school is the virtues led development of the students, no matter how intelligent, what religion or background. I enjoy how students are given the opportunity to intellectually and spiritually develop; helping them to become a good person.

As a Nishkam family, one spark lights another, and that is the beauty behind supporting one another's spiritual and intellectual journey.

SAFFRON KULAR

Excellence in education is doing everything excellently.

LUVPREET TOOR

CASE STUDY: CHANGING THE FOCUS OF CPD

Title: Changing the focus of CPD; how we enhanced CPD to improve our curriculum and our virtues led approach to education

General Area: Continuous Professional Development (CPD), Curriculum Design and Virtues in Education

Author: Andy Brown, Assistant Principal of Teaching and Learning

Why did we change our CPD focus?

Schools cannot be the 'fountain of all knowledge', certainly not on their own. However, schools can now reap rich benefits from the growth of learning communities. ResearchED, The Chartered College, the increasing range and number of educational books and blogs, the development of materials on professional association websites are but a few of the resources now available to schools. It would, therefore, be prudent to 'tap in' to these rich resources and this has been one of the driving forces behind our CPD plan – to arm our staff with the best information, best evidence, best guidance that is available to support them in their work.

What has changed?

Our previous model was dominated by whole school CPD, often covering core priorities of the school and in line with what most schools, typically, do. However, such an approach cannot always support the distinctiveness of specific subjects and the nuances in delivery of these subjects. This year we have given a significant proportion of CPD time back to staff to select personal areas of development. The new approach has split CPD into three strands; one for whole school CPD, the second for department level CPD and the third for individual CPD. This maintained the ability to drive forward whole school improvement whilst, at the same time, providing space for teachers and departments to take ownership of their own development in ways which relate to their own subject knowledge and pedagogical practices.

Why increase the amount of subject specific professional development?

Increasing subject specific CPD has been supported by The Wellcome Trust's 'Developing Great Teaching Report' that states: 'Schools that have the poorest academic or inspection results are the least likely to prioritise subject-specific professional development'; whilst Curee's 2015 report articulates that 'subject-specific CPD ... has a greater impact on pupil outcomes than generic pedagogic CPD'. Improving the teacher's knowledge of their subject and respecting the individual nature of all subjects through our CPD delivery will lead to a better quality of lessons delivered to pupils in the classroom.

What does it look like?

Staff have embraced the freedom to enhance subject knowledge, strengthen an area of uncertainty and reconnect their passion for their subject. We have staff who have attended Saturday conferences from 'researchED' to the UCL's, 'Unpacking the Holocaust'. Teachers are engaging with a variety of subject associations that have included looking at 'Marine Debris and the impact on Iceland' and 'Shakespeare's rhetorical style from Plutarch and Ovid'. Teachers are reading educational research, signing books out of the staff library and engaging with the latest blogs. All CPD is directed toward professional growth, faculty improvement and, consequently, school improvement.

How has this developed our curriculum thinking?

The development of the National Curriculum in the late 1980s had many and varied consequences (intentional and unintentional), one being the relative neglect of curriculum design that was then exacerbated by a 'whole-school' approach to CPD intent upon creating a level of consistency within schools. We, at Nishkam, want to celebrate differences and provide teachers with opportunities to better understand their subject discipline, their craft, by engaging in conversations with fellow teachers or subject experts. We want them to use that enhanced knowledge to better craft our curriculum and the concomitant schemes of learning and assessment opportunities. Faculty Leaders and their staff are best placed to make curriculum-based decisions in their own subject; we believe this is the way to drive improvement in curriculum thinking, develop our outstanding teachers and enhance the quality of education that our students receive.

How has this supported our virtues led approach to education?

Our virtues are embedded throughout our school, manifesting themselves in a myriad number of ways from collective worship to daily reflection. However, after two successful years, we also wanted to consider 'where improvement lies' and further embed faith and virtues into the fabric of the school. Our Trust dedicates five extra, paid, CPD days every year so that staff can develop greater understanding of both faith and virtues. Our CPD offer enables staff to fully explore the thinking and narratives that help support the transmission of key virtues, skills and content to our students. The overall aim is that CPD should assist our staff in accomplishing our vision that they nurture children with values, enable them to grow academically and spiritually and, from there, serve humanity well.

What has been the outcome so far?

The depth and variety of CPD has increased. However, more pleasing, is a culture of engagement with subject disciplines, the fundamental importance of our virtues and trying to put that knowledge into practice. For example, 'researchED' sessions are finding their way into faculty meetings; 'TeachMeet' ideas are being trialled in lessons and academic curriculum thinkers are being referred to in faculty improvement plans. Internally, our first voluntary educational reading meeting had ten attendees, our latest one had twenty-six. The Educational Endowment Foundation refers to making 'best bets' based on evidence. All our evidence points towards effective CPD being specific, personal and closely related to the subject domain you teach; our 'best bet' has been placed and I am excited to review the impact of this.

CASE STUDY: CHANGING THE FOCUS OF CPD

NISHKAM VIRTUES GUIDE

What are our next steps?

I am extremely encouraged by the way the CPD plan has been embraced; however, we are still determined to discover where improvement lies. After an initial review, including a staff consultation, two areas have been identified: specific, low stakes observation and further access to subject specific CPD.

The low stakes observation cycle will identify an area of practice that the teacher would like to improve, support through small teaching communities to select a specific action, and then, finally, an observation to review the success of the action; the school has purchased five in-classroom cameras to support the specificity of this process.

Two examples of developing our subject specific CPD are providing more opportunities to visit departments in other schools and the introduction of department level CPD budgets where staff can source subject specialists to deliver CPD to their department. Our aim is to never stand still; to provide the best environment for teachers to develop, as ultimately, this will provide the best for students.

Link to Learning Rainforest:

Our aim is to deliver CPD that improves the quality of education that our students receive. Chapters based upon 'What does the research say?' and 'Building knowledge structures' have supported our CPD journey — helping to provide the environment for professional development to flourish. The development of teachers' knowledge around pedagogy and the specific subject, we feel, will provide the largest opportunity to positively affect the development of students at Nishkam. There are still many areas that need time to develop; nevertheless, I am excited to see how our CPD provision can support the growth of the school.

The more subject specific knowledge our teachers have, the better they can teach the narratives and virtues inherent in their subject.

ANDY BROWN
ASSISTANT PRINCIPAL OF TEACHING
AND LEARNING

Truth Wisdom Accountability
Trust Awe
Tolerance Cleanliness
Tact Commitment
Simplicity Compassion
Selflessness Confidence
Self-discipline Contemplation
Sacrifice Contentment
Righteousness Courage
Reverence Courtesy
Respect Creativity
Resilience Detachment
Reliability Determination
Purposefulness Devotion
Prayerfulness Discernment
Peacefulness Diligence
Patience Enthusiasm
Optimism Excellence
Obedience Faith
Modesty Forgiveness
Moderation Gratitude
Leadership Helpfulness
Love Humility Honesty
Kindness Justice

LEBANON EVANGELICAL SCHOOL FOR BOYS AND GIRLS, BEIRUT

INTRODUCTION

I am continually taken aback by the reach *The Learning Rainforest* seems to have had, supported largely by the global edu-Twitter community that seems to operate without boundaries. This entry is a perfect example. On hearing that I was planning a trip to Dubai via my Twitter feed, LESBG Principal Steve White contacted me to see if I could fit in a visit to his school in Lebanon on the way. It was one of the most memorable school visits I've made. This is partly because of the spectacular hillside location in Baabda, Loueizeh, up in the mountains outside Beirut. But it was also because of meeting the charismatic Principal, Steve, and his wife Grace, Head of the Primary division of LESBG, enjoying their generous hospitality when I stayed in their family apartment on the school site.

Uniquely among the *Fieldbook* schools, LESBG is literally a family-run school. British by birth but now a Lebanese citizen, 'Mr Steve' White is a central figure in his community having been associated with the school since his father ran it as Principal before him. Steve speaks fluent Arabic but says he never learned the written form of the language. Famously, his father kept the school open, against the odds, at all times during the civil war, at some stages providing a sanctuary for a small group of students who had nowhere else to go. Steve's daughter now teaches in the school and his brother became the Head of another school in Beirut – so it clearly runs in the family. Steve gave me an overview of recent Lebanese history and the ongoing political challenges the country faces. The current period of relative peace and stability isn't something they take for granted. There are daily challenges that most schools around the world do not have to worry about including the rationing of electricity and the supply of water. Every day there is a short-term power cut when the central supply stops and the school generators start up. Every day Steve gets an

update on the school's water levels and will decide when to order a new tanker delivery to top up the supply; this isn't provided by the state because the physical and civic infrastructure isn't in place to do it.

What I found inspiring was the determination of Steve, Grace and their staff, to deliver a first-rate education. There are various context-specific curriculum requirements and social challenges that the school deals with but, in common with all the *Fieldbook* schools, there was a real appetite for professional development. I was given a fabulous reception by the teaching staff – even when they had to attend on an extra Saturday morning to engage with the full programme. We ran through the full Learning Rainforest structure and, as you can see from the case study entries, teachers left buzzing with ideas to implement in their classrooms. Given that some of the contributors are writing in a second language – I've tried to keep their authentic voices in the editing process – the LESBG contributors have done a superb job. It's wonderful to hear how ideas caught their imaginations during the CPD event in a very unique context. There's an honesty to their writing – acknowledging how hard it can be at times to put ideas into practice.

One minor detail of my visit that I enjoyed was learning that, like me, Steve is a physics teacher. Unlike many other Principals, Steve teachers for about three hours every day – he loves doing it too much to give it up! I found a copy of the Feynman lectures in his apartment which, by a nice coincidence, links him to Jim Henderson, Headteacher of another *Fieldbook* school, Archbishop Tenison in London who uses 'Feynman Fan' as his Twitter profile name. Physics teachers united in the Rainforest!

My deepest desire is to see this school populated by a community of learners.
DR. STEVE WHITE

In the school's annual magazine, *Evangazette*, Steve suggests that 'the most pressing need in schools today is to teach students the great importance of being men and women of integrity. Doing the right thing when nobody's watching. Being kind, putting others interests before your own, going the extra mile. These are the key parts of being a whole person. If we want to graduate students that will make a real difference, we need to realize that everything else pales into insignificance against these great attributes of character. I pray that not only will this school be a community of learners but a source of kind and true people.

STUDENT: SARAH BAADARANI

Age and Year Group: 16, 11th grade

Most recent:

School Trip: Rechmaya

Extra-curricular activity: Member of the Student Affairs Organization (SAO), Library Team

Science experiment: Measuring the wavelength of a sound wave

Book/Play studied in English Literature: *How Much Land Does a Man Need?* by Leo Tolstoy

History topic: The fall of the Ottoman Empire

Arts project: Pointillism Project

Learning:

Subjects Studied: Mostly everything with special emphasis on Physics, Chemistry, Biology and Math

Recent learning highlight: My most recent learning highlight is when two of my friends and I organized an entertaining lesson for 3rd graders and taught it. This experience taught me a lot about planning, giving your best, and making the most of an opportunity. It also accentuated the pleasurable innocence of children and offered a chance to relax and be childishly playful.

The most stand-out/interesting/challenging topic you've studied at school: The most challenging topic I enjoyed studying is programming because it expanded my abilities on how to dissect complex problems. Though some found it tedious, I found it fascinating how these unique languages can instruct a computer to undergo certain functions. Learning programming languages shed the light on how code is the literacy of our age.

One of my favourite teachers: I enjoy lessons with Mrs Taline Hawatian who teaches me Math because she advocates students to asks questions continuously as she is also interactive. Not only that, but she always motivates students regardless of their intellect.

A favourite feature of the school: My favourite feature in the school is the integration of autistic students in school activities and lessons. It's very heart-warming to see students with learning disabilities advance in drama, art, PE, and with their social skills after devoting a part of your time to aiding them. Honestly, the best part is when they recognize you and ask for a fist-bump.

STUDENT: GAELLE NASSER

Age and Year Group: 14, 8c
House: Barouk

Learning:

Subjects Studied: English levelled reading

Recent learning highlight: Recently we are learning in our levelled reading lessons how to control ourselves through special reading topics which we read and discuss. Moreover we show our talents listing reading, analysing, as well as listening quizzes, In my opinion the extra reading material that we work on provide us with extra needed knowledge to improve our skills.

The most stand-out/interesting/challenging topic you've studied at school: The two subjects that I personally like and feel challenged when participating in are Math and English levelled reading (ELR). Math is filled of numbers which are my favourite thing and through it I can help build my future major. Furthermore 'ELR' is one of the best; from the day I first started till now all my language in English never dropped under 90% due to advanced vocabulary.

One of my favourite teachers: I enjoy lessons with Mr Jimmy Haddad who teaches me 'ELR' because he gives the chance to each and every single individual in his group to show their talents which were probably hidden.

A favourite feature of the school: One thing that I like strongly and appreciate in this school is that they try their best to teach students that lessons are not only learnt from an academic book but also from life which is a never ending story teaching respect, love, care, share, and last but definitely not least that people suffering from disabilities are not less yet different.

Learning is the foundation of a bright future.
GAELLE NASSER

My favourite feature in the school is the integration of autistic students in school activities and lessons.
SARAH BAADARANI

CASE STUDY: IMPLEMENTING LEARNING RAINFOREST STRATEGIES IN THE JUNIOR SCHOOL

Author: Natalie Hajj Moussa

I am a Junior 3 homeroom teacher and I have been teaching for 17 years out of which 15 years have been as a homeroom teacher for the same grade level. I have always believed in building students' characters and help them mature and grow in confidence. This grade level is very delicate, because here, students are separating from being dependent into independent, and therefore being more responsible for their studies. This is why every year, I try to implement something new in my class, either by reading articles online, or by lessons I have learned from the group of students I had the previous year.

After the Learning Rainforest in Action workshop presented by Mr Tom Sherrington, I got introduced to the following strategies:

1. Using pair work through Think, Pair, Share strategy
2. A new way of students participating through Cold Call
3. Making sure everybody knows the concept in no Opt-Out
4. A new way of improving their cognitive and analytic mind through Probing Questioning
5. Making sure they are ready for pop quizzes through Face It
6. Achieving complete silence through using silent signals.

This is how I implemented **Think, Pair, Share**. My class has thirty students divided into six groups and within the groups there are jobs given to students like the leader and the representative. I always have based my activities on group work. I rarely tried pair work. I was looking for something new to implement in my class and this well-built strategy was the motivation which inspired me. I started using it in all my subjects: Maths, English, Science, and Social Studies. It worked amazingly! I will give an example on applying this method in every subject.

In Maths, I would write a problem on the board to be solved as our starting point in the lesson. We read it together, I ask my students about the operations we learned, then I ask them to think of the given, what is asked for, and how to solve the problem. I time them for a couple of minutes to think about the problem individually. Then, I ask them to pair up in their groups whether with their shoulder to shoulder partner or face to face partner. I time them for another couple of minutes to share their answers and discuss them. During that time, I pass by to check their responses. Questioning is very important as was discussed in the workshop especially probing questioning, so I ask them how they got their answers and why they think this is the best way of solving the problem. I used it in different ways in Maths and with different concepts taught such as visual thinking.

In English, I would give them sentences that have different types of adjectives. Their job in think, pair, share is to find all the adjectives and when they spot them, they decide which type they are (what kind) or (how many). Same as I did in Maths, I did in English.

In Science, students have learned about expanding hot air. Students would be using bicarbonate of soda, vinegar, an empty water bottle, and a balloon. I ask them to think and come up with a prediction of what would happen if the balloon is put on top of the empty water bottle with all the materials in. Then, they pair and share their predictions. Students are very excited and motivated to find out if they nailed it.

In Social Studies, we were comparing different lifestyles in Asian countries. Students were given time to think of a specific number of differences and similarities. Then, they paired and they shared what they had of information that they recalled. I found out that there are lots of advantages in using the method Think, Pair, Share some of which are behavioural and some are academic.

While using the method Think, Pair, Share, students were no longer fighting about who will start first and who will do this or that concerning group work. This means there are less conflicts to solve. Students decide to take turns when revealing and explaining their responses. This method improved students' cognitive skills, because in a way, they are forced to think because they know that they will be paired up to share what they thought about and they know that it is a must. So all students are taking part and are eventually learning from each other because one of the pair should convince them that their way is right. It is very important to note that while pairing up students, I had to think of the way I should pair them and follow a specific criteria in doing that. So average students were paired with challenging students, weak students with average students, impulsive students with calm ones and so on just to keep the balance.

I worked on using **Cold Call** more frequently in almost all lessons, for the first time in my career. As teachers, it is easier to ask a question and encourage everybody to participate while raising their hands, without seeing those who have low self-confidence and wouldn't initiate to participate in any discussion, or the ones that talk during the explanation. Cold Call was a solution for those students. It is a method that would keep all students alert and focused not only the challenged students but everybody. Cold Call paved the way for those students to grow in confidence.

For example in science, when we learned about dissolving, the question was to think how we can know that sugar that is dissolved is still in the liquid and didn't simply disappear. I asked my students not to raise their hands and that I will ask randomly. The students were alert and tried to think. Most of the students' answers were close to the correct answer. So now when I ask my students to think they directly know that I would be calling at anyone to answer and I want their response.

This way they try their best with some prompts and they can answer reasonably. Cold Call took time to implement and took time away in the lesson, and not all that was planned was covered in the lesson, but now this is improving. Cold Call is linked in a way to No Opt-Out. My students are fully aware that even if they don't know the answer, this doesn't mean that they will not know or it is acceptable not to know. They will eventually know because they will have to listen since they will be asked to repeat the answer and re-explain the method. Then the whole class repeats after several individuals.

What most helped my students was **probing questioning**. This type of questions worked to make massive changes in the way the students think: what do you think? Really? Explain, give an example, are you sure? Amazingly, the students started thinking outside the box and this helped improve their analytic and cognitive thinking.

CASE STUDY: STUDENTS LEADING LESSONS

Author: Carla Daher

As mentioned in *The Learning Rainforest*, I recently encouraged students to take the opportunity to explain a lesson. In the past, I have tried this method twice in class 11 and it turned out to be very successful because the students greatly enjoyed the lesson and showed excellent participation. Knowing that it sounds quite good with students when I proposed the idea, the new class were excited to take the role of the teacher for a lesson.

Title: The Social Situation of Modern Science –
الوضع الاجتماعي للعلم المعاصر

Procedure:

Two students, Perla and Hussein, prepared a lesson of Arabic Literature. The lesson centred around how society and science interact with one another in the 21st century. These students explained the lesson and created comprehension questions as well. These questions were designed to test the prior knowledge of the class.

Perla and Hussein divided the work between them. Perla wrote on the board the title of the lesson and highlighted two main ideas mentioned in the text, as an introduction, before reading the text.

≠At first, Perla asked the students: What is the importance of science in today's society?

She received good answers from a number of her classmates. For example, some students mentioned that science has helped us understand more about the world around us. Additionally, students mentioned that it helps to make our life easier. Then, she asked another question: 'What is the importance of the science in the life of the human being?' This time, students were totally involved and interacted very well with the 'teacher'. Students stated that science is important as it helps us ensure a

better future. However, some students also challenged this idea, explaining that science also has negative side effects on society.

Second, Hussein read the text for the lesson and asked the students to give the main idea in each paragraph. Perla wrote the ideas given by her classmates on the board. Some of these comments included: improving home life through technology such as computers, washing machines, and dishwashers not available to other countries, finding better job opportunities, and facing problems in life in a positive way. Then, students started to read each paragraph and tried to explain the main idea in each by themselves.

Finally, after they finished the lesson, Perla and Hussein started analyzing their prepared comprehension questions with the students. They started by writing each question on the board, then they asked the students to reply and answer the questions. The students were fully engaged with the student teachers and greatly enjoyed this lesson and asked to repeat the experience.

Noting that Perla and Hussein adopted my teaching method, they tried to take my role in everything done during that lesson. They did so very well and the class as a whole responded very positively to the experience.

As their teacher, I was so proud of the work that they did. I think it was a beneficial experience for the class, a new one for the students who taught on that day.

Perla and Hussein adopted my teaching method, they tried to take my role in everything done during that lesson. They did so very well and the class as a whole responded very positively to the experience.

CARLA DAHER

So all students are taking part and are eventually learning from each other because one of the pair should convince them that their way is right.

NATALIE HAJJ MOUSSA

STUDENT: MATTHEW SCARBOROUGH

Age and Year Group: 12, Year group: 2006
House: Hermon

Most recent:

School Trip: Lynx; December 2018
Extra-curricular activity: Volleyball
Science experiment: Mar.22,2019; physical and chemical changes
Book/Play studied in English Literature: *Wonder*
History topic: Ancient Rome
Arts project: Pop art

Learning:

Subjects Studied: Math, English, chemistry, life science, Bible, Sp.HGC, computer, physics, art, drama, physical ed., Sp.Arabic, French, and English leveled reading
Recent learning highlight: The geometry lessons are fun for me. By memorizing how to justify, I quickly grasped the concept of how to do it.
The most stand-out/interesting/challenging topic you've studied at school: I enjoyed studying and learning about history. It's very interesting to learn and easy to score high grades in. I like to study it and do extra research about people, places, and things. Overall it is an extraordinary subject.
One of my favourite teachers: I enjoy lessons with Mrs. Rania who teaches me Special History, geography, and civics because in lessons she does something different.
A favourite feature of the school: I like the schedule at school because I never feel like ' I'm so tired of math'. Everything is at the right time for the right amount of time. Also, I feel free during break because there's much to do. At the same time a range of emotions in class while learning.

75

STUDENT: LAURA SAMIA EL MOGHRABI

Age and Year Group: 14, Year group: 2004
House: Hermon

Most recent:

School Trip: As a class, we attended Faraya to go on an educational hike where we learned many facts about nature and its beauty

Extra-curricular activity: As a school we dedicated a specific afternoon for the special Lebanese author Gibran Khalil Gibran.

Science experiment: Many students took blood tests during our biology lesson while we were studying about genetics.

Book/Play studied in English Literature: *The Chronicles of Narnia: The Lion, The Witch and The Wardrobe.*

History topic: The serious Palestine case

Arts project: Pointillism

Learning:

Subjects Studied: HGC

Recent learning highlight: We recently had a civics lesson about the League of Arab States where after the teacher explained specific parts. She would ask a question and we would reply on a postcard she provided us with at the beginning of the lesson.

The most stand-out/interesting/challenging topic you've studied at school: I enjoyed learning about the independence of Lebanon and how it gained it because that showed me how strong and persistent is the Lebanese community and civilization.

One of my favourite teachers: I enjoy lessons with Ms. Rita Keyrouz who teaches me history, geography, and civics because she simply makes these subjects much more interesting due to the unique ways she uses.

A favourite feature of the school: My favorite feature of the school would probably be the great concern and love most teachers have towards their students. Adding to that, the unity between all students is an amazing feature

CASE STUDY: APPLYING RAINFOREST LEARNING METHODS

General: Teaching and Learning
Author: Jimmy Haddad, English leveled Reading Teacher

- Method Applied (Role play) (Think, Pair, Share)
- Group Work and Peer Assessment

Recently I have started implementing new teaching methods acquired from the school's Continuing professional development program to try to move the learning process from passive to active where students are engaged and involved in the lessons, as an 'ELR' teacher I've applied two learning methods so far which are: 'Role play and Think Pair Share'.

In role play what I did is that I gave each student the opportunity to be able to play the teacher's role. They were supposed to read and assign homework, in other words 'contract to read at home', grade the students reading and asking comprehension questions plus analytical ones. Students were in charge of assessing and grading yet none the less keeping the class in order.

The second method I applied is 'think, Pair, Share'. Students were given a special topic to talk or write about then read it out loud. Steps to follow this activity: they first start by brainstorming their thoughts individually writing their ideas on a separate piece of paper then they pair with their assigned group member to discuss it and reach the best outcome possible between them. Once they have reached a final decision they share their work with the class reading it out loud and other students or in this case the other groups are the ones to assess them or the teacher might be the one do it.

These activities were established under 'group work 'conditions which made it a little bit easier for active learning to take place for students are already grouped together and engaged in the lessons. A number of group methods and techniques can be used

to facilitate the learning process. For peer assessment you need to help students first by giving them a clear assessment criteria to build on, give those examples on how to assess, and as a teacher you have to give them feedback at the end.

After applying these methods I realized that a number of points were raised to my attention regarding students' learning enhancement and improvement. Group work for example can be used to promote interaction between students this will help students to develop problem solving skills, better critical thinking skills, better engagement, and create better communication skills. With peer assessment the results were also favourable for the learning process; it encourages students' involvement and responsibility it allows students to see and reflect on their peer assessment.

Link to Learning Rainforest:

From what have been previously presented, I can find a clear connection between the methods I've applied and the Learning Rainforest objectives and techniques, relating to:

- Knowledge
- Assessment
- Establishing the conditions
- Exploring possibilities

The key to engaging professional development sessions is giving me the time to take part in something meaningful for my own development and balancing this with school priorities.
RANIA NAJEM

Tell me and I'll forget. Show me and I may remember. Involve me and I learn.
JIMMY HADDAD

CASE STUDY: APPLYING THE TRAINING TO TEACHING HISTORY

General: Teaching and Learning

Author: Rania Najem, Sp. HGC and ELR teacher in the Senior Department

Throughout my experience as a teacher for the intermediate classes, I always build up my lesson plan beginning with warming up; I do ask prerequisite questions to help the students express their own ideas and share their own experience about the topic so that my students are enriched with all the objectives and requirements before I start explaining the topic. Then, I begin by stating the objectives that the students must attain, after that I start my teaching strategy that comes with the technique of exposing more ideas and try to link them to life and then comes the assessment.

There were a lot of ideas I really enjoyed following from Tom's CPD. The amount of engagement, critical thinking, cooperative learning, problem-solving, and learning, that happened after the workshop fuelled my passion for this type of education and was the guiding light for my work later. I believe that linking professional development to practice is crucial; it needs to have direct effect on students' and teachers' development. It's a big ask for CPD co-ordinators and school leaders, but it should be a priority. However, the effective and inspiring sessions must be part of the whole school development so teachers can see the long-term impact as I did. Training should always link back to the school's aims and values, so everyone will understand the why behind the what. At my school, we try to constantly connect back to our own personal beliefs about what great teaching and learning should look like – sessions are about fundamental values as well as day to day practice. Many of our staff are engaged in their own research and professional reading is part and parcel of the way we keep ourselves informed. I feel it is an empowering way of moving forward.

The key to engaging professional development sessions is giving me the time to take part in something meaningful for my own development and balancing this with school priorities. This cannot be achieved in five inset days throughout the year. Our school with the outstanding professional development models encourages tailored CPD pathways for each individual teacher and support members of staff throughout the year in dropdown sessions and after-school groups.

The Learning Rainforest CPD helped me in exploring ways to teach students with different levels of attainment. For example, engaging students who felt neglected before, in 'missions' where that made them feel brilliant to accomplish. In a unit on the Romans, many students had the opportunity to engage in an extended enquiry to a significant final product demonstrating a range of skills, knowledge and personal attributes, when they were asked to present a project. Applying a knowledge-rich curriculum helped the students to remember all the given information. Eventually, my students had the chance to gain more knowledge and were more confident to encounter different skills.

As a result, my students were able to identify and start key events in history in detail with accuracy. They described events in history in order, at least if not in the exact date but in the exact event order. They were able to make a judgement about an enquiry or issue in history, and state facts that were learnt from the source about the event or the period.

Link to Learning Rainforest:

- Assessment

If I had the chance to mention all the successful methods from the CPD, I would mention them all. Whist I found writing about the outcome, the assessment is something essential to mention. The CPD taught us as teachers how to assess our students effectively.

CASE STUDY: APPLYING THE LEARNING RAINFOREST

Title: Applying the Learning Rainforest training to Geography

General: Teaching and Learning

Author: Rita Keyrouz, HGC for the Lebanese curriculum

In Geography I explained in a previous lesson the spread of population growth based on gender and age in a pyramid-shaped triangle. I also presented a sample format and contents of the pyramid. To begin with, I used the method '**Check for Understanding**' in order to help students deduce the objectives of the lesson. It helped me comprehend that only very few students actually understood the lesson objectives while the majority did not. Thus, I went over the lesson by asking the few students who grasped the objectives and based on their answers I was able to help the majority understand the full objectives of the lesson given.

Unfortunately, the above activity mentioned turned out to be time-consuming when used in 9th grade. Still, it proved effective in testing the pupils' understanding. Next, I showed board signs containing questions about the lesson and asked students to answer in their copybooks. That activity proved to be more effective as it triggered their enthusiasm. It did so since all the wrong answers were corrected by the teacher. It is an approach for others to learn the concepts as well.

Main link to the Learning Rainforest: *Curriculum /knowledge*

During teaching periods I used multiple techniques in different classes. I used '**Cold Call**'; it proved efficient as students thought carefully of their responses before providing accurate answers.

'**Think, Pair, Share**' proved to be useful in certain classes. I found it more difficult with 8th grade but in 10th and 11th grade, it proved to be useful as there was better interaction between them in order to come up with the required answers. I also assigned activities and exercises to strengthen the concepts explained.

To sum up, using various methods of teaching has been enriching for my teaching experience. Different techniques have proven to be quite efficient and practical as they led to better understanding of the concepts of lessons for students in general. I am satisfied with the results and look forward to using new approaches in class in the future.

KING ECGBERT SCHOOL/MERCIA LEARNING TRUST, SHEFFIELD

INTRODUCTION

This *Fieldbook* entry is a wonderful microcosm of the whole enterprise representing some of the best aspects of current practice in the UK system. At the big picture level the account of designing a shared curriculum framework is a fabulous window into the power of inter-school collaboration – the multi-academy trust concept at its best. Then Karl's account of developing retrieval practice in maths and Charlotte's exploration of academic language across the curriculum illustrate the influence of evidence in shaping school development and demonstrate how much detailed thinking is needed to enact real change. Finally, the profiles of Tilly, Shreejana and Ibrahim bring it all to life – three students exploring the possibilities from the diverse set of learning experiences presented to them.

My initial contact with King Ecbert School was through attending the inaugural Mercia Trust conference at Sheffield's magnificent Crucible Theatre. I was immediately impressed by the positive spirit and the bold ambition of the Trust's leaders – the determination for every school to thrive and excel, to collaborate and learn from each other, whilst always maintaining their identities as individual schools. I was also struck by the enthusiasm for research-engagement as different leaders provided some general messages around learning, assessment and curriculum design referencing blogs, books and research papers.

However, the feature of the event that actually moved me to tears was hearing the choir sing. I wrote this on my blog shortly afterwards:

'I watched the students file in, nervous under the spotlights. But then the music started and my attention was drawn to their teacher – conducting from in front of the stage. That look in her eyes – the intense eye-contact and big smile that said: 'Come

on guys; you can do this. You're ready; you're going to smash it' – and then, the most powerful three minutes of non-verbal encouragement you can imagine, willing them through, building up to the finale. The kids got a standing ovation. Of course they deserved it completely, but as the teacher humbly tip-toed out, my mental ovation was for her.'

Wrapped up in the vignette, I see all the aspects of the Learning Rainforest – the nurturing ethos, the challenge and ambition, the discipline of all those rehearsals building knowledge, and finally exploring the possibilities by performing in front of huge audience on a famous stage.

At this school they prepare us to be the best we can be and nothing less.
HEAD BOY

PROFILE

Location: Sheffield, South Yorkshire, UK

Type of Institution: Mixed Comprehensive Academy

Roll/Age Range: 1330, aged 11–18

Year Founded: 1969 as a comprehensive

Motto: 'Achieving Excellence'

House Names: Atlas, Crucible, Henderson, Steel, Kelham (All relate to Sheffield)

Recent/Current School Production: '*Pillowman*' (BTEC Performing Arts students)

Recent significant sports event/triumph: Our PE department were awarded 'Department of the year' this year by the Sheffield Federation for School Sports in recognition of their contribution to sport and participation of students.

Notable quirks/alumni: One of our most notable alumna is Dame Jessica Ennis-Hill who studied at King Ecgbert and went on to study for a degree in Psychology at University of Sheffield and to be an elite athlete, winning gold for Heptathlon in the 2012 Olympics.
England cricket captain Joe Root is also an ex-student.

Paul Haigh
Head Teacher

Every school is unique but King Ecgbert really does feel not quite like any other. The wedge shaped catchment stretches from the city centre of Sheffield to the farms and moorland of the Peak

PROFILE

District National Park which can be seen from the classroom windows. That diverse catchment from inner city terraces through suburbs to country homes and barn conversions indicates the diverse nature of our students; multi-ethnic and very mixed ability and the widest socio-economic range of households you can imagine.

It means our role, to meet the needs of every learner, is our main challenge because their needs are so diverse. We have to have expert subject teachers able to stretch students who go to top universities but those same staff need to employ the best strategies to support those with SEND, those who are disadvantaged and those who don't go home to a family where English is spoken well. The ethos of the school to meet this challenge is all about care – the staff genuinely know and care for each student and care for each other too. Working as such a close-knit team it feels more like a family.

The level of expertise in the staff is high, their commitment to CPD, to reading, to looking at evidence and generating their own evidence of what works best is what keeps the school moving forward. That has taken the school to the strongest point now in its academic history but also creates a thirst for more. The school is constantly on a quest to be better but at the same time focus on well-being of staff and students – it's a challenge but we want to be brave to stop doing the things that don't make a difference.

The success of the school has given it an opportunity to have a system-leading role; starting the Mercia multi-academy trust that comprises six schools and growing and holding Teaching School status. Growing the culture of sharing and collaboration with other schools is the secret to continued improvement of a very strong school that works hard to stay great.

In KES we care.
SHREEJANA KHADKA

I love that I am always busy but that I can also always have a laugh and have some fun!
TILLY HILTON

STUDENT: TILLY HILTON

Age and Year Group: 13, Year 8, King Ecgbert School
House: Atlas
Most recent:
School Trip: Go 4 Set at Sheffield Hallam University – Stations of the Future, we are working with engineers from Arup to design a new station for Sheffield.
Extra-curricular activity: BBC Young Reporter project
Science experiment: Experimenting with reflection of light
Book studied in English: *Romeo and Juliet*, *A Midsummer Night's Dream*
History topic: Transatlantic slavery
Arts project: Lino cutting inspired by mechanics
Learning:
Recent learning highlight: I have recently enjoyed our DT project; automata. It was loads of fun designing and creating our own project. I chose to make a waterwheel which moved a hammer and an anvil. This hands on experience with woodwork has really inspired me to consider a further career in Product Design or Design Technology.
The most stand-out/interesting/challenging topic you've studied at school: I enjoyed learning about the Elizabethan era in History because I love how Queen Elizabeth brought an early form of feminism to Tudor England. We had some great homework which allowed us to explore History in creative and varying ways and overall the topic was interesting and fun.
One of my favourite teachers: I enjoy lessons with Miss Gomes who teaches me Science because during her lessons I feel encouraged to ask questions and learn new things.
A favourite feature of the school: My favourite aspect of school is the number of opportunities available: trips, projects, sports competitions, Maths and Science competitions, lots of chances for me and my school friends to engage physically and mentally with learning outside of schools as well. I love that I am always busy but that I can also always have a laugh and have some fun!

STUDENT: SHREEJANA KHADKA

Age and Year Group: 16, Year 11, King Ecgbert School
House: Crucible
Most recent:
School Trip: Geography trip to Iceland
Extra-curricular activity: Art club
Science experiment: Separating techniques
Book studied in English: *An Inspector Calls*, *Macbeth*
History topic: Weimar and Nazi Germany, Cold war, Elizabethan England, Medicine through the ages.
Arts project: Final project influenced by visits to V and A and Tate Modern Museum and Yorkshire Sculpture Park.
Learning:
Subjects Studied: Triple Science, Maths, English, History, Geography, Art
Recent learning highlight: I managed to paint a landscape of my choice on a large scale and it looked amazing.
I got really good grades in my mocks and now I can do Higher tier for all my Science subjects.
The most stand-out/interesting/challenging topic you've studied at school: We had to do complex molar calculations in Chemistry. It was difficult and complicated but we got there in the end!
One of my favourite teachers: Mr Newton. He cares so much about the students and is willing to do anything to help them learn. He puts so much effort in every lesson and even does research to improve his teaching.
A favourite feature of the school: I came here seven years ago from Nepal and I spoke no English. I benefited from extensive support like literacy work, homework clubs and extra curricular trips. The clubs were organised by school but took place in the community where I live.

STUDENT: IBRAHIM WARSHOW

Age and Year Group: 17, Year 13, King Ecgbert School

Most recent:

School Trip: Sheffield Hallam University trip with my Economics class to use their equity trading systems (Bloomberg)

Extra-curricular activity: Extended Project Qualification (EPQ) in which I wrote a 5000 word investigative essay on the price speculative nature of bitcoin.

Science experiment: Practical Assessment 11 on Transition Metal Complexes in which we used to ligand substitution to identify the transition metal ion of unknown compounds.

Book studied in English: I do not study English literature but the last book I read out of school was '23 Things They Don't Tell You About Capitalism' (by Ha-Joon Chang) which I read to widen my Economics scope beyond school as I hope to study Economics at university next year.

Learning:

Subjects Studied: A-Level Maths, Physics, Chemistry and Economics

Recent learning highlight: In Economics recently we learnt about companies in an oligopoly market system. In the lesson we learnt about Game Theory which has a simple definition but is a complex concept. This was amazing as you could apply it to many decisions in life; the idea of modelling the interaction between two or more individuals in a situation with set rules and outcomes and predicting the most likely outcome.

The most stand-out/interesting/challenging topic you've studied at school: I enjoyed learning about Quantum Physics last year in Year 12 which was by far the hardest topic I had ever come across in Physics and the concept which took me the longest to grasp onto but once I did it was my favourite, especially wave-particle duality within Quantum Physics.

One of my favourite teachers: I enjoy lessons with Mr Newton who teaches me Maths because his lessons are always engaging, and he teaches with so much enthusiasm. You can honestly see how much he loves Maths and always motivates me to try as hard as I can. He will take the time to guide you through something you don't understand whether it's in or out of lesson.

A favourite feature of the school: My favourite feature of the school is the unlimited opportunities. As a sixth former work experience, supper and extra-curricular opportunities are important and essential for our University applications. At this school I receive a minimum of one email a day for a range opportunities from scholarships and summer schools to apprenticeships.

Being part of something great

CLAIRE PENDER

I know at this school there is not a chance of me missing out or being at a disadvantage to other schools. In fact I feel at a position of advantage going on to challenges beyond school. At this school they prepare us to be the best we can be and nothing less.

IBRAHIM WARSHOW

CASE STUDY: DEVELOPING A TRUST-WIDE CURRICULUM

Title: Developing a trust-wide curriculum framework for the Mercia Learning Trust

General Area: Trust Improvement, School leadership of Teaching and Learning and CPD

Author: Claire Pender, Deputy Head, King Ecgbert School

Trust wide collaboration to develop a curriculum framework

MLT, led by CEO Chris French, is a trust of six schools; King Ecgbert School, Newfield School, Mercia School, Nether Edge Primary, Totley Primary, Valley Park Primary.

One feature of our trust is the continuous pursuit of improvement. All our schools are continually focused on the curriculum, teaching and assessment, as obvious and effective areas to concentrate improvement.

At the beginning of the year colleagues from each of the six schools met, as part of a new curriculum working group. The aim was to create a curriculum framework that could be used as an evaluation tool and a catalyst for future school development. Our starting point was to bring examples of good practice from each school based on research evidence. We found that there were similar themes that all of us were focusing on in our separate schools. For example; knowledge retention and retrieval, cognitive load, knowledge instruction, formative and summative assessment, closing the vocabulary gap between our disadvantaged and non-disadvantaged students.

We also shared the research that was informing our areas of focus on and came up with a list of recommended reads for staff in our trust.

Our curriculum framework took shape and was shared trust-wide at our education conference; the first time all staff from the six schools in the trust have come together in one place, at the Crucible Theatre Sheffield! During the morning there were presentations about the trust vision and curriculum matters. We had a keynote speech from Tom Sherrington which reaffirmed many of our ideas and in the afternoon teachers chose from a list of workshops, led by teachers about aspects of curriculum which we deem as essential to building secure learning over time (e.g. learning that sticks and remains in the long-term memory) and the best approaches to achieve this.

There was a general feeling of being part of something great and, as one teacher said, 'It has added further energy to our mission to get the curriculum right for our children'.

CASE STUDY: DEVELOPING A TRUST-WIDE CURRICULUM

Here is a graphic which summarises our framework.

So what are our next steps? Back in schools we are considering our curriculum intent at leadership, phase and subject level. Our CPD plans for the immediate future are based on aspects of the curriculum. All teachers are looking at curriculum design, how it is taught, how it is assessed and how it is sequenced for maximum benefit for our pupils. We are holding a 'MerciaMeet' in the summer term where colleagues will exemplify their work in the classroom based on a feature of the framework – and we are already planning our education conference for 2020!

For the first time in my career I feel like I am part of genuine school to school collaboration, which is open and honest. We have so much to learn from each other and the future is bright.

Link to Learning Rainforest:

The analogy of a rainforest is particularly pertinent to our aligned autonomy as schools in a trust. Our curriculum framework links to many aspects of the Learning Rainforest and especially to the curriculum debate: 'We want our children to have it all: knowledge and understanding across multiple domains; a range of practical and intellectual skills and a range of character traits'

CASE STUDY: EMBEDDING AND DEVELOPING RETRIEVAL PRACTICE

General Area: Teaching and Learning

Author: Karl Newton, Joint Head of Subject (Maths) King Ecgbert School

The journey to the Maths department's current practice regarding retrieval only began a few years ago; it started with a training day where the department were given time to look at a collection of articles on various research from cognitive science. After staff had some time to read and discuss we quickly gathered that 'retrieval practice' seemed like a big thing and we needed to look at this further. Of course, we already knew that students struggle to retrieve knowledge if they haven't seen it for a long time, but this was different. We had strategies to try, approaches to argue about and a sense (with some research to back it up) that we could make a big difference in 'building the core knowledge' for our students.

What does our retrieval practice currently look like?

- **Every lesson starts with some retrieval questions**
  These are selected by the teacher to be based on knowledge which will help students access the new content to be covered in the lesson, as well as some questions that may not be directly related to the lesson to 'keep the plates of knowledge spinning'.

- **Projected from the front or on paper for each student.**
  Some staff like to have students looking at a piece of paper directly in front of them as they feel it can improve focus, others prefer to project from the front. Either way having the questions in the same place every time creates a routine that requires no instruction.

- **10–30 minutes**
  Depending on what new knowledge is being introduced in the lesson there may be more previous content required.

This tends to make the retrieval practice a bit longer for older students, as they will be introduced to more complex concepts building on lots of previous knowledge.

- **Level of desired difficulty**
  If the questions are too 'easy' then the students aren't thinking much, so they aren't learning much; too 'difficult' and they aren't retrieving much and, again, aren't learning much. The magic middle ground of where to pitch the questions requires the most thought, with the expertise and experience of staff key to getting this right. We found each group requires different questions to make them think, there is no easy 'one size fits all' solution.

- **Feedback/response**
  There is an element of formative assessment; most questions students should be confident with answering but, if they aren't, feedback can be instant by a short re-explanation with a few more questions asked of /given to the students or a note taken to re-teach some content. Some staff like to project numerical answers during the activity to allow students to initially self-correct, others prefer to give them at the end. Either way, staff then carefully choose what to select and neglect to give feedback on informed by what they have seen during circulated.

The students seem to really enjoy this; the routine helps for sure and starting a lesson with mostly success increases self confidence, yet I think the fact they know we are trying to help them remember long term and build the core knowledge to allow them access to the more challenging concepts gives them motivation and confidence in us.

CASE STUDY: EMBEDDING AND DEVELOPING RETRIEVAL PRACTICE

What do we choose to retrieve?

Well this is a more complex and challenging question than it appears! Is there a systematic way of spacing and ensuring all previous knowledge is covered? Cue a big spreadsheet trying to systemically model the chaotic process of learning and a bit of flop. The best way we found to ensure we cover all the previous knowledge without treating each student as a sapling in the 'plantation' was to have a list that we can tick when something is covered, making a note (maybe just a colour) of how the class found it so the teacher can decide whether something needs to be re-taught or retrieved less frequently if students are generally fine with it.

Convincing some that spending up to half a lesson on retrieval can be challenging, but when they see it in practice they are soon on board. The focus on responsive teaching and sequencing of knowledge towards new concepts usually captures their attention.

Will we get through enough content? Admittedly some parts of the curriculum go at a steadier pace, but the rewards are reaped later, when teachers don't have to go back to and reteach whole knowledge sequences.

Acknowledgements

To the departmental staff, thank you for continually engaging with research and using this to adapt your practice.

Thank you to the students for having the belief in us when we are changing our practice.

SLT, for allowing this culture of research-driven practice, thank you for giving us the freedom to experiment with these different strategies and approaches.

Finally, to the numerous people out there who are making educational research accessible, including 'The Learning Scientists', the 'Bjorks', Tom, and many more – thank you.

Link to Learning Rainforest:

Suggest how your initiative/improvement journey links to ideas in *The Learning Rainforest*:

- **Plantation/rainforest analogy – school culture.**

  There isn't a 'one size fits all' approach to retrieval practice. Different classes and individual students need different diets of retrieval.

- **Curriculum /knowledge**

  Deciding the sequencing of knowledge required to get to the next steps is essential in any curriculum, taking time to ensure the sequences don't have any missing elements and make the existing ones stronger is only a positive.

- **Assessment**

  Giving staff a vehicle to Find out what students know (more importantly what they don't) and respond instantly or inform future teaching.

- **Building the knowledge structure**

  Giving students the opportunity to retrieve knowledge and build schemas regularly

CASE STUDY: DEVELOPING ACADEMIC LANGUAGE

Title: Developing academic language through a focus on functional grammar

General Area: Teaching and Learning/CPD

Author: Charlotte Bowyer, Assistant Headteacher (strategic lead for EAL and PP students)

To borrow from Wittgenstein, 'The limits of my language are the limits of my world.' We are aiming to do no less than to expand students' language and thus expand their world.

To do this we are developing a cross-curricular approach to academic language, to improve decoding of complex text in reading tasks and its use in writing to express more complex ideas.

The method comes from research done by specialists in the field of EAL (Bernard Mohan, Hounslow Language Services) in which teachers develop strategies to teach the language of their subject simultaneously with teaching content and skills. The real breakthrough comes when teachers see how these are interdependent and build this into each lesson.

Teachers know the vocabulary demands of their subject and have been teaching tier 3 words explicitly. However, beyond vocabulary, each subject has its own form of language. For example the instructions for a science experiment requires the imperative form of verbs (Collect … Measure …). Teachers have studied their subject through further education and absorbed this language without noticing, but students without regular reading or discussion in academic language at home will not absorb it, potentially disadvantaging EAL and pupil premium students the most. Unless we focus more on the language, our students will not be able to apply their learning in the new strengthened GCSEs, because they will struggle to decode the questions and they will score lower marks if they express their answers as 'simple' rather than 'analytical' or 'complex' responses.

The good news is that this language can be taught to all students. The first step is to identify the forms of language within your own subject, which does require some grammatical knowledge. This can be a daunting barrier for secondary school teachers if they completed their own education without formal grammar lessons. English and MFL teachers, plus those who have taught TEFL, tend to have greater confidence and will be asked to take a central role in CPD next year.

We decided to introduce this new approach gradually, starting with curriculum leaders. We have had four meetings this year (45 minutes each). In each one, we have identified one area of language, its role in the language of our subject, and simple strategies to use in lessons.

CASE STUDY: DEVELOPING ACADEMIC LANGUAGE

One language focus has been the modal verb. To demonstrate the 'power' and possibilities of modals, we had a quick discussion about what we **could** do that evening ... what we **should** do ... and finally what we **will** do. Then we looked at the difference the use of modals can make to students' answers, to raise the value and accuracy of their communication, and shared strategies for introducing modals to students and to practise using them.

A few weeks' later I watched this put into effect in a GCSE Drama lesson. Students were giving evaluations of peers' performances. The quality of response was lifted significantly simply by the teacher writing the word 'could' on the board and modelling how this could be used in verbal feedback before students responded.

Another focus has been turning simple sentences into complex ones. First, we demonstrated how language is manipulated to write in more academic sentences: nouns are turned into adjectives to create noun phrases; separate sentences are joined with conjunctions; and pronouns such as 'which' introduce qualifying clauses. Then we looked at an example from a history lesson, in which six separate sentences, showing simple understanding, were re-written as one complex sentence. Although using the language terminology (the meta-language) helps students improve their own writing, students will be able to mimic the more academic form of writing just by seeing 'WAGOLL'[1] and having guided opportunities to practise.

I saw these strategies used in a geography lesson preparing Y11 students to write an exam answer on coasts. The students wrote relevant facts on mini whiteboards (simple level 1 responses), then shared suitable connectives and as a last stage combined their facts in complex sentences which met the marking criteria for the highest band.

We have also looked at the use of visualisers in classrooms to help decode complex text, how to teach the language around information presented in diagrams and different verb tenses. The curriculum leaders are now putting the ideas most relevant to their subject into practice in their own teaching. Later this year they will use part of a training day to share this with their departments so the strategy starts to be rolled out whole school, although some have already used department meetings to share ideas because they are finding them helpful.

We are also working with primary schools within our trust to build our own confidence with grammar. Curriculum leaders have started to visit Y5 and Y6 lessons this term to see the levels of grammar understood by primary students, and in return will deliver a 'secondary ready' lesson to introduce students to the academic language of their specific subject.

Next year curriculum leaders will lead their departments in an analysis of their subjects' language and development of strategies to make its teaching integral to their lessons.

Time, as ever, is a challenge. Time to 'teach grammar' to curriculum leaders, time to develop own strategies, time to share them. At this stage, there is also the perception that there isn't time in lessons to teach language as well as content. We are trying to address this challenge by being selective with the language points addressed in CPD and modelling strategies which are self-evidently useful to gaining higher attainment.

Link to Learning Rainforest:

I think this fits best within **Establishing the Conditions – attitudes and habits for excellence: teaching to the top.**

This approach ensures students from all backgrounds are given the tools to read and write to the highest levels, and stops misdiagnosing simple written work as an indication of low cognitive ability when it is more likely to be a symptom of lack of exposure to academic language.

Unless we focus more on the language, our students will not be able to apply their learning in the new strengthened GCSEs, because they will struggle to decode the questions and they will score lower marks if they express their answers as 'simple' rather than 'analytical' or 'complex' responses.
CHARLOTTE BOWYER

Keep the plates of knowledge spinning.
PAUL JENNER 2019 MATHS CURRICULUM DESIGNER

---

1. What A Good One Looks Like   exemplars.

HUNTINGTON SCHOOL, YORK

INTRODUCTION

I honestly believe that if every school could be as good as Huntington School in York, the world would be a better place. To me, it's an archetypal Learning Rainforest school: inclusive, ambitious, continually seeking to improve, serving the local community, providing a rich, broad curriculum and deeply invested in evidence-informed professional learning. Headteacher John Tomsett is another person I first encountered through social media – his fabulous *This much I know...* blog is a constant source of inspiration; his book *Love over Fear* offers a fabulous vision for pragmatic, compassionate leadership. He's now a close friend and we continually exchange ideas and reflections as we continue on our professional and personal journeys.

My first visit to Huntington was inspired by their work as a research school; I wanted to find out more about their disciplined inquiries and the structure of their fortnightly professional development sessions – the forums described in John's entry below. At the time, Alex Quigley was Deputy Head, running this aspect of school practice – it's no surprise to see him move on to work for the Education Endowment Foundation. Huntington has been at the leading edge of research-engaged thinking and practice for many years.

One of the things I love about John is the importance he gives to maintaining his own teaching. Many of his blog posts describe his own lessons and the ways he has tried to improve his practice. It's fabulous, therefore, to be able to present a case study in which John illustrates the school's use of 'inquiry questions' by writing up his own inquiry. As I've found in so many situations, real school improvement lies in the details of curriculum thinking and the refinement of instructional methods. Here, John shows what it looks like when you try to evaluate something you've tried rather than just go with your hunches.

I am incredibly happy at Huntington School. I intend to stay at Huntington for the sixth form because I can't imagine anywhere else would enable me to achieve good results whilst still maintaining a supportive atmosphere. I am receiving an amazing education.

EXTRACTS FROM AN EMAIL FROM A YEAR 11 STUDENT

**Hello,
My 3 children are at Huntington.
I think the school is terrific.
My kids are happy. I am happy.
I wish I had had the education they are getting. The teaching is great. The 'tone' of the school is great. Thank you!**

ANONYMOUS NOTE FROM A PARENT HANDED TO JOHN TOMSETT WHILST HE WAS HAVING A COFFEE IN TOWN

PROFILE

Location: York, North Yorkshire, UK

Type of Institution: Mixed Comprehensive

Roll/Age Range: 1527, aged 11–18

Year Founded: 1966

Motto: 'Core purpose: Inspiring confident learners who will thrive in a changing world'

Values: Respect; Honesty; Kindness

House Names: Brontë, Cook, Johnson, Wilberforce

Recent/Current School Production: Summer Arts Festival: Art, Drama, Music, Dance carousel

Recent significant sports event/triumph: Finalists in the 2018–19 U16s North Yorkshire football; regional representatives in the Maths Challenge.

Notable quirks/alumni: We are one of the first Research Schools in the country.

John Tomsett
Head Teacher

Our core values are: Respect; Honesty; Kindness. We try to live by those values every day. It isn't easy. We are a fully comprehensive school, with students from right across the socio-economic spectrum. York is an insular city on an insular island. Fully 95% of our students are white British, one of the poorest performing ethnic groups in the country. We stick by our core values and challenge anyone and everyone who finds it hard to live by them.

We try our hardest to educate our students rather than school them. We dedicate an hour a week in Year 10 to a non-examined philosophy course, where we explore the Stoics and all the main philosophers since the likes of Marcus Aurelius, challenging students to understand what it is to be human, what really matters in life and the nature of happiness. And we have always insisted that the vast majority of our students study a Modern Foreign Language at GCSE. When a MFL GCSE was made optional in 2003, we did not accept that so-called freedom, insisting that our students need to have knowledge of a foreign language and culture if they are to be educated.

Lastly, we do not put students first at Huntington. Instead, we put students and staff first. The best thing for students is a well-trained, highly motivated, happy, expert staff who enjoy coming to work. To that end we pour as much resource as we can into training teachers. Our CPD offer is second to none. We benefit hugely from being a Research School; indeed, our practice is underpinned by evidence-informed practice. We only engage in teaching and learning techniques which have the best chance of working according to the evidence.

In essence we aim for the optimal relationship of low anxiety and high standards.

STUDENT: MEGAN TURNER

Age and Year Group: 12, Year 7
House: Cook
Most recent:
School Trip: We went to see Shakespeare's *Macbeth* at the theatre.
Extra-curricular activity: I am on the Read-Write course and have a TA to help me most lessons.
Science experiment: We lit up a light bulb in Science
Book/Play studied in English Literature: *Macbeth*, *Beowulf* and *Holes*
History topic: Henry VII – the Princes in the Tower
Arts project: We have been developing our Doodles Art.
Learning:
Subjects Studied: I am taking lots of different subjects. I have extra English lessons – at least one English lesson a day – but I haven't had any French lessons because I do more English.
Recent learning highlight: I know all the words to *Macbeth* and all the characters. I feel passionate about the play. When our teacher was quoting from the first scene I took over as I had memorised the whole scene by heart. I love acting!
The most stand-out/interesting/challenging topic you've studied at school: I enjoy English because of the stories. I love speaking out and acting. But I find writing hard.
One of my favourite teachers: I enjoy lessons with Miss Townsend because she helps me understand when I have a problem in History.
A favourite feature of the school: I like it that I have a Teaching Assistant in all my classes because they help me during lessons and if I need to go somewhere at break time.

I have participated in many of the York Independent-State School Partnership activities. We went on an ISSP residential in the Lake District last year where we could discuss philosophy, walk in the hills where Wordsworth lived and write ourselves.

JOSH PRINS

I know all the words to *Macbeth* and all the characters. I feel passionate about the play.

MEGAN TURNER

STUDENT: JOSH PRINS

Age and Year Group: 14, Year 9
House: Johnson
Most recent:
School Trip: English Shakespeare trip to York University to see Macbeth
Extra-curricular activity: We have a 'Man Choir' on Fridays after school and I play in Junior Band on Tuesday evenings.
Science experiment: In Biology we did an experiment recently on the effect of a change in pH on the action of enzymes.
Book/Play studied in English Literature: *Much Ado About Nothing* by Shakespeare
History topic: We are currently studying the Holocaust
Arts project: Most recently I performed in Live Lounge in the music department and this summer I will sing at the Arts Festival.
Learning:
Subjects Studied: My Year 10 options are: Music; Religion, Philosophy and Ethics (RPE); History. I will also be studying a Modern Foreign Language.
Recent learning highlight: One lesson recently that captured my imagination was in English. Our task was to write an imaginative response to an image we were given. I have a passion for creative writing and this task allowed me to use my vocabulary and imagination.
The most stand-out/interesting/challenging topic you've studied at school: The topic I enjoyed learning about was Theology in RPE. I enjoy talking about controversial, debatable subjects that you can talk about with others. I found this subject captivating as I learned about many more ideas about what God might be.
One of my favourite teachers: I enjoy lessons with Miss Townsend who teaches me History and is my Form Tutor. She is very enthusiastic about History and allows us to discuss what we are learning about. And I really enjoy the discussions we have in form time.
A favourite feature of the school: I really enjoy all the opportunities our school gives us as students. For example, I involve myself in all the trips and projects in Music. I have participated in many of the York Independent-State School Partnership activities. We went on an ISSP residential in the Lake District last year where we could discuss philosophy, walk in the hills where Wordsworth lived and write ourselves.

In the Music department there are endless opportunities for developing my passion for music, which is largely due to our outstanding teachers.

HOLLY BOYLE

STUDENT: HOLLY BOYLE

Age and Year Group: 16, Year 12

House: Johnson House

Most recent:

School Trip: York School's Music Festival at York University where we joined several primary schools from across the city of York to showcase what we have been working on recently.

Extra-curricular activity: Choir and piano practice

Girls' choir – singing popular songs with all years;

Secret choir – singing art music and chamber pieces; Years 10–13

Science experiment: Measuring the viscosity of fluid in Physics as part of a required practical in the Materials topic.

Book/Play studied in English Literature: *Romeo and Juliet*

History topic: Currently studying the Tudor period 1485–1557 and the Cold War in Asia as part of my History A level

Arts project: 'Live Lounge' and 'Chamber Concert': two evenings where musicians from Years 7–13 play live music to packed audiences – inspiring opportunities to work collaboratively with talented young musicians

Learning:

Subjects Studied: A Levels: French; History; Music; Physics
Optional GCSEs: Drama; French; Further Mathematics; History; Latin Music

Recent learning highlight: Recently I have been working on my History personal study which explores the extent to which Henry VII's foreign policy was successful. I have found this particularly interesting as I am thinking about a career in International Relations. It has been helpful to see how foreign policies have changed over time, from 1485 to the present day.

The most stand-out/interesting/challenging topic you've studied at school: I really enjoyed learning about music theory and Bach's harmony functions. I have one harmony lesson a week where we are given a line of music and we have to arrange the harmony for a soprano, alto, tenor and bass (SATB) choir. It is very challenging as we have to encapsulate the style of Bach through the arrangement of the notes in a four-part chord. It is fascinating how the conventions of Bach Chorales have remained important across time.

One of my favourite teachers: I love my lessons with Miss Townsend who teaches me the Tudor segment of my A level course. She was my History teacher at GCSE and supported me endlessly throughout all the stress and revision. Miss Townsend always makes time to help me improve my work and learn from my mistakes, whilst always making our lessons engaging and intriguing. I was so happy when I found out she was going to be my A level teacher for the next two years!

A favourite feature of the school: In the Music department there are endless opportunities for developing my passion for music, which is largely due to our outstanding teachers. In summer we are holding our annual Arts Festival where students and teachers from all over the school showcase their work. We have an art exhibition, as well as dance, music and drama performances. I always take part in the music performance, because the atmosphere is so special and the final product is hugely rewarding.

CASE STUDY: EVERY TEACHER A DELIBERATE PRACTITIONER

Title: Every teacher a deliberate practitioner: the coherence of evidenced informed CPD

General Area: Evidence-informed CPD

Author: John Tomsett, Headteacher

SUMMARY: We have developed a coherent relationship between school culture, our CPD offer, our Appraisal system and evidence-based practice. This coherence is at the heart of our development as a school. The coherence has taken twelve years of relentless, deliberate work to secure and we are still not where we want to be. Our idealised aim is for every teacher to be a deliberate practitioner, who, when they identify a barrier to students' learning, consults the research evidence in this area of practice, is supported by our Research School team to translate the evidence into classroom practice, implements the change of practice faithfully, evaluates the impact of the evidence-informed change to practice and then makes a decision as to whether to continue with the change to practice or whether they conclude that with their students at Huntington School, this change of practice has no impact and so they stop the change of practice.

The complex process of teaching in a way which helps children learn is an eternally fascinating professional challenge. It is at the heart of what makes teaching an interesting profession. That said, not every school sets up structures to make professional learning as interesting as it is described by Tom in *The Learning Rainforest*:

'*Rainforest* thinking suggests [that]…the whole thrust of Performance Management is to nurture self-driven reflection and professional learning.'

At Huntington we have developed an element of our Performance Management process (we call it Performance *Development*, not Management, to emphasise the supportive, developmental nature of the process) which is imbued with the Rainforest spirit. It is called the Inquiry Question (IQ) and every single teacher has to complete an IQ as part of their annual Performance Development Cycle (PDC).

Our PDC is inextricably linked with our training programme. We have two hours of ring-fenced training time on alternate Mondays throughout the school year. The sessions are called Teaching and Learning Forums or TLFs; we find the two hours by sending our students home early so that the time gained is part of each teacher's contracted hours.

CASE STUDY: EVERY TEACHER A DELIBERATE PRACTITIONER

The TLFs allow teachers and teaching assistants to work on their Inquiry Questions. The steps in Inquiry Question process are well-defined:

- What is my inquiry question?
- What student cohort have I identified for the intervention and why?
- What Pre-intervention and Post-intervention assessments will give me the best results?
- What control factors will best ensure that my inquiry is 'disciplined'?
- What are the limitations and obstacles that affect my inquiry?
- What are the results of my inquiry and how generalisable are they?

The TLF training programme to support colleagues is equally well-defined and detailed:

- September: 1 hour introductory session
- October: 1 hour session on writing inquiry questions
- October: 1 hour session on evaluating your inquiry pre- and post-assessment
- November: 1 hour session for development work
- Jan: Accessing the Evidence – 1 hour session to research further into your chosen intervention
- March: 1 hour session for development work
- May: 1 hour session for writing up your IQ
- May: 1 hour session for writing up your IQ
- June: 1 hour session for writing up your IQ
- September: IQ Festival/Celebration Event

During these sessions colleagues learn about: control groups; treatment groups; identifying variables; faithful implementation; evaluation; qualitative and quantitative data, and how to calculate effect size amongst other nuanced aspects of using an evidence-informed approach to improving teaching and learning. What is especially supportive and makes the whole initiative interesting as a teacher-learner is the support from Research School colleagues. Once you have identified your Inquiry Question, you are provided with a summary of the available evidence relating to your IQ as well as a link to the full evidence papers.

In order to make real the Inquiry Question process it is best to look at an example in detail.

In 2018 I had just five Year 13 students taking the new Economics A level specification. The students had B or B/C targets and the new specification is challenging. The exam essay questions require students to discuss both sides of an argument and then make an evaluation of the evidence in the concluding paragraph.

I decided that my Inquiry Question would be: What impact does **modelling evaluation thinking in real time copying off the whiteboard** in **eight consecutive lessons (the intervention)** have upon the **ability to answer 25 mark 'evaluate' essays (the impact)** for **five mid-attainment Y13 students (the cohort of students)**?

I was directed towards a short research paper entitled: 'Cognitive Apprenticeship: Teaching the Craft of Reading, Writing, and Mathematics' by Allan Collins, John Brown and Susan Newman'.[1]

The paper was illuminating. It transformed my teaching. The first section explores the characteristics of traditional apprenticeship and how they might be adapted to teach cognitive skills in schools; the second section examines three teaching methods to develop in students the metacognitive skills required for expertise in reading, writing and solving mathematical problems, and the final section outlines a framework for developing and evaluating new pedagogies in schools, based on the traditional apprenticeship model.

The paper identifies that 'domain (subject) knowledge…provides insufficient clues for many students about how to actually go about solving problems and carrying out tasks in a domain. Moreover when it is learned in isolation from realistic problem contexts and expert problem-solving practices, domain knowledge tends to remain inert in situations for which it is appropriate, even for successful students'.

In order for my students to use the subject knowledge I knew they possessed, I had to teach them what Collins et al define as '*Strategic knowledge*: the usually tacit knowledge that underlies an expert's ability to make use of concepts, facts, and procedures as necessary to solve problems and carry out tasks'. What I concluded was that I had to teach my students how to think when they write in order to use their economics knowledge in an examination.

I was the expert in the room. I knew subconsciously the skills required to apply my subject knowledge to answer a 25 marker

---

1. The paper was first published in draft in 1987 as Technical Report No. 403 by the Center for the Study of Reading at the University of Illinois, under the title: 'Cognitive Apprenticeship: Teaching the Craft of Reading, Writing, and Mathematics' by Allan Collins, BBN Laboratories, John Seely Brown, Susan Newman and the Xerox Palo Alto Research Center. It is available online at: www.bit.ly/2ILXv96
The final version of the paper was published in the Winter 1991 edition of *American Educator*, under the title, 'Cognitive Apprenticeship: Making Thinking Visible', by Allan Collins, John Seely Brown and Ann Holum. It is available online at: www.bit.ly/2kG7UD7

CASE STUDY: EVERY TEACHER A DELIBERATE PRACTITIONER

essay; the trouble was, I had not consciously taught my students those skills. What I had to do, according to the paper, was 'delineate the cognitive and metacognitive processes that heretofore have tacitly comprised expertise'.

I had to find a way to apply 'apprenticeship methods to largely cognitive skills'. It required 'the externalization of processes that are usually carried out internally'. Ultimately, I had to develop an apprenticeship model of teaching which made my expert thinking visible.

I had to teach my students how to write evaluative paragraphs through repeated modelling of the process where I explain how I write evaluatively deliberately to gain the maximum marks possible.

In response to the research paper, here is what I did: I chose a 25 marker essay question which the students had answered as my baseline test: 'Evaluate, with the use of appropriate diagram(s), whether macroeconomic policy measures can only promote economic growth at the cost of higher inflation.' This is typical of their evaluative paragraphs – brief, general, not answering the question and a repeat of earlier points:

> *To conclude, economic growth will not always lead to higher inflation. This is because, in the Keynesian view, if the economy is below full employment, economic growth can occur without inflation.*

I collated their concluding paragraphs used them as a qualitative benchmark in ready for my evaluation of my intervention.

I then modelled how they could have finished the essay with a highly evaluative paragraph, an extract from which is below:

> In conclusion, whether macroeconomic policy measures can only promote economic growth at the cost of higher inflation depends on four factors: the type of macroeconomic policy; the size of that economic growth; consumers' and investors' levels of confidence and the existing state of the economy.

If the overall levels of confidence in the economy are low – like they were after the economic crash of 2008 – it may take significant levels of expansionary microeconomic policy measures before any growth occurs at all.

I emphasised four key learning points:

1. Address the question directly in your opening sentence and list the key evaluative economic issues;
2. Don't repeat yourself – make new points and cite examples from the real world;
3. Write in a confident, authoritative tone;
4. Use subject specific terminology.

Eight times in as many lessons I modelled an evaluative paragraph and asked the students to write an evaluative paragraph for a different essay title immediately after, in order to embed the model.

The last lesson before the exams, I set the task of writing an evaluative paragraph. Below is the evaluative paragraph from one of the five student. She has clearly written deliberately and evaluatively:

> *To conclude, the extent to which increasing the funds that banks have available to lend will reverse a deflationary spiral depends upon: the confidence of consumers, the size of the increase in bank funds available and the current state of the economy experiencing a liquidity trap, in which, even if the available bank funds did increase, consumers would not reverse deflationary spiral. Furthermore, if the increase of available bank funds only increased by a little amount, it would make little difference to reversing deflationary spiral. Also, if the economy is in such a recession, it is unlikely an increase in bank funds available will result in a reverse deflationary spiral as the current state of the economy is so low.*

So much for qualitative evaluations. Below are two evaluative analyses using data from the final examinations from the OCR website question-level analysis. The initial table identifies the students by initial, rank orders them in terms of prior attainment and then gives their final grade against their minimum expected grade.

Student		Avg QCA score	Avg GCSE score	Grade	Min. exp. grade
B	M	49.84	6.64	C	B
P	F	49.24	6.54	A	B
G	M	49.00	6.50	A*	B
E	M	48.52	6.42	D	B
H	F	47.20	6.20	B	B/C

CASE STUDY: EVERY TEACHER A DELIBERATE PRACTITIONER

Analysis 1: performance on 25 markers vs minimum expected grades

1. Student G: 89% (+2 rank order)

2. Student P: 81% (=)

3. Student H: 66% (+2)

4. Student B: 48% (−3)

5. Student E: 25% (−1)

Analysis 2: performance on 25 markers vs shorter answer questions

1. Student G: 89% vs 80% (25 markers vs shorter questions)

2. Student P: 81% vs 72%

3. Student H: 66% vs 60%

4. Student B: 48% vs 70%

5. Student E: 25% vs 55%

It seems that lower starters who *are* motivated really benefit from the intervention and their performance on extended writing questions is better than their performance on shorter questions. Furthermore, to gain the higher grades you *have* to be able to perform well in the extended writing questions. The data may also emphasise the primacy of domain knowledge – you might learn (even master) the techniques/skills to write an effective 25 mark essay, but if you don't know what you are writing about, it makes no difference…

Every single teacher completes an Inquiry Question like this one – even the head teacher! One benefit of such a comprehensive approach is what is called *reciprocal vulnerability*, identified by Philippa Cordingley as crucial for teacher professional learning: '[a core characteristic of effective professional learning is] the enabling of sustained peer support and reciprocal vulnerability which increases ownership, commitment and a willingness to take risks and to unlearn established assumptions and habits and to develop new understandings and practices.'[2]

The overall impact of the IQ process is incalculable, but one thing it does for certain is to make the job of teaching more interesting. In September 2017 Andreas Schleicher, head of education at the OECD, claimed that we have to make teaching more 'interesting' and more 'intellectually attractive' if we are going to solve the teacher recruitment crisis.

The ultimate success is completing the IQ itself not whether the intervention worked. One of the best IQs has been in MFL where the whole department explored, in one form or another, the impact of short, regular translation practice upon students' writing skills. It prompted the Subject Leader to contact the University of York Languages department who sent a link to a research paper called 'The Bottleneck of Additional Language Acquisition'.[3] The department's collective IQ led them to scale-up the successful intervention the following year.

I met with the Subject Leader of MFL and, without betraying

confidences, she told me that she loves what she is doing at Huntington because it is 'intellectually interesting'. By creating a school which uses an evidence-informed approach – where research findings complement what we already know from experience – we have done two inextricably linked things: improved our students' outcomes and increased job satisfaction.

If we all adopted Rainforest approaches which 'nurture self-driven reflection and professional learning' amongst colleagues, just think what a brilliant school system we would have created!

If we all adopted Rainforest approaches which 'nurture self-driven reflection and professional learning' amongst colleagues, just think what a brilliant school system we would have created!

JOHN TOMSETT

2. P. Cordingley, 'The contribution of research to teachers' professional learning and development', (BERA, December 2013), p. 5

3. Roumyana Slabakova, 'The Bottleneck of Second Language Acquisition' which is a shortened and updated version of a chapter entitled 'What is easy and what is hard in second language acquisition: A generative perspective,' published in *Contemporary Approaches to Second Language Acquisition*, 2013, María del Pilar García Mayo, M. Junkal Gutierrez-Mangado & María Martínez Adrián (Eds.), pp. 5–28. Amsterdam: John Benjamins

HEATHFIELD COMMUNITY COLLEGE, SUSSEX

INTRODUCTION

I heard about Heathfield Community College via two routes. One was through the writing of geography teacher, blogger and author Mark Enser whose output I've admired for some time. His new book *Teach Like Nobody is Watching*[1] is superb – the voice of authenticity; someone who walks the talk in their lessons every day. Mark was also one of the first people to leave a (very kind) Amazon review for *The Learning Rainforest*. He talks about his school's professional culture in very positive terms throughout his writing – so I imagined his school might be a 'Rainforest' type school.

The second route was via Headteacher Caroline Barlow, a leading member of the Headteachers' Roundtable – a group I used to belong to when I led a school myself – and a campaigner around fair school funding. I was delighted to discover that Mark and Caroline's schools were actually the same school! It all made sense. No wonder he is so happy there! As Assistant Head, Becka, describes in her excellent case study account, the provision of dedicated 'collaboration time' is exactly the kind of investment that professional teachers need and value so highly. I also love the idea of the 'Ped Team'.

On a visit to Heathfield last summer, I had an archetypal *Fieldbook* school tour experience with Caroline – that touching and inspiring blend of pride and humility; the story of the journey so far – a mix of triumphs, hurdles overcome, some frustrating barriers remaining and always ambition for doing even better, finding the optimum curriculum breadth-depth balance given the limits of resources. Plus, I got to see Mark in his geography classroom doing his thing!

One distinctive aspect of the school that I found interesting (as well as the gorgeous traditional laboratory benches!) was the school's use of iPads. Through a clever leasing structure, all children have access to an iPad and are required to take it to every lesson. I don't think I've ever seen such practical, no-nonsense, sensible and effective use of 1:1 technology in a school. The iPads were research tools, translators, quizzing tools, stock-clocks and, very simply, presentation tools allowing students to access questions and resources supplied by the teachers. It's so matter-of-fact that, whilst I was noticing them, hardly anyone else mentioned them. Used this well, it's hard to argue with the benefits technology of this kind can offer.

1. Enser, M. (2019)

I'm proud to have this incredible school on my doorstep and only ever see improvements every time I visit.

The ambition, energy and pride of the staff is amazing. There is a clear vision for success and you feel a real determination to get the best for children which means every child has a place and an opportunity to contribute to the school and in doing so develop skills, confidence and knowledge for success in life.

PARENT

PROFILE

Heathfield Community College is a high-achieving rural comprehensive, genuinely inclusive and ambitious for its staff and students. A four year improvement journey has seen the College build on its strengths to make the sum truly more than its individual parts. This has been a hard fought improvement journey against a backdrop of low funding and declining rural services; building community loyalty and pride in the College in the absence of almost every external support structure or resource has required a collective vision and creative leadership.

Visitors remark on the evident high expectations at the core of the schools work, along with a strong moral purpose. Outcomes are high as is staff retention. Students are tangibly proud of their school.

The College has developed an outward looking research-informed approach to pursuing excellence in teaching at the heart of its success. Teachers are empowered and trusted to work collaboratively on continually improving their skills. They are supported to be subject experts, developing mastery in their practice. As a result morale is high and there is a buzz about what happens in the classroom.

Students are proactively engaged in their College, encouraged to be ambitious and develop the knowledge, understanding and leadership skills that will last them a lifetime. Fundamental to the character and ethos of the College is a commitment to developing young people that will thrive beyond College, who have a strong moral purpose, understand their place and responsibility in their community. They value compassion and kindness and are fiercely proud of the College ethos of inclusivity.

In the words of one parent 'Heathfield …provides 'something extra' that money can't buy'

STUDENT: MAEZIE LANE

Age and Year Group: Year 11
House: Heffle
Most recent:
School Trip: Year 11 Trip to Oxford University. On this trip we had a tour of Kings College and learnt about the daily life of a student. This was to encourage us to consider this as a potential place of study, which I am really keen to fulfil.
Extra-curricular activity: Co-funded the Eco Reps
Numeracy Ambassador
Executive Student Council (2 years)
Bronze Duke of Edinburgh in Year 10 and Silver Award achieved Year 11
Science experiment: Dissecting a sheep's heart in Biology. This first the experiment I was brave enough to watch, I found it invaluable to see the elements in their physical form which solidified my knowledge and understanding
Book/Play studied in English Literature: *Lord of the Flies* as a GCSE text. I prefer this text to others as it is a very different social situation and gives an insight into how humanity might work without the constraints of society.
Arts project: Photography
Learning:
Subjects Studied: Geography (Grade 9 Year 10), Photography (Grade 9 Year 10), Music and French
Recent learning highlight: When I studied Geography last year, I learnt about Lagos in Nigeria for the first time. Our teacher showed us a video about the sounds of Lagos and it was incredible. I felt as though my imagination was widened as I was able to wonder about diverse places and cultures across the world. We studied it as a megacity and the development in Lagos, climate and landscape as well as the trade and economic structure, social conditions and ethnic differences.

The most stand-out/interesting/challenging topic you've studied at school: One of the most interesting topics I've studied in school is learning about the Life Cycle of the Sun in Physics. Whilst I found it a challenging topic, I loved how my teacher was able to expand our minds to imagine one of the most fascinating aspects of our Universe. This lesson has truly stood out in my mind.
One of my favourite teachers: All my teachers at Heathfield Community College are my favourite, they are so good! One of my favourite teachers is my English teacher because she is always fully engaged in our lessons and we have a lot of wide ranging discussions on different topics as a class, beyond the texts that we are studying. I feel as though this extends my knowledge of the world we live in and allows me to consider interesting interpretations and reasons that I never would have considered otherwise. It also extends my understanding of the texts we are studying and deepens my knowledge further.
A favourite feature of the school: My favourite feature of the school is the wide range of opportunities that are available for us all to get involved in. We have a breadth of student leadership strands that cover all aspects of the school curriculum. We are able to work towards individual leadership awards (Bronze, Silver and Gold) which have their own bespoke criteria developing our communication, presentation and technical skills along with commitment over an extended period of time. I find them extremely rewarding.

Also, another opportunity within the school is the Duke of Edinburgh's award which has challenged me in all three sections. It is a lot of time commitment alongside my studies, it needs motivation and resilience to achieve the outcomes. The expedition is physically challenging as well as testing teamwork and map reading skills. I volunteered with younger students in my swimming club for the award and overarchingly feel I have learnt a lot about myself in the process.

STUDENT: TIA WHITEMAN

Age and Year Group: Year 11
House: Tower

Most recent:

School Trip: The School Trip that stands out for me is the Physics Trip that I went on when I was in Year 9 to Cambridge University. I remember everything about it from the turning up at school in the dark to taking all the beautiful photos but most importantly it inspired me that maybe one day I could go to Cambridge. It gave me not only inspiration for my further education but the motivation to keep going with my studies and a new found love for science that was always there but hadn't been discovered before. We had a tour of the Cambridge College (Corpus Christi) and had the opportunity to carry out experiments in mechanical physics alongside Cambridge professors.

Extra-curricular activity: I think that during my time at the College my most enjoyable extra-curricular activity has been as a member of the Digital Genius Team. By doing this I have made new friends worked with different people of different age groups and had so many opportunities that I would never have had before. These opportunities have not just been around technology but have included public speaking at EdTech Conferences and leadership experiences supporting other students, staff and parents. These have helped me to gain the skills to become Deputy Head Girl within the college and co-lead our Executive School Council.

Other leadership activities I have been involved in include Numeracy Ambassadors and leading on Parent Learning Walks

Science experiment: A science experiment that stands out to me is Elephants toothpaste, which is a foamy substance caused by the rapid decomposition of hydrogen peroxide using potassium iodine as a catalyst.

It is not an experiment that teachers do very often in the college, due to the chemicals used, but when they do there it creates a great sense of excitement from all the students.

Book/Play studied in English Literature: I think the play that I have enjoyed the most whilst studying English is *Romeo and Juliet*. It is a story that everyone can get empathise with and we can all take part in reading/acting. There are many films that have been produced around the story and therefore it is interesting to see the different ways that the story had been interpreted and how that is portrayed through film and graphics. However it also has themes which have relevance to our age group because it deals with love, family and conflict.

History topic: When studying History at GCSE I think that the most enjoyable topic was Medicine through Time. I found the course very interesting and amazing to see how medicine had developed through to modern day, how it happened and who was responsible for it. I particularly enjoyed the links with Science which deepened my understanding of both subjects.

Learning:

Subjects Studied: History (Grade 6 in Year 10), Photography (Grade 9 in Year 10), German, Design Technology

Recent learning highlight: An outline lesson to me would be one of the lessons where I completed a dissection. For me I find them exciting and interesting, being able to have the organs actually in my hands and investigate further than you can with a diagram. I have furthered my knowledge of hearts, kidneys, eyes and lungs in this way but more most importantly solidified my understanding of the way the body works and is interconnected.

The most stand-out/interesting/challenging topic you've studied at school: For me the topic that I have enjoyed and found the most interesting is the human biology section of my Biology GCSE. This includes topics such as the heart and the lungs. I found this interesting because it really inspired me to want to continue learning and then use that learning outside of school within my own studies. For example being part of the pony club I was able to relate the digestive system of the horse to the feeding programme and needs of the animals at my stables, comparing the differences as well as the similarities. This has inspired an interest that I will pursue to A Level and beyond.

One of my favourite teachers: One of my favourite teachers is Mrs Fielding, my maths teacher because every lesson she inspires me in maths and makes me want to do achieve.

Since having her in Year 8 my love for maths has grown and my inspiration has grown so now I have chosen to continue it further to study it at A level.

A favourite feature of the school: My favourite feature about the school is the feeling of community. By being a part of this school I feel part of a community and that is really important because students are able to achieve more when they feel supported and comfortable.

STUDENT: JOHNNIE WARREN

Age and Year Group: Year 11
House: Cade

Most recent:

School Trip: The trip to Sussex University at the beginning of Year 11 explored life at university and the facilities as well as different options to study. It helped me understand how the transition would work from A Level to university and made the journey ahead clearer.

Extra-curricular activity: Co-founded Lego Club in Year 8 which supports a group to build and model Lego creatively.
Supported other students to also proactively set up their own clubs
Robotics Team: competitions where we build and programmed robots to do a series of tasks, the team were successful up to regional level
Community prefect for Cade House, facilitating house competitions and supporting other students who need help.

Science experiment: Physics: The Motor Effect involved us building an electric generator motor with electromagnets and a DC battery to create a magnetic field which rotated an axle.

Book/Play studied in English Literature: *Romeo and Juliet* is one of my favourites because my teacher allowed us to use drama to understand the play, character dynamics and events better.

History topic: Nazi Germany is interesting to learn about because it helps us see how the past informs our present. To understand how these events happened can help us prevent things happening in the future.

Learning:

Subjects Studied: History, Computer science (Grade 6 in Year 10), Spanish, Drama (Grade 4 in Year 10)

Recent learning highlight: When we were learning static electricity with Mr Cook, he did it in a fun and interesting way so that I understood exactly what he was talking about. He allowed us to feel static electricity by rubbing a balloon on people's heads and seeing the hair stand on end because the negative charge in the hair was attracted to the positive charge in the balloon.

The most stand-out/interesting/challenging topic you've studied at school: Medicine through Time, this was quite hard to understand and remember at first. However the way in which this was taught was interesting and inclusive so we retained the knowledge and were able to understand how disease has been understood and how medicine has developed over time. Biology helps me understand the intricacies such as Germ Theory and I can see the links between science and history more clearly.

One of my favourite teachers: Mr Howard, because his lessons are fun. He makes jokes and uses humour to communicate difficult concepts, communicating the answers to many different topics. I understand far more than I thought I ever would as a result.
He makes it easy to understand. It feels like he is really trying to do his best for the students and the inclusive atmosphere helps me learn much more quickly.

A favourite feature of the school: My favourite thing about the school is that I don't feel overburdened while learning here and the staff, fellow students and even the building itself helps makes me feel like I can stay on top of things. This is different to other schools I hear my friends describe which sound more pressured and more stressful.

We are passionate to provide staff with opportunities to keep improving and develop mastery in 'all things pedagogical and subject specific'; we use every possible means to give staff the time, trust and autonomy to develop expertise in their subject, supported by research informed collaboration. This creates a vibrant, energised and aspirational community of which staff and students are proud

BECKA LYNCH
AHT (TEACHING AND LEARNING)

STUDENT: HATTIE PEMBERTON

Age and Year Group: Year 11
House: Cade House

Most recent:

School Trip: At the start of Year 11 we went to Sussex University. We gained a better understanding of what options there are for university study. We also explored the living accommodation, managing finances and the wide range of facilities. It was very informative and inspiring because it made the connection between the work that was needed to be able to have the opportunity to go to university.

Extra-curricular activity: One Voice Choir: perform at Summer and Carol concerts every year
Swing Band performances
Austria Music Tour

Science experiment: One of the most memorable Science experiments was dissecting pig lungs to understand the different parts of the lungs and understand how they work.

Book/Play studied in English Literature: *Romeo and Juliet* is a widely-known play, it was interesting to understand in more depth how Shakespeare's vision about love, tragedy, family, conflict and relationships translates to the words.

History topic: Nazi Germany is very interesting because it is very relevant to understand how a society moves from a liberal outlook such as Weimar Republic to effectively a dictatorship and the Holocaust through manipulation of the electorate.

Learning:

Subjects Studied: Music, Drama (Grade 6 in Year 10), French, History (Grade 6 in Year 10)

Recent learning highlight: When Mr Beezey, a motivational speaker, came in at the start of Year 11 and talked to us about

STUDENT: HATTIE PEMBERTON

the importance of hard work and the drive that is needed to achieve what we want. It helped me realise the importance of understanding why I am working as hard as I am and what it is all for.

The most stand-out/interesting/challenging topic you've studied at school: At the end of Year 10 the Swing Band went to Eastbourne and performed in public at a large public event. This was quite a daunting experience as a lot of the band had not performed on this scale before.

One of my favourite teachers: Mrs Gully and Mrs O'Connell. Not only did both of them teach us really well but they also cared about our well-being, they made us want to work hard in their separate subjects. They explained things very well and worked very hard so our class was provided with the best resources.

A favourite feature of the school: It feels our school excels in every aspect. It has amazing resources and opportunities of a very high quality. Whether for revision, homework or clubs. There are so many opportunities and the teachers are always there to give up their time to help you.

Also I think a great thing about Heathfield is if the student body have a query or something they think the school needs or could benefit from they also take the point into consideration and most of the time something is done about it. Students feel like they are taken seriously and their ideas and views are respected.

CASE STUDY: COLLABORATIVE APPROACHES TO RESEARCH INFORMED PRACTICE

General Area: Teaching and Learning

Author: Becka Lynch, AHT (Teaching and Learning)

Rainforest vs Plantation: The three-part metaphor:

- **Establishing the Conditions:**
  - **Attitudes and habits for excellence: teaching to the top.**
  - Planning the curriculum: a knowledge-rich curriculum laced with cultural capital, extended learning opportunities.

- **Building the Knowledge Structure**
  - **Principles of instruction: applying the cognitive science.**
  - Feedback and review; securing excellence

- Exploring the Possibilities
  - Projects and hands-on learning, oracy, collaborative activities.
  - Further possibilities: interesting learning opportunities that extend and deepen knowledge.

Three years ago we reviewed our approaches at Heathfield Community College to effective teaching and learning. The driving forces behind this need for change, along with a new leadership team, were our Heathfield Goals. Among others these ensure that our students are *'equipped to enjoy and thrive in their lives'* and ensure Heathfield is genuinely a *'vibrant centre for learning, attracting and retaining the best staff based on career fulfilment, enjoyment and job satisfaction'*. These provided welcome clarity around 'elements' of effective teaching, after what staff referred to as 'initiative overload'.

It was important to ensure our time and efforts remained focused on what was right for our students; to avoid a reactive approach to any new study, idea or theory. This allowed us to ensure that quality Teaching and Learning at Heathfield was, and continues, to be our *'Main Thing'* (Covey).

We were quick to establish a new **Pedagogy Team** who work together to ensure consistent delivery of our teaching and learning agenda. This non-SLT team consists of staff from a range of different career stages. They have additional released time on their timetables to support them in this role. The 'Ped Team' make it their business to read and discuss research on pedagogy relevant to the priorities of the College improvement plan and T&L priorities. They drive the research directly into classroom practice.

From their researched informed perspective, they deliver input to all teaching staff, leading workshops that ensure evidence from research is easily explained and clearly linked to issues

directly relevant to staff. Teachers then reflect upon this further through additional department Continuing Professional Learning (CPL) time. They also discuss this across subjects through their directed **Collaboration Time**. Over the course of the last three years, teachers have had the opportunity to read and explore a range of research including: Allison and Tharby on modelling and scaffolding work that challenges all pupils, Mark Roberts' *Rethinking Boys Engagement*, the work on *Embedding Formative Assessment* by Dylan Wiliam, the SSAT and the EEF, and Alex Quigley's ideas on *Closing the Vocabulary Gap*.

Within **Departments**, meetings have moved away from administrative tasks instead focusing more on subject specific pedagogy. This happens either based on an annual Department Subject Specific Audit which identifies need and skills, allowing for bespoke CPL supported either by identified internal expertise or from external subject based sources. Some recent examples from department CPL plans include, 'spotlight on speaking exams and modelling for success' within MFL and 'making teacher explanations stick' within Geography. In CPL Week bespoke department time, Subject Leaders review subject specific foci and the central Pedagogy Team CPL input at a deeper level with subject colleagues.

This consistent 'whole' staff approach has helped us to clearly see impact, ensuring all our energies are more efficiently directed. Data shows that, since starting **Collaboration Time** in 2016–17, more teachers have become confident in incorporating the Heathfield Pillars into their lesson planning and delivery, leading to greater consistency of teaching and learning across the college. At the end of the academic year 2017–18, Challenge was seen as a strength in 75% of lesson observations, Engagement a strength in 79%, and Independence and Feedback in 66%. Unsurprisingly, we use the lesson observation data to inform future CPL and Collaboration

HEATHFIELD COMMUNITY COLLEGE, SUSSEX

CASE STUDY: COLLABORATIVE APPROACHES TO RESEARCH INFORMED PRACTICE

cycles. The research and structured conversations at Department and Collaboration Time level are broad enough to be able to be applied as most relevant for the individual but the whole College benefits from a clear and consistent dialogue at any one time. This work is underpinned by Appraisal objectives held by all staff which measure not data but staff engagement with pedagogic principles of instruction that are research informed in line with College foci for improvement.

Collaborative approaches

Collaboration is now embedded in our ethos and values at Heathfield, we seek 'a community culture of high aspiration, underpinned by collaboration and compassion' (Heathfield Goals). This is reflected in our structures as well as our habits of working. It is more effective now all Teaching Staff are part of a collaboration team, moving away from our first model of giving staff the choice. A valuable lesson we learnt from Year 1.

Specific '**Collaboration Time**' is now embedded within the timetables for all teaching staff and an established way of working collaboratively. We believe that our most valuable resource is professional dialogue between our teachers, giving time for collaborative planning and reflection with colleagues.

When first established in the context of new specifications and assessments, we were determined to provide opportunities to talk 'all things pedagogical and subject related'. Ensuring all teaching staff have a timetabled hour during the fortnight timetable means staff have the ability to do just that.

The 'Ped team' lead on the development and structure for these collaborative cycles. The image here highlights the 'typical' cycle of these meetings. Within this time staff will, in parallel, discuss their planning for excellent Teaching and Learning linked to our Heathfield 4 pillars of learning, *Independence, Challenge, Feedback and Engagement*.

The pillars, which are also reviewed collaboratively, provide a framework for excellent teaching without being overtly prescriptive. Thus providing the clarity around the 'elements' of effective teaching referenced above. Internal QA of Collaboration Time and subject specific conversations in department minutes show this is a valued and well utilised structure. Following feedback from teaching staff, we adapted the discussion questions used as a focus for the 'discuss' stage meeting to include questions specifically aimed at middle leaders and those

1. DISCUSS
Pedagogical Materials as a Collaboration Team

2. PLAN a lesson with one other person from the collaboration team

3. REFLECT on the outcomes

teaching predominantly KS5. This development allowed a more personalised agenda for those with specific roles.

External review of our practice is important to us too and we engage with the SSAT Framework for Exceptional Education (FfEE) being accredited in 2017–18 as showing 'transformative' practice with regards to our engagement with research and professional learning for our staff.

Collaboration also drives school improvement on a **Whole College** level. Small groups of staff have time to work together and lead on a whole school priority, these are known as **Innovation Teams**. Furthermore, as these are open to members of staff at all levels, from NQT to Head of Department, it means our whole community is driving the '**how**' of our College Improvement Plan.

Since 2016 different groups have helped change understanding and practice on Approaches to Literacy and Active Reading, Boys Achievement, Digital Learning and currently Assessment. Increasingly these groups are linking to external research and networks. Recent work has been or is currently being case studied by SSAI, LkMCo and Apple.

The impact on our staff of working and learning together in these ways has been transformational. The fact that they now have the confidence, knowledge and expertise to engage in regional and national conversations is a testament to the collective strength of the Heathfield staff, their engagement with the craft of teaching and their passion for continual learning and improvement. In a recent 2019 staff voice survey, teachers commented that '*[It is] useful to discuss what colleagues are doing in their subject versus my approach*' and '*Meeting with other teachers from other subjects is so informative… We always leave the session with new ideas to try from each other. Sometimes ideas are so simple and yet so effective.*'

The impact on students has been empowering and inspiring as they know and verbalise that they are taught by experts who are passionate about their subject and powerful advocates for teaching. A genuine '*vibrant centre for learning*'.

Link to Learning Rainforest:

Establishing the conditions: Attitudes and habits for excellence: teaching to the top.

We have a clear culture of aspiration and ambition established at Heathfield, reflected in our goals and habits. We expect excellence from our teachers and our students. You don't need to travel far into our college to be reminded of this, displayed proudly in our main foyer area, we remind all that '*we are what we repeatedly do. Excellence, therefore is not an act, but a habit.*' (Aristotle). Feedback tells us that this is then reflected in the practice and ethos evident in staff and students.

Building the Knowledge Structure: Principles of instruction: applying the cognitive science.

The consistency of the input and structure from the Ped Team into our CPL cycles ensure the research informed discussion of instructions is a whole college conversation.

The Dept CPL and Subject Specific time is driven by a subject interpretation and context of pedagogic and cognitive science research.

The Collaboration teams have Cognitive Science and Principles of Instruction as their core function and content.

The Innovation Teams have to be rooted in the research knowledge that underpins the improvement work on which they are focused.

GORDONSTOUN, MORAY

INTRODUCTION

I have very fond memories of my trip to Gordonstoun. It's such a fascinating school, in the most beautiful Scottish setting, famous for its royal associations and Kurt Hahn-inspired commitment to outdoor education, I was intrigued to discover what it was really like and how they would interpret the various elements of the Learning Rainforest after I presented them in my training sessions. On arrival I was told that, just the day before, the school's own active fire service crew had been on a call-out to deal with a local fire. Imagine that! This is all part and parcel of the school's commitment to service, an integral aspect of their wide curriculum that includes outdoor adventure – on land and sea.

Every student engages in some pretty hardy outdoor expeditions and spends at least a week on board their ship, Ocean Spirit. It seemed that every other person I spoke to was either just back or just about to leave on one expedition or another. My visit coincided with the publication of an Edinburgh University study[1] on Gordonstoun's outdoor education highlighting the value given to it by the alumni. So much goes on during a school day that even the 100 or so day students attend school for over 12 hours a day, sometimes not leaving until 10pm! My guide, a student from a comprehensive in Norfolk[2], had gained a scholarship for the two years of the Sixth Form and was having an extraordinary experience.

It would be easy to be dazzled by all the wrap-around provision at Gordonstoun but, as with any other school, it is actually the day-to-day business of teaching and learning and studying a broad range of traditional subjects that dominates their thinking.

The student profiles give a really good flavour of the breadth of experience the students enjoy. Exploring the possibilities is a big factor at Gordonstoun. However, as the case studies highlight, teachers at Gordonstoun, as elsewhere, are reflective professionals looking for ways to deepen their students' learning – and I was interested to see that the ideas behind 'building the knowledge structure' struck a chord. I love Georgina's account of using modelling to develop students' writing and Alasdair's reflections on the core of his Geography curriculum.

Finally, Caroline's account of her overarching approach to staff development is wonderfully reflective. I love the professional honesty she shows – and I'm really pleased to know that *The Learning Rainforest* has provided some guidance. It wouldn't be hard to tempt me back with or without the trio of treats she has suggested lie in store on my return!

The 'can do' spirit that Gordonstoun has imbued in both of my very different children is amazing, along with a sense of adventure, academic ambition and possibility. They have become courageous, confident and, best of all, kind.

QUOTE FROM CURRENT PARENT

1. Beames, S. Dr. 2018. The nature and impact of Gordonstoun School's out-of-classroom learning experiences. www.ed.ac.uk/education
2. Aylsham High School, led by Headteacher Duncan Spalding, another of the Headteachers' Roundtable group.

PROFILE

Location: Elgin, Moray, Scotland

Type of Institution: Co-educational independent boarding & day school

Roll/Age Range: 550, aged 5–18

Year Founded: 1934

Motto: 'Plus Est En Vous – There is more in you than you think'

House Names: The Junior Boarding house is called Aberlour House. The senior girls' boarding houses are Hopeman, Plewlands and Windmill; the senior boys' houses are Bruce, Cumming, Duffus, Gordonstoun and Round Square.

Recent/Current School Production: The senior production was an adaptation of Homer's *The Odyssey* which was set in the round with a stunning 'wet set'. The Junior School production is *Joseph and the Amazing Technicolor Dreamcoat*.

Recent significant sports event/triumph:
We were proud to achieve 40 team medals at this year's North District Cross Country Championships
As winners of the Highlands and Islands Squash Association's Champions League, we have been promoted to the Premier League. In both our teams are in competition with adult players.

Notable quirks/alumni: Gordonstoun is the only school in the UK with a classroom which takes the form of an 80ft sail training vessel called Ocean Spirit.

Lisa Kerr
Principal

PROFILE

Tom's analogy of nurturing students more as a diverse rainforest than a rigid plantation is a really apposite one for Gordonstoun. Our ethos has always been to impel young people into the widest possible range of experiences so that they can expand their horizons, and more particularly, their sense of themselves as individuals, and of their own potential. But the challenge lies in achieving an appropriate and constructive balance in how we achieve this – between what our students are learning inside and outside the classroom, and the ways in which these environments can and must complement each other.

We have to constantly review and reflect on this – to ensure that those experiences, whether they be on an expedition, on a boat, on stage performing as an actor, dancer or musician, are properly and productively supporting academic endeavour, and vice versa.

Our ambition is to enable our students to fulfil their academic potential of course, but also to supply them with broader life skills. Including the element of service to others as an integral part of the school's curriculum – whether it be as a member of the Volunteer Fire Unit or supporting the elderly and vulnerable in the community – is crucial to this, because it requires our students to look at how they relate to and consider others, themselves and also the wider world. We commissioned some research from the University of Edinburgh into the value of these 'Out of Classroom Learning Experiences' and happily the results concluded that they have a 'lifelong impact' on our students. This has reinforced our belief in, and commitment to, the profound value of this kind of experiential learning.

Our on-going responsibility is to keep these experiences – which are asked of every student, regardless of their socio-economic background, abilities or characteristics – as relevant and meaningful as they can be in a world which is changing with such resolute constancy.

STUDENT: YULY KLINOV

Age and Year Group: 14, Year 9
House: Bruce House
Most recent:
School Trip: Elgin Walkers Shortbread Factory (for globalisation project)
Extra-curricular activity: Kayaking in the school pool
Science experiment: Putting leaves under a microscope to see the stomata (Biology)
Book/Play studied in English Literature: *Macbeth*
History topic: 19th Century USA
Arts project: Large model in the style of Pop Artists like Claes Oldenburg
Learning:
Subjects Studied: Art, Biology, Chemistry, Computing, Dance, Design, Drama, English, French, Geography, History, ISC, Latin, Maths, Music, PE, Physics
Recent learning highlight: Writing a History essay on the impact of European settlers on Native Americans. I learnt a lot and it was a great opportunity to express some opinions on Manifest Destiny. I also enjoyed using the information and having my own explained answer to a thought-provoking question.
The most stand-out/interesting/challenging topic you've studied at school: Composite materials in Chemistry. We've done some interesting experiments, such as making pykrete, and I've learnt about how various materials interact and combine usefully.
One of my favourite teachers: Mr Richardson, my English teacher. He is very funny and entertaining, but we still get through all our work.
A favourite feature of the school: The size and beauty of the campus. It's been a home away from home to me for over three years and I don't think I will ever get tired of it. There is so much vibrant plant life and the variety keeps boredom at bay.

STUDENT: LIBERTY BLACKWOOD

Age and Year Group: 16, Year 11
House: Hopeman House
Most recent:
School Trip: Expedition to Glen Affric
Extra-curricular activity: Playing French Horn with the school Concert Band
Science experiment: Light Intensity and Photosynthesis
Book/Play studied in English Literature: *Romeo and Juliet*
History topic: The English Civil War
Arts project: A monologue from Caryl Churchill's Top Girls
Learning:
Subjects Studied: English Literature and Language, Maths, Combined Science, French, History, Drama, Latin
Recent learning highlight: Recently, I had a drama lesson in which we rehearsed an extract from Caryl Churchill's 'Top Girls'. As it's set in a small 1980s kitchen, we started to set up a small set, with a few props: cups, counters, bottles and so on. It was amazing how quickly and thoroughly this enhanced our performances and the world we had been struggling to portray.
The most stand-out/interesting/challenging topic you've studied at school: The most interesting topic that I've studied at school is the International Relations unit of History, which focuses on conflicts across 20th century. I found learning about previous events such as the Soviet-Afghan war really deepened my understanding of the world today, and what has led up to wars in my lifetime.
One of my favourite teachers: I enjoy lessons with my Latin teacher, Mr Kirkwood, because he teaches what is commonly preconceived as a very difficult subject in a relaxed and patient manner. He manages to make daunting ancient texts come alive through humour and teamwork.
A favourite feature of the school: My favourite feature of the school is the music department. There is a fantastic sense of encouragement and joy as well as achievement and discipline. I really appreciate how it pushes me to take new musical opportunities, such as new instruments or more difficult pieces.

STUDENT: JORDI BROWN

Age and Year Group: 17, Year 13
House: Gordonstoun House
Most recent:
School Trip: Round Square Regional Conference, Denmark
Extra-curricular activity: Model United Nations
Science experiment: Physics A Level Core Practical investigating oscillations on a spring
Learning:
Subjects Studied: Maths, Further Maths, Physics
Recent learning highlight: Studying Decision in Further Maths has been particularly interesting as the use of algorithms in graphs and linear programming have many practical applications. Additionally, the problem types are very involved and thought-provoking.
The most stand-out/interesting/challenging topic you've studied at school: I enjoyed learning about nuclear and particle physics. We have looked at the conservation of mass/energy in nuclear decay, as well as the function of cyclotrons and linear accelerators.
One of my favourite teachers: I enjoy lessons with Mr Martin who teaches me Physics because of the use of practicals to teach Physics concepts – for example, the use of dice to show the spontaneous and random nature of radioactive decay.
A favourite feature of the school: Sail Training is perhaps one of my favourite things about Gordonstoun – it's incredibly challenging and I spent much of my time on Ocean Spirit (the school yacht) being incredibly seasick. However, the views were unparalleled and the resilience instilled in me is something that I can apply to my A Level studies.

Sail Training is perhaps one of my favourite things about Gordonstoun – it's incredibly challenging

JORDI BROWN

Mr Kirkwood manages to make daunting ancient texts come alive through humour and teamwork.

LIBERTY BLACKWOOD

The campus has been a home away from home to me for over three years and I don't think I will ever get tired of it.

YULY KLINOV

CASE STUDY: HOW WE USED METACOGNITION AND MODELLING...

Title: How we used metacognition and modelling to improve creative outcomes.

General Area: Teaching and Learning

Author: Georgina Black, Head of Media Studies and Teacher of English

Having read *The Learning Rainforest* one of the key areas that stood out to me was the use of modelling and metacognition in the building knowledge area of the process. I, like many other teachers, am happy to set various tasks for the students, while not necessarily so happy to have a go myself. The use of modelling and metacognition has been a really positive experience, especially when encouraging creative outcomes in both English and Media Studies. It is something I have done before, but in a much more unconscious manner; now I am doing it deliberately.

For example, while teaching creative writing to my Year 10 English class, I was struggling to get the students to move from the childish 'recount' type story, with a linear narrative, to the more detailed descriptive writing required on the exam paper. After using lots of different 'better writing' stimulus, anchor charts, verb charts and slow writing techniques, still nothing much changed. But once I modelled the beginning of a story, based on an image, on the board, suddenly the students knew exactly what I wanted. While I modelled the writing, I explained why I was making the decisions I did. The outcome was some of the best writing I have seen from this level of set, it felt like instant and easy success.

There is a difficulty with this technique and one which means I would not use it all the time, for all the success it provides. When teaching exam style answers, I have found modelling to be less successful, as students, particularly less confident ones, will approach a model as if it is a perfect answer and just copy it. I have found that using metacognition techniques more helpful in these cases, explaining carefully and logically the thought process behind and extended analysis response, gives the students the toolkit to model their own thinking on, rather than modelling the answer. This process takes repeated sessions and lots of positive encouragement, but has proved successful.

In another situation, while working on the practical assessment with my Media Studies students I have adapted the course content I was already using to be more metacognitive. Our chosen NEA expects students to produce a music video and website, with accompanying planning and research. Students are given a checklist of tasks they need to complete and a series of deadline and are left to work independently. Some of the students struggle with long time frame and managing their time, but I have found this has improved when an element of metacognition has been added, allowing them to understand exactly what they will eventually get out of their work. Students are often about short term gains, but taking a more metacognitive approach allows them to begin to see the long term benefits of their work. For example, spending time going over the specific wording of the mark scheme and explaining it, allows them to understand how their storyboarding will allow them to gain specific planning marks. Again, this is nothing new, it is just a conscious effort to show the thinking, rather than just hoping they will somehow pick up on it.

Link to Learning Rainforest:

- Building the knowledge structure

CASE STUDY: EXPLAINING, MODELLING, METACOGNITION, CHECKING FOR UNDERSTANDING

General Area: Teaching and Learning

Author: Alasdair Monteith, Teacher of Geography and Climbing Instructor

The route ahead seemed challenging and exciting at the same time, it wasn't quite clear what would be encountered; whether we were adopting the right approach or what the end result would be, but we ploughed ahead nonetheless.

...OK, exaggeration aside, the similarities between winter climbing and teaching are more apparent in a place such as Gordonstoun than anywhere else I have had the pleasure of working.

The specific teaching uncertainty I am referring to above was the new GCSE and A level Geography specifications that we began teaching, as thousands of other colleagues did around the country, in September 2016. Reflecting on that first year of the new course and my five years in teaching, I realised that my focus had been too heavily centred on delivering the content – reviewing the syllabus like a lawyer would review a legal document. Not enough time was given to considering the effectiveness of delivery, the extent to which my students understood each element of a topic, and the tools that I could deploy to check understanding. It seems obvious now, but at the time my Head of Department and I were really concerned about the time pressure and getting every topic covered, particularly with the GCSE course.

Since that first year I have really focused on a variety of elements that Tom puts under 'Building the knowledge structure'. I teach Geography because I am passionate about global affairs, physical process and the world in general. I enjoy spending hours reading up on the latest twists in geopolitics and world affairs so that my lessons are interesting and current, but I realised that this

is wasted passion if the appropriate modelling and framing of the topic, supported by rigorous knowledge, is not passed on effectively to students. I have gone back to the drawing board (literally with some physical geography processes) to ensure that technical processes such as the formation of a meander or the tricellular model are clearly explained, modelled (sometimes in a variety of ways) and then time dedicated to enabling the students to apply the knowledge, before testing them. This could be through targeted questions, so that we have more two way explanatory dialogue, formal methods of testing with exam questions, or quick quizzes at the beginning of the lesson; something I have found very effective at encouraging recall of information and ensuring it enters long term memory. I created a little crib sheet with a few retrieval practice examples to stick on the side of my computer to prompt me into making these practices a core part of my teaching everyday.

Alongside this I have looked to develop the students' independent learning through the development of a department website. Department resources, from Powerpoints to documents and worksheets are stored in Google Drive and then linked directly to an appropriate section of the website. This ensures that students can access relevant information during and after the lesson and has been particularly powerful for both EAL, who can instantly translate key terms, as well as higher ability students who can be stretched with a wide variety of selected reading from sites such as The Economist and FT. I have certainly found that having technology to hand helps with engaging and encouraging students with a range of abilities.

So, to finish with a link back to climbing. I am also a Rock Climbing Instructor (RCI) and run sessions at the school's indoor climbing wall and the local cliffs. Establishing routines and

cementing information is vital from a safety aspect, but tasks such as belaying a climber correctly and tying into the rope require practice and understanding. Too often I felt that my younger climbing groups were just not getting these essential skills learnt and applying them as rigorously as I would have liked. By applying the same memory drills, thinking about the language I use to convey information, and the modelling I demonstrate actions with, I feel that the climbing sessions have become even more effective – and the students' understanding has reached new heights!

Link to Learning Rainforest:

Suggest how your initiative/improvement journey links to ideas in *The Learning Rainforest*:

- Plantation/rainforest analogy – school culture
- Curriculum /knowledge
- Assessment
- Establishing the conditions
- Building the knowledge structure
- Exploring possibilities

By applying the same memory drills, thinking about the language I use to convey information, and the modelling I demonstrate actions with, I feel that the climbing sessions have become even more effective – and the students' understanding has reached new heights!

ALASDAIR MONTEITH

The outcome was some of the best writing I have seen from this level of set, it felt like instant and easy success.

GEORGINA BLACK

CASE STUDY: FROM FIREWORK TO INFERNO – THE IMPACT OF THE LEARNING RAINFOREST ON INSET PLANNING AND DELIVERY

General Area: CPD

Author: Caroline McCallum, Director of Teaching and Learning

Since becoming Director of Teaching and Learning three years ago one of my greatest challenges has been how to ensure that INSET actually makes a difference to real teachers and real students in real classrooms. Of course, simply sharing practice in-house when structured well is incredibly impactful and enriching. However, in our geographically isolated school (in northern Scotland but providing an English curriculum and exams), we all need challenging external stimuli to ensure we aren't retreating into our own echo-chamber or educational bubble. It is too easy to opt for speakers who are simply entertaining; it might cheer up staff for the day but makes absolutely no lasting impact on learning outcomes. Also, even if the speaker is incredibly inspiring with excellent ideas, to keep the momentum through subsequent CPD is a feat of endurance. The firework that I refer to in my title you might recognise from Tom's blog post in which he calls some CPD a 'bang then a whimper' and seemed to completely sum up some of my own failed CPD planning in recent years.

We invited Tom to the school in 2018 for INSET and this was many of our teachers' introduction to the Learning Rainforest construct, with only a handful having previously read the book. The workshop was a resounding success with a real buzz in the room, even my most cynical staff were engaged. Yes, you all recognise these teachers sitting back in their chair with their arms folded 'come on then, try and impress me' attitudes! However, I had seen this positivity before – how could I sustain this energy and deep thought, moving out of the hall and into lessons?

The first thing that spurred me was the day after where I received countless emails and colleagues visiting my office to say how

much they had enjoyed the INSET but also 'what next?', 'how can we start doing things differently?' and 'when can he come back?'. The latter question made me think – do we actually need Tom to come back straightaway? Can we not take this on, move it forward and make it our own?

So, after some thought, I decided to rip up my existing INSET plan and start again, this time using the themes, chapters and sub-headings from *The Learning Rainforest* as inspiration to create a future structure for all our T&L INSET. The beauty of Tom's approach is that, generously, he doesn't claim all the ideas as his own and includes other like-minded educational theorists, moving fluidly from Martin Robinson's *Trivium* to Barak Rosenshine's 'Principles of Instruction', meshing this together with his philosophy in the way that we all naturally do in with our own professional learning.

So, the new academic year started with workshops on 'Establishing the Conditions' with some elements extracted from *The Learning Rainforest* but personalised to our school and current priorities. I must admit I was a bit apprehensive, as following Tom is a tall order, but it seemed to actually work! With little convincing, staff immediately saw the connections and understood the premise; this meant we could get to the bottom of things straight away with strategies, approaches and deep discussion – the 'folded arms' had not returned...yet.

Onwards and upwards, this workshop was quickly followed by a 'Learning Rainforest' edition of our in-house T&L newsletter and it was easier than ever to find contributors. Next, I overhauled our 'Lunch and Learn' CPD sessions with staff being encouraged to pick up on sub-headings and the smaller details of the book to frame their sessions. We have since covered some of 'Building the Knowledge' in workshops, this time combined with new research

on cognitive psychology, which complemented the theme very well. This is where we are now – I am just planning another start-of-term session on 'Building the Knowledge' and the whole process seems so much easier.

However, will it last? Only time will tell and perhaps we can question that the 'novelty' value is currently in force, but I strongly doubt this as every time I (and others) read the book there is a sentence or a word that sparks a new focus. As Tom purports, it is not about changing our practice but enhancing and making the tweaks so that every minute in the classroom counts. There has been a new dynamic in our CPD provision with much positivity so far. If it wanes, I might tempt Tom back up to see what we have achieved, with the promise of shortbread, bracing walks and lots of whisky.

Link to Learning Rainforest:

This piece reflects how the overall Learning Rainforest approach has been adopted in our approach to Professional T&L.

As Tom purports, it is not about changing our practice but enhancing and making the tweaks so that every minute in the classroom counts. There has been a new dynamic in our CPD provision.

CAROLINE MCCALLUM

THE LEARNING RAINFOREST

WHAT DOES RESEARCH SAY?

" IT'S IMPORTANT TO DEVELOP AN UNDERSTANDING OF EDUCATIONAL RESEARCH; ITS SCOPE AND LIMITATIONS. IT'S NOT 'ANYTHING GOES' OR 'WHATEVER WORKS FOR ME'; THERE ARE STRONG MESSAGES THAT EMERGE FROM THE COMPLEXITY.

" THERE'S A CONSENSUS EMERGING FROM COGNITIVE SCIENCE AND EDUCATION RESEARCH IN GENERAL. I HAVE MADE THREE CATEGORIES:

■ CLIMATE: RELATIONSHIPS, EXPECTATIONS AND MINDSETS ALL PLAY AN IMPORTANT ROLE.

■ PRINCIPLES OF INSTRUCTION: PEDAGOGICAL CONTENT KNOWLEDGE, QUESTIONING, GUIDED AND INDEPENDENT PRACTICE AND EFFECTIVE FORMATIVE FEEDBACK.

■ MEMORY AND BUILDING KNOWLEDGE: IT'S IMPORTANT TO GIVE PRIORITY TO TEACHER-LED INSTRUCTION THAT EXPLICITLY BUILDS LONG-TERM MEMORY.

" THE IDEAS BEHIND THE LEARNING RAINFOREST METAPHOR APPEAR TO BE SUPPORTED BY THE EVIDENCE FROM RESEARCH.

HOW DOES ASSESSMENT WORK?

" WE NEED A REAL PARADIGM SHIFT AWAY FROM MACRO SUMMATIVE DATA TRACKING TOWARDS AUTHENTIC FORMATIVE ASSESSMENT.

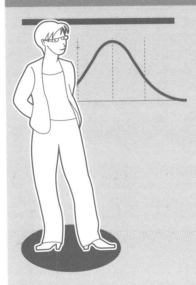

" STANDARDS ARE ALWAYS DETERMINED BY REFERENCE TO THE BELL CURVE WHETHER WE LIKE IT OR NOT.

" "DEFINING THE BUTTERFLIES IS THE GOAL IN EVERY CONTEXT. WHAT DOES EXCELLENCE LOOK LIKE AND HOW DO WE COMMUNICATE THAT TO STUDENTS?

" LOW STAKES HIGH-FREQUENCY TESTING IS A POWERFUL FORM OF FORMATIVE ASSESSMENT.

" AUTHENTIC ASSESSMENT HAS DIFFERENT FORMS IN DIFFERENT SUBJECT DISCIPLINES. IMPOSING A GENERAL GRADE SYSTEM LOSES THE INFORMATION THAT SUPPORTS ACTUAL IMPROVEMENT.

" 'RESPONSIVE TEACHING' REQUIRES USING STRATEGIES THAT ELICIT INFORMATION ABOUT WHAT STUDENTS HAVE LEARNED AND GIVING THEM FEEDBACK THAT MOVES THEM FORWARD.

CRAMLINGTON LEARNING VILLAGE, NORTHUMBERLAND

INTRODUCTION

Cramlington Learning Village has had a national reputation in England for a long time; it was one of the first schools given the Leading Edge designation by the SSAT and was lauded for its commitment to staff development and innovation in various areas of the curriculum. I once saw Ken, the Deputy Head who has written the case study, give an excellent conference presentation on Cramlington's CPD impressive programme which remains one of its central features. I've always held the school in high regard and was very pleased to be asked to visit and deliver a session to staff about the Learning Rainforest. An added bonus was getting the chance to meet Jamie Thom and see him in action – albeit very briefly. Jamie is another teacher-author who I admire immensely; his book *Slow Teaching*[1] provides a wonderful alternative perspective on what can feel like a frenetic business.

I loved my tour of the school with Ken and Wendy. It has an extraordinary campus where the 'village' aspect is vivid. The Junior Learning Village for Years 7 and 8 has an innovative open plan science 'plaza' where you can see multiple lessons happening simultaneously in the various linked spaces; there's a central covered 'street' that creates a great community feel and they even have their own mini-Eden project; a proper biome with some wonderfully exotic plants growing that students study in science and use as a stimulus in art.

In Ken's account below, he uses the rainforest metaphor to tell the school's more recent story. They've been on a roller-coaster with the flawed English accountability system, suffering a huge (disproportionate) knock and then bouncing back. It's been a tough process that has made the school re-evaluate certain

approaches, perhaps rebalancing the blend of instructional and student-led 'personalised learning' elements of the learning. Some of the ideas in *The Learning Rainforest* around building a more secure knowledge platform for exploring possibilities, seemed to resonate strongly with staff during the training and this is echoed in the idea of schema-driven planning and the 'wall' that Ken illustrates, drawing, as I do, on Doug Lemov's work in Teach Like a Champion.

I love the school's description of itself as pragmatopian! You can sense their idealism at every turn on a visit to the school – but they're also hard-headed about the process of improvement – always with that deep investment in staff development at the forefront.

PROFILE

Location: Cramlington, Northumberland

Type of Institution: Academy – Comprehensive with mixed intake

Roll/Age Range: 2000, aged 11–18

Year Founded: 1969

Motto: 'Where the science of learning meets the art of teaching'

Recent/Current School Production: *Back to the 80's*

Recent significant sports event/triumph:
2018 National Cup runners up at girls football (U-16 level)

Notable quirks/alumni: Ross Noble, Comedian

Headteacher: Wendy Heslop

We are a school with a 'pragmatopian', optimistic outlook.
WENDY HESLOP

To be a practitioner at Cramlington Learning Village is to be CPD'd to within an inch of your life – I mean that in a good way!
MATHS TEACHER

Ken Brechin
Deputy Headteacher

Cramlington Learning Village is a very warm and relationship centred organisation. Despite having 2000 students on site, it feels like a much smaller school. We are the only high school serving the town of Cramlington and we are committed to supporting and challenging all of our students, each with their own talents, abilities and aspirations – 'personalisation, not normalisation' is what we aspire towards.

There is a strong culture of professional development at the school. Our teachers are always hungry to learn, they like to talk

PROFILE

about teaching with colleagues and we nurture this through weekly, two-hour professional development sessions for all. CPD programmes are planned to challenge and support teachers at every stage and age.

We are a school community who have pulled together through very challenging times in recent years. A period in special measures had the potential to devastate the foundations and DNA of the school. By staying together as a community, and with good help and support we were able to steer our way through these turbulent times and emerge stronger as an organisation.

We are a school with a 'pragmatopian', optimistic outlook. Our feet remain firmly on the ground. We strive to give our students the best day to day experience that we can, while also remaining outward looking and receptive to ideas as we dream of the possibilities we can explore for our young people.

STUDENT: HOLLY SWAN

Age and Year Group: 15, Year 10
Most recent:
School Trip: Art trip to Boggle Hole
Extra-curricular activity: Drama
Science experiment: Density of non-linear objects
Book/Play studied in English Literature: *Dr Jekyll and Mr Hyde*
History topic: Elizabethan England
Arts project: Architecture
Learning:
Subjects Studied: Art, Music, History, Photography
Recent learning highlight: Working on my recent photography project and learning about different artists and incorporating them into my own work. It really helps me to develop my photography skills when I look at these artists because I learn from them.
The most stand-out/interesting/challenging topic you've studied at school: I enjoyed studying Germany in History because it was interesting to see how the war affected the people of Germany.
One of my favourite teachers: I enjoy lessons with Mr Gray who teaches me Maths because he has helped me progress far and is really funny; he makes maths easier to understand.
A favourite feature of the school: My favourite feature of the school is the support you receive from teachers. They all try their hardest to make sure you do well and understand everything.

STUDENT: THOMAS MCDOUGALL

Age and Year Group: 12, Year 7
Most recent:
School Trip: A trip to the Basketball
Extra-curricular activity: Golf and Badminton
Science experiment: Ray boxes – Investigating Reflection and Refraction
Book/Play studied in English Literature: *Romeo and Juliet*
History topic: The Middle Ages – The Norman Invasion
Arts project: Land Art
Learning:
Subjects Studied: ICT, Spanish, Food technology and CREATE (Music, Media, Drama)
Recent learning highlight: I thought I had really learned something important from the middle ages topic as it made me respect all of the things we get today.
The most stand-out/interesting/challenging topic you've studied at school: I enjoyed studying about Biology because they teach me a lot about animal behaviour and I also like studying about middle ages as we learn how people used to live back in the day.
One of my favourite teachers: I enjoy doing lessons with my PE teacher, Mr Paterson, as he inspired me into golf!
A favourite feature of the school: I really love that the school has great facilities for PE so we are always doing PE whether the weather is bad or good. I also appreciate that I am asked to play golf for the school.

I really love that the school has great facilities for PE.

THOMAS MCDOUGALL

Mr Gray has helped me progress far.

HOLLY SWAN

CASE STUDY: CONSERVATION OF THE RAINFOREST DURING CHALLENGING TIMES

Author: Ken Brechin

How do you keep the Learning Rainforest alive when you have been placed in special measures and you are battling for your survival as a school? Among the many challenges that you face when you are placed into a category of concern – when there are short term fires to put out, a cloud of uncertainty above your head and the pressing need to implement quite dramatic change across an organisation – is the predicament that the very heart and soul of the school might get lost along the way.

As a school we have always taken great pride in our Learning Rainforest culture, which had been cultivated, grown and tended over decades, which saw the school develop a national reputation for innovative approaches to teaching and learning and be judged as 'outstanding' four times in a row in the period between 2007 to 2015.

Everything changed when we were placed in special measures in July 2015. These were lifted in February 2017 when the school, with largely the same staff and students, was judged as being good.

A special measures judgement places an almighty question mark over everything that you do and have ever done to get to that point. Nothing can be off the table in terms of tearing things down and ripping things up in order to meet the expectations of dramatic change.

So how do you keep the rainforest alive in challenging times? What do you hold on to and what do you change?

Keeping the soil fertile and the conditions for learning rich.

A key element of the model of teaching and learning at the school has been to actively create a positive classroom climate. The school has an ethos underpinned by positive, warm relationships and encourages classrooms which foster engagement and curiosity. We were hugely concerned that the trauma and stress of special measures would start to harm the roots of the rainforest.

We adopted the philosophy of 'let the leaders do the worrying, let the teachers teach to their passions'. We know the reasons why teachers enter teaching can be lost in a maze of accountability, marking and pressure, but fundamentally most of us enter teaching because of a passion for two things: working with young people and our subject. Ensuring teachers keep connected with this most basic of motivations can have a real impact on how they feel about their work on a daily basis. The classroom is our empire to translate to others this palpable joy and enthusiasm for the content of our lessons. Where else do we have the privilege of selfishly indulging in waxing lyrical about the wonders of our subjects?

In our learning walks around the school at this time, we had often anticipated that we would pick up a sense of teachers and students grinding their way through their day, and ploughing through specification content for the next assessment or with summer exams in mind. We also feared that teachers being on 'red alert for a visit' would have a repressive effect on the culture and climate in our classrooms.

Our efforts as senior leaders to shield teachers from the stress of special measures was not without success. In fact, it was a frequent observation that the climate in the classrooms was still palpably one of enthusiasm, curiosity, passion for learning and, well, joy. We made a concerted effort to share positive stories and good practice around 'banishing the blues' from our classrooms and great practitioners like Jamie Thom, Zoe Taylor and David Gray were hugely proactive and visible in sharing ideas and strategies to keep the learning soil as fertile as possible and infectiously lift the climate in classrooms, even when the focus of lessons shifted into drill and practice for assessments.

Some tips that were explicitly shared by Jamie, Zoe and David:

- Set the tone at the start of lessons, explain how you are going to be covering some fascinating things today, share your passion for what students are going to be exploring for sixty minutes. This is your moment to capture them!

- Have one thing in every lesson that you are going to get very excited about. It might be a student's answer, a particularly troublesome formula, it might be an experiment. It has to be a light bulb moment that gets you hugely excited, convey it in your language. Lose all inhibitions for that moment, show how you can be moved by the content of your lesson.

- Be armed with a dizzying array of words that translate your passion: fantastic, outstanding, amazing, brilliant, wonderful, superb, splendid. Vary these each lesson to keep your students guessing.

- Show off the depth and detail of your subject knowledge; students love feeling that they are in the hands of a confident expert. Build a sense of mystery about your knowledge, hold back from revealing everything. When they see that you are a master of your subject they will be hanging on every word, desperate to hear your knowledge nugget for today's lesson.

- Use hand gestures and movement around the classroom to illustrate your excitement and enthusiasm.

- Search for the best qualities in every student. Look for opportunities to recognise and value their qualities. Remember to thank them for their contributions.

CASE STUDY: CONSERVATION OF THE RAINFOREST DURING CHALLENGING TIMES

- Use inclusive language to build a positive community. 'Together', 'support' and 'team' set a positive tone.

- Good learners never run out of questions. They are never satisfied with how much they know about anything. They are motivated by questions—the ones they still can't answer, or can only partly answer, or the ones without very good answers. Make use of question walls to co-construct future learning. This will foster a sense of curiosity and interest in your subject.

- Treat the end of a lesson like an Eastenders cliffhanger (cue theme tune). Provide closure with every lesson, e.g. 'Next time we will...', 'Please read...', 'Share one new thing you learned today...' or 'Find a video clip that shows...' This is a great way to build anticipation and a reason for students to be excited about coming to your next class!

All of these tips were shared via our in-house teaching and learning magazine *The Muse* which is available online via www.cramlingtonmuse.wordpress.com

Keeping the conditions for learning fertile was a significant step in ensuring that the quality of teaching at the school could flourish, even when the forest was on fire around us.

Building knowledge through schema-driven planning.

For 20 years, our approach at Cramlington Learning Village was to invest lots of CPD time carrying out collaborative planning around individual lessons. Over time we had built up a bank of over 3000 lesson plans across the full range of subjects, all of which followed a consistent structure, with each lesson representing the wisdom and experience of two or three subject teachers. In terms of supporting newer teachers to the profession, as well as non-subject specialists, the resources gathered online were incredibly

helpful and promoted consistency in quality, approach and a language of teaching which went a long way towards our success as a school in the period between 2000 and 2013.

However, the approach was not without its flaws. While the lesson plans were always meant to be regarded as a starting point for planning, sometimes teachers were overly wedded to the lesson plans and attached resources, with not enough individual thinking and adapting taking place to meet the needs of their own classes. We also wanted to adjust the lenses that teachers were looking through when planning, with less focus on the small details and resourcing of lessons, and more time taken to harness the deep knowledge of the subjects they teach. We wanted more of the collaborative planning time to be spent on discussing and planning for the ways students think about the subject content, to identify students' common misconceptions, and to evaluate the best way to sequence our schemes of learning so that knowledge is built effectively and held onto over time.

Changing course dramatically from the successful ways of the past is a difficult thing to do, but the special measures judgement gave us permission for us to let go of the things that we had once so much invested in. It is like clearing a part of the forest to keep the whole forest alive and so that something better and more wonderful can grow.

Our approach to planning shifted away from collaboratively planned individual lessons, to a collaborative, medium term approach to planning, rooted in pedagogical content knowledge, followed by individual personalisation to meet the needs of students.

Map it out first – make schema.

In our training we encouraged staff to make schema of their subjects. This involved working in groups to think their way through their subject content, reflecting not just on how the knowledge should be taught but also on how they engaged with the subject as learners themselves. These are great, high energy moments to witness, seeing teachers spark off one another, using their expertise to establish the core knowledge which underpins concepts in other topics. During these collaborative sessions a schema of knowledge is created which forms the medium term plan – the sequence of how knowledge will be built upon, challenged, developed and applied.

To ensure consistency we developed audit tools to ensure that our schema-driven plans:

- take into account and build on prior learning.

- take into account potential misconceptions and difficulties in teaching key concepts – and strategies to expose these.

- identify how teaching allows for memorisation, retention and recall (e.g. low stakes quizzing, recap activities).

- identify the vocabulary and key words necessary for success alongside teaching strategies for new vocabulary.

- identify how students will be assessed.

CASE STUDY: CONSERVATION OF THE RAINFOREST DURING CHALLENGING TIMES

Watering the rainforest through the 'teacher wall'

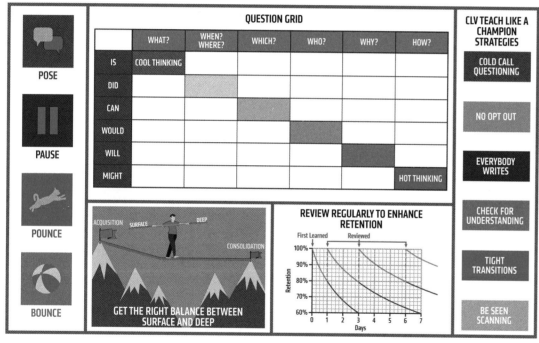

Of these, 'Check for understanding' serves as a reminder to not let too many minutes go by before checking for student understanding and progress, so that no student is left behind and misconceptions are not allowed to take root.

The retention of knowledge graph: as well as serving as a visual reminder to us that timely review of the main concepts is key to shallowing out the 'forgetting curve' – this graphic features on the teaching wall so we can use it with students. Our students are like wet cement – if we can imprint upon them early that they need to review their learning consistently, we stand a better chance of building a culture of revision across the school, which is all-important in the landscape where final examinations are the norm.

The final part of the teacher wall serves as a reminder to teachers about keeping balance in their teaching – that for students to engage deeply and love their learning – we do need to create opportunities where we get students learning in different ways through projects and open-ended enquiries, through debate and deeper engagement.

Conservation of the rainforest during difficult times.

All of these strategies were developed and implemented while the school was going through a very traumatic, but thankfully short, period of intense difficulty. During this time, when it felt that we were fighting for our identity, for the heart and soul of the school, a key battle was to prevent our own Learning Rainforest from being completely torched and cleared. While some of the rainforest may have a different shape and density than it had before, the roots, trunks and canopy remain strong, ready for whatever lies ahead.

With approximately 120 teachers on the staff, each brings their own talents and energies to our core purpose of giving our students the best possible chance for success. Ensuring that the culture of the rainforest pervades so many classrooms is a challenge, requiring lots of small inputs and positive degree changes over time. One positive influence has been the development of our own 'teacher wall' which is displayed in every classroom. In our experience, there is real strength in the students being exposed to a shared and consistent vocabulary of teaching and learning.

A quick tour of the wall:

There are two sections on building questions – the 'pose, pause, pounce, bounce' strategy is a strategy that works particularly well in our classrooms as does the question grid, which is aimed at ensuring there is good balance in the number of higher and lower order questions being asked by both staff and students.

Of the many, many 'teach like a champion strategies', we have focussed on a few that have the most impact in CLV classrooms.

THE LEARNING RAINFOREST IN PRACTICE

ESTABLISHING THE CONDITIONS

ATTITUDES HABITS FOR EXCELLENCE

C 1 JOY, AWE AND WONDER

C 2 TEACH TO THE TOP

C 3 RIGOUR

C 4 PITCH IT UP

C 5 PYGMALION

RELATIONSHIPS AND BEHAVIOUR

C 6 FOSTER RELATIONSHIPS: POSITIVE, CARING AND DEFINED

C 7 ESTABLISH ROUTINES FOR EXCELLENCE

C 8 SIGNAL, PAUSE, INSIST

C 9 POSITIVE FRAMING

C 10 USE THE SYSTEM AS A LEVER, NOT A WEAPON

C 11 SILENCE IS GOLDEN

C 12 KFFP PERSPECTIVE

PLANNING THE CURRICULUM

C 13 BIG PICTURE, SMALL PICTURE

C 14 PLAN THE STEPS

C 15 SPECIFY THE KNOWLEDGE

C 16 OBJECTIVES v TASKS

C 17 SCAFFOLDS AND STABILISERS

C 18 SKILLS AND DRILLS

C 19 BUILD THE WORDS, PLAN THE READING

C 20 BUILD A TIMELINE

EXPLORING THE POSSIBILITIES

BUILDING THE KNOWLEDGE STRUCTURE

ESTABLISHING THE CONDITIONS

CHACE COMMUNITY SCHOOL, ENFIELD

INTRODUCTION

Of all the *Fieldbook* schools, my contact with Chace Community School was initiated the most directly through the Learning Rainforest. I didn't know much about the school at all until Deputy Head, Tanya Douglas, sent me some images of their staff CPD noticeboard via Twitter. Right in the centre is a large-scale Learning Rainforest tree with the three labels clear to see: Establishing Conditions, Building Knowledge and Exploring Possibilities. I was absolutely thrilled because this was the first time I'd seen a school adopt the structure as a CPD model so comprehensively. I arranged a visit to meet Tanya and Headteacher, Daniel Bruton, to find out more and to make a contribution to their staff CPD process.

Daniel's brief account of the school context conveys the mix of honesty, humility and can-do spirit that I have come to admire so much in the *Fieldbook* leaders that I've met. The school had clearly been through a tough period when he came in as Head, albeit with many strengths to draw on, and it was interesting to hear how focusing on the quality of teaching has been a key driver in their improvement process. Tanya's case study explains the details of the approach they've adopted, working through each of the Rainforest elements term by term, with some lovely subject-specific examples. Obviously, the ideas I present in the book are drawn from a range of sources but it's so interesting to hear how useful it has been to have a common framework providing a shared language around which a raft of development work can revolve. If *The Learning Rainforest* can provide that, I couldn't be happier.

I'm a big fan of events where staff showcase their work; as well as sharing the specific ideas themselves, it helps to reinforce the culture of professional learning and that sense of working with common purpose. Some of the examples Tanya gives are where teachers have explored some 'Mode B' strategies. As ever, it will be the way these blend with the default diet of instructional Mode A teaching these teachers normally provide – rather than a simplistic 'good idea/bad idea' dichotomy. I'd love to visit one of their Teaching and Learning Hub showcase events in the future.

Generating interest and inspiring self-belief in students is not always easy, particularly when the school is under pressure to improve results, but I very much hope this will continue to be part of their experience

YEAR 7 PARENT

PROFILE

Location: Enfield, London, UK

Type of Institution: Mixed Comprehensive Community School

Roll/Age Range: 1219, aged 11–18

Year Founded: 1956

Motto: 'Aiming to be the best we can be'

Recent/Current School Production: *Lady Crimble's County Cake Off*

Recent significant sports event/triumph: Girls futsal team made it to the National Finals, finishing top 8 in the country.

Notable quirks/alumni: Richard Moon, United Nations Diplomat

Daniel Bruton
Headteacher

I never went out looking for headship, but headship found me. At the time the school was not only mourning the retirement of an established and much loved Headteacher, but was also in a cycle of declining outcomes and a loss of confidence from the community; a damning Ofsted report could have been the final nail in the coffin. In fact, the lowest point for me was when students came to my office to point out the name of our school in the Daily Mail's list of 'most failing schools'.

And yet, there is and always has been so much that is great about Chace. Authentic comprehensive values alongside a commitment to all students' entitlement to a whole curriculum offer. At Chace, 'everyone valued equally' means the majority of learning is still

PROFILE

mixed ability. Staff really invest in the school, work hard, and we are a cohesive team – there is still a regular contingent of colleagues who meet up on a Friday evening.

So the challenge was and remains the same. How do we reinvent ourselves whilst retaining all that is great about the school? At the heart of it, there were only really two challenges – convincing the whole community that we could meet this challenge together and convincing the teachers that although they worked incredibly hard, their teaching just wasn't having the desired effect. In hindsight it all sounds quite simple, but in reality the emotional impact was exhausting – we paid a high price in the first couple of years and I really couldn't have done it without the encouragement and support of my team and Chair of Governors.

In the second full year, we used *The Learning Rainforest* as a template for our focus on teaching. The themes were consistent with the work we had already started on teaching and little by little we have returned to being the great school that we deserve to be.

STUDENT: LOTTIE

Age and Year Group: Year 11
Most recent:
School Trip: French trip to Paris
Extra-curricular activity: Senior Netball Team
Science experiment: Using quadrats on the school field to count the number of species in a set area
Book/Play studied in English Literature: *An Inspector Calls* by J.B. Priestley
History topic: Weimar Germany
Arts project: Drama – group piece and monologue '*Five kinds of silence*'
Learning:
Subjects Studied: Sociology, History, Drama, French and core subjects
Recent learning highlight: My imagination was captured when I studied Weimar Germany. We learnt about systems of government and a different way of governing a country, proportional representation, and how this could be used in the UK. It also inspired my passion for government and politics, which is something I want to pursue at A level and in the future.
The most stand-out/interesting/challenging topic you've studied at school: I enjoyed learning about Nazi Germany in Year 9 because we learnt about the concentration camps. The teacher brought the topic to life by showing videos and he took risks to not shy away from showing us content that was difficult at times.
One of my favourite teachers: I enjoy lessons with Mr Halford who teaches me History because he teaches with such enthusiasm and passion for his subject that is passed on to us.
A favourite feature of the school: Being a diverse community school promotes openness and understanding at Chace. The teachers are always willing to help and support us if we need anything and focus on people coming out as better people and not just having good grades.

STUDENT: DYLAN

Age and Year Group: 14, Year 9
Most recent:
School Trip: Art trip to the Victoria and Albert Museum
Extra-curricular activity: Maths club
Science experiment: Using equipment to understand different types of energy
Book/Play studied in English Literature: *Of Mice and Men* by John Steinbeck
History topic: Nazi Germany
Arts project: Photography using sweets
Learning:
Subjects Studied: English, Maths, Science, RE, Lifeskills, History, Geography, PE, Art, Music, Drama, MFL, Technology
Recent learning highlight: When we studied Of Mice and Men in English we learnt about segregation between the different sexes and races and how different people were treated. It taught me how much we have changed and that I have more rights in life and work. The text moved me because it made me think if things had not changed what my future could be like.
The most stand-out/interesting/challenging topic you've studied at school: In music I couldn't really play the keyboard as I had never played an instrument before Secondary School. Practising since Year 7 was hard but I have built up skills and can now play quite well. Although I still make mistakes, lessons are fun and I have achieved a lot as I can now play this instrument.
One of my favourite teachers: I enjoy lessons with Ms Wilson who teaches me Science because she has taught us since Year 7 and knows every student, our weaknesses and what we need to focus on to be better. She is patient and helped me grasp chemistry really well because she has developed my maths skills in my chemistry work.
A favourite feature of the school: My favourite thing about the school is the pastoral care we get from Form Tutors. My Tutor really cares about us and because she is a maths teacher we can go to her outside of maths lessons and she will help us with things we don't understand. My Form Group is also really close, we trust and support each other and this helps us with our learning.

CASE STUDY: USING THE RAINFOREST TO ENSURE LESSON TIME IS USED PRODUCTIVELY

General Area: CPD

Author: Tanya Douglas, Deputy Headteacher, Teaching and Learning/Staff Development

A continued area of development for our school has been to ensure teaching is consistently good, leading to improved outcomes. We are proud of the journey we are on to get closer to this goal and have had great buy in from students, teachers, middle and senior leaders to continue to improve what happens every day in every classroom for the young people we are responsible for.

This year we have gone about designing a Professional Development (PD) programme under the umbrella of 'planning to use time in lessons productively' as our monitoring highlighted that gains could be made in this area. In particular, focusing on our whole school non-negotiables which include knowing the students, having high expectations and planning accordingly.

To bring the PD theme to life we decided to use the Learning Rainforest metaphor to consider the key features of what goes into effective planning to ensure that all lesson time is productive. Our Chace Lead Teacher (CLT) team had already read the book and the common sense, practical strategies were in line with our already established philosophy of teaching in our school and agreed it would provide a great backdrop to have maximum impact. In the summer term we put together the plan, mapping out the year, half term by half term, staff briefing by staff briefing, development time and twilight to design a programme around the three parts of the metaphor.

We decided that establishing the conditions was an important starting point for the first half-term in autumn. A big focus of our September INSET was to address curriculum

planning and our expectations for every lesson; knowing each individual student and planning for their needs; planning one challenging learning objective and scaffolding to ensure access for all; and establishing positive relationships and routines from the first lesson. Following this, we used our weekly staff briefings to drive home some of the key messages and in one of our briefings provided a 'bridge task' for teachers to choose an aspect of establishing the conditions that we had been addressing, share it with someone else in the faculty and get them to be a 'nudge buddy' to ensure they commit to doing it. The impact of our work was clear; our first whole school learning walk in November highlighted high expectations in planning alongside positive behaviour for learning leading to lesson time being positive and productively used.

As challenge and high expectations were a key priority for us, we decided to host an event in our Teaching and Learning Hub in October around high expectations. This was a two day event featuring a gallery of work from our current Year 7s' best Primary School work and projects they completed as part of their transition to our school. We also hosted two discussion forums – 'KS3: The wasted years?' and 'Challenge'. The intention was to showcase what our KS3 students are capable of, the work they can produce and how in turn we need to ensure when planning we are teaching to the top and having the highest expectations of what our young people can do. The feedback from the event was extremely positive; we had around 60 teaching and support staff visit the event leaving comments in the visitors' book such as 'a reminder to keep expectations high' and ' great idea to show, share and raise the bar'.

For the second half term, **we launched the PD theme of Building the Knowledge Structure** with our staff. Following

an introductory session on the theme, we used a twilight PD session to zoom in on four key areas; feedback and review, homework, metacognition and recall and retention. As part of the twilight, our CLT team delivered key messages and teachers collated information on a capture sheet including how they could use some of the practical strategies in a lesson. The outcome would be that in January we would carry out developmental peer observations focusing on how we used the strategies in lessons, but also a Teachmeet to showcase learning. To ensure buy in and get commitment from all staff our Teachmeet used a spinner that randomly selected teachers to give micro presentations, meaning everyone had to be ready to share how they used the PD. To consolidate some of the ideas from the Learning Rainforest metaphor, we hosted another twilight PD session delivered by Tom Sherrington. The session developed the ideas from *The Learning Rainforest* and what we had focused on for the year.

The Teachmeet in January and feedback from staff made clear that there was a huge amount of professional learning that had taken place during this part of our PD programme. The micro presentations showed that teachers really had engaged with building the knowledge structure and applied some of the ideas in their teaching.

In March, we held another event in our Teaching and Learning Hub called 'The Power of PowerPoint'. This was an opportunity for us to explore how we build the knowledge structure with our students without increasing cognitive overload. The event focused on the idea that PowerPoint is an aid in our teaching, but is not the teacher, therefore slides crammed with text that we read out or expect students to focus on whilst we teach can be counterproductive. Furthermore, our teaching should be the main vehicle we use to explain and model, not our PowerPoint

Ms Wilson knows every student and what they need to do to be better.

DYLAN

The teacher brought the topic to life and took risks.

LOTTIE

CASE STUDY: USING THE RAINFOREST TO ENSURE LESSON TIME IS USED PRODUCTIVELY

or flip presentations. During the event we asked provocative questions to staff like 'Does teaching without slides make you a better teacher?' and 'Is it okay to have lots of writing on a slide?'. The event was, once again, very well received by staff and we asked teachers when leaving to consider what they would do differently. We received comments such as 'I am going to teach a lesson without PowerPoint/flip' and 'I will consider the layout of slides to ensure they do not contain unnecessary information and discuss verbally/through questioning before a slide is shown'. A few weeks after the event a member of CLT received an email from a member of staff that really sums up what the event hoped to achieve:

Hi, just wanted to drop you a few lines about the PowerPoint stuff we were talking about a few weeks ago. I've tried minimising ppt use with my Year 10 classes in Sociology and in English. With my English class, this has been boosting their independence as they've had to do most of the work finding the information themselves. I also had a revision lesson with my Sociology class where I didn't use any slides at all! This got me thinking more creatively so we ended up doing lots of group work revision – including some competition on the whiteboard (which also meant that they were really active throughout the lesson!). Thanks so much for all the brilliant ideas and the support.

With the second half of the Spring term came **our opportunity to use the PD programme to Explore the Possibilities with staff. We introduced the idea of Mode A and B teaching**, and reflected honestly that our default of Mode A gave us room to be more creative in what we do. So for our Spring twilight, teachers opted into a session that would provide a platform to get creative and, dare I say, go off piste! The sessions included online learning,

creating independence through project work, playing detective and group work and at the end of each session our teachers and teaching assistants wrote a postcard of what they would commit to trying in the classroom around the different themes.

On our return from the half term break, we hosted a Teaching and Learning Hub event to showcase how teachers had explored the possibilities with their learners and found more opportunities for Mode B teaching. The event included a gallery of around 20 examples of how teachers across the different subject disciplines had tried something new.

In geography, students had the opportunity to play detective through a mystery lesson to find out why so many people died in the Haitian earthquake. For the starter activity, students had to guess what was happening in the picture, but only small sections of the picture were revealed at a time. Students were then given a series of questions to solve by the end of the lesson using the clues planted around the room. This investigation made students more curious and motivated as they had to work things out for themselves without being told.

In art, the teacher used group work to support collaboration and understanding of the painter Degas. First students worked in groups of four to brainstorm their analysis of a Degas painting. They then recreated the paintings using a freeze frame of themselves in their group. The aim was to focus on the body language and facial expressions of Degas' work. The class then drew a couple of the groups from first hand observation. They then used this to add more to their original analysis as they had delved deeper into the painting. The outcome was greater engagement in the lesson and understanding of the painter. Using the group work and freeze frame activity brought the paintings to life.

We also had two lunchtime forums hosted by teachers as part of the Hub event; one on online learning using Google Classroom and the other on using project work in drama. **In drama,** students used class and homework time to carry out an independent exploration into the Blood Brothers. Students were given options for the project such as an in depth character exploration, an investigation into a theme in the play or to become a designer. Each option had a clear outcome, for example, giving a verbal presentation, creating costumes, making model boxes and recording a performance. The project had clear deadlines, success criteria and links to component 1 of the GCSE which requires students to use technical drama language with accuracy. The outcome of the project was a gallery to showcase all of the projects. Students left the lesson excited by their learning and wrote postcards about what they had learnt from the process such as 'I have a better understanding of the characters', 'I can now write a question on the themes in Blood Brothers with confidence' and 'I feel more able to answer a 4 mark question in the GCSE'.

So, with the final half term of the year our professional development plan has gone back to where it all starts; the planned curriculum. Colleagues will be spending time reviewing what we intend to get from our curriculum and whether our plans and teaching actually achieve it. And in the spirit of sharing excellence, we will be showcasing our curriculum in a final Teaching and Learning Hub event at the end of the year. We have also asked staff to reflect on their professional development over the year and created a display in the staff room of staff postcards outlining the impact PD has had in their classroom.

CASE STUDY: USING THE RAINFOREST TO ENSURE LESSON TIME IS USED PRODUCTIVELY

CPD Review of the year

Thinking back over all of the CPD that you have been involved in (reminder of all sessions below), what has had the greatest impact on your practice? All materials used are available on #ChacePD. Use the other side of this postcard to give us some information including examples of how your practice has been influenced by participation in this year's CPD programme. Please take some time to consider this thoroughly and include as much detail as possible. If you would like to share some examples of work that students produced as a result, please do attach a copy. Once completed, simply put your postcard into DS's pigeon hole.

CPD themes/ events	Detail
Establishing the conditions	Planning to use lesson time productively Non-negotiables then sessions on: Questioning/marking and feedback/challenge/differentiation
Hub event 1	Sharing examples of Year 6 work = high expectations
CPD: Building the knowledge structure	Recall, retrieval, HW, feedback and DIRT, metacognition
Teachmeet	Sharing good practice from above sessions. The Spinner!
CPD: Exploring the possibilities	Mode A vs Mode B teaching. Group work/projects/playing detective/Google classroom
Hub event 2	Examining Powerpoints – Cognitive overload
Lesson drop-ins	Sharing good practice from peer observations etc.
Re-establishing the conditions	Sessions on: Relationships/Mental health/Reluctant writers/Form tutor/ADHD
Hub event 3	Sharing practice from "Exploring the possibilities"
NQTs +	Lesson study +
Other CPD	e.g. coaching programme, external courses, reading about pedagogy.

Link to Learning Rainforest:

Using the metaphor of the rainforest to map out our professional development for the year has provided an engaging and thought provoking backdrop for what we do in the classroom everyday. The rainforest analogy has 'just worked' for us and we have 'zoomed in' on the different aspects of establishing the conditions, building the knowledge structure and exploring the possibilities that are relevant to us.

Using the metaphor of the rainforest to map out our professional development for the year has provided an engaging and thought provoking backdrop for what we do in the classroom everyday.

TANYA DOUGLAS

CASE STUDY: ESTABLISHING THE CONDITIONS THROUGH COACHING

General Area: CPD

Author: Hugh Halford, Head of Government and Politics, High Starter Co-ordinator

As a long standing member of the teaching staff I am passionate about improving teaching and learning at my school. For this reason, I joined the newly established Coaching Team. The rationale was for experienced teachers to establish a coaching relationship with other members of staff in the school. This is also in the context of our school's journey towards being a good school and providing the best education for our learners.

To have an impact on improving teaching in the department I lead I was paired up with a recently qualified teacher to coach who would be teaching Government and Politics. A fundamental part of this process was to use the rainforest to generate discussion and strategies to use every week in his teaching. As the coaching began in the Autumn term, we started by looking at areas of establishing the conditions. Before any meeting, my coachee gave me areas that he wanted to develop in this teaching, an example being in his pastoral role as a tutor, establishing routines. From this I found aspects of the rainforest, alongside my own experience, that he could try out with his form group. Similarly, he was keen to generate excitement in his lessons, so we looked closely at the idea of how to instil 'awe and wonder' and 'pitching up' in the classroom. One strategy he used with a Year 9 class was to expose them to A level content through reading materials and assessment questions. This made the students more resilient as they felt more comfortable in their ability to take on challenges independently.

Our coaching relationship lasted for eight weeks. In this time we explored a number of aspects of the rainforest ranging from behaviour management to subject knowledge and pedagogy. As the process continued it was clear to see the strategies being trialled and being successful which emboldened the teacher to take risks and try new things. This drove home to me the principle of not putting a lid on student potential. An example of this was seeing my coachee, who was working on relationships with his form group, lead a successful high level debate on global political theories. The students were clearly engaged and inspired by the challenging nature of the content.

Although our coaching formally ended at the end of the Autumn term, we continue to discuss teaching and learning informally. In the Summer term, to see if there has been lasting impact we will be re-establishing our coaching for a few sessions. Although the process of coaching is time consuming and an addition to our teaching roles, it reminds me of the importance of collaboration and reciprocal learning. I have learnt as much from the coachee as he has learnt from me and the rainforest has been a great tool to support the process.

EXPLORING POSSIBILITIES

BUILDING KNOWLEDGE

ESTABLISHING CONDITIONS

ST STITHIANS COLLEGE, JOHANNESBURG

INTRODUCTION

The most recent school encounter to feature in *Fieldbook* was with St Stithians Boys' Prep in Johannesburg, South Africa, one of the family of schools that form St Stithians College. As with several other entries in the book, this began with an exchange on Twitter. Deputy Head Lester Lalla contacted me and we began to discuss the Learning Rainforest and idea that I might travel to South Africa, combining some work at his school with attending the 2019 Cape Town researchED event. I knew the timing would be tight to fit in a visit before *Fieldbook*'s publication, but we have managed it.

St Stithians has some interesting connections with other *Fieldbook* schools. The school's founders originate from Stithians in Cornwall, not too far from St Austell where Penrice is located. The 15 stars in the St Stithians badge echo the 15 bezants found on the historic Cornish flag. The school is a member of the Round Square group of independent schools, named after the famous 'round square' building at Gordonstoun where the group held its first conference in 1967. 'Saints' as it is often referred to, is an impressive place with magnificent sports facilities – including 11 cricket pitches and a football pitch installed especially for use by the Australian 'Socceroos' team during the 2010 World Cup. At night the school's on-site Higher Ground restaurant provides a magnificent view of the Sandton business district skyline across the valley.

As with many other independent schools in South Africa, St Stithians is undergoing some philosophical change, adapting to maximise its contribution to social change whilst maintaining its traditions and standards. It was fascinating talking to Headmaster Jakes Fredericks and Deputies Lester Lalla and Gavin Olivier about their perspectives on the country's continuing political turbulence and economic fragility which provide the backdrop against which educational reform takes place. It was moving to

hear Lester, responding to my questions, describing growing up under the Apartheid regime, living with travel restrictions and racial segregation, and then accompanying his parents to take part in the first democratic elections in 1994 when they queued for five hours at the polling station. In the modern South African context, the school's philosophy is informed by a strong sense of moral purpose – to educate a generation of future leaders who will contribute to on-going national development. They recognise the privileges they enjoy as a fee-paying school whilst remaining committed to playing a role in the system beyond the school gates; alongside various outreach programmes, they've secured increased racial diversity in the student and staff body as part of a deliberate strategy to extend opportunities more widely and this looks set to continue.

One of the fascinating aspects about St Stithians, captured brilliantly by Lester in his case study, is that they are wrestling with their own version of the progressive-traditional debate. In keeping with recent national trends where the rhetoric of '21stcentury learning' has been given high value, the school has publicly promoted its values-led progressive outlook very explicitly in its literature. At the same time, however, there is now a growing commitment to the need for teachers to be research-engaged, embracing ideas about effective instructional teaching amongst their other strategies. I was delighted to learn that the school had purchased a copy of The Learning Rainforest for every member of staff and, during my visit, it was clear that many of the ideas had resonated with teachers in different ways. Lester's piece is highly quotable but I particularly like this idea: *We plan for learning, not simply for learning experiences*. That encapsulates the essence of 'building the knowledge structure' and it has been wonderful to follow Lester's exploration of this in the teaching at St Stithians.

A boys' school by intention.

JAKES FREDERICKS
HEAD OF SCHOOL

St Stithians College, an older school by South African norms, is rooted in nourishing traditions and values. In this ecosystem of five individual schools located on 105 hectares, we have the opportunity to live out our motto of One and All. We value and celebrate the distinctive character of each of our schools and recognise the strength and beauty of our collective College.

As a Boys' Preparatory, we exist to develop the character and potential of each of our boys through rigorous academic, sport, cultural, leadership and service programmes.

ST STITHIANS COLLEGE, JOHANNESBURG

PROFILE

We strive to develop fertile conditions for learning by investing in relationships and in instructional practices that best support learning.

The rich, enacted curriculum has an intentional focus on the interests and wonders of boys through the use of story, literature and music, however this is carefully managed and negotiated.

Domain specific knowledge and skills are valued, and these are given right of place in our curriculum and approach.

As a truly transformative South African school we are enriched by the cultural and racial diversity of our many stakeholders. This is the type of variation we seek for our learning rainforest – a culture which values trust and challenge and places our teachers at the vanguard of their own development and practice.

STUDENT: RICHARD LESCHNER

Age and Year Group: Year 12, grade seven

Most recent:
School Trip: Tour to England
Extra-curricular activity: Maths club
Science experiment: The solar powered school hat
Book/Play studied in English Literature: *Holes* by Louis Sachar

Learning:
Recent learning highlight: We had a recent lesson in English on World War 2. We learnt how gruelling life was and how the Allies ultimately beat the Germans. The way it was taught brought the history to life. It was fascinating.

The most stand-out/interesting/challenging topic you've studied at school: I have recently been learning the concept of simple algebra. It has captured my attention because it is a bit like solving a puzzle with only numbers and one correct answer at the end. I enjoy the challenge.

One of my favourite teachers: I enjoy lessons with Mr De Buys who teaches me English. The way he teaches the lessons is so inventive and fun. He has incredible knowledge on the past, literature and poems which contributes enormously to his lessons. I always look forward to the lessons because you never know what he will come up with next.

A favourite feature of the school: The schools culture department is phenomenal and I am given endless opportunities to participate in all sorts of school events and tours, even though I am not good at sport. There is an amazing choice of instruments, choirs, bands, drama and public speaking to partake in.

STUDENT: CORBIN BOUWER

Age and Year Group: Year 13, grade seven

Most recent:
School Trip: Rugby trip to Penrynd
Extra-curricular activity: Maths club
Science experiment: Does gravity effect weight or size more?
Book/Play studied in English Literature: *Holes* by Louis Sachar

Learning:
Recent learning highlight: My recent learning highlight was learning about volcanoes and natural disasters. How they affect our way of life and how we have adapted.

The most stand-out/interesting/challenging topic you've studied at school: I have recently been learning about integers which was challenging because it is a side of maths that I have not explored before.

One of my favourite teachers: One of my favourite teachers is Mr Lalla who teaches me natural sciences. The reason I chose Mr Lalla is because he believes that it is not about the marks but about how much we learn through our mistakes and supports each and every student.

A favourite feature of the school: The facilities in our school are top of the range and convenient which makes things easier.

CASE STUDY: A RETURN TO GREAT TEACHING

General Area: Teaching and Learning

Author: Lester Lalla, Deputy Head

A growing number of South African independent schools are adopting progressive educational ideologies and practices. This is driven by increased competition within the sector, rising unemployment, a sluggish economy and the need to develop so-called 21st century skills for the marketplace. Inquiry based learning, project based learning and cross-disciplinary modular teaching are the drivers of macro curriculum reform.

This was my reality as a teacher and curriculum leader. We spent many hours designing units that would improve student agency, engagement and critical thought. 21st century educational rhetoric was at the heart of our ambition and practice. This, we believed, was necessary for the development of future entrepreneurs, professionals and industry leaders.

To some degree, we were successful, however, you don't know what you don't know. Tom's Learning Rainforest opened new vistas of knowledge and instructional techniques which we reflected on honestly and critically.

In a masterful way, Tom is able to inhabit the seams of educational discourse without resorting to binary outcomes.

What was evidently lacking in our practice was a rigorous focus on what Tom calls Mode A teaching. I returned to my natural science class the next year determined to build a solid knowledge structure. I applied the principles of cognitive science and effective instruction. What followed was simply wonderful – I rediscovered my love for teaching and a by-product of this was awe and wonder for my students. My prep time was drastically reduced, and I felt more confident tracking the progress of my students.

Concepts, important terms and pronunciation were taught explicitly which is especially important because English is a second, third and/or fourth language for a number of our students. High quality content and multimedia were made available via Google Classroom and in hard copy. Questioning became a major part of the learning process. I dedicated a significant amount of time developing my questioning techniques. It was amazing to witness the improvement in their responses throughout the year. In addition, frequent, low-stakes assessment became commonplace. Technology was a great enabler in this regard. While this may rightly appear to be 'normal teaching' in any classroom, it required careful planning, iteration and persistence.

A greater focus on Mode A teaching gave me the confidence and opportunity to engage in some Mode B strategies.

In the first term of their Grade Seven year, my students undertake an independent scientific inquiry of their choice. This is underpinned by the study and application of the scientific method. This project is particularly exciting for my boys as they get to showcase their work at our annual fair. It attracts a great deal of foot traffic and admiration.

Rather than letting them loose and hoping for the best, this is a carefully managed and scaffolded process. Students engage with the scientific method, one step at a time. This includes a reading, worked examples and independent practice. This knowledge is later applied to their own inquiry and investigation.

I am often amazed to witness the quality of work on display and the confidence with which my students share their learning and experience. This would not be possible without a dualistic approach that places knowledge at the heart of our curriculum.

Using Tom's Learning Rainforest model and the principles of cognitive science, we are reimagining our collective vision for teaching and learning in the following ways:

- Ensuring that **there is fluency and coherence to our curriculum**. Whilst we have a fairly tightly prescribed national curriculum, we are planning the sequencing structure which will ensure the development of strong schemas. This is a particular priority in subjects which have a vertical knowledge structure.

- **We all teach for memory**. No longer will we pit knowledge against skills. We have a collective responsibility to ensure our students encounter our domain specific knowledge in an engaging and lasting way. Retrieval practice and regular drills will be a common feature of all classrooms.

- **We plan for learning, not simply for learning experiences**. A great criticism of inquiry-based learning and the like, is the dominant focus on activities and engagement instead of learning. We will invest our future time and energy in strategies that are well-worn and effective instead of those which appear populist and trendy.

There is no doubt that The Learning Rainforest has taken our staff on unique and individual journeys. For some it has provoked a return to good practice, whilst for others it has introduced a new world of educational research and instruction.

In the spirit of The Learning Rainforest, we have not reduced these principles to checklists or performance criteria. We want teachers to be in the driving seat of their own practice and development. They should allow evidence to inform their practice and engineer success for all their students.

CASE STUDY: A RETURN TO GREAT TEACHING

After years of plantation thinking and edu-fads, it is a joy to witness the diversity and maturation of our practice.

Our enriching rainforest is evident in the broad and stretching curriculum our boys are exposed to. Languages, Mathematics, Sciences, Humanities, Technology and the Arts are well established disciplines in our tapestry of learning.

Expression of this can be found in our thriving cultural programme which is comprised of our choirs, music ensembles and whole school drama productions. In addition, our boys participate in 16 seasonal codes of sport. The focus here is skills development and mass participation.

A young man's schooling experience at St Stithians Boys' Preparatory is rounded by community engagement, an intentional focus on character education and the round square discoveries.

Through this holistic approach to education, we endeavour to develop future engaged citizens who will make a contribution to the landscape of South Africa.

Link to Learning Rainforest:

- Mode A and Mode B teaching
- Diversity of approaches
- Rainforest thinking

I rediscovered my love for teaching and a by-product of this was awe and wonder for my students.

LESTER LALLA
DEPUTY HEAD

GIVING BACK: THE THANDULWAZI MATHS AND SCIENCE ACADEMY

Having visited South Africa in September 2019, concluding my *Fieldbook* tour with my visit to St Stithians I feel more strongly than ever that, with all the privileges I enjoy in my work, I should do more to give back. I was thrilled to hear about the work St Stithians does through its Thandulwazi programme, created in 2005 to improve the quality of Maths and Science teaching and learning in public high schools.

The key objectives as described on the programme's website are:

- Operating a Saturday School on the St Stithians College campus, providing extra tuition to Grades 9, 10, 11 and 12 students who self-select to attend these classes from a large number of high schools in greater Johannesburg, and in particular from under-resourced districts. The curriculum focuses on Mathematics, Physical Sciences, Life Sciences, English and Accounting.

- Facilitating the training of new teachers through an internship programme which places trainee teachers in the schools of St Stithians College. There is a special focus on areas of critical teacher shortage, such as Maths and Science; English; and Early Childhood Development (ECD)/Foundation Phase. The interns are mentored by senior teachers of St Stithians.

- Creating an in-service teacher development programme for educators teaching across the educational phases. Teachers are drawn from over 400 schools across greater Gauteng, and workshops focus on improving teaching skills and methodologies; classroom management; and integrating technology into teaching and learning. Special attention is given to key learning areas: numeracy/Maths; language and literacy; Natural Science; technology; and leadership.

- Providing scholarships to highly talented students (from the group described as historically disadvantaged South Africans), enabling these students to enrol in schools of excellence, such as St Stithians College.

"Education is my passion, specifically Mathematics and Science education, and I am committed as Head of the Thandulwazi Academy to impact the lives of teachers and students as we create the future of our beautiful country" Mr Velaphi Gumbi, Head Of Thandulwazi

I am delighted to inform readers that I will be contributing half of the *Fieldbook* royalties to the Thandulwazi programme together with an additional contribution from John Catt Education Ltd such that 15% of all book sales revenue will be donated to this excellent initiative.

THE RISE SCHOOL, FELTHAM

INTRODUCTION

It meant a lot to me when, back in 2017, I was invited by Helen Ralston and her predecessor Sarah Roscoe, to visit The Rise School to work with their staff on assessment and feedback. It was early in my new career as a consultant, where my Learning Rainforest ideas were still taking shape and I was excited to be invited on the basis of some of the ideas I'd shared via my blog. In common with other schools in the *Fieldbook*, the school has had its fair share of challenging early wobbles – but is also now blessed with some amazing assets. As well as inspiring leaders – Helen's passion for her work never ceases to amaze me – they have impressive new buildings with the kind of specialist multi-sensory and soft-wall rooms and autism-specific equipment that mainstream schools just don't have. The staff are fabulous – and it's no easy task to assemble a team of people with the necessary subject specialisms to deliver a broad secondary curriculum as well as the dispositions needed to thrive in a special school context where classes are very small and students' learning needs are so complex.

(I'm thrilled to hear that Matt Pinkett, co-author of *Boys Don't Try?*, Twitter's @positivteacha, has joined the team.)

I've visited a couple of times now and as a mainstream teacher nearly my entire career, I found it eye-opening to see how I could find a class of five or six Year 8 students studying science or English, each with very individual autism characteristics that would not be remotely discernable to a casual observer. Teachers' knowledge of their students is so subtle. I was fascinated by the range of techniques deployed including, for example, 'deep touch pressure vests' that some students wear very tightly to reduce their anxiety levels.

The discussions I've had with Helen have been wide-ranging – something she alludes to in her case study introduction. The Rise

is 'Rainforesty' through and through. However, I'm very pleased she elected to focus on assessment because it's an area that a lot of schools are currently wrestling with and the Rise perspective throws light onto some complex ideas in a very interesting way. If you have a small cohort-school, where each class and year group has students with a wide range of learning needs and where expectations around following a mainstream curriculum are high, how do you begin to define 'success', 'excellence', 'progress'? There is no neatly solid set of standards to compare with and yet these students are entitled to be taught in a way such that allows them – and their parents – to understand what the standards are, where aspirations are high and challenges are authentic – just like anyone else.

I love Helen's account – blending her leadership thinking with the details around her assessment thinking in her typical reflective and research-informed style. Helen is one of the most well-read school leaders I've met as has been evident in our discussions. 'Ambitious about Autism' is a great name for the trust that The Rise belongs to and I think that comes through loud and clear in the case study.

PROFILE

Location: Feltham, West London

Type of Institution: SEND school for pupils with an EHCP for Autism

Roll/Age Range: 100, aged 4–18

Year Founded: 2014

Motto: 'Be Proud, Be Kind, Be Resilient'

Recent significant sports event/triumph: Carnegie Mental Health – Gold Award

Helen Ralston
Head of The Rise School

The Rise is a pretty unusual school occupying the middle space on a spectrum of provision between mainstream schools and our colleagues in SEND provisions who support young people with more complex or profound needs.

Opened in 2014, The Rise's vision is to deliver the national curriculum to age-expected outcomes and qualifications but within a highly specialist environment to allow pupils with autism to flourish and achieve. We place equal importance on achieving academic and social progress: balancing rigour alongside carving precious time in our curriculum for nine trips per year and lessons on mental health and wellbeing – a particular challenge for people with ASD.

PROFILE

We genuinely believe our school provides 'the best of both worlds!'

If you wandered around our school (and you should, we love visitors!) you would see classes of eight pupils accessing a curriculum you would recognise from mainstream: factorising brackets, analysing *An Inspector Calls* and doing practicals on force and extension in our Science lab. You might wander past a pupil who is taking a self-regulatory break outside the classroom. They might have a sensory toy or a timer. You might overhear a teaching assistant talking through a situation with a frustrated pupil, offering them the appropriate space to process their anger, perhaps our gym or rooftop garden with guinea pigs!

You would certainly witness calm and productive learning environments, The Rise has come on quite the journey to reach this point.

When it opened in 2014 the school faced a 'perfect storm' of challenges. This meant that the initial school development priority between 2015–2016 was to secure safe and respectful behaviour, alongside engaging lessons that pupils wanted to be in. By 2016, lessons as a distinct unit, were now successful. Therefore the focus shifted to joining individual lessons up into coherent terms and years and to begin to focus on assessment. Evaluation revealed that now pupils were experiencing highly successful 'years' but these weren't joining up across years – you might have a superb Year 5, but that wasn't built upon what you had learnt in Year 4, and It wasn't informing what you learnt in Year 6.

This is the point from which our case study is taken.

STUDENT: FINLEY

Age and Year Group: Year 8

Most recent:

School Trip: Clink Prison, London Bridge

Extra-curricular activity: Football and Board games

Science experiment: Balance and Forces

Book/Play studied in English Literature: *A Midsummer Night's Dream*

Arts project: We have been thinking 3D Paper Mache sculpture of food. My group made a large burger with multiple layers that we then painted it to make it look like our design.

Learning:

Subjects Studied: English, Maths, Science, Computing, Weaving Wellbeing, Citizenship, Yoga, PE, Food Tech, Music, Art, Swimming

Recent learning highlight: A recent learning highlight has been basketball in PE because I really enjoy playing basketball. I have good dribbling skills and enjoy working on improving my shooting.

The most stand-out/interesting/challenging topic you've studied at school: I really enjoyed learning about hockey because I'm good at hockey. I am able to control the ball well with the hockey stick and have a good understanding of team play and how to support my team-mates.

One of my favourite teachers: I enjoy lessons with Holger who teaches me Science because Science is one of my strengths.

A favourite feature of the school: One of my favourite things about The Rise is Golden Time (P6 on a Friday) where you get 45 minutes of free choice, if you've completed your homework.

STUDENT: JOJO (JONATHAN)

Age and Year Group: Year 6

Most recent:

School Trip: The last trip I went on was to Windsor Swimming Pool which was great. We also go to Crane Park to learn about nature and conservation every week.

Extra-curricular activity: On Mondays I go to cooking club.

Science experiment: We used light boxes to measure the angles of incidence and reflection.

Book/Play studied in English Literature: In English we have been doing story writing which was fun. We have recently read *Gangsta Granny* by David Walliams and *Hatchet* by Gary Paulse.

History topic: We are learning about the Ice Age.

Arts project: We are learning about the elements of art and different artists such as Picasso and Van Gough.

Learning:

Subjects Studied: English, Maths, Science, Computing, Weaving Wellbeing, PSHE, Yoga, Topic, PE, Music, Art, Swimming

Recent learning highlight: A recent piece of learning that I have really enjoyed was Maths 'Fluent in Five' which is where you need to use different techniques at the start of the lesson.

The most stand-out/interesting/challenging topic you've studied at school: I have really enjoyed learning at Crane Park and learning about the London Wildlife Trust.

One of my favourite teachers: I enjoy learning with Lee, Philly and Adam who are very kind.

A favourite feature of the school: My favourite thing about The Rise school is our school pets (guinea pigs Ginger and Spice) and having friends.

I love my school because I have kind friends and don't get bullied anymore.

ELLIE

STUDENT: ELLIE

Age and Year Group: 8, Year 4

Most recent:

School Trip: Science museum – it's so fun there
Extra-curricular activity: Cooking and Robots
Science experiment: I made elephant toothpaste
Book/Play studied in English Literature: *The Phantom Tollbooth*
History topic: The battle of Hastings
Arts project: I decorated a picture frame using pasta

Learning:

Subjects Studied: English, Maths, Science, Computing, Weaving Wellbeing, PSHE, Yoga, Topic, PE, Music, Art, Swimming
Recent learning highlight: Looking at the evolution of Mickey Mouse in animation.
The most stand-out/interesting/challenging topic you've studied at school: I really enjoyed learning about the Ancient Greeks in topic.
One of my favourite teachers: Sam and Lee because they have the best lessons and are super kind.
A favourite feature of the school: The playground is my favourite place to be at school.

CASE STUDY: AUTHENTIC ASSESSMENT: NOT FORCING SQUARE PEGS INTO ROUND HOLES

Title: Authentic assessment: not forcing square pegs into round holes

General Area: Assessment

Author: Helen Ralston, Head of The Rise School

The Learning Rainforest at The Rise

A significant number of Rainforest themes permeate our thinking and subsequent curriculum and assessment model. I could have written a case study on a range of Rainforesty aspects:

- How we went about selecting the content for the intended curriculum – a stimulating but also potentially overwhelming process
- The template we designed in order to capture C15: Specifying the Content
- How we're implementing K16: Teaching for Memory at The Rise
- The process of 'Establishing the Conditions' and 'Building the Knowledge' for the staff – the CPD process that has underpinned the entire rebuild

However, the area I wish to explore in greater depth is the issue of authentic assessment: how to allow different subjects to execute formative and summative assessment in ways that respect their unique disciplines but share a common understanding of the evidence; to as Tom puts it, generate 'feedback in the form most useful for a particular discipline, whatever that looks like' (p131).

Previous Assessment Procedures at The Rise

As explained above, and by no means a problem unique to The Rise, we realised that there was a lack of coherence between years in terms of the curriculum content we were delivering. This was matched by a fairly haphazard approach to assessment with teachers designing their own assessments to cover the material they had chosen to deliver over the previous half-term.

Authentic Assessment: The Rise's Journey

To address this, we made it a priority in our school development plan with these targets:

- The curriculum will provide clear pathways from KS1-KS4, enabling access to KS5 opportunities.
- Assessment will be purposeful, and skilfully used as, and to inform, learning opportunities at The Rise.

I engaged in a sustained research phase in order to ensure the model that would be created was 'evidence-informed.' The process for sharing with, and engaging, staff is detailed below.

CPD: A Tight Approach

Having pulled my thoughts into a model that approached clarity, I planned to launch it with the teachers on three separate 'Teacher Away Days' in March, May and June 2018. These days were a vital component in the rebuild process to ensure that staff had a common, rich CPD basis for this rebuild with time between sessions to complete follow up work and thinking.

A risk was that over the months of research, I had gradually come to an understanding of a range of concepts, ideas, terminology but that I may now 'blitz' the staff. Therefore, in February 2018 I began to drip feed short extracts from Dylan Wiliam, Daisy Christodoulou, Peps Mccrea, Andrew Percival, Carl Hendrick and Robin Macpherson – never more than a page or two. I modelled some of the key principles such as 'retrieval practice' by setting up low stakes formative quizzes for the teachers on the readings.

The table below summarises the Away Days and the content covered, most detail below is given to Away Day 3 which focused on assessment.

February 2018 onwards	**Drip feed key readings** with the purpose of familiarising staff with key concepts and terminology that would be explored in greater depth during the teacher away days.
March 2018	**Teacher Away Day 1** AM – Share the rationale for why we needed to create a centralised curriculum spine. PM – Work on developing the long term plans for each subject.
May 2018	**Teacher Away Day 2** AM – Share, justify and evaluate the long term plans created. AM – Share the rationale for the curriculum overview template that act as medium term plans that specify the key content for each unit. PM – Work on creating the curriculum overview templates.

CASE STUDY: AUTHENTIC ASSESSMENT: NOT FORCING SQUARE PEGS INTO ROUND HOLES

June 2018	Teacher Away Day 3
	AM – Share the rationale and evidence behind our assessment model, engage in CPD on assessment pillars: purpose, validity, reliability and value.
	PM – Work on creating formative and summative assessments for Autumn 2018 term.

CPD: Tight Principles

We began the third teacher Away Day by reading James Pembroke's *Tes* article 'Don't Drown in Data' – essential reading in my opinion. Pembroke's succinctly analyses assessment's place in the educational landscape between 1988 and current day: 'taking into consideration that schools had, since 1988, always been given a methodology of assessment [levels] and thus had no expertise in creating new assessment systems, was it any surprise that [once this methodology was removed] the assessment tools created were so often not fit for purpose?'

This provided a reassuring, non-judgemental platform from which I proposed that we would need to both re-think our assessment practices and engage in assessment-oriented CPD.

The Rise's approach to assessment is summarised in this diagram, which is 'on top' of a helpful diagram in Wiliam's Principled Assessment Design pamphlet:

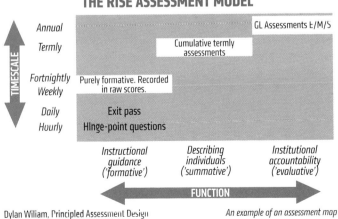

THE RISE ASSESSMENT MODEL

Dylan Wiliam, Principled Assessment Design

An example of an assessment map

There were some aspects of 're-thinking' that I had done in the creation of the above model. Therefore, I relatively quickly shared these changes and the rationale:

- We were ditching objective based tracking
- We were ditching the use of descriptors that are overlaid on top of raw performance such as 'beginning, developing, secure, extended'
- We weren't going to use a flight-path model

A central principle underpinning our new model was the deliberate divorce of summative and formative assessment products. Christodoulou argues hugely persuasively that by trying to get one assessment product to generate a useful formative consequence and a useful, reliable summative consequence it does neither well. Staff spent time on the Away Day reading extracts from *Making Good Progress*.

Furthermore, we spent time broadening our understanding of the functions of formative assessment:

1. To check something has been learnt/understood correctly in the first place
2. To prevent it from being forgotten over time
3. To become increasingly fluent/automatic in the execution of this piece of knowledge or skill

This third function links to another valuable point made by Christodoulou: getting pupils to repeatedly produce the complex 'end product' (mock-paperitis!) is not necessarily the most helpful form of practice in order to help them progress. Formative assessment can lend itself well to deliberate practice whereas summative assessments are more appropriately *generic* practice. Nick Wells summarises this clearly: 'There are, therefore, times when we need to drill our students in the really granular elements

of our subjects to be able to provide them with high impact, immediate feedback, and I believe, times when we need to allow them to play something more akin to the full match.'

Having unshackled formative and summative assessment, but understanding the burden that a summative assessment now shoulders (to produce a shared meaning across multiple contexts and audiences) then it is necessary our summative assessments are up to the job.

This meant introducing the team to the 'four pillars of effective assessment:' purpose, value, validity and reliability.

Three middle leaders had undertaken the Assessment Lead online CPD programme from Evidence Based Education over the course of 2017–2018 and therefore selected key messages to share with the wider teaching team.

In terms of improving our design of summative assessments, they zoomed in on the pillars of purpose and validity.

With regards to the latter, my colleague introduced the team to new learning on the concepts of 'construct irrelevant variance' and 'construct underrepresentation' – both of which put the validity of the inference you're trying to draw from the assessment at risk:

- Construct irrelevance is when the test assesses things that are not relevant to the construct – and example would be where overly wordy questions are hindering pupils from demonstrating their ability on the maths construct that you're intending to assess and draw inferences about.
- Construct underrepresentation is where the test is not assessing a wide enough range of the construct – this is why GCSEs are often conducted over multiple papers... six for the new combined Science!

CASE STUDY: AUTHENTIC ASSESSMENT: NOT FORCING SQUARE PEGS INTO ROUND HOLES

The teachers were given this checklist to aid the design of more robust summative assessments:

ASSESSMENT VALIDITY CHECKLIST:

1. Identify and write down the purpose/the end use of this assessement.
2. List the constructs/outcomes to be included in the assessment.
3. Decide the best tool:
   - 3.1 Identify if you're using a difficulty or quality model of assessment (or a mixture).
   - 3.2 Identify potential activities/questions for the construct you're assessing which are able to effectively measure a pupil's ability.
   - 3.3 Review the validity of your assessment by checking the above for construct irrelevance – is there anything that would distract/obscure their performance?
   - 3.4 Structure your assessment to capture a pupil's ability through a reasonable and ethical assessment with a balance of low and high order questions/accessible open wording for essay questions.

The afternoon, as well as subsequent directed meeting time, was dedicated to creating relevant formative and summative assessments.

Subject-specific execution: a loose approach

A generous allocation of tightly designed CPD time had generated shared understanding of the fundamentals of effective assessment. Whilst, of course, this would need to be revisited and deepened over time, I was pleased with the confidence with which staff were now talking about assessment and raring to apply it.

This stage was the danger zone – the moment when as a school leader I needed to stare down my (quite normal I think) urge for 'consistency' and allow teachers the space to apply the principles in a way that respected their subjects. It's clearly ridiculous to think that authentic, useful assessment will look the same in Art, History and Food Tech. It's clearly a source of frustration to be stifled by a system that is clearly incongruent with the core business of your subject… but nevertheless the school leader's thirst for consistency can be insatiable.

I remained steadfastly flexible and was subsequently pleased with how our different subject leads have created assessment models that are each different, but each clearly exhibiting an understanding of the principles we had covered in our training.

I take five different subjects as examples below. Please note that this 'formalised' formative assessment is, of course, in addition to the wealth of ongoing, organic formative assessment that you would expect to see in any classroom via questioning, instant feedback etc.

ENGLISH/HISTORY ASSESSMENT MODEL

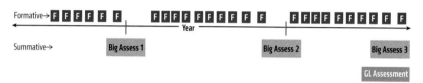

English and History – both subjects that assess with a qualitative model – have adopted a largely similar approach: weekly/fortnightly formative assessment that can take any format in order to generate genuinely useful, diagnostic information; summative assessments that are termly, each covering a larger domain of material so that they are cumulative. The assessment year concludes with a standardised assessment from GL which will allow us to do some benchmarking of our small, SEND cohorts against national age-related performance.

MATHS ASSESSMENT MODEL

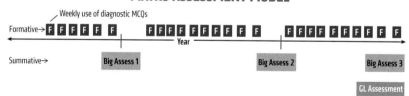

Maths differs from English in their formative use of Craig Barton's incredible diagnostic multiple choice questions every week. Equally, the design of their summative assessment will use the difficulty model.

SCIENCE ASSESSMENT MODEL

> Assessment doesn't look consistent across each subject. What is consistent is the understanding of the evidence underpinning each subject's assessment decisions.
>
> HELEN RALSTON

CASE STUDY: AUTHENTIC ASSESSMENT: NOT FORCING SQUARE PEGS INTO ROUND HOLES

I was originally uneasy about Science's use of 'end of topic' tests which I felt could provide the unhelpful *illusion* of long term learning because pupils performed well in a test immediately after having spent 5–6 weeks on that material. However, they have pre-planned weekly retrieval practice using a combination of Adam Boxer's retrieval roulette and Kate Jones's retrieval grids. Therefore they are mitigating against pupils forgetting material over the long term in their formative, rather than summative, assessments.

FOOD TECH ASSESSMENT MODEL

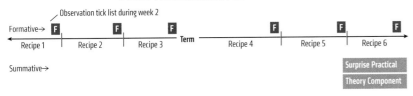

Over the course of a full term, pupils study 5–6 recipes spending two weeks on each recipe. Therefore the formative assessment is an ongoing observation ticklist that is used during the second week as pupils more independently execute the recipe. Carefully sequenced recipes allow pupils to revisit and consolidate similar concepts and skills.

The termly summative assessment has two components: a theory component and also a 'surprise practical' in which the teacher will select any of the previous recipes covered to be independently produced.

PE ASSESSMENT MODEL

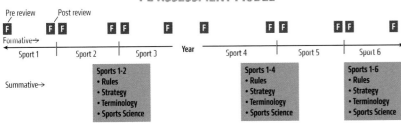

Each half-term there is a different focus sport. The formative assessment takes place through a pre and post review of pupils' competency at a range of sport specific components, knowledge and skills.

The summative assessment is paper based and covers rules, strategy, terminology and sports science questions. Each term it grows to become cumulative with questions on all preceding terms.

To conclude, assessment doesn't look consistent across each subject. What is consistent is the understanding of the evidence underpinning each subject's assessment decisions – the very act of creating these subject specific models demonstrates this. And that, for me, is enough. More than enough.

This approach to assessment isn't perfect; the more you open the Pandora's box of assessment the more you realise that perfection isn't an attainable goal. It's easy to be daunted by the complexity of the task and find yourself wishing for the good ol' days where you uncritically used the national curriculum levels. However, what I do know is that The Rise teachers are more thoughtfully, purposefully and skilfully using assessment to support pupils' learning. I do know that we're spending less time on the 'data decisions' (guess work!) that serve the needs of stakeholders beyond teachers; for parents and governors, we're keeping the time cost-benefit firmly in mind and being honest about what we can and can't infer from our data.

We will spend the next few *years* (at least) regularly refining our decisions about curriculum content and assessment; it's a long journey and we've only just begun – but it feels like the right direction of travel.

References

Christodoulou, D. Making Good Progress.

Pembroke, James. Don't Drown in Data. www.bit.ly/2IS5vFr

Ralston, H. A template to trigger and capture improved thinking about curriculum and assessment. www.bit.ly/2kdhqgH

Wells, Nick. Real vs. Gummy Assessment www.bit.ly/2kHlvce

Wiliam, Dylan. Principled Assessment Design (SSAT).

The drip feed authors/extracts mentioned:

1. Memorable Teaching – Peps Mccrea
2. Why Educate – Dylan Wiliam
3. Assessment Validity and Reliability
4. Memories are Made of This – Dylan Wiliam
5. Confessions of a Curriculum Leader – Andrew Percival
6. Extract from Memory & Recall Chapter of What does This Look Like in the Classroom – Carl Hendrick & Robin Macpherson.

Link to Learning Rainforest:

Chapter 5 – Assessment

LONDON ACADEMY, BARNET

INTRODUCTION

When Paddy McGrath, the London Academy Executive Headteacher, agreed to submit a case-study for the *Fieldbook*, I was thrilled. Paddy was, I think, just the second person to contact me to arrange some consultancy work after I left my job so, on a purely personal level, it means a great deal to me to include them here. Housed in one of the first purpose-built academy buildings, London Academy makes a big impression from the moment you arrive: a massive atrium runs along the main building; classrooms and offices and the library have glass walls creating a sense of openness. Meeting Paddy and his colleagues was inspiring and, on each of my visits, I came away bursting with ideas – it's a goldmine of innovation in the running of a large, complex comprehensive school.

Some ideas related to reading. Every tutor group in Year 7–9 started school half an hour early so that they read together every day: that's 150 minutes of reading time per week – extra! This was coupled to lunchtime tutor periods where reading interventions based on the Toe-to-Toe scheme took place for those that needed it. It's typical of their big thinking, removing logistical barriers to make things happen.

Another distinctive initiative was geared towards raising aspirations to go to university. The school organises a trip to a university for every student in Year 7–9, every year – a massive undertaking. They have excellent behaviour management systems and had nailed some of the logistical challenges with centralised detentions that I know lots of other schools struggle with. Student behaviour was now a strength in the school having previously been regarded as a challenge.

I was also impressed with their high frequency, low stakes systems for quality assurance: a process called '10 for 10' where 10 leaders would each drop in on 10 lessons by different teachers

with a focus on 10 identified students, one per lesson, every 10 days. That's 100 students and teachers in total. This was all mapped in advance but with leaders having the freedom to plan their set of 10. This meant they really knew what was happening in quite a systematic way. Teachers got feedback on the specific agreed focus for the cycle.

Paddy is one of those leaders who just quietly and humbly gets on with the job without shouting loudly about what he and his team do; the recognition comes largely from their own sense of achievement. But I think it's an inspirational school that lots of people could learn from. I certainly wished I had visited while still a Headteacher. In this case study, Paddy and Amy describe their thinking as their assessment system has evolved over several iterations.

PROFILE

Location: Edgware/Barnet

Type of Institution: Mixed Comprehensive

Roll/Age Range: 1500, aged 4–19

Year Founded: Opened as Academy in 2004 predecessor school 1896

Motto: 'Leaders for Tomorrow'

Principal: Alex Warburton

Paddy McGrath
Executive Head

Why we exist?

We exist to develop Leaders for Tomorrow in both our students and staff. Many of the families we serve have traditionally fallen short within the education system we seek to transform tradition by providing opportunities to develop them into Leaders for Tomorrow. As a community we are committed to the principle of continuous improvement, to keep getting better at getting better one iteration at a time. Our motto applies equally to staff and students and we are very proud to have developed Leaders at all levels and indeed lost many to other school and into their own Headships. Our work with children is underpinned by a belief that children should be seen as children deserving of Structure, Love and High Expectations.

There are opportunities such as university trips to Oxford and Cambridge, Brilliant Club and work experience.

IOANA BIVOLARU COZMA

I enjoyed learning about how the world develops in relation to economic and social priorities.

HAMEEM AHMED

STUDENT: HAMEEM AHMED

Age and Year Group: 15, Year 10

Most recent:

School Trip: Geography Field Trip to Stratford
Extra-curricular activity: Gym
Science experiment: Flame Test
Book/Play studied in English Literature: *Macbeth*

Learning:

Subjects Studied: English Language and Literature, Mathematics, Physics, Biology, Chemistry, Sociology, Business Studies, French and Geography

Recent learning highlight: During my lesson in science, the teacher demonstrated how specific junk food such as Doritos produces energy for the body during respiration. This enabled me to imagine how my body functions.

The most stand-out/interesting/challenging topic you've studied at school: I enjoyed learning about how the world develops in relation to economic and social priorities because it allowed me to understand how things are interconnected across the world and that things are not insular.

One of my favourite teachers: I enjoy lessons with Mr Lomas who teaches me Geography because he engages us in the lesson and makes the subject interesting and exciting.

A favourite feature of the school: I really like the diversity within our school community and the fact that everyone gets on with each other from different backgrounds. I also like the different types of tests that we do in subjects as they happen frequently but I like them as they force me to remember what I've learnt.

STUDENT: IOANA BIVOLARU COZMA

Age and Year Group: 15, Year 10

Most recent:

School Trip: Houses of Parliament
Extra-curricular activity: Speaking, Writing and Poetry Workshops
Science experiment: Metal Reactions
Book/Play studied in English Literature: *Macbeth, An Inspector Calls* and *A Christmas Carol*
History topic: Superpower Relations and the Cold War

Learning:

Subjects Studied: English Language and Literature, Chemistry, Biology, Physics, Maths, French, History, Psychology, Spanish

Recent learning highlight: There was an English lesson where we had to analyse and compare poems. I feel that this allowed me to express my creativity skills and at the same time practise essay writing. Through this lesson, I was able to see how independent I can be and how useful it is to trust your imagination.

The most stand-out/interesting/challenging topic you've studied at school: I enjoyed learning about health in Biology because I feel like it's a useful thing to know, especially nowadays, where teenagers tend to be oblivious towards mental, social and physical health.

One of my favourite teachers: I enjoy lessons with Ms Parekh who teaches me Science because she makes the lessons interesting. She teaches us a way that is comfortable to us, rather than following a step by step structure.

A favourite feature of the school: London Academy has great opportunities. This school focuses on preparing us for the future instead of just finishing school. There are opportunities such as university trips to Oxford and Cambridge, Brilliant Club and work experience.

STUDENT: LUCY EDWARDS

Age and Year Group: 15, Year 10

Most recent:

School Trip: Houses of Parliament
Extra-curricular activity: Speaking, writing and poetry workshops
Science experiment: Metal reactions on Bunsen burners
Book/Play studied in English Literature: *Macbeth, An Inspector Calls, A Christmas Carol*
History topic: Cold war and super power relations
Arts project: Magazine cover project

Learning:

Subjects Studied: English Literature, English Language, Maths, Chemistry, Biology, Physics, Spanish, History, Health and Social Care, Graphic Design

Recent learning highlight: In English language we learnt how to write stories and we wrote our own pieces based on our lives, experiences and emotions. We also learnt how to write cover letters for applying for jobs and work experience.

The most stand-out/interesting/challenging topic you've studied at school: I enjoy in biology learning about health, disease and different treatments and causes of disorders that affect parts of the body like the cardiovascular system and the causes of different cancers.

One of my favourite teachers: I enjoy lessons with Mr Wilson who teaches me English language and literature because he makes our lessons fun and interesting and we hold debates on different topics and he teaches us on current issues and gets us to write our own opinions on particular topics. We also get regular feedback that helps me improve.

A favourite feature of the school: My favourite part about the school is that we as a school accept everybody for who they are and we do not allow people to bully on any basis like race or religion. I also like the opportunities we get for things such as university trips and clubs such as debate mate and different sports teams.

STUDENT: OSKAR JARZA

Age and Year Group: 15, Year 10

Most recent:

School Trip: Trip to Houses of Parliament
Extra-curricular activity: Piano lessons
Science experiment: Chemical Flame Test
Book/Play studied in English Literature: *A Christmas Carol*
History topic: Cold War

Learning:

Subjects Studied: Core (Maths Science English RS), French, History, Computing, Media Studies

Recent learning highlight: French lesson where I felt that I really understood the conjugation of everything. An epiphany moment.

The most stand-out/interesting/challenging topic you've studied at school: I enjoyed studying/learning about electricity in physics as it explains how a large variety of things work in everyday life.

One of my favourite teachers: I enjoy lessons with Ms McKenzie who teaches me Media because her lessons are enjoyable and engaging.

A favourite feature of the school: Our school has a lot of revision classes and schemes like The Brilliant Club that give extra opportunity to higher achieving pupils. The school also organises a lot of trips to various universities in order for student to see what post-secondary education looks like.

In French, I felt that I really understood the conjugation of everything. An epiphany moment.

OSKAR JARZA

My favourite part about the school is that we as a school accept everybody for who they are.

LUCY EDWARDS

CASE STUDY: MOVING AWAY FROM OUR DEPENDENCE ON 'JUNK DATA'

General Area: Assessment

Authors: Amy Castle, Assistant Principal, and **Paddy McGrath**, Executive Head

For a number of years, we had a half termly whole-school assessment cycle. Staff entered either grades (GCSE & A Level) or sub-levels (Key Stage 3) alongside a judgement as to whether students were making Good, Appropriate or Not appropriate progress towards target grades. We reported this to students and parents half termly. This approach started back in 2001; attainment in the school was low at this point and we were classed as a school facing Challenging Circumstances. This status paved the way for us to become one of the first sponsored academies in 2004. The main driver behind the approach was to develop an aspirational culture within the school. However, the system over time became less effective as the culture strengthened, weaknesses developed in the quality of data collected. Assessments weren't necessarily standardised across a cohort and, in addition, inconsistencies of approach across and within subjects as to what constituted the grades or levels awarded meant we were collecting and analysing a lot of 'junk data'.

Although the approach had merit in developing the culture of the school alongside getting teachers thinking about assessments, it served little in terms of using data deliberately either to inform teaching between lessons or to deliver higher leverage feedback for students. We began changing our approach in 2015 through a series of iterations:

Iteration 1 2015:

We began our current journey having exhausted our excel skills with conditional formatting!

- Number of Assessment points: 6
- Content of assessment: Purely on what had just been taught
- Target Setting: Used FFT[1] to generate targets for KS4 and ALPs[2] for KS5 but no targets set for KS3.

We looked at planning backwards from either A level or GCSE, considering the curriculum skills/concepts/knowledge each student should master by the end of each year. We were clear that we wanted to have a curriculum that provided progression and not just the use of GCSE criteria at KS3. In addition we considered grouping these into subcategories similar to Attainment Targets within the national curriculum e.g. Maths; Number, Geometry and Reasoning & Algebra. The basis of each assessment would allow staff to assess against objective but then further across sub category as to how secure students were in each. This in practice was quite complicated and something that we started but didn't explore fully.

Iteration 2 2016

- Number of Assessment Points: 6
- Reporting: Percentage achieved, Ready to Learn Grade & Comparison with Average Percentage for Prior Attainment Band.
- Content of assessment was just on what had been taught

We kept with the principle of backwards planning and highlighting the curriculum skills/content and knowledge required for each Year. We collected just a percentage achieved on each assessment. As a way of benchmarking this we chose to consider the prior attainment of each student. This helpful in particular for KS3

---

1. FFT: Fischer Family Trust; a widely used UK data analysis tool using national attainment data comparing student outbaseline assessments to predict likely future outcomes.
2. ALPS is the A Level Performance System – another tool for post-16 students used to set aspirational outcome targets.

CASE STUDY: MOVING AWAY FROM OUR DEPENDENCE ON 'JUNK DATA'

students who we would have traditionally compared progress against target, but, as no targets are sets we wanted a simple way to benchmark individual scores.

The prior attainment of the school is significantly below the national average. We used Jesson bands[3] to group each Year group into quintiles to allow for comparisons to be made relative to not only the average for teaching group but also the average of prior attainment band. We were concerned about the 'age' of using the Jesson methodology as it was a bit dated but wanted to use an external anchor so as not to lower expectations on ourselves. As the new KS2 scores have come through we have used FFT to generate High. Middle and Low Prior attainment bands we then further split this to form six prior attainment groups. We do have a proportion of students who arrive without KS2 data so we sue a combination of Reading Age data and Teacher assessment to place them into a prior attainment band.

Iteration 3 2017

- Number of Assessment Points: 4

- Reporting: Percentage achieved, Ready to Learn Grade & Comparison with Average Percentage for Prior Attainment Band.

- Content of first three assessments were just on content taught over that teaching cycle. Fourth assessment was cumulative based on entire content of the year.

We introduced a clearer structure to the academic year with the year being split into cycles. The first three cycles have the following structure: Weeks 1–8 teaching of content. Week 9

assessment week and Week 10 re teach week. Cycle four 9 weeks of teaching and one week as assessment week. Limitations of this increased teacher workload of having all assessments in one week and planning for effective re-teach meant that quality was impacted.

Iteration 4 2018

- Number of Assessment Points: 3

- Reporting: Percentage achieved, Ready to Learn Grade & Comparison with Average Percentage for Prior Attainment Band.

- Content of each assessment is cumulative.

Moving this academic year to the leanest possible assessment structure. The move from 6 to 4 to 3 assessment points in the year to avoid 'junk data' which isn't used to inform teaching. Also allows time for teachers to cover a broad curriculum. Utilised a CPD day at the end of each assessment cycle to allow for assessing and planning for re teach week to ensure greater quality and consistency of practice across the academy.

The CPD days have also offered opportunities for collaborative planning in departments, so that colleagues can evaluate the impact of the curriculum taught that term. They have also been used for meetings with subject leaders where class data can be discussed, and actions agreed for re-teaching. Focus has been on 'higher-leverage' effective whole class feedback, rather than targets and actions for individual students in each class.

We have also spent time creating standardised assessments and conditions in each year group to increase the validity and

reliability of the data gathered (this was variable before). CPD has been used to train teachers to use summative and formative assessment effectively – e.g. an understanding of the difference between learning and performance; how to sample from the curriculum and agreeing clear structures for reteach lesson; how to consolidate core content throughout the year. CPD to support these days has included: clear structures for planning meetings and data meetings; opportunities to roleplay and practise conversations with colleagues; a framework for data analysis for each class; lesson structure for effective whole class feedback.

Assessments have been cumulative, so assessments will test content from the whole year, to encourage students to revise the 'core content' from each unit they study and view their curriculum as a 'whole' which builds their knowledge and skills each year, rather than a collection of disconnected units. We have tried to raise the profile of assessment week, introducing self-quizzing throughout the year and explicit teaching of effective consolidation and revision strategies, as well as providing space for quiet revision in the exam hall after school for all year groups (not just exam year groups).

The focus this year has been on using assessment to inform our planning and teaching, but as a single school we need to develop strategies which will help us to understand comparative attainment of each cohort. This is a challenge as a stand-alone academy. We also need to develop better ways to identify 'outliers' – students who are significantly underachieving early on in the curriculum and map better provision and support for these students.

---

3. A tool devised by David Jesson in the early 2000s whereby, instead of using whole cohort averages, cohorts are broken down into say five bands of prior attainment so that outcome measures can be seen in more detail relative to students' starting points.

CASE STUDY: MOVING AWAY FROM OUR DEPENDENCE ON 'JUNK DATA'

Iteration 5 2019

- Number of Assessment Points: 3
- Reporting: Percentage achieved, Ready to Learn Grade & Comparison with Average Percentage for Prior Attainment Band.
- Content of each assessment is cumulative.

We're keeping the same structure but we also want to:

- Develop better systems to intervene early with students who underachieve using the average percentage for prior attainment bands and create systems and structures which will help us to intervene and then track effectively. This will prevent the 'intervention/catch up culture' at GCSE.

- Develop the expertise of curriculum leaders so that subject experts can plan assessment and curriculum carefully to assess and consolidate 'core content' at each assessment point. Develop a shared language and expertise around effective assessment – reliability, validity, sampling which will enable subject leaders to have more meaningful conversations with line managers.

- Look at how we can better use assessment within lessons and between lessons to inform teaching – develop clear approaches to 'exit tickets' and the collection of raw data in-between assessment points. E.g. writing good multiple choice/knowledge questions and developing ways to help teachers use these efficiently to inform planning and feedback (without creating extra burden on workload).

- Explore possible collaboration with other schools to compare student attainment and progress with them.

Our approach to developing our assessment structure has been to focus upon making better use of formative assessment within and between lessons focussing upon feedback that provides the highest impact for the student. In a similar approach we have refined our approach to teacher development working with our ex-colleague Josh Goodrich from Oasis Academy Southbank we have worked with him in developing the online tool www.powerfulactionsteps.education. The tool helps teachers and coaches select high impact action steps designed to help teachers practise and perfect skills before using them in a lesson.

Link to Learning Rainforest:

- Our assessment structure supports the 'leanest possible tracking'

- Our assessment structure has been designed primarily to contribute to the learning process through feedback. The focus at each assessment point is to make inferences about student learning and use this to inform planning of the curriculum through reteach week and throughout the next term.

- Every lesson includes a retrieval do now to capitalise on the testing effect. We have ensured that 'quality model' subjects like English and History also include knowledge based recall questions as part of their assessment and feedback cycle.

- Three assessment points 'samples' from the curriculum taught to avoid 'teaching to the test' which often happened when assessments occurred every half term. Assessments are infrequent to ensure that teachers have the maximum time for teaching a broad curriculum.

- For summative tests, conditions are standardised across each subject.

- Next year we want to develop a clearer approach to formative assessment between the assessment points, collecting raw data and using this for responsive teaching.

- Removal of a requirement to 'mark every two weeks' to have subject leaders design 'feedback policies' which are suitable for their subject areas. The focus is on 'whole class feedback' rather than individual targets for individual students.

THE LEARNING RAINFOREST IN PRACTICE

BUILDING THE KNOWLEDGE STRUCTURE

EXPLAIN, MODEL, PRACTICE, QUESTION, FEEDBACK, ASSESS

K 1 EXPLAINING

K 2 MODELLING AND METACOGNITION

K 3 CHECK FOR UNDERSTANDING

K 4 PROBING

K 5 GO DIALOGIC

K 6 THINK, PAIR, SHARE

K 7 WHOLE-CLASS RESPONSE

K 8 MULTIPLE CHOICE HINGES

K 9 GUIDED PRACTICE

K 10 SAY IT BETTER

FEEDBACK AND REVIEW

K 11 VERBAL FEEDBACK

K 12 RESPONSIVE TEACHING

K 13 MARKING: KEEP IT LEAN

K 14 WHOLE -CLASS FEEDBACK

K 15 CLOSE THE GAP

K 16 TEACH FOR MEMORY

K 17 DAILY, WEEKLY, MONTHLY REVIEW

K 18 FACE IT

K 19 LEARNING BY HEART

K 20 HOMEWORK = GUIDED STUDY

ST ANDREWS INTERNATIONAL SCHOOL, BANGKOK

INTRODUCTION

I've known Roo Stenning for longer than anyone else featured in the *Fieldbook*. We worked together as young teachers and pastoral leaders at Holland Park School – an experience I describe in *The Learning Rainforest*. We both learned a lot in that environment. Roo then went off to Thailand and, 20 years later, he is still there, living and working in Bangkok, heading up the High School at St Andrews International. I subsequently met up with Roo at an IB conference in Singapore when I was working in Jakarta. Always passionate about his subject, geography, by then he was also a passionate advocate for the IB and, as his case study illustrates, that passion remains strong.

I had the great fortune of being able to visit St Andrews in the summer of 2018 when I delivered some training for the staff and ran a small conference based on the Learning Rainforest. I had some fabulous discussions about the research-informed elements of instructional teaching and the role of specified knowledge within the curriculum; this is always interesting with IB schools where there is an emphasis on inquiry in the language of the organisation.

Together with the more detailed student profiles, this case study is a superb account of the richness, depth and rigour the IB offers, with arts right at the heart. Of course there are issues around government policies and school funding but all caveats asides, for me the IB remains the international gold standard for what a holistic curriculum can be. Roo has done an excellent job linking his thoughts to the Learning Rainforest – the connections are clear, both in spirit and in the detail. Reading this makes we want to go back to school and do the IB – probably at St Andrews! It's a fabulous example of what 'exploring the possibilities' can mean.

Students are confident to express themselves freely, their questions are valued and teachers give them space for their own thoughts and ideas.

YEAR 10 STUDENT – TO INSPECTION TEAM

PROFILE

Location: Bangkok, Thailand

Type of Institution: International School

Roll/Age Range: 1900 students, aged 2–18

Year Founded: 2001

House Names: Akha, Karen, Lahu, Yao – Hilltribes from Northern Thailand/South-East Asia

Recent/Current School Production: Primary: *Annie*
High School: *Bugsy Malone*

Recent significant sports event/triumph: It was great that our Under 13 Girls and Under 15 Boys both won their BISAC (Bangkok International Schools Activity Conference) Basketball Tournaments in our first year of competing with at this new, higher level, against all the biggest international schools, both British and US curriculum, in the city.

Roo Stenning
Head of High School

We try, more than any school I know, to live up to our Mission Statement:

'Our mission is to provide an inclusive, international education in a safe, happy, supportive and stimulating environment, where all the needs of the individual learner are met. Students are inspired to be the best they can be, enabling them to become responsible global citizens.'

Since the school began, we have been a small, friendly school, where all students have been welcome. Every year we continue to expand and develop our provision for those students with additional needs, allowing students with an even greater range of needs to benefit from a St Andrews education.

It is very important to us both that meeting 'all the needs of the individual learner' also means meeting the needs of those students who are aiming for the very highest International Baccalaureate Diploma Programme scores, and the world's best universities, and that inspiring students 'to be the best they can be' also means inspiring them to be the best trumpet player, footballer and friend that they can be and is not just focused on academic attainment.

The school has grown significantly in recent years, especially since we opened our new High School site in August 2017, but our commitment to a happy and supportive environment, where teachers know and relate to students as individuals, understanding that teaching and learning depend on positive relationships, in which teachers always act as role-models to the students and the students are confident that the teachers always have their best interests at the heart of everything they do, has not changed.

STUDENT: MICHELLE SOH HUI XUAN

Age and Year Group: 16, Year 12

House: Yao

Learning:

Subjects Studied:

Higher Level: Economics, Geography, English Literature, Mandarin Chinese B

Standard Level: Maths, Biology.

Extended Essay:

- Subject: Economics.
- Topic: The impact of palm oil production in a state in Malaysia
- Reasons: As a Malaysian and as someone who grew up surrounded by palm trees, I am sympathetic towards the palm oil producers and local workers, whose lives are at stake if they become unemployed. At the same time, as someone who cares about the environmental sustainability, I am conflicted about my stance and would like to find out whether the drawbacks outweigh the benefits/ advantages of palm oil production and vice versa.

Most recent:

CAS/Extra-curricular activity: CAS:

Creativity: Organising the St Andrews' Model United Nations (STAMUN) conference. Sustainability Group leaders.

Action: I have enjoyed trying out yoga and fitness. I would like to take this opportunity to try other sports that I have no or limited experience in, such as rugby and boxing.

Service: The TT Club, which is a social club where students meet new people and interact with IB students who also help to informally mentor the younger students. Sustainability Group is looking to organise a trip to Taco Lake in partnership with Trash Hero Thailand for a trash clean up.

School Trip: Geography Internal Assessment trip to Khao Yai. The research question that was being investigated was about how river characteristics change downstream. Before the trip, students first had to come up with at least two hypotheses regarding a river's characteristic, to either prove or disprove the Bradshaw Model. During the trip, we worked in groups to collect data for measurements of the river's discharge, velocity, slope angle, etc. to be analysed afterwards.

Science experiment: For my group's Group 4 Project (another IBDP requirement), we came up with a model of a hydroelectric generator which could be installed in the pipes in the school, which would transform the kinetic energy of rainwater that falls on the school roof and turn the energy into electricity for the school to use. This project may save the school some electricity and is better for the environment as electricity can now be from a renewable resource.

Book/Play studied in English Literature: *Chronicle of a Death Foretold* by Gabriel Garcia Marquez

History/Humanities topic: Macroeconomic objectives and policies

Arts project: For Community Action Week, I helped out with an activity where we turned old, unused shirts into recycled cloth bags.

Recent learning highlight: One of my favourite high school experiences has been participating in the Scholar's Cup programme. The World Scholar's Cup is an academic competition that is split into four main components: essay writing, multiple-choice quizzes, team debates, and a team quiz. Last year, my team made it to all three rounds: regional, global, and the Tournament of Champions, which has been a highlight of my High School career because I can learn about subjects which I do not take for the IB, such as History,

in a fun way. I also enjoyed meeting people from all over the world during the global and final (Tournament of Champions) round.

The most stand-out/interesting/challenging topic you've studied at school: I enjoyed learning about the different historical, social, and cultural contexts behind the literary works that I have studied in Literature thus far, including the novels *Kitchen* by Banana Yoshimoto, *The Handmaid's Tale* by Margaret Atwood, *Persepolis* by Marjane Satrapi, *Perfume* by Patrick Suskind and so on.

One of my favourite teachers: I enjoy my lessons with Ms Libby who teaches me Geography because her teaching is balanced with a good mix of seriousness and fun, which encourages me to work hard and do my best in Geography.

A favourite feature of the school: The multitude and diversity of opportunities that are available. I have had many opportunities to explore and experience a variety of topics and activities, from attending a Student Leadership Conference in Vietnam back in 2017, to attending a UNICEF Student Summit in New York last summer.

Talent means nothing, while experience, acquired in humility and with hard work, means everything.

PATRICK SUSKIND IN PERFUME

STUDENT: ILESH NILESHKUMAR VORA

Age and Year Group: 17, Year 12
House: Akha

Learning:

Subjects Studied:

Higher Level: Maths, Physics, Chemistry, Economics
Standard Level: English Lang/Lit, Mandarin Ab Initio
Extended Essay:

- Subject: Physics
- Topic: Modelling Quantum Mechanics – Analysing Quantum Tunneling
- Reasons: I have always wanted to gain some intuition in the mind-bending field of quantum mechanics. And, some of my favourite sci-fi films have these quantum mechanics concepts.

Most recent:

CAS/Extra-curricular activity: CAS:

- Tutoring (Creativity) – My student, who studies at Mahidol University, scored a 4.9/5 in her Application of Calculus in Economics exam – she was at a D before I lent her a hand.
- Choir (Creativity): Performing in the Christmas concert
- House Team Captain (Creativity): Hosting the first House Assembly of the year, and the Teacher Karaoke Competition.
- Student Voice (Creativity, Service): Re-writing STAs Appropriate Use of Technology document
- Sustainability (Creativity, Service): Hosting Community Action Week
- Fitness (Action): I beat my deadlift record
- Track (Action): I have improved my stamina substantially
- Rugby (Action): Still in the learning curve...

School Trip: Service Week – School for the Blind

I get the opportunity of helping blind children for a week. This allows me to develop a side of me that has yet to be fully developed – patience and care.

Science experiment: Measuring chlorine concentration in swimming pools

Book/Play studied in English Literature: *1984* by George Orwell, *Chronicle of a Death foretold* by Gabriel Garcia Marquez

History/Humanities topic: Economics – Theory of Firm

Arts project: Choir Performance: Christmas Concert

Recent learning highlight: My Maths IA requires me to create an entirely new way of thinking. I am looking at Cartesian functions that are being projected onto a sphere. Trying to imagine this was very challenging, and so it forced me to use technology – GEOGEBRA – to program something that I was incapable of imagining.

The most stand-out/interesting/challenging topic you've studied at school: I enjoyed learning about polarization in Physics. This topic encapsulates the weirdness and the counter-intuitive nature of reality. Learning about this topic forced me to put some common-sense aside, and treat it like a baby learning the alphabet. The complexity and the concept's applicability really stood out to me.

One of my favourite teachers: I enjoy lessons with Mr Matt who teaches me Physics because of his child-like enthusiasm, and his ability to communicate effectively, making difficult topics a walk-in-the-park. Furthermore, the pace at which he makes us work is perfect – not too fast, and not too slow either. Lastly, his relevant tangents and Physics challenges keep me engaged at all times.

A favourite feature of the school: The dose of healthy competition between students, and seeing selflessness amongst many students not only strengthen my friendships but also encourages me to push myself, and bring others with me – there is a symbiosis between the students at school.

> **Selflessness amongst my peers does not only strengthen my friendships but also encourages me to push myself, and bring others with me.**
>
> ILESH NILESHKUMAR VORA

STUDENT: CHARLOTTE GANDOSSI

Age and Year Group: 17, Year 12 (Sj)
House: Yao

Learning:

Subjects Studied:

Higher level: French A Literature, English A Literature, Psychology
Standard Level: Math studies, Biology, Spanish B (online)
Extended Essay

- Subject: Psychology
- Topic: How different types of parenting will affect a child's behaviour, especially violent behaviour.

Most recent:

CAS/Extra-curricular activity:

Creativity: Planning our Service Week at Boon Choo Centre in Sattahip. I am part of the activity planning and the fundraising group.

Activity: I am part of the Varsity Touch Rugby Team and also play Community Touch Rugby on Monday nights.

Service: During holidays or weekends my family and I join a reforestation group, Green Event, to plant trees around Thailand. Every Green Event trip we plant trees through sling shots, as it helps us cover a larger surface.

School Trip: Pre-service week survey trip to Boon Choo Home, in Sattahip

Science experiment: My most recent science experiment would be my Biology Internal Assessment. It is a mix between Chemistry and Biology as there was titration and different types of chemicals involved.

Book/Play studied in English Literature:

English Literature:

- *Chronicle of a Death Foretold* by Gabriel Garcia Marquez

> **One of my favourite features of St Andrews school is the wide diversity in students ... The school does a great job at making everyone feel included.**
>
> CHARLOTTE GANDOSSI

STUDENT: CHARLOTTE GANDOSSI

French Literature:

• *Chronique d'une mort annoncée*, Gabriel Garcia Marquez

Chronicle of a Death Foretold is originally written in Spanish, and translated into English, French and other languages. I find that it is easier to read *Chronicle of a Death Foretold* in French, as Spanish and French have a similar sentence structures.

History/Humanities topic: Psychology:
In Higher Level we are learning about Human relationships and the social responsibilities whereas in Standard Level we are learning about the cognitive approaches to understanding behaviour.

Recent learning highlight: My favourite lesson is Spanish online, with Senora Revalyn. I enjoy it as I can work at my own pace and it is a different atmosphere to having classes in a typical classroom.

The most stand-out/interesting/challenging topic you've studied at school: Personal connection to the language and Spain, as my grandfather spent his last couple years in Spain. Spanish is the class I stand out the most, as I get to show the love I have for the language. I believe that I stand out in Spanish as it is similar to French.

One of my favourite teachers: I enjoy lessons with Mr Jean-Claude who teaches me French because it makes me feel at home. French is my first language and I was enrolled in a French school until I moved back to Thailand in Year 9.

A favourite feature of the school: One of my favourite features of St Andrews school is the wide diversity in students, from kids who do not come from an English speaking countries and do not speak English, to kids with special needs. The school does a great job at making everyone feel included.

CASE STUDY: THE IB DIPLOMA PROGRAMME AT ST ANDREWS

General Area: Curriculum Design

Author: Roo Stenning, Head of High School

The UK's Department for Education recently launched its Consultation on post-16 qualifications that include plans to withdraw public funding in England for 'qualifications that overlap with T Levels or A Levels', which they want to become the 'qualifications of choice for 16- to 19-year-olds'.

As you have seen from the student profiles above, the IB (International Baccalaureate) Diploma Programme is our 'qualification of choice' and the foundation upon which we have built our Senior Studies (Years 12 and 13) programme – Our tenth cohort of IB Diploma Programme students are currently taking their final exams.

The IB Diploma Programme ensures a broad and balanced education for all students until Graduation and entry to university, with students studying subjects from six subject groups, as shown in the diagram below, still called the Hexagon by many experienced IB Diploma Programme teachers. All students must study two Literature and/or Language courses, a Humanities subject, a Science and Maths, with the sixth subject being either an Art or an additional Language, Humanities or Science course. Most students study three subjects at Higher Level (HL) and three at Standard Level (SL), but some, like Ilesh and Michelle, chose to study four subjects at HL.

CASE STUDY: THE IB DIPLOMA PROGRAMME AT ST ANDREWS

Within this framework a huge amount of flexibility is possible, as you can also see from the student profiles, with Ilesh, Michelle and Charlotte focusing on the Sciences, Humanities and Languages respectively, but also studying subjects that they would be very unlikely to be studying alongside these in a three or four A-Level model, with our profiled Scientist also reading Chronicle of a Death foretold and studying Mandarin and our profiled Economist/Geographer and Linguist also studying Maths and Biology.

As well as these six subjects, all students are required to complete the three elements of the Diploma Programme Core: Creativity, Activity, Service (CAS), a 4000 word Extended Essay and Theory of Knowledge (TOK).

Creativity, Activity, Service (CAS) means that all students are involved in a huge range of extra-curricular activities, whether in school, on trips or outside school in evenings and weekends, challenging themselves and planning, reviewing and reflecting thoughtfully on both outcomes and their personal learning. While the Creativity (see below) and Activity projects are extremely valuable, and Ilesh, Michelle and Charlotte illustrate the huge range of different projects that our students are involved in, having all students committed to Service Learning is fundamental both to the IB's mission 'to create a better world through education' and our 'Students are inspired to be the best they can be, enabling them to become responsible global citizens'. This week all three students are preparing both for their End of Year 12 exams and for Service Week the following week, during which all Year 12 students work on a Service Project that they have been fundraising for all year, either in Bangkok or around Thailand.

The 4000 word **Extended Essay** is a real challenge but one that enables students to investigate a topic of special interest to them, either related to one of their six subjects or based in World Studies, which allows them to approach a topic of global significance, illustrated in a local context or contexts, using an interdisciplinary approach. Students work very independently on their Extended Essays, meeting with their supervisor for three reflection sessions including a final viva voce, and this is excellent preparation for their future lives as undergraduates.

Finally, **Theory of Knowledge** asks students to reflect on the nature of knowledge, and on how we know what we claim to know, especially in their other Diploma Programme subjects. The subject is organised around discussions of how eight different ways of knowing (WOKs) – language, sense perception, emotion, reason, imagination, faith, intuition and memory – work in eight different areas of knowledge (AOKs) – Maths, Natural Sciences, Human Sciences, History, The Arts, Ethics, Religious Knowledge Systems and Indigenous Knowledge Systems – with students assessed through an oral presentation, in which they apply their TOK thinking in the exploration of a knowledge question extracted from real life situation, and a 1600 word essay, in which they show their TOK thinking skills in the discussion of a more conceptual prescribed title. The May 2019 prescribed titles were as follows:

1. 'The quality of knowledge is best measured by how many people accept it.' Discuss this claim with reference to two areas of knowledge.
2. 'The production of knowledge is always a collaborative task and never solely a product of the individual.' Discuss this statement with reference to two areas of knowledge.
3. Do good explanations have to be true?
4. 'Disinterestedness is essential in the pursuit of knowledge.' Discuss this claim with reference to two areas of knowledge.
5. 'The production of knowledge requires accepting conclusions that go beyond the evidence for them.' Discuss this claim.
6. 'One way to assure the health of a discipline is to nurture contrasting perspectives.' Discuss this claim.

All of this is underpinned by **the IB Learner Profile**, shown in the centre of the diagram above, which aims to develop students, and teachers, who are Inquirers, Knowledgeable, Thinkers, Communicators, Principled, Open-minded, Caring, Risk-takers, Balanced and Reflective. Teaching is inquiry based, with a strong emphasis on students finding their own information and constructing their own understandings, focused on conceptual understanding, with clear links to both local and global real-life contexts and examples, and emphasises collaboration, both between students and between students and teachers.

While the IB Diploma Programme is demanding, our commitment to inspiring students 'to be the best they can be' and our belief that all students can benefit from elements of the programme means that each year the vast majority of our Year 12 students will begin on the full IB Diploma Programme as described above.

Our commitment to being inclusive and meeting 'all the needs of the individual learner' does not end at IGCSE, however, and we guarantee all of our students a pathway to Graduation, and are therefore responsible for creating the conditions that enable every student to succeed at post-16 qualifications. Each year some students begin with a timetable made up of a combination of IB Diploma courses and a growing range of BTECs, with one of our Five Year Plan Working Groups currently investigating the introduction of the International Baccalaureate (IB) Career-related Programme (CP) which more formally combines IB Diploma courses with a different CP Core and career-related study.

Why would that not be any school's 'qualification of choice'?

ROO STENNING,
HEAD OF HIGH SCHOOL

CASE STUDY: THE IB DIPLOMA PROGRAMME AT ST ANDREWS

Whatever non-Diploma pathway they follow, these students will always be fully involved in Creativity, Activity, Service, both 'enabling them to become responsible global citizens' and, as the IB's Mission Statement says, 'to develop inquiring, knowledgeable and caring young people who help to create a better and more peaceful world through intercultural understanding and respect.'

Why would that not be any school's 'qualification of choice'?

Link to Learning Rainforest:

- Plantation/Rainforest analogy – school culture.
- Building the knowledge structure
- Exploring possibilities

Tom discussed the IB Diploma Programme in several places in *The Learning Rainforest*:

'It's an exceptional curriculum in my view, combining rigour and depth with breadth. The Creativity, Action, Service programme and Theory of Knowledge components ensure that strong core values and critical thinking are interwoven with the subject content; the curriculum whole really is greater than the sum of its component parts. I loved it.'

I believe that the IB Diploma Programme, especially as it is enhanced at St Andrews, is a great balance between the Plantation and the Rainforest, and so leads to a balance between Building the knowledge structure and Exploring possibilities at a number of levels.

The Diploma Programme provides both an over-arching structure, in terms of both the 'Hexagon' and the Core and in individual subjects, with clear expectations from the IB of the content to be taught, and the philosophy and pedagogy, and ends with a series of rigorous exams, but there is also a huge amount of

freedom, both for students and teachers. Within this structure, students can choose from a huge variety of subjects, in different combinations and at Higher and Standard Level, and have a great deal of freedom, in both their Internal Assessments in individual subjects and in their Creativity, Activity, Service (CAS), their Extended Essay and their Theory of Knowledge (TOK) essay and presentation, to really construct their own Diploma Programme, as well as their own understandings, as they move through the two year programme, enhanced by the IB's emphasis on inquiry, local and global real-life contexts and examples and collaboration described above.

As Tom also wrote in *The Learning Rainforest*, in a Rainforest school, 'Learning and achievement are recognised in the widest possible sense. It is understood that learners will have all kinds of talents and skills, personal goals and interests and in the Rainforest, these all have value. The curriculum has embedded within it a layer of learning that makes teachers and students focus on dispositional, attitudinal development that enables them to self-nourish their intellectual and emotional lives.'

Creativity, cultural capital and 'the most challenging intellectual experiences a student can have'. Definitely worth five hours a week.
ROO STENNING
HEAD OF HIGH SCHOOL

To develop inquiring, knowledgeable and caring young people who help to create a better and more peaceful world through intercultural understanding and respect.
IB MISSION STATEMENT

PENRICE, ST AUSTELL, CORNWALL

INTRODUCTION

Located just up the hill from the historic Charlestown with its famously well-preserved 18th century Georgian harbour, Penrice Academy is a great school, emanating a kind of self-confidence that comes from having a stable, experienced staff team and a clear sense of purpose. I made my first visit to deliver a Saturday training session on curriculum design for middle leaders at Penrice and some of their partner schools. On arrival you are greeted by walls of huge photographs, both outside and inside, that project the image of a lively active school; this is a place where things happen; where the opportunities are fabulous. As I arrived, a group of students were setting off on a Duke of Edinburgh expedition with some of the staff.

During the training we discussed the Learning Rainforest concepts of Mode A and Mode B teaching, the various ways of delivering a knowledge-rich curriculum with built-in stretch and challenge, and exploring the 'hinterland' that weaves core concepts together into richer, more cohesive whole. Returning six months later, it was fascinating to work more closely with some teams to see how their curriculum thinking had taken shape – linking their ideas on paper to what we saw in the classroom. Led by Lucy, Jenni and Rebecca, the curriculum has developed superbly. All three accounts communicate a deep desire to push the school forward with an earnest and honest process of self-reflection providing a starting point.

It's difficult to summarise but examples that impressed me included the development of a Penrice maths mastery model built around an anchor problem for each lesson, a process of students journaling their learning – an amazing kind of metacognitive diary – and some lovely contextual references, such as the Babylonian calendar and its link to 360 degrees in a circle. In science, they have established a set of wonderful knowledge-rich topics to hang the content from – such as Arctic exploration. Across the curriculum, they have established an excellent problem-solving feedback process called 'over to you' that compels students to think hard about areas for improvement, rather than having it spelt out for them every time. There's a lot more going on but the general spirit is one where teachers are continually seeking to deepen their students' curriculum experience in interesting, innovative ways, in keeping with their overall values and ethos. It's incredibly exciting and rewarding hearing how the Learning Rainforest has supported Penrice on its journey.

PROFILE

Location: St Austell, Cornwall

Type of Institution: Mixed Comprehensive

Roll/Age Range: 1400, aged 11–16

Year Founded: 1950

Motto: 'Every child succeeds. Every child is valued. Every child is challenged. Every child is supported'

Recent/Current School Production: *The School of Rock*

Recent significant sports event/triumph: 8.30–3.00, 1150 students on the school playing fields for a spectacular sports day. All included in events ranging from Boules to archery to staff student relays.

Notable quirks/alumni: Every year we teach 290 Year 11 students how to ballroom dance. They learn eight classic dances and during their Year 11 ball they are very proud to show off their skills.

Lucy Gambier
Vice Principal

Penrice Academy is an absolute pleasure, with one overwhelming strength: The students are fabulous!

We are a large oversubscribed secondary school with a truly comprehensive intake. We work incredibly hard to provide a well-rounded holistic education for all our students. We are very proud of our school's fundraising ambitions, last year raising over £15000 for Cornwall Hospice and previously raising over £25000

for a small village school in Africa. At these moments that you see the whole school community working together towards one purpose and one goal that you, see the school at its very best!

We are very proud of our exceptionally high expectations of students and staff. At times this can alienate some parents but it allows all teachers to teach their subjects, with joy and passion. We offer an extensive support structure for students, parents and staff to enable all to be ready for the challenges which life can and does bring.

We inspire all our students to be aspirational for their future and to enjoy the opportunities that Penrice Academy offers. We encourage all students to take part in Penrice Plus: a diverse range of extra-curricular activities every Wednesday from Debating to Board Games, from The Farm to Boat Building. At the end of the summer term, we see all students exploring new horizons, locally, nationally or internationally during Curriculum Enhancement week.

I must confess I was concerned as Billie isn't the most engaged pupil but his teachers were encouraging as well as constructive with their feedback. Billie was really glad he came and it was good for him to hear that the world isn't against him! Thank you all very much!

YEAR 7 PARENT FOLLOWING PARENTS EVENING

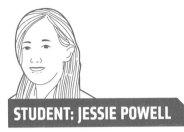

STUDENT: JESSIE POWELL

Age and Year Group: 15, Year 10

Most recent:

School Trip: Local college visit on Monday, we are going on another one tomorrow. We also all went to Universities recently.

Extra-curricular activity: I played in the school cricket team last week.

Science experiment: We did an exo/endothermic reaction experiment.

Book/Play studied in English Literature: We are currently studying *An Inspector Calls.*

History topic: We are currently studying Elizabethan society

Learning:

Subjects Studied: English, Maths, Triple Science, Spanish, History and Catering

Recent learning highlight: In History we were learning about how Britain changed after the Spanish Armada. It was great because we did a variety of tasks, all linked to GCSE questions and techniques. We had to think hard and I really feel I can succeed at these questions.

The most stand-out/interesting/challenging topic you've studied at school: I enjoy studying History because it explains why things are as they are in the modern world and how our society has formed to be what it is today.

One of my favourite teachers: I enjoy lessons with Miss Oddy who teaches me Spanish because she is enthusiastic, she makes the lessons interesting and one lesson is never the same as the next.

A favourite feature of the school: The different sporting opportunities that you can do. You can try completely new ones all year round. It is an important part of the school and what it offers students.

STUDENT: JED SCRACE

Age and Year Group: 12, Year 7

Most recent:

School Trip: Big Bang festival in Exeter

Extra-curricular activity: Painting and drawing techniques after school on a Thursday

Science experiment: Bottle rockets – ours went the furthest!

Book/Play studied in English Literature: *Roof toppers*

History topic: We are doing our own project at the moment. I am doing Roman entertainment.

Arts project: We are looking at two artists and using their techniques in our own work.

Learning:

Subjects Studied: Maths., English, Science, Drama, Art, Catering, Geography, History, PE, French, Class, Computer Science

Recent learning highlight: We play a catchphrase game in Maths, it helps us learn in a quick way and helps us to remember things we did before and helps it to stick in our heads.

The most stand-out/interesting/challenging topic you've studied at school: I enjoyed learning about cells in Science because it is interesting to learn about the things in our body, that there are different types and different sizes.

One of my favourite teachers: I enjoy lessons with Mr Smith who teaches me Maths because he is easy to learn stuff with and does fun activities.

A favourite feature of the school: Geography is brilliant because it is all about things that we do in our everyday life. I have learnt about topics that make sense of things in my world.

CASE STUDY: MOVING AWAY FROM PROGRESS 8

General Area: Curriculum Design and Timetabling

Author: Lucy Gambier, Vice-Principal

Over the past five years working as a Vice Principal (Academic) I have been very focused on students' outcomes, responding to the accountability measures of Progress 8 that were introduced alongside the new reformed GCSEs introduced from 2016. This pushed our school towards only teaching subjects that featured on the DFE approved list and supporting teachers to meet the demands of the new specification examinations.

However, over the past 12–18 months, we have broadened our thinking around student outcomes, and as we start to develop our thinking and our understanding, education has become more exciting, more relevant and more meaningful. Reading *The Learning Rainforest*, the evolution of the Ofsted framework and having Tom in for a Super Saturday (CPD days for middle and senior leaders across our teaching school alliance) has given us the knowledge and understanding to begin on a journey as a school to break away from the unnecessary constraints that we had around our students. We are very excited to be on the beginning of a journey that allows us to offer the very best for each of our students.

Link to Learning Rainforest:

Hinterland knowledge is a real driver in developing the understanding of our teachers and middle leaders.

Thinking with a blank canvas about the purpose, the importance and the fundamentals of each subject as a unique learning experience.

Education becomes more exciting, more relevant and more meaningful.
LUCY GAMBIER
VICE-PRINCIPAL

I have learnt about topics that make sense of things in my world.
JED SCRACE

We had to think hard.
JESSIE POWELL

137

CASE STUDY: RAISING ASPIRATIONS THROUGH AN EXPERT CURRICULUM

Title: 'Raising aspirations through an expert curriculum' at Penrice Academy

General Area: Curriculum Design/ CPD

Author: Mrs Rebecca Challis, Extended Leadership team: Curriculum and Head of Geography

At Penrice Academy I was tasked with the role of reviewing and developing the school curriculum; our 5-year journey. I attended an ASCL conference based on new and old thinking about curriculum design and of course read up on Amanda Spielman's thoughts and Ofsted's recent viewpoints and documents on how the curriculum will be judged.

At Penrice however, I felt that it was more about our story, about our geographical context and what we wanted for our students. Our school is situated in a coastal town with high levels of poverty and the town itself lacks vision. I think therefore many of our families have low aspirations for themselves and their children. The curriculum we offer has to be right for them, to tackle these issues.

My research involved reading books on how children learn, such as Arthur Shimamura's book *MARGE*[1] and *Understanding how we learn* by Sumeracki and Weinstein[2]. I also follow; among others, Spielman and Tom Sherrington on Twitter. It was Tom's book *The Learning Rainforest* that really gave me clarity of thought and helped me to design an 'intent, implement and impact' programme for the school. (Ofsted)

Penrice has a very productive team of teachers who work hard and who care very deeply about the students that attend. The heads of department teamwork together regularly to discuss whole school issues such as teaching and learning, marking and feedback etc. and now we felt ready to discuss the curriculum.

I needed to first look at the current offer. I used the curriculum plans that were on our website. These it seemed were just lists, tables of 'stuff' to be taught. We needed to go deeper, to actually think about what we wanted Penrice students to learn and why. Some departments had begun changing their plans. English, for example, had already reviewed their offer and had created an inspiring range of exciting topics and learning. Science had spruced up their KS3 curriculum so that it inspired a love of science and exploration. I wanted other departments to start thinking about their plans in the same way.

---

1. Shimamura, A. (2018)
2. Sumeracki, M. et al (2018)

As part of the process, I wanted to create a strapline for the school. I asked for input from Senior Leaders, Heads of Department and the Headteacher. I set them a task entitled 'what is the point of' and they had to write down why their subject/ school was important. I think this helped to set the scene and gave them the motivation and passion needed to then think more deeply about their subject and its place within the whole school learning environment.

Having received these and of course rewarded the winner with a bottle of wine, I worked closely with our vice principal and of course involved the HODs in coming up with our strapline: 'Raising aspirations through an expert curriculum'. It took some time and I think I did lose my way at one point having been overwhelmed with so many different viewpoints.

On reading Tom's book and listening to his CPD I felt more focussed and created a CPD event for all teachers and HODs to attend which enabled them to reflect on their current provision, RAG-rate it (red-amber-green) and really think about the 'what' and the 'why'. I gave them time to reflect and time to plan forward.

My next steps are to review the curriculum using some of the Ofsted statements to support this process. I will work with HODs to do some learning walks, work scrutinies and to gather student voice responses. I would love to see Penrice become a model of excellence where deep thinking about our curriculum can be seen clearly in lessons and in the progress and ultimately learning / knowledge of our students when they leave in Year 11.

Link to Learning Rainforest:

For me *The Learning Rainforest* gave a clear overview of the idea of a knowledge-based curriculum and how it could be achieved.

I was especially inspired by this: 'School cultures need to feel liberating, invigorating and inspiring' and 'This is what it should feel like to be a great teacher...a designer of great learning.' I think that this should rekindle every teacher's passion about their expertise, their knowledge and how this can be developed in the children sat in front of them every day.

I used this in my CPD session to get everyone thinking about the importance of the curriculum journey. 'Great teachers design the curriculum based on a deep understanding of the learning process. Great teachers design lessons to MAXIMISE the opportunity for students to understand concepts, develop skills and deepen their knowledge.'

I ensured that the HODs and staff understood that curriculum design therefore needs thought, deep thinking, discussion and planning. It should be a team process whereby all teachers have an input. This is why my CPD allowed each individual time to think about this: I asked them to think about their 'subject guarantees'. 'What would you include in the teaching of your subject?' I felt it was important that they could and may want to bring in some 'hinterland' knowledge into their teaching such as the context of 'Charge of the Light Brigade' or the industrial revolution when teaching about economic change in the UK. They may feel it important to teach about the little ice age when doing 'A Christmas Carol' or Leonardo de Vinci when teaching about the heart in science. The idea of hinterland knowledge really struck a chord with me as a HOD because it made me question not only my own hinterland knowledge but also my team's. Were they expert enough to teach what I want them to teach and, if not, what was I going to do about it? How would this impact on my curriculum design and ultimately lessons taught?

CASE STUDY: RAISING ASPIRATIONS...

During the CPD session the staff went on to answer a series of questions based on Tom's thoughts on curriculum design. I felt this part was particularly challenging yet the staff responded confidently due to the preparation we had done. The final part of the session was when HODs could go onto evaluate their curriculum and really unpick their journey and think more deeply about the 'what, when and why'. I feel that using the text and quotes, questions and ideas from the book supported them. I had great feedback from this part of the session and many HODs felt this was time well spent.

I have met each HOD since the session to talk through their ideas and thoughts. They are now tasked with the creation of a vision for their curriculum and of course an updated and 'expert' based curriculum plan.

Use every opportunity to share our cultural capital.

JENNI ODDY
ASSISTANT PRINCIPAL

Your specialism is very important. We are not teachers in a generic nebulous sense but are teachers of specific knowledge and skills.

MRS REBECCA CHALLIS
EXTENDED LEADERSHIP TEAM:
CURRICULUM AND HEAD OF
GEOGRAPHY

We at Penrice are indeed taking the student on a journey to expertise.

MRS REBECCA CHALLIS
EXTENDED LEADERSHIP TEAM:
CURRICULUM AND HEAD OF
GEOGRAPHY

CASE STUDY: DEVELOPING CULTURAL CAPITAL

General Area: Teaching and Learning/CPD

Author: Jenni Oddy, Assistant Principal. Lead of Teaching and Learning and CPD.

Something that struck a chord with me during a CPD session run at our school by Tom, based on *The Learning Rainforest* was the concept of cultural capital and the gaps in student experience. Reading the book cemented this for me, as it was a reoccurring theme throughout. As a rural school in Cornwall we are a long way geographically from pretty much everywhere; this means that the experiences of our students are often limited by living where they do.

My brain started processing the potentially enormous impact that actively developing cultural capital in our teaching and curriculum could have on our students. The book references that one of the challenges teachers and school leaders face is to address the layer of inequality for disadvantaged students. I feel our personal challenge as a school is to create experiences for our young people through our curriculum design and the delivery of it, which allow them to experience the same things as a student living in a multicultural city; ensuring the best possible outcomes for each and every one of them. I have a staff body with a wealth of 'life experience'. It is time to tap into that!

My first step was to drop into lessons with this as my focus. I saw some brilliant things as always, but I was struck by how much we, and I absolutely include myself in this, assume knowledge. We teach our curriculum content really well, but we regularly miss opportunities to expose our students to cultural capital.

Next, I closely scrutinised my own teaching. To me it is important to lead by example and so my practice was my next 'starting point'! Looking at my teaching objectively, I saw myself assuming students had a certain level of understanding of Spanish culture, geography, climate, history and an inbuilt understanding of common grammatical structures and rules. Unsurprisingly my students did not have this knowledge. I built a series of lessons where I included cultural capital and hinterland knowledge at appropriate intervals. On adapting my own teaching to include these elements, knowledge, motivation and progress all increased. My Year 9 students had some interesting discussions about the Spanish education system and students then used this knowledge in a GCSE style question, making their work far more creative and gaining them more marks than previous pieces of writing in school.

So, having done my research around the school, experimented in my own classroom to gain some evidence, our next steps are to develop a cultural capital CPD programme for all student facing staff aimed at closing the gap for our students. Tom is continuing to work with us and this will be a focus for some whole staff training followed by workshop sessions during the year to revisit and embed our practice.

Link to Learning Rainforest:

- Building the knowledge structure
- Exploring possibilities.

NORTHAMPTON PRIMARY ACADEMY TRUST (2 PRIMARIES)

INTRODUCTION

The idea for this two-in-one case study came from Tom Rees, erstwhile Education Director of NPAT and former Headteacher of one of the featured schools. Using the Learning Rainforest structure as a guide, it showcases some of the workings of an excellent multi-academy trust and the way common ideas take different form in schools at different stages of their development.

I came across Tom, Anna and NPAT through different routes. Tom is another fabulous teacher-author, one of several featured in the *Fieldbook*. He has been one of my go-to sources for insights about primary education for some time; his 2018 book *Wholesome Leadership*[1] provides a superb guide to running any school in what I'd regard as a true 'Rainforest' spirit. The book's key message is embedded in the tagline: the heart, head, hands and health of school leaders. I recommend it strongly. It's no surprise that Tom has now moved onto work full-time with Ambition Leadership, where his expertise will influence emerging leaders far and wide.

I met Anna, rather coincidentally, when we were both involved in supporting the visit of some Chinese teachers from Jiangsu province. Anna ran a brilliant, highly interactive drama workshop for the visitors at the Lings Primary School – a school which had a strong tradition of using drama in the curriculum and is now another member of the NPAT family.

Last year I was invited to meet Tom and Anna, with CEO Julia Kedwards, at the central NPAT offices to discuss some of their work around curriculum and assessment and then to deliver some cross-MAT training on the Rosenshine principles. I was impressed with their determination to work with the schools through a balance of disseminating the strong ideas and beliefs held at the centre with respect and recognition for each school's strengths and need for autonomy. I think this comes across in the different responses provided by Sarah and Joanne in the respective accounts of the Rectory Farm and Simon de Senlis stories. For me, the spirit at work at NPAT characterises exactly how a multi-academy trust should be.

---

1. Rees, T. (2018)

PROFILE — RECTORY FARM PRIMARY SCHOOL

Institution Name: Rectory Farm Primary School

Location: Northampton

Type of Institution: Primary School – Part of Northampton Primary Academy Trust (NPAT)

Roll/Age Range: 210, aged 4–11

Year Founded: 1979. Opened as an academy in NPAT – February 2017

Motto: 'Growing minds, shaping lives'

House Names: Red, Yellow, Blue and Green

Recent/Current School Production: *The Tempest*

Recent significant sports event/triumph: Training our Young Leaders to run our whole school Sports Day – they were magnificent!

Sarah Heslop
Headteacher

A walk throughout our school will show a calm, purposeful and happy learning environment where staff demonstrate high aspirations for children's achievement. Our ethos, 'Growing Minds, Shaping Lives', is reflected in the commitment we show to knowing every child and relishing the challenge of guiding them through their primary phase of education. As well as great teaching, we place a strong emphasis on Sports, The Arts and Personal, Social and Emotional Education in order to broaden horizons and develop a growing understanding and knowledge of the world and all it has to offer!

The Cherry Tree Room is a Nurture Group facility based in Rectory Farm Primary School. We aim to provide a flexible, early intervention resource which is responsive to children's needs in terms of their social and emotional wellbeing. We do this by providing learning experiences at a child's developmental stage, with a focus on play, emotional literacy and social skills.

We very much value the contribution parents can make to their children's education and recognise that effective partnerships are essential. Parents are always most welcome into school to help or to discuss their child's progress or any matter of concern.

At Rectory Farm we are happy, have mutual respect and work hard. It is a privilege to be headteacher of this very special school and, I believe, a wonderful place for children to start their educational journey

Educating the mind without educating the heart is no education at all.
ARISTOTLE

STUDENT: MACIE

Age and Year Group: 11, Year 6
House: Yellow Team

Most recent:

School Trip: Longtown
Extra-curricular activity: Dance club, gymnastics club, basketball club, football club, cricket club, ukulele club, netball club
Science experiment: Chocolate – we were challenged to think of our own question to investigate
Book/Play studied in English Literature: *Pig Heart Boy* by Malorie Blackman
History topic: The Ancient Greeks
Arts project: World War Two dance

Learning:

Recent learning highlight: Learning about the heart. Cutting open a lamb's heart and finding the four different chambers. I learnt what's inside, like the superior vena cava, the inferior vena cava and the aorta. I didn't know anything about this before. My teacher talked to us about it and then we could choose between various texts to find out more.
The most stand-out/interesting/challenging topic you've studied at school: I enjoyed studying/learning about 'Natural Disasters' because I learnt about blizzards, Tsunamis, volcanoes etc. and we learnt about where in the world these disasters happen.
One of my favourite teachers: I enjoy Miss Green's maths lessons because she is really supportive. She doesn't give answers away – she asks me questions so that I can work it out for myself and then it clicks in my brain!
A favourite feature of the school: I've had a lot of opportunities like residentials at Longtown and Grendon – we all faced fears and challenged ourselves. I was really nervous about going and didn't think I'd do any of the challenges but I ended up doing them all!

Also all the sports tournaments and competitions. Every time we come off the pitch, our coaches were really supportive and encouraged us by telling us what to do to improve.

I also really love writing...at the moment we're working on Flanimals where we're making our own Flanimals e.g. their habitat, diet, are they in danger of extinction? I like it when we integrate our writing and art work for a presentation piece. Using watercolours, you can make different colours from just one colour!

STUDENT: MIA

Age and Year Group: 10, Year 5
House: Red

Most recent:

School Trip: Stibbington – we dressed up in WWII costumes and learnt about evacuees, and different jobs people had then.
Extra-curricular activity: Third Space Learning (maths club), basketball, netball
Science experiment: Mixing vinegar and baking soda to make an explosion
Book/Play studied in English Literature: *The Shaman's Apprentice* by Lynne Cherry
History topic: WWII
Arts project: Drawing flowers in my own style

Learning:

Recent learning highlight: Maths. Since I've been in Year 5 I've changed and I love Maths. I'm now confident with 'Fluent in Five'(mental arithmetic)
The most stand-out/interesting/challenging topic you've studied at school: I enjoyed studying/learning about The Mayans because before I didn't know they existed!
One of my favourite teachers: I enjoy Mrs Shields' maths lessons because she explains maths really well. She puts an example on the board so we know what to do and then we practise using that.
A favourite feature of the school: The school has helped me a lot – helped me to get healthy – they bought me a fit-bit!

I spent time in Cherry Tree Class (nurture) and the adults there helped me to feel more confident. We always had a healthy snack so I learnt about new foods like pitta bread and kiwi.

The adults in Cherry Tree Class helped me to be better at making friends and not falling out – we had lots of relationships games which helped me to know what to do.

Rectory Farm Primary School has put everything in place for me.
MIA

RFPS is full of fantastic experiences.
MACIE

PROFILE — SIMON DE SENLIS PRIMARY SCHOOL

Institution Name: Simon de Senlis Primary School

Location: Northampton, UK

Type of Institution: Primary School, part of Northampton Primary Academy Trust (NPAT)

Roll/Age Range: 440, aged 4–11

Year Founded: 1994

Motto: 'Making a dent in the universe'

House Names: Knights, Wizards, Unicorns, Dragons

Recent/Current School Production: *The Amazing Adventures of Super Stan* by The Players who are our drama club.

Recent significant sports event/triumph: Mrs Haigh, our Special Unit Teacher/Leader recently won the Northamptonshire 'unsung hero' award for her work to support children and staff across school.

Notable quirks/alumni: We are a Flagship School for Inclusion.

Joanne Fennelly
Headteacher

Simon de Senlis is a happy and successful primary school in East Hunsbury, Northampton with around 430 pupils on roll. We are an inclusive school and have a Special Unit for 12 children with complex learning difficulties, whom we are immensely proud of. We are driven for all children to succeed both academically, socially and emotionally. We do this through a commitment to trust and high expectations between staff, pupils and families. The learning atmosphere at SdS is exceptionally positive and we believe in children behaving well because they receive an intrinsic feeling of pride when doing so. We also use rewards and praise, along with clear routines and structures to allow all to achieve.

We believe that all children should receive great teaching and will leave our school with the academic foundations for success in the future. Alongside this, we offer our children a wide range of learning opportunities through Sport, The Arts, Drama and Technology which help to develop their creativity, confidence and well-being. Leadership is a key skill that children develop whilst on their learning journey at SdS and have many opportunities to become leaders throughout school. These vary from being a digital leader, a school council member, a playground leader or a house captain.

As we continue on our learning journey, as staff and pupils, we look forward to the future – it's definitely bright at SdS!

Learning here is really good. You learn lots in different ways. The curriculum is set out well with knowledge organisers given out to children at the beginning of a unit. The teachers regularly go back over things that we have already learnt to help us learn more. Feedback from teachers helps us to learn from our mistakes. We learn things in a fun way and teachers always challenge our thinking. We know what we're aiming for in our learning. I love it here.

YEAR 5 CHILD

STUDENT: ELLEN

Age and Year Group: 7, Year 2
House: Yellow Wizards

Most recent:

School Trip: The canal at Stoke Bruene
Extra-curricular activity: Dancing
Science experiment: Which material is the most waterproof?
Book/Play studied in English Literature: *Romeo and Juliet*
History topic: The Great Fire of London
Arts project: Learning about Vincent Van Gogh

Learning:

Recent learning highlight: We wrote a letter in the style of 'The day the crayons quit' which was really fun.

The most stand-out/interesting/challenging topic you've studied at school: I enjoyed studying/learning about The Mayans because before I didn't know they existed!

One of my favourite teachers: I enjoy lessons with Miss Gedney who taught me in Year 1 because she is kind, she is a great teacher and she leads the choir.

A favourite feature of the school: I love learning about the world – we learn about really interesting people and places.

STUDENT: STANLEY

Age and Year Group: 11, Year 6
House: Yellow Wizards

Most recent:

School Trip: Going to a Sikh gurdwara
Extra-curricular activity: Summer games
Science experiment: Making polystyrene
Book/Play studied in English Literature: *Kensuke's Kingdom*

Learning:

Subjects Studied: All!

Recent learning highlight: Going to the Sikh gurdwara and learning about Sikhism. I enjoyed studying/learning about Sikhism because I found their beliefs very balanced and interesting

The most stand-out/interesting/challenging topic you've studied at school: When learning about the First World War, we visited northern France and visited the trenches where the Battle of the Somme took place.

One of my favourite teachers: I enjoy lessons with Mrs Rosevear who taught me Maths. She was strict and pushed me to do well.

A favourite feature of the school: I love the school field.

I enjoyed studying/learning about Sikhism because I found their beliefs very balanced and interesting.

STANLEY REES

CASE STUDY: SCHOOL IMPROVEMENT IN A PRIMARY MAT

Authors: Tom Rees (Education Director, NPAT), **Anna Carter** (Trust Lead for English and Teacher Professional Learning), **Joanne Fennelly** (Headteacher, Simon de Senlis Primary School), **Sarah Heslop** (Headteacher, Rectory Farm Primary School)

Setting the Scene

NPAT is a growing multi-academy trust of eleven primary schools in Northamptonshire with a free school opening in 2021. One of the early MATs formed in 2012, the partnership is one built on collaboration and ambition with a vision to achieve 'extraordinary things' for its communities.

NPAT has a proven track record at improving the quality of education in some of the most challenging primary schools in the county, sponsoring three schools in need of a home in the last two years. Since the trust was formed seven years ago, all inspections have been good or outstanding in the MAT since its inception despite eight of the eleven schools having previously been in an Ofsted category at some point in the past 10 years.

An introduction from Tom & Anna...

As part of the Education Team at NPAT, we have the enormous privilege of working across the eleven schools in the trust. Although all our schools are all primary, situated in the same town and with much in common, each setting has its own individual context and character. Around three years ago, as we started to establish a central education team, we found ourselves scratching our heads at the challenge of building an education strategy across such diverse schools, all with different wants and needs. Having both been in the game long enough to know the risks and rewards of advising and directing schools to take on new strategies, we wanted to be more informed about our strategy. It was at this point, we started to pay closer attention to research and evidence.

The two schools featured here are Simon de Senlis Primary School and Rectory Farm Primary School.

Simon de Senlis joined the trust in 2015 with Tom Rees in post as full-time headteacher from 2012 until 2016 when Joanne Fennelly became Head of School and Tom became Executive Headteacher. Joanne then became the substantive headteacher in 2018 when Tom became Education Director for NPAT on a full-time basis. Prior to joining the trust, Simon de Senlis had been through a challenging few years, having been judged as Requires Improvement by Ofsted in 2013 before being judged as a good school in 2014.

Rectory Farm was NPAT's first sponsored school joining the trust two years ago with Sarah Heslop in post as headteacher. Sarah had formerly been Deputy Headteacher at Weston Favell C of E Primary, one of the founding five members of the trust and joined the school at a time of significant challenge without a Headteacher and in an Ofsted category. Rectory Farm is a one form entry primary school situated in the Eastern District of Northampton which is an area of high deprivation. The school comprises of predominantly white British children, with one third coming from minority ethnic groups. 50% of children come from low income families and are entitled to Pupil Premium funding.

We have shared their stories using the analogy of the Learning Rainforest: Establishing the Conditions, Building the Knowledge Structure and Exploring the possibilities. We have great pleasure in sharing them with you.

Establishing the Conditions

Simon de Senlis and Rectory Farm are at varying stages of their school development journey so 'establishing the conditions' manifests in different ways.

At Simon de Senlis, Joanne and her team spent time reading and researching current thinking around curriculum, learning and cognition. They learnt more about knowledge and memory, and spent time questioning the established practices at the school. Having rationalised this into change, they felt ready to move on from the previous model of curriculum that existed at the school

In tune with the Learning Rainforest metaphor, they knew paying attention to the conditions and climate would be essential for change to be effective. **In Joanne's words**:

'After a continuous search for improvement and reading much research into education and learning, we become more interested in the science behind learning and memory. Could our growing understanding of cognitive science be helpful for us in enabling children across school to become better learners? How should our thematic curriculum develop as a result?

CASE STUDY

We came to realise that the future for learning at Simon de Senlis should include more emphasis on clearly identified knowledge, attention to more direct methods of instruction and the reintroduction of subject integrity. This was a shift from the curriculum model we had developed over the previous five years and meant we had to ask ourselves difficult questions about well-intentioned features of our approach such as 'wow days', our emphasis on 'the theme' and our understanding of creativity. Whilst memorable themselves, were these approaches helping children to still retain the knowledge and skills we aimed for in years to come? Were they helping children to transfer and apply this learning across other areas of the curriculum?

Thought was given to how this change would be managed with staff. We were in the fortunate position of having an established staff who were passionate about their roles and always had the interest of the children at heart, no matter what. But we needed them to think in a different way and perhaps break away from existing viewpoints.

Staff training began in earnest throughout the Autumn term of 2017 and we learnt about Cognitive Science: reading about how knowledge is developed, the role of working and long-term memory and the theory of retrieval. Teachers were given quality time to plan, with on-going support from SLT, and a realistic implementation timetable was agreed. In order to create the right conditions for changes to practice, we decided to focus initially on just two subject areas, History and Geography. Once staff began to implement new approaches, SLT began to monitor how these subjects were developing. Through learning walks, book looks and conversations with staff, there was clear evidence of a change in learning taking place.

In the Spring term, through conversations with staff about cognition and learning, it became clear that they needed further training and that we needed to revisit, deepen and embed teachers' own knowledge. It seemed that staff did not feel an ownership of this new curriculum so a further round of CPD was vital. The conditions were established however it was important that we continued to build knowledge, understanding and ultimately ownership.'

For Sarah at Rectory Farm establishing the conditions started with staff morale and children's behaviour in a school in an OFSTED category. As a Head arriving in a turnaround situation facing daily complex challenges, her focus had to be different.

Sarah thinks back to this period:

'In my previous school, good behaviour was a given; children showed positive attitudes to learning, and they understood the importance of working hard. There a clarity around expectations for behaviour shared by staff and pupils. It quickly became apparent that this was not the case at Rectory Farm. Children lacked resilience and reacted badly to any challenge from adults. Even the children with the potential to be the highest attainers had no access to good role models and structures that would enable them to flourish. Effective learning and teaching was almost impossible in this environment; the established ethos was one in which low-level behaviour was normal and accepted.

Staff morale was generally low but this wasn't a reflection of the teachers' commitment to their jobs. The culture of poor behaviour and being unable to teach was exhausting and demotivating. I found it relentless and had to work really hard to get to a place where teachers could get down to the core business of teaching.

I knew that I needed to harness some key strengths among the staff from which I could draw much-needed allies including a strong deputy headteacher and some highly-committed, talented teachers. Recruitment and retention were at the top of my agenda. I knew I had to get the right people to stay 'on the bus 'if the school was to improve.

I made the decision to teach for half a day myself; with the purpose of understanding this school from a class teacher's point of view so that teachers knew that I really understood the same frustrations and levels of exhaustion that they were experiencing. We began to make small positive changes that the children were hugely appreciative of. This was a humbling experience, as surely, this was their entitlement? These 'light bulb' moments became more and more frequent. The children's excitement and growing sense of pride gave us the drive to keep going and work even harder on our school improvement journey. These deep-rooted behaviour issues, however, continued to be our main barrier to making progress. In response we developed a set of school values and a behaviour system that was clearly visible, simple and focused on positive outcomes. We were started to uproot the old and reseed for new growth.'

Building the Knowledge Structure

After working to establish the conditions for change, both schools then paid attention to the professional learning of their staff and prioritising CPD opportunities.

As a trust, we've reflected that many of our school improvement initiatives of the past have asked teachers to change their methods and approaches without necessarily building a shared knowledge and understanding of why these approaches are effective. Within the trust, as part of a strategy to develop more expertise in teachers, we wanted to ensure a high bar of training, ensuring that teachers had the knowledge and rationale that sat behind any new classroom or curricular approaches.

We began to make small positive changes that the children were hugely appreciative of. This was a humbling experience, as surely, this was their entitlement?

SARAH HESLOP
HEADTEACHER, RECTORY FARM
PRIMARY SCHOOL

CASE STUDY

Joanne reflects on this phase of development at Simon de Senlis.

'We spent the majority of the Summer Term's staff meetings following a structured approach to enable the staff to have two things: a greater knowledge of cognitive science and more ownership of the curriculum. I was increasingly confident this would have an immense positive effect on the teaching and children's outcomes. I also knew it was going to take time.

The first few sessions were spent reading current research on cognition and learning, including Rob Coe, *What Makes Great Teaching*, John Sweller's *Cognitive Load Theory*, The Learning Scientists' *Six Strategies for Effective Learning* and Rosenshine's 'Principles of Instruction'. Staff broke into small groups, summarised their understanding of the research and fed back to the whole group. The following week staff were encouraged to trial some small changes in the classroom and then shared their successes and challenges during the following CPD session. The emphasis was on personal development and as an SLT, we tried to keep the stakes low in terms of any monitoring and checking. Staff were beginning to understand learning through the lens of cognitive science; the next step was to develop this in more detail within our own curriculum.

During the following 4 CPD sessions, we arranged staff into three curriculum groups: History, Geography and RE. The groups were led by the subject leader and had a selection of staff that represented the whole school from EYFS, to Year 6 and including our Special Unit. The remit of these groups was to revise the whole school curriculum map for each subject area, using the National Curriculum as a starting point. It started as a mammoth task but was one which was so important to complete in order for the teaching staff to feel an ownership of the curriculum. Within

these sessions we would commit time to look at examples of other curriculum work taking place across the county. Clare Sealy became a favourite with her blog posts on Cognitive Load, The 3D curriculum that promotes remembering and The Importance of Automaticity, along with other primary leaders such as Jon Hutchinson and Andrew Percival.

As the weeks went by the groups collaborated together and went back to previous research and knowledge that had been learnt. There were rich discussions and debates amongst colleagues and there was clear and vivid transition of understanding of the way forward for a more knowledge-rich curriculum at that time.

During these weeks, each working group edited their whole school curriculum map and it became clear that there were vertical and horizontal links that could be made across the Geography, History and RE curriculum. Clare Sealy's 3D curriculum was becoming a reality and one that the staff had decided upon themselves rather than being directed to. The outcome of those weeks was a Geography, History and RE curriculum with clear vertical and horizontal links. Across both History and Geography there was to be a clear focus on the power of rule, along with democracy, and how this had an impact on the development of human geography and settlements. RE was to have vertical links across school on places of worship: their similarities and differences, religious artefacts and actions of respect.

The next step was for staff to put this knowledge to work within their classroom. This meant adapting medium-term plans, sequencing these into a series of lessons and developing resources such as knowledge organisers and quizzes to support the delivery. By September 2018, a year on from our original introduction of a knowledge rich curriculum, staff had taken on ownership and had a much-improved understanding of cognition

and learning. They were ready to put this new curriculum into action. Our staff's knowledge structure was building.'

At Rectory Farm, huge steps had been taken to create a calmer environment with better classroom behaviours. Despite this, there were still regular escalations of high-level behaviours derailing learning and keeping leaders away from their core business of improving teaching. In particular, there were children with specific identified needs who required more specialised support.

The next part of the journey was in two strands: firstly, to develop the school's pastoral approaches further including establishing a nurture provision and secondly, to work on some core areas of the curriculum to ensure children were gaining important foundational knowledge and skills. Building the knowledge structure through effective professional learning was the approach of the leadership team.

In Sarah's words:

'I found myself at a point where after making an initial impact, I was finding making further change difficult. I had a clear idea of my vision based on my previous school and what worked there, but was discovering to my peril, that to simply transfer all the 'success stories' into my new context wasn't going to work. I realised I needed to think more strategically and selectively about what this school in this context needed.

We were finding that while our approaches to embedding our school values and improving behaviour were working for the large majority, we still had a significant number of children with attachment difficulties, whose social, emotional and mental health needs were more complex and needed additional support. To address the challenge for more specialist pastoral provision, we took the decision to develop a nurture provision in the school.

There were rich discussions and debates amongst colleagues and there was clear and vivid transition of understanding of the way forward for a more knowledge-rich curriculum at that time.

JOANNE FENNELLY
HEADTEACHER, SIMON DE SENLIS
PRIMARY SCHOOL

CASE STUDY

Not having experience of nurture provision to build on, I knew we needed to learn more so we set out a journey to build our own knowledge in this area. We visited other schools and settings, read around the topic of nurture and attended formal training. We also made strong appointments to lead the nurture provision and utilised some of the expertise in our staff, including colleagues with degrees in psychology.

Although I felt under pressure to implement this provision quickly, I was determined to do it properly and this meant waiting until we had the right knowledge and expertise in place. Alongside our professional learning, we found the community rallied around this project. Through the kind donations of local charities we raised enough funds to convert a once dreary ICT suite, into a warm inviting and homely room in which to base our nurture provision.

At the same time, we were investing heavily in our teacher's CPD. If we were to going to raise standards, we needed to utilise the curriculum more effectively to develop children's literacy as a priority and this meant being really rigorous and intentional about the approaches we used. Specifically, we invested in whole-staff training for phonics, handwriting and mathematics approaches. This was expensive but we knew to have impact, we needed all teachers to access training – we didn't want a situation where one teacher with expertise was expected to disseminate this across the school.

Ensuring high quality, productive and relevant CPD, both from within school and using expertise within the Trust, was crucial in raising morale amongst our staff. Networking with colleagues in Trust schools also served to build a sense of belonging and comradery. Well planned appraisals were useful in addressing individual needs and identifying training opportunities. Staff were feeling valued.

During this phase, difficulties with recruitment continued to challenge us but, gradually our culture was changing and once we'd succeeded in enticing candidates through the door, our vision and ethos was clear for all to see and people bought into our commitment and drive to improve the school and decided to stay! We were strengthening our staff team.

Although a developmental phase, there were still 'difficult conversations' to be had along the way. 'You get what you tolerate' is a phrase which regularly comes to my mind and I was determined to address areas of concern without delay.'

Exploring the Possibilities

Both schools' journeys started by establishing the right culture and conditions in and then prioritised the development of shared knowledge and expertise through well-planned professional learning. In this next phase, we see how teachers and schools are starting to explore the possibilities their shared expertise allows. In both cases, although still with contrasting contexts and areas of focus, we can see the value of alignment within a staff; a careful balance of shared principles, intentions and knowledge which is cultivated to allow the confidence and agency to get better.

On the next phase of curriculum development **at Simon de Senlis**, Joanne continues:

'During the academic year 2018–2019 we have continued to think hard about the curriculum. This has involved visits from the SLT to schools who are further ahead on their curriculum journey on the journey than us, along with attending conferences and talks. This has allowed us to continue our discussions and allowed us to support staff further. Alongside our school-based development, our work has flowed into the wider curriculum development

across NPAT. This has led to some joint curriculum thinking and development across all eleven schools in the trust with training opportunities for staff to learn more about curriculum development, vocabulary and cognitive science.

We have concentrated on the enacted phase of our curriculum development, delving further into conversations with staff about the balance of declarative, procedural knowledge and conceptual knowledge as we revise our approaches in the classroom.

We further seek to explore possibilities within the curriculum and have just began to apply the skills taught in English, within non-fiction writing, to a final written piece at the end of each unit of work across either Geography, History or RE. Our next development for the coming term – How to ensure children have a conceptual knowledge of the subject they have learnt? How can the children now apply their knowledge of Geography, History or RE to the impact this has had on our life or may have on the lives of others to come? These will be wider, broader, philosophical and ethical questions that will be added to the knowledge organisers and will be debated as the children's knowledge develops.

Another important point for us is that a knowledge-rich curriculum remains one rich in enjoyment and experience. Enrichment opportunities remain a deliberate inclusion within our approach and experience days are built into the curriculum as opportunities for children to extend and apply what they have learned in the classroom and seek further inspiration. For example, residentials have ranged from residential visits to the Norfolk Coast when Year 4 were learning about coastal erosion in Geography and a week residential trip to Northern France to The Somme for Year 6 children learning about World War One. Enrichment days include a History Off the Page visit for Year 3 to apply their knowledge of The Romans, a trip to the local

These will be wider, broader, philosophical and ethical questions that will be added to the knowledge organisers and will be debated as the children's knowledge develops.

JOANNE FENNELLY
HEADTEACHER, SIMON DE SENLIS
PRIMARY SCHOOL

CASE STUDY

synagogue for Year 2 pupils and a visit to the local church for Reception children. The positioning of these types of days has altered as a result of our curriculum approach. Whereas before, we may have used these as a hook to try and inspire the children at the beginning of the topic, now we find children are more engaged as they know and understand more about the places they visit later in the unit.

It was a privilege recently to discuss the curriculum with children across school, their thoughts and comments were mature and showed an understanding of the changes we have put into place. When asked how they feel about knowledge organisers, one Year 5 girl replied, 'They're great, we take them home and I learn the facts, the teachers quiz us on the knowledge and I'd like more of these for each subject.' When asked about the experience days and where they are placed within the term, one Year 4 boy replied, 'Of course they're planned after we have learnt lots of information, it would be silly to have them at the start of the unit when you didn't know anything and if it was at the end you might not have time to find out anything else.'

When asked about a written report of their knowledge at the end of the unit, one Year 3 girl replied, 'I am writing a report about the religion Christianity to share with other people, as I know lots about this religion I have lots to say and I can compare it to Judaism because I know lots about that too.'

As Mary Myatt says, 'For the education system to reach coherence on the curriculum, it's going to require teachers in schools to engage in the conversation; it's a journey we need to share if we're going to deliver a curriculum we understand and believe in.'

At Rectory Farm, a tipping point had been reached. With a calm and purposeful climate established across the school and more effective teaching approaches being used consistently in the classroom, the culture had become one centred around learning. Staff morale had improved and collaboration was becoming key as teachers explored the possibilities together.

In Sarah's words:

By September 2018, we had established a team of highly committed and effective teachers. With behaviour in a much better place and a shared set of core approaches through good training and development, I was able to draw more on the expertise within the school to set the agenda and teachers really started to help develop each other more organically within this environment.

Our Nurture group has now been successfully running for 18 months and has enabled children to develop and progress within this bespoke provision. Transition back to mainstream, after an agreed period, is sensitively managed and to date all children who have transitioned are thriving back in the classroom.

Collaborative planning and peer-to-peer lesson coaching have become drivers in developing a whole team culture where together we were raising standards. Feedback between teachers is now commonplace, it happens all the time as part of our culture and is very much a shared solution-finding conversation, based on improving outcomes for children. The coaching approach ensured teachers were really 'owning' their professional development. Doug Lemov's 'Teach like a Champion' was (and still is) a useful point of reference for us all and approaches such as 'Track the Speaker' and 'No way out' are now an integral part of teaching and learning at Rectory Farm.

Monitoring of learning and teaching had traditionally been the job of SLT. At this stage, we have been able to invite teachers one by one to take part in learning walks and monitoring activity. The positive impact of this was quickly evident and we wished we had done this sooner. Firstly, teachers really enjoyed being involved and learning from the practice of others. They learnt from seeing the progression in children's learning from year to year and were empowered to see strategies and approaches we had discussed at staff meetings in place in classrooms other than their own. Everyone took away an improvement point of their own and the process has proved to be another building block in strengthening teacher confidence and our whole school sense of team.

Weekly staff meetings soon became a forum for sharing our knowledge for the benefit of everyone. Meeting time was also allocated for reading and research, and over time this has driven ownership of individual CPD. Self-reflection is becoming common place, with staff looking at where they want to take their practice in the future. We have now reached the point where teachers are impatient for feedback; everyone can see that our school culture is changing and with it the drive for each of us to be the best we can be. A sense of 'we're all in this together' is emerging and continues to be an important factor in our continuing success; staff voicing this to be an important element in team building and wellbeing.

Collaborative planning and peer-to-peer lesson coaching have become drivers in developing a whole-team culture where together we were raising standards.

SARAH HESLOP
HEADTEACHER, RECTORY FARM PRIMARY SCHOOL

MARKETHILL, ARMAGH

INTRODUCTION

I think the Markethill *Fieldbook* entry provides an exceptional account of a school on a mission. Their ambition, the clarity of purpose and the rigour in the approach are breath-taking and this comes across vividly in their writing. If you were to meet former Principal James Maxwell and his successor, James McCoy, this would come as no surprise. They have taken their time to engage with research, to explore the ideas of a range of key thinkers, to visit other schools and then assimilated these ideas into a powerful vision for their own knowledge-rich curriculum.

As James Maxwell describes, there is a sense in which the school has felt the need to row against the tide of the prevailing philosophy in the context they are operating in. They communicate a strong pioneering spirit as that's how they feel about the work they're doing. Northern Ireland is fascinating and complex in relation to the traditional-progressive values axis with the political, social, academic selection and faith-based divisions an ever-present backdrop for the work schools do. Markethill is very close to the border with Ireland and, very quickly on my visit, references to the history of the 'troubles' and the current challenges of Brexit came up. However, whilst other schools are engaged in initiatives based around more 'progressive' social integration and collaborative practices as a means to foster peace and deeper integration, James and James are firmly of the view that empowering children in a traditional manner, with deeper, more secure knowledge, is the best way to achieve this in the long run. The theory is that, if education is the key to peace, then the best thing schools can do is focus on delivering the best quality education possible, using research-informed instruction and a knowledge-rich approach.

James McCoy's account of the implementation of the English Mastery programme devised by Ark Schools in England gives a clear flavour of the thinking – and it's lovely to see this reflected in the students' profile comments. When a Year 7 student spontaneously mentions that 'we had to get to grips with hard ideas like looking at the Tenor, Vehicle and Ground of a metaphor', as Kingsley does, you know something very interesting is going on. James also captures the central importance of a professional culture backed up by a tangible investment in staff knowledge. On my visit, I was impressed with the baseline knowledge of many staff; they seemed way ahead of the game compared to many other schools I visit. James Maxwell has since gone to be Principal of Carrickfergus Grammar School and James McCoy has gone to be Principal of Lurgan Junior High School, however, the very able staff of Markethill High School continue their journey along the knowledge-rich route, convinced by its efficacy in enhancing the life chances and opportunities of all its pupils. I'm sure it will go from strength to strength.

PROFILE

Location: Markethill, Co. Armagh, Northern Ireland.

Type of Institution: Mixed all-ability

Roll/Age Range: 520, aged 11–16

Year Founded: 1959

Motto: Crede ut Perficias – 'Believe to Achieve'

House Names: Gosford, Glendinning, Witherow and Magowan

Recent/Current School Production: *Practically Perfect/Aladdin*

Recent significant sports event/triumph: Under 16 Girls' Northern Ireland High School Champions in Hockey; Under 14 Girls' Northern Ireland High School Champions in Hockey; Ulster Cross-Country Champion, Jodie McMullan, 2018; Gemma Gillanders – District Champion in Discus and Hammer; Year 7 Girls' District Relay winners; Rosie Jennings, winner of District Shot Putt; Jack Armstrong – District Discus winner.

Notable quirks/alumni: First school in Northern Ireland to introduce the Ark Schools' English Mastery curriculum at Key Stage 3; First school in Northern Ireland to achieve Silver award from the Teacher Development Trust. One of the first schools in Northern Ireland to introduce a knowledge-rich curriculum. A school polytunnel to promote the study of Agriculture and animal husbandry. The Sky Sports' Teacher of the Year Award held by Miss Poole. Pearson highly commended Teacher of the Year award held by Mrs Hargan. International 2G hockey pitch. Holder of the International School Award from the British Council.

James McCoy
Acting Principal

Receive my *instruction* and not silver; and *knowledge* rather than choice gold.

PROVERBS 8:10

PROFILE

Markethill High School is a thriving, exciting, ambitious and thoroughly aspirational non-selective Controlled school which is currently ranked as one of the top five non-selective Controlled schools in Northern Ireland. Situated on a spacious site adjacent to the town, the school has a strong Christian ethos and works in partnership with local churches. It also enjoys very strong community links. In 2017 the Education and Training Inspectorate of Northern Ireland concluded that the standards and outcomes at Markethill High School were 'significantly above' those in similar schools.

In 2018 the Controlled Schools' Support Council undertook a case study on the School such is the huge increase in the performance of our boys at GCSE. In the last four years, the number of boys attaining 5 or more GCSE's at A*- C has risen from 70% to 92.4%. The number of girls achieving the same statistic in 2017 was 98%.

The school aims to offer pupils a world-class education, reinforced by the most robust research-based evidence into high quality learning and teaching. In 2018 Markethill High School became one of the first schools in Northern Ireland to introduce a unique knowledge-rich curriculum for Year 7 pupils. It has also become the first school in the country and one of only 59 across the UK to adopt an English Mastery Curriculum for its pupils.

The purpose of the school's new knowledge-rich curriculum is to ensure our pupils have the strongly-rooted core knowledge and consequent domain-specific skills in order to enrich their educational experience and empower them to access the next stage in their education, find suitable employment and participate in society. The values which are embraced at Markethill High School such as respect, tolerance, responsibility, honesty and community spirit remain a constant and unshifting element embedded within the history and future of the school and are central to the school.

Good, better, best. Let me never rest until my good is better and my better best!
KINGSLEY

I love Markethill High School – our school is an exciting adventure!
JENI

STUDENT: JENI

Age and Year Group: 12, Year 7
House: Glendinning

Most recent:

School Trip: Lurgaboy Outdoor Education Centre
Extra-curricular activity: Drama Club
Science experiment: Making your own Sherbet
Book/Play studied in English Literature: Shakespeare – *A Midsummer Night's Dream*
History topic: Health in the Middle Ages
Arts project: Music project on 'The Musical' as a genre

Learning:

Subjects Studied: English, Maths, Science, French, History, Geography, Religious Studies, Music, Art, Technology & Design, Learning for Life and Work, Home Economics, PE

Recent learning highlight: One of the most memorable lessons I have had in school was an English lesson where we were studying the original text of *Oliver Twist* – the part where Nancy is killed. I really enjoyed the way our English teacher read the passage; it was so exciting to hear. We were all on the edge of our seats – it really got our attention because it is such a dramatic scene in the novel.

The most stand-out/interesting/challenging topic you've studied at school: I enjoyed studying *A Midsummer Night's Dream* in English after Christmas because it was challenging. Our teacher explained many literary techniques that Shakespeare used and we learned many interesting things about Shakespeare's life and the Elizabethan era. We learned about life in Athens through the play and we also studied the features of Shakespearean comedy. The funniest part in the play was when Bottom had a donkey's head and Titania fell in love with him!

One of my favourite teachers: I enjoy lessons with Miss Muldrew, who teaches me Geography, because Miss Muldrew explains things in detail so that we understand. We can listen to her explanation of the topic we are looking at and then when we do the written work, it is easier because she models what a perfect answer would look like. Her instructions to us are easy to understand and she has a good sense of humour, so she makes learning fun.

A favourite feature of the school: My favourite feature of this school is English Mastery. We get to learn English at a 'first-class' level from day one. We are learning knowledge and how to write analytical essays which will help us when we come to GCSE level. I really enjoy our Grammar lessons, where we get to infer what happens from the pictures and then write about them using the techniques we have learned. It is a real challenge to get all of the 'Mastery Checks' correct!

STUDENT: KINGSLEY

Age and Year Group: 12, Year 7
House: Gosford

Most recent:

School Trip: Lurgaboy Outdoor Education Centre
Extra-curricular activity: Drama Club
Science experiment: Making your own sherbet
Book/Play studied in English Literature: Dickens – *Oliver Twist*
History topic: The Normans
Arts project: Music project on 'The Musical' as a genre

Learning:

Subjects Studied: English, Maths, Science, French, History, Geography, Religious Studies, Music, Art, Technology & Design, Learning for Life and Work, Home Economics, PE

Recent learning highlight: One of the most memorable lessons I have had in school was a History lesson where we learned how to build a clear timeline. We learned about the different people who have come to Ireland and later on, when we were looking at 'The Normans', we were able to locate the Normans on the timelines that we created. I love the way our History teacher explains things clearly on the board.

The most stand-out/interesting/challenging topic you've studied at school: I enjoyed studying poetry in English in the summer term because it was very challenging. Our teacher said that we were doing GCSE level work, but that we could manage it. We had to understand difficult language and had to get to grips with hard ideas like looking at the Tenor, Vehicle and Ground of a metaphor. I can now understand common metaphors that are used every day.

One of my favourite teachers: I enjoy lessons with Miss McConnell, who teaches me Home Economics, because they are hands-on lessons and Miss McConnell explains things to us in small steps, giving us the information that we need to know in our knowledge organisers. Miss McConnell always makes sure that everyone understands and takes time to make sure that everyone does their best and achieves their best.

A favourite feature of the school: A favourite feature of this school for me is the use of knowledge organisers. These are good as they contain all of the important knowledge that we need to learn. When I self-quiz using my knowledge organiser, I am able to learn key facts about a subject and help myself prepare for GCSE. They also help us to recall information in exams.

CASE STUDY: ENGLISH MASTERY AT KS3

Title: How and why we introduced the knowledge-rich 'English Mastery' programme at Key Stage 3

General Area: The introduction of Ark's 'English Mastery' at Key Stage 3

Author: James McCoy, Acting Principal and English Teacher

The Parable of the Sower', which we read of in Matthew Chapter 13, is a cautionary tale against all those who believe that seed can grow in stony ground. The story outlines how when the sun comes, the product is 'scorched' because it has 'no root' and 'withers away' as a result. At Markethill High School, we have learned that if the seed of skill is to grow, it needs to be embedded in a rich, knowledge-based soil and nurtured in an environment which encourages plenty of practice. Without strong roots in subject knowledge and practice, pupils will never be able to demonstrate skill.

We believe that improving literacy scores with our pupils is the best way of ensuring that they are able to access all parts of the curriculum. To this end, we introduced English Mastery – a knowledge-rich curriculum for English at Key Stage 3. The first school in NI to adopt this approach, we felt that it was necessary because too many of our pupils were getting to GCSE level without the core knowledge that they needed in order to succeed. Sure, we had put several interventions in place at Key Stage 4 to combat this, but it seemed logical to put the intervention in place earlier in the educational pathway of each pupil – hence our move towards English Mastery! Its introduction has seen the bar for stretch and challenge set very high indeed, with pupils studying classic texts in great detail and having grammar taught in a specific fashion in English lessons.

Daisy Christodoulou and Amy McJennett who designed the programme have done so in a way as to ensure that knowledge is sequenced, that recall and practice are deliberately focused on and that schemas are built. So far, the programme is very successful, with pupils, in the majority of cases, able to write extensively about texts and able to express themselves much clearer because of their knowledge of grammatical structures. Anecdotally, many of our English teachers have commented on how some of our first years are producing work of comparable standard to some good GCSE pupils. Assessment to date has been very pleasing. Some pupils are performing well and there is clear engagement with the texts – evidenced by the quality of written responses.

The English Department in Markethill consists of a lively bunch of professionals who are passionate about improving the life chances of all pupils, and so, when we embarked on the planting of English Mastery within the culture of the school, we did so with energy and enthusiasm. We meet during lunchtime once a week and over our sandwiches and coffee, we discuss the many difficulties, challenges that the programme throws up, as well as the many benefits that we have had the joy of witnessing. Initially, there were many discussions about timetabling implications from the introduction of the programme. Curriculum time in Key Stage 3 is a mixture of statutory requirement and breadth of study. English time needed to increase to allow for the effective teaching of the model, so time devoted to other subjects was affected, but this was necessary if real progress was to be made. We felt guilty that teachers of other subjects might feel threatened because their subject's time was reduced but presenting the clear rationale for cutting time is the best way to assuage fears and reassure staff of the moral imperative for doing so.

The programme provides many resources for us and we have found that most of our lunchtime chats have focused on HOW we teach and not WHAT we teach. This has, in turn, renewed our

CASE STUDY: ENGLISH MASTERY AT KS3

emphasis on effective pedagogy and has enabled all teachers within the department to share best practice. As a result, the level of professional dialogue has undoubtedly been raised and as a team, we actively share our *highs* and *lows*. It's important to learn from our mistakes, yes, but it is also important to celebrate the successes. The latter, unquestionably, has been the quality of examination answers from pupils!

Our approach in English has always been underpinned by Research Lesson Study, (our school's chosen vehicle for professional development), and throughout the year, gradually observations of each other's lessons have increased. We are keen to get things right, we are keen to work together and we are keen to enhance the collegial spirit between us, because we know that is when we will perform at optimum levels. Making sure that high quality professional development is available to all teachers in the department is central to growth. We have invested time and money in sending staff to England for training and have engaged in numerous English Mastery webinars – all helping to create subject experts and promote best practice. We have therefore learned from each other and from the English Mastery representatives in England.

Have pupils enjoyed the challenges that have been laid for them? Throughout the year, we have monitored their assessment scores, but we have also tracked their enjoyment of literature through questionnaire responses. Indeed, the majority of pupils demonstrate real enthusiasm for the subject and tangible enjoyment of texts that they have studied, is witnessed across a range of fora – not least of all our Family Lunch, where pupils have openly and voluntarily discussed aspects of the literature they have studied, at the lunch tables!

The structure of the programme is such that children are *instructed explicitly*, that knowledge is *spaced* and *interleaved*,

and *self-quizzing* and *practice* are built into the very fabric of the course. These methods mean that when pupils are assessed, they succeed and we have found that this success breeds further success – once they taste success, they want some more! This has been a real joy to watch.

Parents too have positively commented on the effectiveness of the programme. Where some parents have older children in year groups further up the school, some have conveyed the idea that their younger child is more advanced at this stage of their secondary school career than where their older child would have been a few years ago, such is the difference that they can see in the new approach. We also organised Parents' events so that they understood the rationale behind the approach and how they might best help their child at home.

Northern Ireland's revised curriculum incorrectly, we believe, placed skills at its root, at the expense of knowledge, but we have proved this year that real skill in English is a mixture of knowledge and practice. By implementing English Mastery, we are undoubtedly travelling against the flow of the current, but we will continue to do so, 'boats against the current' of the revised curriculum because we know that to be the best way to expedite success at Key Stage 3 and beyond.

Crede ut Perficias! – Believe to Achieve!

Link to Learning Rainforest:

The English Mastery approach adopted is a perfect example of 'building the knowledge structure' and the level of challenge provided is clearly 'establishing the conditions'. This applies to staff and students, with the CPD approach adopted to support staff in delivering the programme.

CASE STUDY: KNOWLEDGE-RICH CURRICULUM IN YEAR 7

Title: How and why we introduced a knowledge-rich curriculum in Year 7

General Area: Developing a Knowledge-Rich Curriculum

Author: James Maxwell, former Principal

Last year we introduced a new curriculum for Year 7 pupils – one which promotes subject-specific knowledge as a precursor to domain-specific skills; one which emphasises the need to embed core knowledge in long-term memory; one which promotes explicit instruction with strong links to Rosenshine's Principles of Instruction and one which values the great importance of formative assessment/responsive teaching/low-stakes quizzing. It marks a slight change of emphasis away from Northern Ireland's Revised Curriculum, and away from an unwieldy and unworkable Key Stage 3 assessment system based on much-maligned level-descriptors.

Increasingly, direction in our school has been shaped by educational research. Our revised Learning and Teaching Policy from 2015 was shaped quite firmly on the Six Principles of Great Teaching outlined in Allison and Tharby's excellent book *Making Every Lesson Count*, with further input from the writing of David Didau amongst others. Our journey to a knowledge-rich curriculum actually started two years ago when we read Daniel Willingham's seminal book *Why Don't Students Like School?* It was a game changer which led us onto other great educational literature such as Daisy Christodoulou's *Making Good Progress* and Peps Mccrea's *Memorable Teaching*. A staff training day in August 2017 focused on some of this literature, and as a result the decision was taken to embed the following three maxims as the crux of our learning and teaching principles in our new School Development Plan:

* Subject-Specific Knowledge must precede domain-specific skill

* Memory is the residue of thought

* Assessment is the bridge between learning and teaching

In October 2017 we gave staff a folder of research and a day to read from home (or Costa Coffee, or the top of a mountain – it didn't matter, as long as they read!). The folder was arranged in sections based on the above maxims, and included the writing of Daniel Willingham, E.D. Hirsch, David Didau, Peps Mccrea, Daisy Christodoulou, Katharine Birbalsingh (*Battle Hymn of the Tiger Teachers*) and Joe Kirby, amongst others.

At the same time, we launched a staff professional development portal in which we brought together as much of the current articles and research linked to the development of knowledge-rich curricula as we could.

CASE STUDY: KNOWLEDGE-RICH CURRICULUM IN YEAR 7

We were fortunate enough to be able to send staff over to visit the Michaela School in Wembley, Barry Smith at Great Yarmouth Charter Academy and to visit Daisy Christodoulou in London. These visits helped to shape our emerging concept of a curriculum which would reduce the Matthew Effect[1], close the knowledge gap and ensure our children had access to a curriculum which was coherent, cohesive and apt to ensure many doors remain open for them and that the aspiration of attending higher education for all pupils – should they wish – becomes a reality. No labels, no limits, is our mantra.

As part of our preparations, we spent a long time focusing on what our Knowledge Organisers should look like. Not aesthetically – although we spent time looking at aesthetic strategies for the presentation of KOs which avoid cognitive overload – rather in terms of content, of course. Martin Robinson's book *Trivium21c* shaped our discussions on what knowledge we should be teaching our children and should be represented in the KOs. Eventually we decided on the following as our benchmarks:

- The core knowledge our children need to know for future success
- The best of what has been thought and said in the discipline in question
- Cultural capital (e.g. in Physics the fact that Northern Ireland's Dame Joycelyn Burnell Bell co-discovered the first radio pulsars, or in English the writings of Seamus Heaney).

We also discussed at length how this knowledge would build cumulatively across the key stage.

At the same time, we reinforced our understanding of Explicit Instruction, using Rosenshine's Principles, and evidence/research in relation to a child's journey from novice to expert. Children in our classrooms are not experts, and yet the NI Curriculum encourages teachers to get pupils to 'think like scientists' or 'think like historians' etc. on occasions. This, of course, is endeavoured in the NI Curriculum through teacher facilitation, group work, 'kinaesthetic learning' and independent research/thinking skills/personal capabilities. For us at Markethill High, explicit instruction is about the teacher teaching from the front, imparting their knowledge in a direct manner and using low-stakes formative assessment to identify misconceptions, gauge progress and respond appropriately. We believe in purposeful drill, rehearsal and spaced/interleaved recap. We believe in the power of worked examples (we would recommend Craig Barton's book *How I Wish I'd Taught Maths*, as well as his excellent podcast with Greg Ashman on this matter). As a result, we have procured high-quality visualisers for every single classroom in the school.

And so, in August 2018, our new knowledge-rich curriculum was introduced with a visit from Tom Sherrington to undertake staff training on Mode A + Mode B teaching – a concept from his book *The Learning Rainforest*.

A year in? How are we getting on? Well, our children have their Knowledge Organisers out in every subject. They self-quiz every evening for 20–30 minutes. We created a self-quizzing step-by-step for parents and pupils. Our pupils undertake IXL self-quizzing and much Quizlet self-quizzing also. They have learned poetry by heart, in our belief that we must return pupils to the notion of learning poetry for the great wealth of learning experience it brings and for the purposes of cultural capital.

Whilst early days, and whilst a small number of children have struggled a little with organisation and the establishment of routine, after a year we are already hearing anecdotes of pupil knowledge being much more solid and even advanced than in previous years, and this is even starting to be noticed in test scores. Indeed, my own Year 7 class have been internalising PROFS (Past – Reasons – Opinions – Future – Subjunctive) structures as part of their French. After a year, they can recite some subjunctive structures in French, as well as clearly articulate (in French) the academic register for accents and their purpose. When it comes to explicitly teaching the structures at a later stage, their automaticity of multiple structures in long-term memory will have forged patterns which will allow them to think more deeply – and creatively – in the discipline than students who do not have this automaticity.

It is our firm conviction that this curriculum will close the knowledge gap and narrow the Matthew Effect at arguably one of the most important junctures in a child's education. For Markethill High School, there is no going back, and the glass ceiling fast approaches.

Link to Learning Rainforest:

Establishing the conditions by designing a knowledge-rich curriculum.

Building the Knowledge Structure – through effective instruction, attending to long-term memory.

Mode A vs Mode B teaching

It is our firm conviction that this curriculum will close the knowledge gap and narrow the Matthew Effect at arguably one of the most important junctures in a child's education

JAMES MAXWELL
FORMER PRINCIPAL

Crede ut Perficias! – Believe to Achieve!

JAMES MCCOY
ACTING PRINCIPAL AND ENGLISH
TEACHER

---

1. Matthew Effect: Those already with the most knowledge also then gain the most knowledge.

THE LEARNING RAINFOREST IN PRACTICE

EXPLORING THE POSSIBILITIES

PROJECTS AND HANDS-ON LEARNING

P 1 HANDS ON

P 2 AMBIGUITY AND UNCERTAINTY

P 3 PLAY DETECTIVE

P 4 DEEP END

P 5 GROUPS: GOALS AND ROLES

P 6 PROJECTS

P 7 KEEP IT REAL: AUTHENTIC PROJECTS, PRODUCTS, EXPERIENCES

P 8 GET CREATIVE; LEARN TO CHOOSE

P 9 'DAZZLE ME ': KEEPING IT OPEN

P 10 OFF-PISTE

FURTHER POSSIBILITIES

P 11 CLASS FORUM

P 12 RECIPROCAL TEACHING

P 13 FLIPPED LEARNING

P 14 ONLINE TUTORIALS

P 15 CO-CONSTRUCTION: SIDEKICKS

P 16 INDEPENDENCE: TOOLS AND TRICKS

P 17 STRUCTURED SPEECH EVENTS

P 18 DEBATE

P 19 THIRD TIME FOR EXCELLENCE

P 20 EXCELLENCE EXHIBITION

LES QUENNEVAIS SCHOOL, JERSEY

INTRODUCTION

I first discovered the power of Twitter as a means of making connections across the world of education back in 2012 when I started using it to share my blog posts. Very early on, I came across an account called @pekabelo, a kind, engaging teacher sharing ideas about projects, art and general education and leadership issues. This turned out to be the account of Pete Jones, Assistant Headteacher at Les Quennevais in Jersey. For a long time, Pete was top of my list of 'people I know from Twitter that I'd like to meet in person'. Ideas we discussed online included 'excellence exhibitions' and transition. I shared some ideas from my school where we ran a British Museum project and I remember Pete posting images of his beach-based version and the school's fabulous 'excellence wall'. Finally, in 2018, the opportunity arose for me to travel to Jersey for the first time, to work with the Les Quennevais science team and deliver some whole-school CPD on the role of oracy. It was wonderful to meet Pete and Headteacher, Sarah in person. It was also great to hear that ideas from *The Learning Rainforest* resonated so strongly with the philosophy of the school.

The education system in Jersey is fascinating and rather complex for a small island, with various tiers of selection. Les Quennevais is one of the few non-selective, non-fee-paying schools that serves its local community without special advantages. However, over recent years, as Sarah describes with characteristic passion in her entry below, the school staff have done a phenomenal job creating a reputation that increasingly makes it the school of choice. The two contrasting case studies give us a feel for the reasons for that. Pete's story of the beach-themed transition project creates an image of a place where curriculum thinking is bold and ambitious; where teachers are inspired by what they're doing, creating something that is knowledge rich, interdisciplinary and holistic, leading to very strong learning outcomes. Emilio's story captures some of the rigorous thinking that underpins the curriculum in English, as an example of the depth of thought that runs across the school in general. The school can't afford to be half-hearted given all the competition it faces and you can tell from these accounts that they don't ever do things by halves.

The great community spirit of the school is lovely to experience on a visit. There are some schools you feel you could just hang out in happily all day and this is one of them. I'm delighted to know that their long-promised move to a brand new purpose-built school on a nearby site is in full swing, including a new location for the school's amazing multi-screen immersive exhibition space – it's one of the most amazing things I've ever seen in a school. 'Joy' is one of the cornerstones of the Learning Rainforest philosophy so it's fabulous to see that 'excellence and enjoyment' are coupled together in the school's new motto. I'm certainly looking forward to a return visit when the new buildings open.

PROFILE

Location: Jersey, Channel Islands

Type of Institution: 11–16 States' mixed

Roll/Age Range: 696, aged 11–16

Year Founded: 1965

Motto: 'Learning to be your best – through excellence and enjoyment'

House Names: McKeon, Tranter, Watts

Recent/Current School Production: *Oliver!*

Recent significant sports event/triumph: Year 7 Island champions – Netball and Football
Year 8 – Rugby champions
Year 11 – Rugby champions

Quote: "When I think back on my time at Les Quennevais it has been nothing but positive. It has illustrated the type of student I am: the community makes me feel like I'm part of something special and that I can make a valuable contribution to the school. Teachers motivate and encourage all students at every opportunity to make the workload manageable and engage them to want to learn. Year 11 in particular has been a year when the support and nurture of teachers has been most needed. Our teachers truly care and often hold revision sessions, making themselves available to students to unlock our potential, whilst setting realistic expectations as to what we could achieve. Even though I will not experience the new school and its facilities, it fills me with joy knowing that the future students of Les Quennevais will be given the very best experience in this new centre of excellence. Thank you to every single person who has made the journey at Les Quennevais one we will remember with great fondness." – Year 11 student.

Notable quirks/alumni: Several years ago students started the hashtag #AlwaysQuennevais – meaning that a part of them will always belong to our school. We have embraced this as a school, for students to know that even when they leave, they are always part of the Les Quennevais family.

Sarah Hague
Headteacher

2013 signalled a seismic change for me and as it turns out our school. This was the date that, as a newly appointed Headteacher myself, and my Leadership Team set about radically transforming the learning culture of our school, from within. I have chosen the words 'from within' quite deliberately. Firstly, as a Leadership Team, we were all employed, albeit in different parts and positions, within Les Quennevais School; a school which we were already fiercely proud to be part of, and just wanted to really let fly! 'From within' also because Jersey is a peculiar jurisdiction. An offshore environment where 60% of the Island's children go to fee paying schools and the option of a transfer to a States' grammar school at the end of Year 9 for those who meet the criteria.

My mission and drive as a teacher in Jersey and new educational leader has always been to ensure our school is a school of first choice for all our families, and a school which reflects a strong commitment to making a tangible difference to the young people in our community, who the system can actually divide.

PROFILE

In order to do this, we knew we had to raise standards and outcomes, drive ambition and aspiration and create and define a culture and ethic of excellence in everything we do. We adapted our school aim from 'Learning to be your best' to 'Learning to be your best – through excellence and enjoyment'.

As school leaders we set about dramatically addressing the professional culture of the school, placing the importance and need for a strong curriculum at the heart of the school. Having a driven and committed Senior Team who bought heavily into a clear vision, that they still uphold today, allowed us to move forward rapidly. Crucial to our success was creating and assembling a strong body of Middle Leaders. Middle Leadership is the engine room of the school and with a good balance of high quality CPD and an acceptance of accountability, Middle Leadership here has emerged as an impressive collective. This in turn has allowed leadership to be distributed at every level and thus curriculum development has become rich and challenging and outcomes for students have significantly improved. As a school that has been described as 'not just going the extra mile for its students, but also the extra 10 miles!' – developing a high performing guidance team alongside strong curriculum leads, has secured professionals who are committed to doing all they can for all our students but particularly the most vulnerable.

Attendance has dramatically improved to become the highest of the States' 11–16 schools, with lowest suspensions and behaviour incidences. With two consecutive attainment and progress outcomes and results at GCSE breaking Island records for 11–16 schools, I feel we are beginning to turn our vision into a reality. All our students leave with improved life changes and pathways available but with a strong sense of belonging to our school.

At times the journey to get to this point has felt impossible, but never lonely. That has been as a result of assembling a strong team, all with different skills and views, but who are part of a collective endeavour to deliver our vision and support each other, because it matters to our kids! It's easy to get distracted from your main thing and my mantra of 'keep your main thing your main thing' was at times, laughable – but it worked. We learned the importance of measuring and evaluating everything and if it's not working, change it. The professional culture that we set out to create is highly visible from the moment you enter our building. From our frontline staff in reception, to our support staff, site staff and teachers – we all work on our school not in the school. There is a collaborative culture and network of teams who all work on and contribute to aspects of school improvement, with teaching and non-teaching staff working on innovations together.

Our Teaching for Learning (T4L) Team consists of Senior and Middle Leaders, mainscale teachers and NQTs. A Journal Club, reading and discussing the latest research emerged from staff themselves, highlighting how CPD has moved on from being solely directed by SLT. Staff take more than 'responsibility' for their own CPD, they take an active interest in it. When our T4L team present briefings on Friday morning before school, there is standing room only and people are rarely late because they know they are going to get 15 minutes of a quality presentation, that they may be able to use in the classroom. Our intervention culture is formidable and effective.

As we plan a move to a brand new building, our challenge will be to keep this momentum and cherish and nurture the special culture that permeates our school. There have been huge highs and lows, but resilience and ambition have kept us going. You also need a bit of luck in this game and I am both blessed and lucky to have a team of outstanding and committed professionals around me, because you cannot raise a community alone, it needs an army!

This experience; the planning, the expectations and the joyful outcomes helped permeate a new vision for what the curriculum could be.

PETE JONES
ASSISTANT HEAD

I am both blessed and lucky to have a team of outstanding and committed professionals around me, because you cannot raise a community alone, it needs an army!

SARAH HAGUE
HEADTEACHER

Curriculum development has become rich and challenging and outcomes for students have significantly improved.

SARAH HAGUE
HEADTEACHER

STUDENT: ANNABELLE BOWER

Age and Year Group: Year 7, Tutor group 7Q

House: Watts

Favourite moment: The Great British Blake Off! I performed the poem 'Angel' which I had learnt by heart. I was so nervous to speak, but I got up and spoke in front of the whole year group and guest judges. The experience really raised my confidence.

Favourite science experiment: Chromatography using skittles in a tray of water.

Favourite teacher: Miss Brooks because she is understanding and will always help us if we need it. I have really engaged with Shakespeare this year. Acting out the scenes in class helped me understand the language.

Favourite History unit: I loved learning about Boudica and how she managed to defeat the Roman Empire.

Favourite subject: Art. I have really enjoyed learning how to paint properly in my first year at Les Quennevais using the techniques of Monet and Van Gogh to create realistic paintings. It has been great fun!

Favourite literature: I loved William Blake's *London* Poem. How he expresses what life was like for the people of London at that time and his clever use of metaphor.

THE LEARNING RAINFOREST FIELDBOOK

STUDENT: ISAAC SEYMOUR

Age and Year Group: Year 7, Tutor group 7Q

House: Watts

Favourite moment: Inter-House music competition. I performed my own drumming solo, which I loved!

Favourite bit of the curriculum: Population in Geography. It has helped me understand migration, immigration and why the population of the world is rapidly increasing.

School Trip: In RS we went to the local church and explored the meaning and design behind different bits of the church.

Favourite science experiment: Exploring Distillation through extracting water from a can of coke.

Favourite teacher: Mr Spencer – my Geography Teacher. Every area of Geography is accompanied with fun tasks, lots of encouragement and help if required.

Favourite books: *The Hunger Games* trilogy. Fast paced, full of action and constantly engaging.

The word 'ominous' is met for the first time in Year 7 as students study *The Iliad*, it comes into prominence again in Year 8 when Bill Sikes is encountered in *Oliver Twist*

EMILIO CHAIN-LOPEZ
HEAD OF ENGLISH

CASE STUDY: CURRICULUM STORY – THE TRANSITION PROJECT

Author: Pete Jones, Assistant Head – Teaching and Learning, Les Quennevais School

Over the past five years, the curriculum in so many subject areas at Les Quennevais has been slowly and carefully transformed through the diligent hard work of our expert subject leaders and by developing a culture that has relentlessly focused on the quality of learning experiences we want for our students. Five years ago, our rainforest was in need of nourishment. It wasn't barren, but it was neglected and not brimming with beautiful specimens. To extend the metaphor, the roots of the curriculum lacked the depth needed for strong growth and our ability to nurture the kind of experiences we wanted for our students was difficult to visualize let alone provide the right conditions for the growth of a beautiful, varied and complex Learning Rainforest.

Transition is one of the key areas to get right when considering the curriculum experiences of our students. Too often, the lesson experiences during transition in secondary schools is an afterthought. Exam season has ended, the sun is generally warm and shining and we begin to think about the long holiday that lends us an opportunity to refresh and tend to the rainforest. Transition, however, is a huge deal – especially for the students themselves. The movement from one school to another, with a different and growing population of children, often a different stance on teaching and curriculum can be daunting and a real challenge for many of our youngest students. For students at the top of their primary schools, with many accomplishments and responsibilities under their belts, to move to a new school can feel like starting their education all over again. That initial experience is absolutely vital to get right; to establish the conditions to belong and flourish. Like most schools, our new students have two days in July where they visit the school before starting in September. I want every child to leave Les Quennevais after those two days filled with new, rich knowledge, an abundance of excitement and ambition for the next five years ahead.

We have built a curriculum experience based around the theme of beachcombing – we are a small island surrounded by beautiful beaches after all! Different subjects become involved each year, but some experiences stay the same. In English, students study a variety of descriptive writing relating to the sea. To add genuine awe, our digital immersive space is used to recreate the sensory experience of being on the water's edge with beautiful excerpts of poems and literature spoken by our students at the touch of a wall. In art, students explore how artists are inspired by the sea; from Da Vinci's bird's eye view of the Italian coast to Anthony Gormley's 100 cast iron figures spread out over Crosby beach. Students then have the opportunity to create their own responses to the sea using inks and bubble printing. In Science, students conduct experiments to see how wetsuits work, take part in a chromatography rock pool mystery and look

at seaweed and grains of sand under a microscope. The students absolutely love the opportunity to get hands-on in the science labs! Other subjects help out each year to create an unforgettable two days. Design Technology made pewter cast jewellery inspired by coral out of cuttlefish bones last year; Languages described beach scenes in French; Geography were looking at why Jersey is shaped the way it is and looking at the effects of plastics in the sea; History created a timeline of events in one of our small harbour villages, from the Vikings to the Nazis; Maths explored how to measure the grains of sand on a beach and we are now getting close to every department having an opportunity to deliver a curriculum experience relating to the beachcombing idea.

This was one of the 'catalysts' for change at our school in developing a beautiful rainforest for our students to wander through. This experience; the planning, the expectations and the joyful outcomes helped permeate a new vision for what the curriculum could be. This wasn't to say that we were to go down a thematic approach to curriculum design, but it helped staff cast off the shackles of the past. To set a new course with a focus on a knowledge-rich curriculum alongside memorable experiences for our students to engage with.

A homework booklet with ideas for possible tasks inspired by their two days with us is given to all students which has a wide range of possible responses, alongside a knowledge organiser for each subject to help them refer to their new found knowledge to their Summer project. Early in September each year, we have an exhibition day where we take over the whole ground floor of the school. In a single morning, an exhibition of 170+ student's work is carefully displayed. In the afternoon, students spend time looking at each other's work and providing feedback to each student. Subject experts look at specific content and awards are given. Parents and primary school

CASE STUDY: CURRICULUM STORY...

teachers are invited in after school to gaze in awe at our youngest students responses to the homework project.

There have been some quite remarkable responses over the past few years. One student who found an old piece of cast iron on the beach – which after further investigation turned out to be part of a Victorian diving board – provided the stimulus for a wonderfully in-depth exploration of the Victorian era of one small fishing village on the South West coast. Another student studied bird migration to and from Jersey, creating a beautiful world map with migratory routes alongside stunning, meticulous drawings of all the different birds as well as life-size papier mache models. We have had a range of projects which started life as beach cleans, with illuminated sea monsters, lifeguard stations, working clocks, tables and lamps all made from the debris washed up on our beaches. Not only are these functional objects, but an important reminder of the issue of plastics within the sea.

The resulting exhibition is a wonderful opportunity for our Year 7s to genuinely feel like they are part of our family. All too often, whole school displays are filled with older students' work, but having this opportunity to share the passion and determination of our youngest students is so important. Not only does it provide a wonderful beginning and recognition for our new Year 7s, but every year, it provides a really powerful reminder of what our youngest students are capable of. The work every year just seems to get better and better.

The transition process is one small way in which we have secured a more solid footing in our own rainforest. Departments across the school are now brimming with knowledge-rich, experience-rich curriculum models, which just keep growing as the roots dig deep and we continue to explore the fertile ground we are beginning to grow from.

CASE STUDY: AN EMERGING FIVE-YEAR WRITING CURRICULUM IN ENGLISH

Author: Emilio Chain-Lopez, Head of English, Les Quennevais School

Five years ago the English department decided to design a five year curriculum prioritising the teaching of writing. Such a curriculum, we felt, should emerge from an understanding that writing is a cognitively complex task, something that responds well to deliberate practice. In order to achieve this we had three areas of focus – a writing trivium if you will.

Taking our cues from Exeter University's influential 'Grammar for Writing' project, we realised that teaching grammar, particularly the grammar of the sentence could help give students a tool to reflect both on the choices they made in their writing and on the choices made by the professional and canonical writers they encountered over five years.

We selected an array of sentences from literary texts ranging from Victorian novels through to modernist and postmodernist fiction. We also made selections from classic genre fiction including the works of Raymond Chandler and Ursula K Le Guin. An important factor in our choice of sentences was the use of parallelism. We privileged sentences in which the syntax had been deliberately patterned, sentences that proudly proclaimed their artifice from the rooftops. For example, a sentence by Elizabeth Bowen using a pattern of three prepositional phrases, or a sentence by Philip Pullman in which the definite article is repeated three times in increasingly detailed clauses in order to describe a scene. We found that these syntactic patterns, once shared and discussed, could be imitated in a range of contexts. The repetition of the definite article might originally have been used to bring a startlingly complex universe to life but it might also animate a non-fiction piece about fake news.

If sentence grammar was to provide one useful strand, then the teaching of various aspects of narratology provided us with another. A successful writing curriculum would not only acknowledge the sentence level choices made by successful writers, it would also aspire to make students aware of the structural choices open to writers too and encourage them to use them in their writing. Rich and varied reading, supported by lively discussion would be the royal road to this kind of awareness. Drawing on the work of academic narratology, stylistics and the veritable cottage industry of creative writing instructional texts, we created a glossary of structural devices that would come to inform our teaching and enrich our students' reading and writing over five years. We reasoned that if students knew how fictional worlds are built, they might just become more adept at building their own.

The final part of our writing trivium was vocabulary. Vocabulary remains a hot topic in teaching discourse but we were mindful of simply 'bolting-on' generic lists of tier 2 vocabulary in the quest for eloquence.

Instead, we carefully selected words from the rich texts in our curriculum to be explicitly taught and revisited. By encountering the same words in different contexts over time, it was felt that students would gain a greater depth of understanding. Once words were selected it became possible for us to track individual vocabulary items across the five years of our curriculum. For example, the word 'ominous' is met for the first time in Year 7 as students study 'The Iliad', it comes into prominence again in Year 8 when Bill Sikes is encountered in 'Oliver Twist' and again when the Martian war machines wreak havoc in 'War of the Worlds'. In Year 9 the word returns during the study of 'Woman in Black' and war poetry. By the time students meet their Key Stage 4 texts it is hoped that their understanding of the word has been productively expanded. Depth through greater breadth was our rallying cry in this area.

Sentences, narrative structure and vocabulary all come together in our Key Stage 3 and 4 compositions. The composition is a weekly extended writing task undertaken by all students in the school. It is a further, essential expression of the fact that consistency, routine and teachers with the capacity to effectively teach English enable our writing curriculum to function effectively. All composition tasks contain word, sentence and structural level success criteria. The words are from our bank of curricular tier 2 vocabulary items, the sentences include a selection of our patterned forms and our structural choices might relate to setting, conflict, flashbacks or another of the items from our glossary of narrative devices. Wherever possible the topics of the weekly compositions reflect our curriculum. In Year 8 students currently studying 'The Rime of the Ancient Mariner' might complete a composition on ghost ships. In Key Stage 4 the GCSE literature texts provide even further scope for literary escapades and all along the five year path students are practising the knowledge and skills prioritised by our writing curriculum.

ST JOSEPH'S PRIMARY, PENARTH, SOUTH GLAMORGAN

INTRODUCTION

Back in March 2017, Scottish educator, David Cameron, set up a gathering of people involved in education from each of Scotland, Wales, England and Northern Ireland for an event called 'Four Countries' – neatly enough! They wanted to invite a member of the Headteachers' Roundtable group as part of the English delegation and I was quick to volunteer – not least because it entailed a trip to Edinburgh where my daughter is at university! It is the one and only time I could ever say that I was 'representing England'! In a similar fashion, representing Wales, was Gareth Rein, Headteacher of St Joseph's, one of the pioneer schools in the Curriculum for Wales initiative. Interestingly, a key figure at this small conference was Professor Graham Donaldson himself, the author of the 'Successful Futures' report that Gareth mentions in his case study.

It was particularly fascinating to discuss the Curriculum for Wales initiative with Gareth because, possibly against the grain of the general thrust of the initiative as it is often characterised, he was extremely passionate about E.D Hirsch's ideas about core knowledge and the role of cognitive science, with a trip planned to Virginia where he would meet Dan Willingham and Hirsch in person. We had a great discussion about the role of the actual knowledge content within the 'areas of learning and experience' and the 'purposes' that take prominence in the Curriculum for Wales structure. It's interesting to discover just how much remains up for grabs in this process; the structure leaves it wide open for schools to develop their curriculum content in myriad ways; St Joseph's pioneer status is fully justified in that regard.

Last year I had the opportunity to visit St Joseph's to run a training day for Gareth's staff and other leaders around the Cardiff area, sharing the Learning Rainforest concept which seems to support this blend of purposes and a knowledge-rich curriculum very well, if leaders opt to choose that direction. As Deputy Head, Laura, describes in her excellent account, the St Joseph's four-part structure for their Domain Units are a superb way of incorporating rigorous knowledge within a wider framework, perhaps pointing the way for how Curriculum for Wales could develop. She outlines how it links with all three parts of the Learning Rainforest metaphor very clearly.

In Gareth's case study, it's wonderful to see how student voice is given such a high profile through the School Parliament and how this links so strongly to the whole school's vision and values. For sure, one of my favourite student *Fieldbook* contributions comes from Annie in Year 6: *My favourite feature would have to be the School Parliament, but as I am the Prime Minister, I probably would say that.* How many children could say that?!

PROFILE

Location: Penarth, Vale of Glamorgan

Type of Institution: Roman Catholic Primary School

Roll/Age Range: 240, aged 3–11

Year Founded: 1877

Motto: 'Jesus: in our hearts, in our minds, in our living, in our learning.'

House Names: St Cadoc, St Non, St Tydfil and St Teilo

Recent/Current School Production: *The Wizard of Oz.*

Recent significant sports event/triumph: Winner of the St Joseph's Annual Rugby 7s Tournament in 2015, 2017 and 2018.

Quote: "Over the past few years, we have been on an interesting and sometimes challenging journey in redesigning our school. We constantly evaluate the curriculum, ensuring pupils are secure in their knowledge and confident in their ability to apply this in interesting and purposeful ways. We have been spurred on by the positive comments received from our pupils and their families, many of whom appreciate that we are on this journey together. We value open discussion and feedback around aspects of the curriculum and act upon this in order to provide rich learning experiences for the pupils in our care."

Jenny Dunstan. Year 5 teacher and ALNCo.

Notable quirks/alumni: St Joseph's School is situated in over seven acres of grounds, that include woods, an orchard, a pond, and meadow, and is the only maintained school in Wales with an observatory, housing a high-powered telescope.

Gareth Rein
Headteacher

St Joseph's is a Roman Catholic school where we support and guide our pupils in mind, body and spirit to live the Gospel as beacons of light to the world. During this unprecedented time of great change in our education system, we maintain focus on the formation of the whole person by aiming for our pupils' intellectual, physical and spiritual development.

Since January 2017, St Joseph's has been one of around 170 Pioneer Schools that have been writing the new Curriculum for Wales through a ground-breaking co-construction approach. Wales is the first country to entrust the construction of its curriculum to the teaching profession and the enterprise has received attention from around the world. This exciting work, which followed the 2015 publication of Professor Graham Donaldson's seminal report 'Successful Futures', has been the catalyst for much innovation in Wales and, early on, our school set out to construct a robust, progressive and coherent curriculum that would be knowledge-rich, develop skills securely and provide exciting experiences for all learners so that we may open minds and broaden horizons.

Soon after the publication of Successful Futures, we consulted all stakeholders to help us to develop a shared curriculum vision for our school. We asked pupils, parents, governors and staff members, '*By the time they leave St Joseph's School, what should*

PROFILE

pupils know, be able to do and what attributes should they have?" We shortened this to 'Know, Do, Be' in discussions and used the data in the creation of our long-term curriculum map.

After three years of continuous development, implementation and review, the school has made much progress with this work and our teachers have improved their collective understanding of the importance of curriculum design and mapping. In addition, we have developed our staff members' knowledge of the application of cognitive science in the classroom through carefully planned professional learning opportunities. On this journey, we have been influenced by the work of prominent figures such as Daisy Christodoulou, Dan Willingham, E.D. Hirsch, Doug Lemov, Dylan Wiliam and, of course, Tom Sherrington.

STUDENT: ANNIE

Age and Year Group: 11, Year 6
House: St Cadoc

Most recent:

School Trip: National Museum, Cardiff
Extra-curricular activity: Piano lessons
Science experiment: Conditions for plant photosynthesis as part of our Rainforest Domain Unit
Book/Play studied in English Literature: *Macbeth*
History topic: The Renaissance
Arts project: Whole class Mona Lisa collage

Learning:

Recent learning highlight: At the end of the Astronomy Domain Unit, we invited parents in to school to learn about what we had studied. We shared some astronomy facts we had learned, played games and displayed our space art-work. Our parents really liked our work and we loved showing it to them.

The most stand-out/interesting/challenging topic you've studied at school: We studied the early twentieth century and I learnt a lot about what life was like in Wales and the U.K. at this time. I also learned about the sinking of the Titanic and how the passengers were separated by class; like society at that time.

A favourite feature of the school: My favourite feature would have to be the School Parliament, but as I am the Prime Minister, I probably would say that. We have Government Groups, like the Healthy Schools and Learning Spaces Ministries and we learn about things like the UNCRC. All children in KS2 are in a group so all are able to have an impact on the school. With the Parliament, it is not just the teachers who have a say in the school, but the pupils too. We all have a voice.

STUDENT: THOMAS

Age and Year Group: 9, Year 4
House: St Teilo

Most recent:

School Trip: Cardiff United Synagogue
Extra-curricular activity: Rugby
Science experiment: Reaction times and reflexes as part of our Characteristics of Animals Domain Unit
Book/Play studied in English Literature: *Wind in the Willows*
History topic: The Founding of Rome
Arts project: Roman Mosaics

Learning:

Recent learning highlight: One recent piece of work that captured my imagination was when we made Roman Shields. I enjoyed using the paints and linking my knowledge of Roman soldiers and their weapons to the art-work.

The most stand-out/interesting/challenging topic you've studied at school: I have especially enjoyed learning about the Romans recently because we had an immersion day when we tried different Roman foods and did exciting activities. I like learning about the Roman army and learning lots of facts about the founding of Rome and the lives of Romans. I have been very excited by this Domain and am very good at the work.

A favourite feature of the school: My favourite feature is the school grounds. We get to go outside a lot and I learn more outside. I really like the playing fields and all the facilities we have. I like that we can learn together and help each other.

I like that we can learn together and help each other.
THOMAS

With the Parliament, it is not just the teachers who have a say in the school, but the pupils too. We all have a voice.
ANNIE

STUDENT: COLM

Age and Year Group: 10, Year 5
House: St Cadoc

Most recent:

School Trip: Llantwit Major beach and coastline
Extra-curricular activity: Irish Dancing and Ballet, but these are out of school activities
Science experiment: Tectonic plates using crackers as part of our Geology Domain Unit
Book/Play studied in English Literature: 'The Highwayman' poem by Alfred Noyes
History topic: Age of Exploration
Arts project: Fossil Sketches

Learning:

Recent learning highlight: My favourite piece of work this year was writing a story for the Eisteddfod competition. We used a Welsh Changeling tale as our inspiration and I loved creating my own version. This was a highlight because I love writing and being creative.

The most stand-out/interesting/challenging topic you've studied at school: I enjoyed working on The Highwayman poem. Breaking it down and studying each part was extremely interesting and challenging. The poem is great and it really amazed me to learn more about it.

A favourite feature of the school: I love our Holy Week liturgies. This year, I took the part of Jesus in our Good Friday liturgy. I really liked preparing for this and took the role very seriously.

I also love how we keep trying to improve school life, like the changes to lunchtimes in the hall with family lunch and to our curriculum. Things keep getting better every year.

I also love how we keep trying to improve school life, like the changes to lunchtimes in the hall with family lunch and to our curriculum. Things keep getting better every year.

COLM

CASE STUDY: ST JOSEPH'S SCHOOL PARLIAMENT

General Area: Pupil Voice and Citizenship

Author: Gareth Rein, Headteacher

A 2014 summer review of our School Council concluded that it was not fit for purpose and that its work had resulted in almost no discernible benefit for pupils in the school over the previous few years. When such a conclusion is reached in a school, leaders have three options:

1. Stop doing the thing
2. Do the thing better
3. Do something else

Welsh Government regulations mandate that all maintained schools must have a School Council to provide pupils with an opportunity to '*discuss matters relating to their school, their education and any other matters of concern or interest*', so Option 1 – stop doing the thing, was not possible. Option 2 – do the thing better, seemed plausible and we decided to delay the class votes for the 2014–2015 School Council until we had constructed a plan for improvement. In the usual ways, we looked inward and starting chatting about what could be done to improve our School Council and looked outward by researching online and consulting with others.

I spoke with quite a few local headteacher colleagues and each told me that their School Council didn't really achieve much and that they simply paid lip service to the regulation. Interestingly, many headteachers reported that other pupil groups within their schools, such as Eco Committees and Digital leaders, were more impactful than the School Council and this reflected the findings of our online research. If these groups were working well across Wales, why weren't the School Councils?

After a few weeks of investigation, I had an epiphany: the pupil groups were succeeding because they had a reason to exist. The work of the Eco Committees was authentic and through these groups pupils were making a difference in their schools. School Councils, in contrast, were talking shops where little was achieved and no time was given to act on any concerns that were shared and on any decisions that were made. This led to Option 3 – do something else: create an ambitious, purposeful and inclusive School Parliament. By creating multiple pupil groups, each with a raison d'être, the St Joseph's School Parliament would enable pupils to not just '*discuss matters relating to their school, their education and any other matters of concern or interest*', but to plan and take actions that would impact positively on their experiences in school.

Since the establishment of the first St Joseph's School Parliament in autumn 2014, our pupils have achieved more than we could ever have expected from the model.

GARETH REIN
HEADTEACHER

CASE STUDY: ST JOSEPH'S SCHOOL PARLIAMENT

St Joseph's School Parliament Model

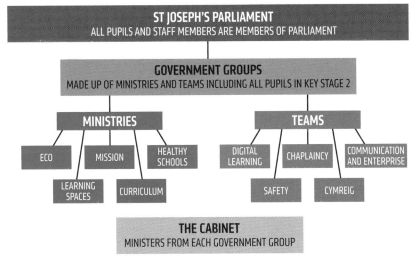

The St Joseph's Parliament is an umbrella organisation for work undertaken to achieve three aims:

1. Improve the school
2. Improve the local community
3. Help to achieve the United Nations' Global Goals

All pupils and staff members in the school are members of the Parliament and, as such, have rights and responsibilities in helping to achieve the three aims. Most of the work is undertaken by pupils in Key Stage 2 who are assigned to pupil groups known as Government Groups. When planning the Government Groups initially, staff members and pupils listed all of the areas of school life about which pupils could work to make a difference. Initially, ten Government Groups were established and these were subdivided into two categories – Ministries (greens) and Teams (reds). The structure of the Parliament can be seen in the model diagram.

In the first week of the academic year, all pupils in Key Stage 2 complete an application form outlining which Government Group they would like to join and stating why and how they believe they will serve this group well. The group size and age range is important as we have found that groups of 10–15, including pupils from Year 3 to Year 6 work best (as Tom says, be conscious of the Ringelmann effect[1]). A staff member acts as a facilitator for each group and, again, this works best if the teacher or teaching assistant is able to have a say in this allocation.

At the outset of the enterprise, we decided that if we were to value and respect the work of the Parliament, it must be given time during the school day and meetings would need to take place weekly throughout the year. At their first meeting, the group is reminded of its responsibilities and members elect a Chairperson to lead its work and a Secretary to keep minutes of each 40-minute meeting. The two elected officials also represent their Ministry or Team in the Cabinet, which oversees the work of all groups and holds each to account.

During the first few meetings, the groups think about how they can help the school to improve, how they can develop links with the local community and how they can help to achieve the Global Goals. There is a blend of adult directed tasks that help pupils to learn about the United Nations Convention on the Rights of the Child (UNCRC) and the seventeen Global Goals to provide focus for their work, and pupil-led conversations about what they would like to achieve in the year. Action plans are written through genuine co-construction and the adult facilitator provides a steer, but ideas mostly come from pupils. By the end of the first half-term, each of the Chairpersons presents their group's action plan

to the Cabinet, whose members discuss the targets and provide feedback about what is acceptable and advise what changes should be made.

The Cabinet meets fortnightly throughout the year to receive reports from the groups about their work and their progress towards meeting their objectives. Ministries and Teams provide information in alternate meetings so that Chairs and Secretaries report only once a month. This allows sufficient time between reports for the groups to have made progress against their action plan and provides an opportunity for discussion and challenge from other Cabinet members. These 30-minute meetings take place during lunchtime as Cabinet members understand that with power and privilege comes service and responsibility. The Parliament's Prime Minister, who is elected by all pupils and staff members each September, chairs Cabinet meetings and they are supported by a Deputy Prime Minister and the Headteacher, who is the Cabinet facilitator.

When setting objectives for their action plans, pupils are invited to be ambitious and creative to solve problems under the three broad Parliament aims. These open ended tasks result in wide-ranging and aspirational goals, about which pupils are enthused and motivated. To achieve their objectives, pupils undertake projects that require the setting of strategy and success criteria, role allocation, and budget and time planning. This is a joint enterprise where all group members, including the staff facilitator, harness their capabilities to maximum effect. These purposeful opportunities to develop pupils' wider knowledge and skills are also excellent vehicles for developing literacy and numeracy, such as oracy and number application, and digital competency through structured and unstructured activities. The richness of discussion and debate during Cabinet meetings is often staggering and the excellent listening habits,

---

1. The Ringelmann effect is the tendency for individual members of a group to become increasingly less productive as the size of their group increases

CASE STUDY: ST JOSEPH'S SCHOOL PARLIAMENT

developed intentionally during lessons, are evident in the ways in which Cabinet members provide both affirmative and critical feedback. Under a School Council model, by Year 6 only a minority of pupils will have participated, but in the St Joseph's model, all pupils serve their school for four years and develop understanding of service, responsibility and accountability.

Since the establishment of the first St Joseph's School Parliament in autumn 2014, our pupils have achieved more than we could ever have expected from the model. Each year, all Government Groups achieve nearly all of the ambitious objectives that are set under the three Parliament aims and the Cabinet fulfils the statutory requirements set out in the Welsh Government regulations in a more meaningful and effectual way than any School Council could. Each year's Parliament's achievements are too many and varied to list here, but suffice to say that their work has been sufficiently successful to gain the attention of our local AM[2] and MP, who both requested visits to the school to attend Cabinet meetings and, without any publicity, we receive multiple calls each term from schools wishing to learn about what we do. During the last five years, we have shared our model with over thirty schools directly and many of these have shared it with others so that the St Joseph's School Parliament model has been adopted and adapted by at least fifty schools in Wales with the numbers growing each year.

Link to Learning Rainforest:

There are elements of the three Learning Rainforest aspects of Establishing the Conditions (C), Building the Knowledge Structure (K) and Exploring Possibilities (P) in the St Joseph's Parliament, but the model is most closely aligned with Exploring the Possibilities. The potential for the model to enable pupils to take part in Projects and Hands on Learning – P1 to P10 – are limitless and there are many opportunities for exploiting Further Possibilities: P11 to P20.

Of the twenty P strategies, we most often use:

P5 Groups, Goals and Roles
P6 Projects
P7 Keep it Real
P8 Get Creative; Learn to Choose
P9 Dazzle Me
P15 Co-construction.

---

2. AM: Assembly Member

CASE STUDY: CURRICULUM: DESIGNING TWO ENVIRONMENTS

Title: Curriculum: Designing Two Environments: An approach to curriculum design

General Area: Teaching and Learning and Curriculum Development

Author: Laura Taylor, Deputy Headteacher

In his 2012 book, *When Can You Trust the Experts*, Daniel Willingham links Herbert A. Simon's design terms 'inner and outer environments' to the mind of a child and the wider classroom experience respectively. Over the past few years, St Joseph's School has used the concept of crafting a designed school through the thoughtful construction of these two environments. We use findings from cognitive psychology, to inform our curriculum design and lesson planning for inner environment development. For the outer environment we principally use Doug Lemov's Teach Like a Champion 2.0 for improving pedagogy and classroom culture and research findings about learning spaces to establish the physical conditions in which our pupils learn. In this short Case Study, I will provide information about a four-stage Domain Unit approach that we designed to support the development of the inner environment.

At St Joseph's School, we are designing a knowledge-rich curriculum that is inspired by E.D. Hirsch's U.S. Core Knowledge Curriculum, but is rooted in Welsh and U.K. content. Through detailed whole school mapping, we ensure that the curriculum is coherent, rigorous and progressive, so that lessons build knowledge, develop skills and provide experiences to open minds and broaden horizons.

The St Joseph's Domain Unit approach has been designed in line with the new Curriculum for Wales, which aims to seek connections between the six Areas of Learning and Experience[3] (AoLE) where appropriate. The approach is interdisciplinary in organisation but a strong focus on disciplinary knowledge is retained. For instance, in the Year 6 Rainforests Unit, we cover aspects from four of the six AoLE, but the links are relevant and purposeful. To ensure that there is integrity and rigour to all aspects of this work, the school devised an effective four-part structure for Domain Units which is followed from Reception to Year 6:

Stage 1. *Engagement and Immersion*

We provide immersive experiences to engage, enrich and excite learners and develop their interest in the domain.

Stage 2. *Knowledge Acquisition*

Pupils are provided with a foundation of factual, conceptual and procedural knowledge through a variety of activities and experiences.

Stage 3. *Build up to Writing*

We use five steps to build up to a piece of extended writing in each Unit. These are 1. Hook and features, 2. Plan and practice, 3. Draft, 4. Edit, 5. Publish.

Stage 4. *Application and Exit Celebration*

Pupils apply what they have learned in a variety of ways and situations and celebrate what they have learned, often with a wider audience.

At the Unit outset, a domain knowledge organiser, which is used during all four stages, is shared with pupils and parents, and teachers provide opportunities for pupils to immerse themselves in the topic through texts, videos, hands-on experiences, stories and a variety of engaging methods. These experiences stimulate pupils' interest and this leads effectively onto stage 2 where the teacher builds the knowledge structure and develops pupils' understanding through Read Alouds, including Dual Coding and Concrete Examples,

---

3. Expressive Arts, Health and Well-being, Humanities, Languages, Literacy and Communication, Mathematics and Numeracy, Science and Technology

CASE STUDY: CURRICULUM: DESIGNING TWO ENVIRONMENTS

Elaboration, outdoor learning, homework, visits and visitors, research and experimentation. The curriculum is structured in a way that enables pupils to build on prior knowledge and develop schema, and frequent reference is made to previous domains and learning experiences. Through frequent retrieval practice and low stakes testing throughout the Unit, pupils are provided with opportunities to reinforce their learning and teachers gather meaningful data via whole class marking and provide purposeful feedback that informs future learning.

At Stage 3, pupils from Year 2 to Year 6 complete and publish a piece of extended writing linked to the domain. For each Unit, teachers and pupils follow a five-step process that includes the teaching of the purpose and conventions of the text type and genre. Since the introduction of the Domain Unit approach, we have found that pupils' extended writing is richer, more ambitious and is technically better. This is because pupils' domain specific knowledge is so well embedded in their memory they have something to write about and are, therefore, able to focus on the quality of the writing rather than having to divide their attention.

During the final stage, there is a blend of teacher directed and pupil choice activities. Pupils are able to take their learning further by researching areas of the domain that they found particularly interesting or undertake an enquiry. As a class, pupils then choose how they would like to demonstrate and share what they have learned during the Unit, often to a wider audience. Across the school, pupils have chosen to compose music; write poems, wikis and stories; create iMovies; complete research projects; and craft artworks, all of which have been shared with their peers, parents or online.

There are aspects of the four-stage approach that will require refinement as it is used over a longer period and, presently, teachers sometimes feel the work is a little rushed in their aim of completing all planned Domain Units during the year. Such feedback is helping us to make changes to our long-term mapping and our curriculum will evolve and improve as we work together. We are only a few years into working in this way, but already standards are higher than they have ever been in the school and pupils are thriving.

STAGE 4 APPLICATION & EXIT CELEBRATION	→	Pupils apply what they've learnt to new situations and celebrate their learning with a wider audience.
STAGE 3 BUILD UP TO WRITING	→	We use five steps to build up to an extended piece of writing: 1 - Hook and features, 2 - Plan and Practice, 3 - Draft, 4 - Edit, 5 - Publish.
STAGE 2 KNOWLEDGE ACQUISITION	→	Pupils need a foundation of factual, conceptual and procedural knowledge to underpin their learning.
STAGE 1 ENGAGEMENT & IMMERSION	→	Learning should engage, enrich and excite learners. We provide immersive experiences to develop their interest in learning.

Link to Learning Rainforest:

The four-stage Domain Unit approach described in this case study is aligned closely with Tom's Rainforest Analogy. By Establishing the Conditions through excellent relationships, habits for excellence and the carefully planned curriculum, teachers provide strong roots on which to Build the Knowledge Structure. The approach also provides opportunities to Explore the Possibilities through projects and hands on learning and gives teachers and pupils the freedom to go off piste, get creative and exhibit excellence.

At St Joseph's School, much of our professional learning is based on developing a common understanding of the application of cognitive science in the classroom and a common approach to teaching and learning. *The Learning Rainforest* has been extremely helpful in this regard, as Tom provides excellent explanations of essential strategies and learning theories. St Joseph's School considers itself a learning organisation where teachers are encouraged to engage in reading, research and debate, and of the many texts we have read, teachers are in agreement that *The Learning Rainforest* most closely reflects our school and what we are trying to achieve.

At St Joseph's School, we are developing a knowledge-rich curriculum that is inspired by E.D. Hirsch's US Core Knowledge Curriculum, but is rooted in Welsh and UK content.

LAURA TAYLOR
DEPUTY HEADTEACHER

SCHOOL 21, STRATFORD

INTRODUCTION

In drawing up a list of schools to include in the *Fieldbook*, School 21 was firmly in my mind from the very beginning. A key reason is that founder and Executive Head, Peter Hyman has had a big influence on my thinking over the last few years, often challenging my biases. In 2017, I shared some draft chapters from *The Learning Rainforest* with him and he didn't agree with everything I was saying but, nonetheless, encouraged me to be more bold in expressing my own opinions without trying too hard to be even-handed. He helped me find my voice. Peter himself has strong views about the importance of a holistic, contemporary curriculum and offers an important critique of narrow interpretations of what a knowledge-based curriculum might mean. He thinks that children in the UK take far too many exams; exams that have too much influence on the curriculum as a whole. His 'head, hand and heart' philosophy, as mentioned in the case study and as I describe in the curriculum chapter of *The Learning Rainforest*, is powerful in its depth and clarity as an alternative curriculum framework.

I first met him when we delivered a conference session together in 2016 where, at his suggestion, we employed a technique called 'provocations'. Rather than presenting our views to the participants, we wrote a list of 10 stimulus statements and engaged everyone in a discussion around them, basing our input on their responses. The list included things like 'Speaking matters as much as reading and writing' and 'Character can't be taught but it can be engineered'. This technique for generating discussion was just one of many that teachers use in the amazing oracy programme at School 21.

When I visited School 21 it was for a parents' evening. But, unlike many schools where this would feature teachers at desks talking to individual students' parents, the event was a showcase of learning. I saw fabulous writing in the primary school – sophisticated pieces drafted and crafted to a standard far beyond the norm; students in Year 9 standing on soap-boxes reciting revolutionary speeches as part of a history-drama collaboration; wonderful large-scale chess boards with clay heads as chess pieces based on key figures from the cold war – from a project linking art and history. There was a music and science collaboration; some fabulous work in technology and a group of students talking about their weekly work experience or authentic community service projects. The curriculum at School 21 is fabulously creative – and demonstrably knowledge-rich. The foundations have been laid for a magnificent school.

The case study here outlined here by Daniel, Kate and Amy, illustrates the detailed thinking that has gone into the School 21 oracy programme. I love the focus on listening and the problematic issue of 'me' listening. The framework presented is excellent; it's no surprise that School 21 is the go-to source of inspiration for many teachers and leaders looking to develop similar programmes in their schools.

A work in progress...but maybe that's the point.
OLI DE BOTTON

PROFILE

Location: Stratford, East London

Type of Institution: 4–18 'free school' with comprehensive admissions

Roll/Age Range: 1200, aged 4–18

Year Founded: 2012

Motto: 'Empowering young people to take on the world'

Recent/Current School Production: *Hairspray, Woyzeck*

**Oli de Botton
Headteacher and co-founder**

School 21, a 4–18 school for boys and girls, was founded in 2012 in the heart of Stratford, East London. The founders, Peter Hyman, Oli de Botton and Ed Fidoe, were united in a belief that education needed to be done differently if children were to be ready to live and learn well. The mission is for children to leave the school empowered to take on the world; so the curriculum is designed to nurture the 'head', the 'heart' and the 'hand'. A curriculum of the ' head' helps children grapple with the big ideas of subject disciplines – evolution, revolution, the aesthetic – whilst securing key facts and skills. A curriculum of the 'heart' asks children to find out who they are so they can make informed

PROFILE

choices about their future. A curriculum of the 'hand' fosters a hands on approach and prioritises creativity – starting from the arts subjects but going well beyond. All these strands are joined together by a philosophy of teaching and learning that prioritises dialogue so children can learn to talk and learn through talk. Oracy sees children discuss, explore and challenge – pupil to pupil and teacher to pupil. This work has been amplified by Voice 21, the school's charity, which is working with over 1000 schools across the country to embed oracy.

An emphasis on dialogue is important not just for the classroom but for the staffroom. School 21 believes teaching is an intellectual as well as practical profession that requires an engaged discourse to keep it vibrant. So teachers are encouraged to blog about their work, present 'viva' style papers to their colleagues in place of performance management and professionalise themselves through turning their work in modules for other teachers to learn from.

Seven years in, the school is full and making strides with lots still to do including working out how to innovate at scale and getting the balance right between teacher and student autonomy and consistency of practice.

STUDENT: MALA

Age and Year Group: 8, Year 4

Most recent:

School Trip: Salesforce Tower to deliver my Spark Speech

Extra-curricular activity: Choir on a Friday and performing arts club on Saturdays at School 21 to prepare for my role as the genie in Aladdin.

Science experiment: My last science experiment was to investigate how sound travels. We used different materials and distances to find out how sound travelled best between two polystyrene cups.

Book/Play studied in English Literature: *Goodnight Mister Tom, Butterfly Lion, Kensuke's Kingdom, Goodnight Stories for Rebel Girls, Coraline, Early Modern Rulers,* 'The Listeners' (Walter de la Mare)

History topic: 'How can we give a new voice to Newham's war stories?' We studied the Second World War, using the grounding text, *Goodnight Mister Tom.* We then used historical sources to find out how Newham, our local borough, was impacted during the war. Our product was to host a local walking tour, where we retold residents' war stories at the sights where bombs hit.

Arts project: 'How are families shaped by where they live?' I had a choice to study geographical case studies from either China, Brazil or Kenya. After choosing Kenya, we learnt about different families across the country. We then created printing blocks where we developed symbols to reflect the family's life. We drew the family and printed our symbols as their clothes.

Learning:

Subjects Studied: All primary subjects – MFL – Spanish

Recent learning highlight: For our project, 'How can we give a new voice to Newham's war stories?' we wrote a newspaper article about city children being evacuated from their homes and arriving in the countryside. I liked this style of writing because we had to research real facts. We re-drafted our work and our final piece was presented like a real newspaper.

The most stand-out/interesting/challenging topic you've studied at school: Presenting my Spark Speech at Salesforce Tower was challenging because we had to perform a two-minute speech about a challenge in our life so far. Before presenting our speeches, we practised our oracy skills with secondary students. After I performed my spark speech, even though I was really nervous, I felt on top of the world.

One of my favourite teachers: I enjoy lessons with Ms McCartney when she teaches me maths because if I struggle to understand at first she always explains things in a new way to help me understand. She draws lots of pictures on the table to help!

A favourite feature of the school: I am lucky because I get to be taught by my class teacher and some secondary school teachers. The secondary teachers teach me PE, Spanish and Music. Now that I am in KS2 we also get real novels in Shared Reading and they are so interesting. Our project and Storytelling are always linked and this makes learning much easier to remember.

Aspire to inspire before you expire.
ZAKARIYA

After I performed my spark speech, even though I was really nervous, I felt on top of the world.
MALA

STUDENT: ZAKARIYA

Age and Year Group: 13, Year 8

Most recent:

School Trip: Portugal
Extra-curricular activity: Chess, Debating, Football And Table Tennis
Science experiment: Acids And Alkalis
Book/Play studied in English Literature: *We See Everything* (William Sutcliffe)
History topic: Civil Rights Movement
Arts project: Tangram Puzzle

Learning:

Recent learning highlight: My trip to Portugal where we got to collaborate with a group of people from a completely different culture and we learnt new ways of logical and innovative thinking. It gave me a new perspective on the way I think and I wholeheartedly believe it was so beneficial.

The most stand-out/interesting/challenging topic you've studied at school: In our school we have coaching where we discuss current social issues that affect us, such as LGBT rights, or Philosophy, and this is pivotal to creating a narrative for scenarios which aren't talked about and should be talked about.
Another thing is that we utilize all the technology we receive and most students have an iPad ready for living in the 21st century.

One of my favourite teachers: Mr Pardoe because he always finds new way to keep the content interesting. Also he has a lot of general knowledge and I have gained lots of learning from him.

A favourite feature of the school: The openness that exists is second to none. Imagine going to a school where I feel I could tell my teacher about any problems I face. Imagine having a family like a coaching group who trust and are trusted. Imagine coming to school every day to see your second family. This what all schools should be like.

STUDENT: ANGELINA

Age and Year Group: 12 (13 in a few days), Year 8

Most recent:

School Trip: Watching a performance of dance
Extra-curricular activity: School performance of *Hairspray*
Science experiment: Exploring different Acids and Alkali
Book/Play studied in English Literature: *We See Everything* by William Sutcliffe
History topic: Civil Rights
Arts project: Tangram Puzzles

Learning:

Recent learning highlight: One of the lessons that really stood out for me was making a song by writing specific lyrics about things to do with suicide and although it was very hard I enjoyed it nonetheless because it was fun to make music with my friends.

The most stand-out/interesting/challenging topic you've studied at school: I enjoyed studying/learning about diversity in coaching and philosophy in coaching because I prefer to have deep probing conversations where I can talk and explain my opinion openly.

One of my favourite teachers: I enjoy lessons with Ms Wall who teaches me Music because I like learning how to play new instruments and discovering timeless bands. Also because it's a subject I can sing in.

A favourite feature of the school: One of the features that I like about School 21 is that it's very modern and cutting edge. They do things differently and provide opportunities that other schools don't.

STUDENT: AIYSHA

Age and Year Group: 18, Year 13

Most recent:

School Trip: University Fair
Book/Play studied in English Literature: *Paradise Lost* and *The Duchess of Malfi*
History topic: Witch hunting in early modern Europe

Learning:

Subjects Studied: History, English Literature and Government and Politics

Recent learning highlight: My most recent learning highlight was creating my EPQ[1]. I researched the British Empire by exploring not only the information that is available but I also pushed myself and went to India where I used the history of my family as the basis of my exploration. During the process I refined my research skills as well as my dissertation writing skills.

The most stand-out/interesting/challenging topic you've studied at school: I enjoyed studying witch-hunting as it was a topic that has been interpreted by many historians and therefore there is a lot of rich content that was available to assess. It was also challenging as the topic is complex and I had to develop my own perception of the topic whilst evaluating other arguments.

One of my favourite teachers: I enjoy lessons with Ms Davey who teaches me Politics because her lessons are very interactive and collaborative so I always feel challenged and I feel like my opinion is always developing during the lessons. I also enjoy the focus on specific information that Ms Davey puts into her lesson to ensure that we stand out when we write essays.

A favourite feature of the school: I love the focus that the school has on oracy and well-being. Students are taught to be fluent and confident in the ideas through collaborative learning and therefore we are able to develop ideas alongside helping others develop their ideas too. We also take our time to ensure we are feeling calm and collected so that we can focus on being less stressed.

---

1. EPQ: Extended Project Qualification

CASE STUDY: THE DIALOGIC SCHOOL: HOW ORACY CAN DRIVE A SCHOOL FORWARD

Title: The dialogic school: how oracy can drive a school forward

General Area: Teaching and Learning and Curriculum Development

Authors: School 21 Oracy leads: **Daniel Thomas, Kate Barron, Amy Weerasekera**

At School 21, Oracy has been a foundational pillar since the start. It shapes the curriculum, teaching and learning and our approach to well-being. Oracy, which we understand as learning to talk and learning through talk, has been a bottom-up movement with teachers collaborating together to give it depth. Our co-constructed vision, developed over the years sees 'every teacher a teacher of oracy.' This means we want every classroom to be a dialogic space where pupils are challenged and supported to learn through talk. No matter the subject, we believe talk is at the heart of engaging children in the learning process and help them make sense of challenging concepts. Talk is not for talk's sake: teachers think deeply and deliberately about the use of talk in lessons based around three core principles: expectations, intentionality and reflection.

What does it look like in practice?

Exploratory talk

Exploratory talk is the pedagogy through which pupils learn in the classroom: children collaboratively explore, constructively build on and challenge each other's ideas to deepen their thinking and understanding. Walk into a classroom and you might see five-year-olds in a traverse giving each other feedback on vocabulary choices; seven-year-olds using 'fed-in-facts' to come to a shared agreement about what a group of ancient Greek artefacts might be and how they may have been used; a group of Year 4s passionately engaged in group discussion about who Shackleton should have taken on his perilous journey to Elephant Island; Year

8s using a story map to articulate the process of evolution or 15 A-level students engaged in a Harkness discussion, debating the extent to which Theresa May is a true conservative.

In this way, the teaching of skills and knowledge are fused together: children build subject knowledge whilst developing vital skills in communication, collaboration, critical thinking and creativity, to name a few.

Presentational talk

Initially working with Professor Neil Mercer from Cambridge University, we developed a framework to support more explicit teaching of oracy across four strands: physical, linguistic, cognitive and social-emotional (see below). This has helped students reflect on their own talk and has helped teachers support improvements:

ORACY SKILLS FRAMEWORK

CONTENT
- Choice of content to convey meaning & intention
- Building on the views of others

STRUCTURE
- Structure & organization of talk

CLARIFYING & SUMMARISING
- Seeking information & clarification through questions
- Summarising

SELF-REGULATION
- Maintaining focus on task
- Time management

REASONING
- Giving reasons to support views
- Critically examining ideas & views expressed

VOCABULARY
- Appropriate vocabulary choice

LANGUAGE
- Register
- Grammar

RHETORICAL TECHNIQUES
- Rhetorical techniques such as metaphor, humour, irony & mimicry

VOICE
- Fluency & pace of speech
- Tonal variation
- Clarity of pronunciation
- Voice projection

BODY LANGUAGE
- Gesture & posture
- Facial expression & eye contact

WORKING WITH OTHERS
- Guiding or managing interactions
- Turn-taking

LISTENING & RESPONDING
- Listening actively & responding appropriately

CONFIDENCE IN SPEAKING
- Self assurance
- Liveliness & flair

AUDIENCE AWARENESS
- Taking account of level of understanding of the audience

| PHYSICAL | LINGUISTIC | COGNITIVE | SOCIAL & EMOTIONAL |

CASE STUDY: THE DIALOGIC SCHOOL: HOW ORACY CAN DRIVE A SCHOOL FORWARD

As a school with a mission to develop young people who make a positive impact on the world, we have a moral purpose to ensure advocacy and agency: that our pupils have something to say and our confident and articulate enough to say it. This requires providing opportunities in a wide range of contexts in front of a wide range of audiences over their 4–18 journey. A child at this school will experience this in a multitude of ways every single year, whether it be as storytellers, tour guides, actors, documentary presenters, sports commentators, performance poets, campaigners, activists, orators etc. In addition, every child writes and delivers a speech at pivotal transition points along their journey: in Years 4, 7, 9 and 12. These link to our school values: openness, humanity, community and responsibility, using the following enquiry questions as stimuli:

What has been difficult for me and how did I get through it?

What does my voice say about me?

How can I use my voice to contribute to my community?

How can I use my voice to move people to action?

Listening

As our oracy journey has progressed, listening has become a stronger imperative. As the crucial counterpart to talk, it requires explicit teaching and lots of practice (just as talk does). The school's initial approach to teaching 'active listening' through a focus on eye contact and body language has been rethought to champion the idea that listening is in the *response*. Too often we get caught up in '*me*' listening: listening just to make a comment that relates back to ourselves or not really even listening at all; just making eye contact to make it appear we are listening, but with something else on our minds altogether. To support this, we have created a 'listening framework', which breaks listening skills down across the four strands but also encourages us to listen through 'micro' and 'macro' strands: on a micro level we might listen through the physical and linguistic strands for the body language or the powerful words. Through the cognitive and social-emotional strands we might listen for the main message or the values the person is conveying matters to them.

Another initiative has been the introduction of 'listening buddies' for both staff and students as a way of 'checking-in and out' to provide a safe space in which to be heard and to mentally/emotionally cleanse. Thinking more purposefully about listening has enabled us to think more deeply about the tension between talking to win and talking to blend: the latter demands an ability to listen effectively so that we can elaborate on our own and each other's ideas, challenge ourselves and each other, justify our own points of view and reason with each other: that is the making of citizens who shape a productive and positive society.

Oracy as Culture

Oracy is a key building block for the wider culture at School 21. The centrality of oracy (speaking *and* listening) permeates everything we do as a school community and how we do it. One crucial aspect of achieving this has been to embed a shared language across the school. All staff and students use the same language: we discuss 'the four strands', 'talk guidelines' in the form of 'building on', 'challenging ideas' and 'inviting others to contribute', we all use 'protocols' such as the 'traverse', 'onion', 'trio' or 'nest', we ask 'silent summarisers' to feedback on discussions they hear and 'talk detectives' are used to reflect on the quality of talk heard in the room. We talk about 'strong circles' as an inclusive way of engaging with each other in various communities, whether it be in class, key stage assemblies, coaching circles (student and staff) or saying goodbye to members of staff who are leaving. Having a shared language has been fundamental to creating coherency and consistency at School 21, especially on a 4–18 scale.

Oracy is also at the heart of professional development. Every School 21 teacher is trained in the core principles of oracy pedagogy as soon as they join the school through a day's training delivered by the school's oracy leaders in conjunction with Voice

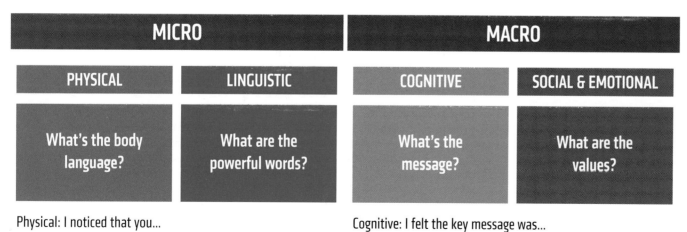

Physical: I noticed that you...
Linguistic: One word that really stood out was...

Cognitive: I felt the key message was...
Social & Emotional: You clearly value...

CASE STUDY: THE DIALOGIC SCHOOL: HOW ORACY CAN DRIVE A SCHOOL FORWARD

21 – the social enterprise that has been developed out of the school. This is then built on throughout the year through ongoing CPD. No matter the focus of the CPD (whether the content be specifically oracy-focused or not), every CPD session is delivered using oracy techniques.

Our headteacher, Oli de Botton, is a passionate advocate for the dialogic staffroom as well as the dialogic classroom. He affirms that teaching 'is an intellectual as well as practical profession that requires an engaged discourse to keep it vibrant. Teachers I work with are energised by conversations about the craft and feel professionally valued when their reflections can be accumulated into a robust evidence base about what works.' This is evident in the design of our CPD. Over the course of the year, CPD is dedicated to the following: craft presentations (where teachers present 'what they are working on' to the community), lesson studies in coaching trios and a range of action research modules (staff can elect which they attend). Lesson studies are designed with an emphasis on giving constructive feedback whereby staff choose protocols with which to receive this feedback in the form of 'keep, lose, introduce', 'I like, I notice, I wonder' or 'People, Process, Content' for example. Staff blog voluntarily in their spare time, be it about their work or opinions about the system on a wider scale.

Oracy as a movement

School 21's commitment to oracy goes beyond classroom practice as teachers take part in key oracy events across the year aimed at spreading the word to other schools. At the end of the Autumn term in 2018, School 21 held its third Teach Meet focused on oracy. Each of the teachers presented for two or five minutes on an area of their oracy practice from their classroom. This culminated in an evening rich in talk, where a range of skills and strategies were shared with attendees from a variety of schools. At the end of the spring term the school hosted its second Great Oracy Exhibition. The day was attended by over 500 guests who spent their day taking part in teacher led workshops, observing students' oracy outcomes and listening to panels discussing the big questions around oracy.

Beyond the walls of School 21 the movement continues to develop due to the incredible work carried out by Voice 21. Voice 21 was founded by the School 21 Foundation, the innovative charity behind School 21 and they work with teachers and schools to train and support them to place oracy at the core of their teaching practice. They created a network of oracy hub schools, creating a nationwide community committed to furthering the movement of oracy.

How did we get here?

...With difficulty and we are by no means where we want to be. Over the years though we have found a number of things particularly helpful (and a number of things unhelpful)

What's worked...

- Making the case for oracy in both practical ways and in ways that speak to the mission of the school. The value of oracy has been its depth. It starts with improving talk in the classroom and very quickly becomes something more profound as it touches on curriculum design, how teachers collaborate and the purpose of the school.

- Co-constructing the 'what' of oracy. When we started we weren't entirely sure of the contours of the agenda. A breakthrough moment was when we came together to define good talk through the four strands. The strands aren't gospel but they give us a shared language about what we were seeking to teach and how we would assess it.

- Giving teachers autonomy over the 'how' of oracy. Once we established what it was, teachers used the four strands framework to 'riff' off, coming up with a range of tools and protocols (e.g. talk detectives, silent summarisers, consensus circles, talk roles etc.) Over time this has developed into an extensive toolkit

- Making all CPD oracy CPD. The oracy toolkit promotes purposeful talk and so it seemed natural to use it to improve how the adults in the organisation talk and learn from each other

What hasn't worked...

- Prioritising showcase oracy as opposed to oracy that is purposeful and enhances thinking. We see oracy as intrinsic to the learning process so all talk needs to be intentionally planned. Occasionally over the years we have slipped into having, for example, an onion formation of students because it showed oracy rather than thinking why that formation would support cognitive stretch

- Focusing too much on oracy and not enough on listening. Many voices can grow into a cacophony unless we help students really hear what others are saying. We were more successful when we shifted the concept of listening from performative i.e. seeing if children are sitting upright and facing the teacher, to seeing proof of listening always being in the response. We found that children can appear off task while really listening and reverse.

PARLIAMENT HILL SCHOOL, CAMDEN

INTRODUCTION

It's impossible to tell the story of Parliament Hill without referencing my personal connection to the school via my wife Deborah O'Connor who is Deputy Head at the school and a science teacher. Through her eyes, I probably know more about Parliament Hill than any other school; it's a very special place that she has loved from the moment she arrived, working alongside Headteacher Sarah Creasey and her predecessor Sue Higgins. Deb and I have accompanied each other on our respective journeys through the Learning Rainforest, spending endless hours debating and sharing ideas over many years as we've engaged with teaching and learning in different contexts – both as leaders and in our own classrooms. The Learning Rainforest strategies include FACE It – an approach to building knowledge that was developed at Parliament Hill. It's just one of several ideas that Deb has given me over the years and I'm delighted that the school now features in the *Fieldbook*.

Parliament Hill embodies so much of what The Learning Rainforest is about, securing excellent outcomes for a supremely diverse population of North London girls, through a magnificent blend of aspirational 'no glass ceiling' values, an inclusive ethos and technical research-informed understanding of how to secure deep learning. Parliament Hill is proud of being a sought-after, fully comprehensive, inclusive Camden school, one of very few secondary schools to resist the need for a school uniform. As well as playing a key role as a member of the LaSWAP Sixth Form consortium, it's a prime example of a successful local authority school with a distinctive identity. Located at the edge of Hampstead Heath, typical of many inner-city schools, its leafy surroundings mask the range of social issues and the scale of deprivation many of their students experience; a context that makes their success all the more impressive. This year, a

significant new classroom block was opened, taking the school's facilities to another level, with the modern and traditional buildings dovetailing together to great effect, Learning Rainforest style!

This is the kind of school that inspires loyalty. A sense of belonging matters and, at PHS, they take that very seriously. *High Achieving and Happy*. I just love the power and simplicity of that motto. I also love the pride they take in the 'Parli Girls' and 'Parli Learning'. To be a 'Parli Girl' suggests being an assertive, confident, modern young woman ready to take on the world. That's the spirit that comes across in this case study alongside the curriculum thinking and commitment to professional learning that underpin every educational success story.

PROFILE

Location: LB Camden, London, UK

Type of Institution: Girls' Comprehensive

Roll/Age Range: 1300, aged 11–18 (inc. La SWAP sixth form)

Year Founded: 1906

Motto: 'High Achieving and Happy'

Recent/Current School Production: *High School Musical*

Recent significant sports event/triumph: We won the Camden Shield this year – again.

Notable quirks/alumni: We don't have a school uniform. Dua Lipa is an ex Parli girl.

Headteacher: Sarah Creasey

> **Thank you from the bottom of our hearts for the truly wonderful time you have given our girls. There is hardly a day passes when we don't think about how fortunate we have been to land in the most perfect school. It is hard to pinpoint exactly why the girls have all been so happy there but I think it is something about getting what seems just the right balance of a good academic education without a sense of pressure; genuine embracing of all types of diversity and the most lovely environment that allows the girls to thrive as exactly who they are.**
>
> PARENT OF THREE PARLI STUDENTS

Deborah O'Connor
Deputy Headteacher

Parli is a truly comprehensive girls' school with a very diverse intake reflecting our inner London location. We are very proud of our strong ethos which values and respects the rich cultural and ethnic diversity of our community. Relationships are strong and we like to think of ourselves as a happy school where everyone feels a sense of belonging. We are also a high achieving school with over 40 % of our GCSE grades at grade 7 or above this year. We aim daily to live up to our 'High Achieving and Happy' strap-line.

All schools have faced challenges in recent times and the sheer volume of curriculum change schools had to deal with was

PROFILE

STUDENT: ARIELLA BEAZLEY

daunting. Here at Parli we were also in a never-ending stop-start building programme. However we were excited at the chance to really look at our curriculum and our vision for our students. We decided that ultimately we want our students to become 'truly independent learners' and have been working out exactly what that means and how we can achieve it for the past few years now. We debated whether or not to include the word 'feminist' in our aims – we did. And we thought carefully about the wellbeing of our students and the need to address the mental health challenges faced in our community.

We began with the curriculum looking at threshold concepts, sequencing of knowledge and development of memory. And now, four years later, we are working in subject specific teams designing ways to deepen their learning, to really 'work' their knowledge so it becomes flexible and more powerful. In today's world we want our students to be able to argue confidently using evidence, distinguish a fact from an opinion and ask the right questions.

And we have finally moved into our long-awaited fabulous new building – the Kite building, a name chosen by the students. The kite represents their ambitions to aim high, take risks and have fun while they do it. Our students are becoming increasingly aware of the impact they have on their own outcomes. We have challenged them and they have grown in resilience as a result; the more they do, the more they can do. But we are a community which also endeavours to balance achievement with the need to support the wellbeing of students and teachers – we are proud to be a school with time to play, laugh and celebrate one another in all aspects of our diverse community.

Age and Year Group: 12, Year 7

Most recent:

School Trip: We visited the Globe theatre this year and it was my favourite trip. We had a tour and saw behind the stage and the trapdoors. We saw the costumes they would have used in Shakespearean times. We didn't see a play but we got a really good idea of what it would have been like to see a play in those times.

Extra-curricular activity: I have been class rep, a co-planner (we work with teachers to help them plan learning activities) and an anti-bullying ambassador. Also I have been part of STEM club, Movie club and Creative writing club. And I joined the Debate Mate club too. I have taken part in assemblies and given speeches to parents. In my spare time I am in a band with friends from school.

Science experiment: My most memorable science experiment was when we made parachutes with paper bags and we used raw eggs to investigate which one gave the greatest air resistance. We dropped them out of the window on the top floor to see which ones let the eggs break.

Book/Play studied in English Literature: *The Breadwinner*, Deborah Ellis. It is about Afghanistan and the Taliban. A little girl is looking after her family and trying to keep them safe in very difficult circumstances.

History topic: I really enjoyed learning about Eleanor of Aquitaine. She was married very young and had a child at 13. Her child was taken away and she had to fight to get him back. Eventually she made her son king and got all her land back. She was a very strong woman.

Arts project: I also really enjoyed Comedia del Arte in drama. A large part of it is improvisation. It is done in silence and depends on exaggeration and facial expressions. It was really fun to do.

Learning:

Subjects Studied: English, Maths, Science, Geography, History, French, RE, Citizenship, Music, Drama, Art, DT, PE, Swimming and Dance

Recent learning highlight: In English we were adapting *A Midsummer Nights Dream*. I made my version quite dark. We used persuasive writing and lots of literary devices such as pathetic fallacy. So I mentioned the weather and contrasted sunny and stormy weather to link with the characters emotions.

The most stand-out/interesting/challenging topic you've studied at school: In RE we were looking at Buddhism which was really interesting. We were talking about whether or not it is a good thing to take away all the things you are attached to – even your family. It really made me think quite deeply about whether or not I would want to be a Buddhist and what it really means.

One of my favourite teachers: I enjoy lessons with Ms West who teaches me RE because she makes sure that no one's beliefs or religion are judged but also lets everyone express their ideas. She teaches really well.

A favourite feature of the school: I really like the diversity at Parliament Hill. And one of the best things about the school is the people. And all of the clubs and opportunities to get involved in things outside lessons.

I liked the fact that the plot could be related to today's events if you just twisted it around a little bit.
MADLYN SINTIM-MISA

She makes sure that no one's beliefs are judged but also lets everyone express their ideas.
ARIELLA BEAZLEY

STUDENT: MADLYN SINTIM-MISA

Age and Year Group: 15, Year 10

Most recent:

School Trip: We went to the National Portrait Gallery to see an artist called Nina Mae Fowler who works in charcoal. She taught us how to use the material and I liked it as I don't use charcoal much but having her teach us made it seem more possible. And I was surrounded by really good friends which made the trip even more enjoyable.

Extra-curricular activity: I always do quite a lot of self-taught art at home – it gives me a real sense of self-accomplishment when I have taught myself something. And I really do love art and know I need to practise as much as I can to improve as much as I can.

Science experiment: The crystallisation experiment in chemistry was fun. We made copper sulphate crystals. The method was fun and easy to follow and you got a cool substance at the end to study.

Book/Play studied in English Literature: I actually did quite like *Jane Eyre*. The protagonist went through a struggle to gain respect and experienced lots of self-discovery and even though she was lower class she managed to gain respect from upper class men and women. I liked the fact that the plot could be related to today's events if you just twisted it around a little bit.

History topic: I really enjoyed the Whitechapel unit, specifically learning about Jack the Ripper. It was so interesting the way in which Jack was always one or two steps ahead of the police. And it was also interesting to find out how the police force was structured so differently in those days from the police today.

Arts project: In drama for our last exam performance we had to choose a stimulus – we chose loneliness. We devised a play about how loneliness can affect all types of people. We got a lot of very positive feedback and we were really proud of what we achieved with the finished play.

Learning:

Subjects Studied: English, Maths, Double Science, History, Citizenship, Drama, Art and Dance leaders

Recent learning highlight: My recent drama test was a highlight as I do sometimes find it confusing and had been finding it hard to use all the terminology correctly. I was really pleased I got a good mark in the most recent test and I was pleased I had improved in my use of drama terminology. I think it has taken a while for it to become familiar this year but I feel positive about next year now.

The most stand-out/interesting/challenging topic you've studied at school: Probably in citizenship when we studied voting, democracy and how MPs are elected and represent their constituencies. It was challenging with a lot of information to retain. I made lots of small notes to cope with the large number of facts. I was quite motivated to learn about politics and how countries are run – I think it is really important to know about these things.

One of my favourite teachers: Probably Ms Brogan – her teaching style makes it easier to understand citizenship and cope with all the new words and ideas. She always gives us everyday examples to help explain new ideas, e.g she explained devolution in terms of a married couple and that really helped.

A favourite feature of the school: I love the back field and being there out in the open with fresh air – just hanging out with friends in the sun. I have so many nice memories of being there and the back field has a really good positive energy.

CASE STUDY: DEVELOPING OUR CURRICULUM

Title: Developing our curriculum to support the journey to independence

General Area: Learning and Teaching

Author: Deborah O'Connor, Deputy Headteacher T&L

We began a major review of our curriculum in 2015 when subject areas identified their threshold concepts and began to carefully sequence knowledge to support memory and retention. We recognised the need to build our students' cultural, social and learning capital and reduce the gaps which can open up for our disadvantaged students.

Making the explicit connection between effort and success is so important for our students, in particular for many of our disadvantaged students who sometimes have quite fixed ideas of their ability and are more likely to lose confidence as learning becomes less structured.

As we increased the knowledge demands of our curriculum we had to address our own skills in supporting that knowledge acquisition and skilfully using assessment to support the process. We began by introducing ideas from Willingham, Bjork and Sweller as well as many others and our team of lead practitioners worked with groups of teachers on metacognition, memory, oracy and questioning. Last year all teachers completed an Inquiry project engaging with research and reflecting on their own practice. Now we feel all teachers are in a position to engage with research and evidence within their teams. The belief that we are all constantly looking to improve as practitioners and that we can support one another to do so underpins our professional learning at PHS.

We have very much encouraged subject areas to take the lead on their own journeys. Our three core subject areas had very different needs in terms of their curriculum development, pedagogy and assessment practices. Here they share a snapshot of the work they have undertaken and their ambitions for the future.

The science story: Anoushka Lester, Head of Science

I remember our Year 11 science lessons at PHS six years ago – characterised by a frantic focus on coursework completion and an extremely high level of dependence on the teacher. Wails of "what do I write?" echoed around the labs. And when it came to the exams many of the girls didn't know how to revise science or what to revise or even that you *could* revise. Intervention sessions were frequent and involved revision by osmosis – the students were present but simultaneously passive and panicked. So a loud sigh of relief followed the demise of coursework and we began phasing out

CASE STUDY: DEVELOPING OUR CURRICULUM

interventions and tackling the elephant in the room; the teachers were doing most of the work and the students needed to know how to do more work for themselves.

In science, sequencing the curriculum to support effective memory development was the key area for us. We quickly moved from simple knowledge checklists to study guides providing knowledge and fact quizzes. The fact quizzes formed the basis of our assessments. How can you not get 80% if you already have the questions? We think that was a key moment for our students – when they realised 80% was possible with just a little effort. And when you get a small taste of success you want more. Creating opportunities for success became the way we structured our assessments.

There were going to be times they struggled – mock exams were difficult and grades were often disappointing but the message was always "green pen it, just find 10 extra marks". If they wanted to retake they could do it after school. And we continued to refine our revision resources. We aren't in a position to provide them with textbooks and in fact textbooks wouldn't suit some of our students. So we invested time in making home-learning booklets and study guides and exam packs; opportunities to quiz yourself repeatedly and practise, practise, practise.

Resilience grew as the students realised that they had the power to do something about their achievement. They were in control, they knew how to remember facts, how to practise their application skills, how to hone their exam technique.

These days we have more students who know how to revise, who tell younger students not to worry about science exams because "you just have to revise". Of course we still have students who highlight the whole study guide, who spend hours making

flashcards and then carry them around for months. But we challenge and explain and model revision all the way from Year 7 to Year 11.

Our challenge now is to find the best ways to make them think deeply and use their knowledge in challenging contexts, sharing their questions and conclusions with confidence. Questions we are asking ourselves this year focus around making best use of our new science labs, the role of practical work and using investigations to enhance learning, always staying aware of what it is we want them to learn.

Maths at Parli: Carly Sugarman, Head of Maths

Our maths GCSE results at Parli had been lagging behind English for some time. Consultants were called upon, schemes and textbooks were purchased, books were scrutinised and lessons observed endlessly. Our maths results did begin to improve and we are now looking at positive and rising progress scores for the past two years. The GCSE results still lag behind English and science but progress of 0.3 this year is really pleasing. Importantly the department has identified what it thinks works. They have a long-term strategy and are confident that the results will continue to improve.

1. One of the key areas to work on was the **behaviour** of the students – getting the conditions right. We knew that behaviour is extremely important in a successful maths lesson. Our students love to talk, they love to share their opinions but in maths we needed them to also be able to listen to the teacher share a carefully constructed explanation and worked example. So small things were established like teachers seating students to face the board, all lessons starting promptly with a Do Now activity and

maths teachers regaining their control over listening and discussion activities.

2. We ran focus groups with students to find out where some of the negative attitudes to maths were coming from. Students told us that they couldn't revise for maths and had little idea how to improve. If they felt they were unable to do maths they believed that would never change. These attitudes were more frequently encountered with disadvantaged students and in lower prior attaining groups but were present to some extent across all groups. We decided to show the students that **practice and repetition** was the key in building basic maths confidence. We introduced a Do Now exercise called Nothing New, Just Review (NNJR) and all lessons began with 4 questions on the IWB, often one from last lesson, one from last week, one from last term and one from last year. This modelled to the students that topics had to be revisited and practice improved performance leading to greater fluency.

3. Similarly we found many students did not value **home-learning** in maths and the marking load was leading to some debate in the department over the value of home-learning. We decided to make home-learning booklets to provide many practice questions and we also invested in Hegarty maths. We reviewed our assessment policy to make it clear what was expected to be marked and that most home-learning would be self-assessed. We established that all teachers had to value the completion of home-learning but that did not mean marking every question.

4. We reviewed schemes of learning and used ideas from Sweller on **cognitive load** and read widely as a department to develop strategies which supported **problem solving** without producing cognitive overload issues. We established

We do not believe that a broad and exploratory curriculum and exam success are mutually exclusive: we aim to succeed by balancing the needs of our students

KATE TREACY
HEAD OF ENGLISH

CASE STUDY: DEVELOPING OUR CURRICULUM

that fluency with skills would be developed first in a new topic and then those skills used in increasingly complex and linked problems.

5. We reviewed our **assessments** to ensure that students could see the link between practice and success. We simplified assessments to use more low stakes testing and topic tests. We reduced the amount of high stakes full GCSE paper assessment. And we reported only marks and discouraged the award of grades. This made students focus on small improvements rather than losing hope because they had got "a grade 3 – again".

6. We established a **numeracy** registration when students would present puzzles and numeracy problems to solve with their tutors. We encouraged all subject teachers to speak positively about maths and model a 'can-do' attitude.

And our results are improving, pupil focus groups reveal a much more positive attitude. Maths home-learning is seen as useful and having purpose. Now students will say 'maths revision is fine – you just practise'. Of course they sometimes still give up too easily and they don't always do enough home-learning but they are so much better.

Our English curriculum: Kate Treacy, Head of English

We are unapologetic about our modern, feminist English curriculum and feel that we strike a balance between introducing students to the foundations of the Canon and giving our students the tools they need to analyse and question the very complex world around them.

We believe that fostering cultural capital is not just reading the great writers (although this is of course important to us) but is also having the confidence and skills to question, debate and make active choices as consumers of culture.

Our KS3 curriculum ranges from reading complex 19th century novels such as Great Expectations to exploring the impact of celebrity culture on the media and news.

At KS4 we have made brave choices for the core Literature texts in Jane Eyre and the Short Story anthology, believing that these texts offer all our students the opportunity to grow as readers and thinkers. We aim to strike a balance between creativity and rigorous improvement of core skills.

We do not believe that a broad and exploratory curriculum and exam success are mutually exclusive: we aim to succeed by balancing the needs of our students. We are very happy to say that this has been reflected in the high academic success of our students right across the ability range.

Link to Learning Rainforest:

The Rainforest analogy expresses how we allow our subject areas to flourish and meet their own specific needs. We have a set of shared values and a commitment to engaging with research and evidence informed practice. But we know that no one style fits all subjects. We allow them to take ownership of their curriculum choices, assessment strategy and pedagogy. Just as a rainforest is strong and balanced as a result of its species diversity, we know we are stronger when we allow subjects to find their own way, as long as we are supporting one another and putting the students' learning at the centre of everything we do.

CASE STUDY: THE WELLBEING PROJECT

General Area: Wellbeing

Author: Donna Billington, Assistant Headteacher and SENDCo

Having had a school counsellor working within the school for many years, in 2010 we decided to scale up our mental health and wellbeing provision in response to an increase in mental health related issues among students. We successfully secured funding for three years to fund the post of 'Wellbeing Project Manager'. The Wellbeing Project Manager qualified as child and family psychotherapist in 2018. The Wellbeing Project supports the mental health of students and when the funding came to an end in 2018, the school committed to funding the post for the future.

The project has four key areas:

- Daily break and lunchtime drop-in space
- Emotional wellbeing sessions
- Referral to child and adolescent mental health services (CAMHS) including in school CAMHS worker
- Mental health focused workshops

The Wellbeing Project seeks to identify and support any student within the school who has a mental health need by providing emotional wellbeing sessions in school, or by referring to CAMHS or another specialist external service. Students access the Wellbeing Project through self-referral or having been referred by a member of staff, a peer, or by their parents. All referrals are discussed at a social inclusion panel which is attended by the Wellbeing Project Manager, the Senior Leader for Inclusion (Chair), the head of year, the senior leader linked to the year group, and the safeguarding officer. Individual social inclusion panels for each year group are held fortnightly. The purpose of the social inclusion panel is to decide on the most appropriate support for a student and to monitor any interventions that are in place.

The following feedback is from students who regularly attend the drop-in:

> "The wellbeing room has helped me find new friends and has become a place where I can share my opinions and feelings freely as I know that they will be appreciated. I enjoy coming here because I can be myself free of judgement. Most of the time it is a quiet place where I can personally reflect on my thoughts and it has overall improved my self-esteem."

CASE STUDY: THE WELLBEING PROJECT

"The room is important because it is a calm and comforting space to read and to think. It's separate from all the drama and stress of school life and gives me a time to think before I go to lessons so I am able to focus on them."

Emotional wellbeing sessions in school comprise of:

- Guidance sessions with the Wellbeing Project Manager. This could be a one-off session as and when needed, or regular short-term or longer-term sessions.

- Mental health assessment by the Wellbeing Project Manager to ascertain if additional support is needed, and if so what support would be most appropriate.

- Weekly counselling, psychotherapy or art therapy provided by the Wellbeing Project Manager or a member of the therapy team she manages (part-time school counsellor, volunteer trainee child counsellor, volunteer trainee art therapist, volunteer trainee psychotherapist).

- Parent work provided by the Wellbeing Project Manager.

The most common reasons for referral to Wellbeing Project sessions are: family issues, peer relationships, low self-esteem, anxiety, parental mental health, being a young carer identity issues, eating disorders, self-harm, depression, and suicidal thoughts. All therapists and counsellors have their clinical work supervised according to professional or training standards.

"My weekly therapy sessions offer me an opportunity to reflect on my feelings so I have a clear mind, allowing me to focus at school." Year 10 student who is in local authority care and who is currently in therapy.

"The wellbeing room is a space that offered me support when I had therapy. It's a place that has been familiar to me and I have gone to since the beginning of year seven and continued to go to during break and lunch times since finishing therapy. The therapy I had really helped me to understand the things I was thinking or things that had happened. My therapist helped me a lot at a time when I was really struggling." Year 8 student who has ended therapy.

In addition to emotional wellbeing sessions the Wellbeing Project runs mental health focused workshops. The groups that we have run in the last 12 months include: arts and social skills, Bright Minds Bright Moods, Empower, CBT and an emotional resilience group. During last spring and summer terms we took up the invitation to participate in Camden's peer mentoring programme. Twelve students from year nine were recruited as peer mentors and trained to provide peer mentoring support to twelve students from year seven. The programme was delivered by a local youth organization Fitzrovia Youth in Action, in partnership with Mind in Camden and the Tavistock and Portman NHS Trust. Student feedback was positive and included the following comments:

"I found it educational, it was helpful to hear other people's life experiences and responses to situations." Year 9 student

"I enjoyed meeting everyone and seeing what I am good at and what I had progressed in. Also I enjoyed the activities because they made me even more confident and I was able to try and learn new things in different ways and to express myself." Year 7 student

Link to Learning Rainforest:

Establishing the conditions for students to feel safe means they are more likely to risk making mistakes. We want our girls to feel secure enough to explore, to have the resilience to withstand the struggle but to recognise when to ask for help and know-how to find it. We want them to experience that support within our community and we believe that they will then be more able to support others.

The *wellbeing* room has helped me find new friends and has become a place where I can share my opinions and feelings freely as I know that they will be appreciated. I enjoy coming here because I can be myself free of judgement.
STUDENT AT PHS

ST ANDREW'S HIGH, LANARKSHIRE

INTRODUCTION

I first encountered Mark Healy, Deputy Head at St Andrew's High School and the author of their *Fieldbook* case study, through my early interactions on Twitter. He was always someone who brought a healthy blend of intellectual rigour and grounded realism to any debate. Mark is a true enthusiast; passionate about teaching and learning, knowledgeable about the research and absolutely committed to the process of professional development. As well as having an interest in evidence-informed teaching in common, we have both shared the experience of working in international schools – Mark spent a number of years in Hong Kong before returning to Scotland.

It's amazing how little English people usually know about the education system in general, north of the border in Scotland. Following the 'Four Countries' event described earlier in *Fieldbook*, I've now worked at a few schools in Scotland and my daughter still attends university there but still I need to remind myself of all the differences at the level of organisational structures, the nature of the qualifications and some of the terminology. However, happily – and obviously enough – the fundamental challenges are exactly the same. Teaching is teaching! Mark first invited me to Scotland to contribute to a conference for North Lanarkshire Headteachers, in 2018. I was joined by Professor Becky Allen and teacher training expert, Harry Fletcher-Wood. I remember that each of us independently mentioned the work of Graham Nuthall – the Hidden Lives of Learners – as one of the key reference points for our thinking. I sensed from discussions that day that research-engagement at school level was not as far down the road as people would have liked but that the appetite was there.

Earlier this year, Mark asked me to lead a training day for the St Andrew's staff. It was a real joy to contribute to the journey that he captures so well in his case study. They have taken the process of professional learning extremely seriously, very deliberately embarking on a long-term journey from the beginning. Mark's piece is so quotable. I love the idea of 'slow leadership' and that 'teaching is learning'. I also love the opening sub-heading: *The Beautiful Risk of Education*. Perhaps better than anyone else I can think of, Mark articulates an acute awareness of the simultaneous power and limitations of educational research. This informs a CPD culture and process where teachers are invited to learn about what research says and to build it into their practice without it ever being enforced, imposed or directed. There's an honesty about the validity and challenge of 'implementing the research' that is not always present. It's lovely to make another connection via the work of Oliver Caviglioli. Mark had commissioned Oliver to produce some high quality displays to help promote research-informed thinking in the school and he has included a sample here.

PROFILE

Location: Coatbridge, North Lanarkshire

Type of Institution: Mixed Comprehensive

Roll/Age Range: 1360, aged 11–18

Year Founded: 2006

Motto: 'Domine Dirige Nos – Lord Guide Us'

Recent/Current School Production: *Songs from the 80s*

Recent significant sports event/triumph: Highest number of medal winners at the recent NLC County Sports.

Quote: This email was to try and put into some form of words that the vocal and physical support provided to M was crucial to his well-being going forward and he has managed his first step into life with some real positivity under difficult conditions which were provided by a caring group of teachers employed at St Andrews and this is some small way to testimony their commitment to our son which my family will never forget and I am sure my son M will never forget.
(Mr and Mrs G., Parent of M.G.)

Notable quirks/alumni: St Andrew's High School (2006) was born from the proud legacy and traditions of St Patrick's and Columba High Schools. We look back with pride and forward with hope and faith.

Mr Mark Healy
Deputy Head Teacher

The Beautiful Risk of Education

As a provocation, it is difficult to find consensus on the principal aims of education. Improving the quality of our education systems to meet economic imperatives and drivers may be a rather utilitarian view for some, but for many, it carries real life currency. Similarly, increasing formal levels of attainment and achievement in order to widen opportunities and choices for our pupils holds significant traction as a key aspirational aim of our school community. These seem to resonate with the aims of a Curriculum for Excellence and National and Local Authority Improvement Priorities, such as closing a poverty induced attainment gap and developing our young workforce. Most importantly however, they resonate with our school community, with our school contexts and with our school values.

Walking the Words of our Values

We are a very proud Catholic Secondary school that espouses a Gospel-based values system that informs everything we do within the Faith Life of this school. Crucially, our Gospel values – Human Dignity, Community and Participation, Care for Creation, Dignity in Work, Solidarity and Peace and Reconciliation – act as our values filters in the relationships we build and the ethos we create in our school community, both within and beyond the immediacy of the classroom. They also frame how we have tried

PROFILE

STUDENT: REBECKAH MUIR

to keep learning and teaching the main thing in a world of ever increasing intensification and valorisation of teacher roles beyond the classroom. How we engage in professional learning as a community is framed also by these values. If teaching is learning, the values of building relational and cultural capital with our pupils should sing majestically in consonance with our teachers also.

Quality Learning and Teaching

What makes someone an excellent teacher? What makes a lesson very good? What makes another lesson less good? Such provocations should rightly generate a long list of diverse responses, some within our locus of control, some merely within a locus of influence. Certainly our values and ethos should play a vital role as key ingredients of whatever good looks like. We believe also however that excellent can be framed as consistently good with an intrinsic motivation to want to get better. This is not to highlight a deficit model, but a shared belief that 'every teacher can get better, not because they are not good enough, but because we can all improve.' D. William

Age and Year Group: 17, S6 (Year 13)

Most recent:

School Trip: New York & Washington
Extra-curricular activity: Netball Team/District Team
Science experiment: Specific Latent Heat experiments
Book/Play studied in English Literature: *Macbeth*
History topic: JFK
Arts project: Macbeth book cover

Learning:

Subjects Studied: English/Psychology/Business Studies/Geography/Maths/Modern Studies/PE/ Advance Modern Studies

Recent learning highlight: In Modern Studies Higher Assignment, I focused on a topical educational issue at present: trying to understand the factors that explain a poverty induced attainment gap. I found this incredibly insightful and also tragic at the same time. Socio-economic status has a large impact on peoples' future and it seems so inequitable at times.

The most stand-out/interesting/challenging topic you've studied at school: I enjoyed studying/ learning about memory in Psychology as it's integral to our identity as human beings. It's something we take for granted, yet when there are abnormalities to memory processes of encoding or recall, we see very clearly the devastating impact it can have. This was especially highlighted in the case study of Clive Wearing.

One of my favourite teachers: I enjoy lessons with Mr Mullen in Social Subjects (Humanities) because he is funny and engaging yet when you leave his classes you really feel as if you have learned more than you knew from the beginning of the lesson. He always begins lessons with retrieval practices from previously learned material and this was so helpful as the year progressed.

A favourite feature of the school: I loved my experience of six years at High School. There was a very caring attitude from staff and you always felt teachers had a genuinely had your best interests at heart. I especially loved our enrichment trips and went to Italy twice and New York – really fond memories of my school years.

I will always remember with great fondness my time at St Andrew's High School. So many memories join together and they will stay with me all my life.

ALANA CAREY

I will always look back fondly on my time at St Andrew's and felt teachers genuinely cared about me as a person and wanted the best future for me.

REBECKAH MUIR

STUDENT: ALANA CAREY

Age and Year Group: 17, S6 (Year 13)

Most recent:

School Trip: New York & Washington

Extra-curricular activity: Netball Team/District Team

Science experiment: Replication of Brewer and Treyen's investigation into the role of schema on reconstructive memory. It was really interesting.

Book/Play studied in English Literature: *The Great Gatsby*

History topic: USA and Gun Control

Arts project: Inquiry into mental factors that affect physical performance

Learning:

Subjects Studied: English/Psychology/Business Studies/Geography/Maths/Modern Studies/PE/Advance Modern Studies/Religious, Moral and Philosophical Studies

Recent learning highlight: In my RMPS Assignment, I focused on the relationship between Science and Religion. It focused on the compatibility of The Big Bang Theory and religious thought. It was so interesting and helped open up a world of thought that never crossed my mind. Mr Cassidy was so good at teaching as always recapped material in retrieval practice and gave concrete examples and exemplars of excellent practice.

The most stand-out/interesting/challenging topic you've studied at school: I enjoyed studying/learning about the Stanford Prison Experiment in Psychology. Understanding how context and situation can have such a massive influence on our thoughts and behaviours was so eye opening and made me realise that good people can indeed do 'evil things'. I enjoyed resisting social influence as a way of trying to better understand how we can resist such negative social influences.

One of my favourite teachers: I enjoy lessons with Miss Barr in Physical Education. Her lessons are so well organised and you knew she had put so much time, energy and effort to make the lessons interesting and well structured. She would always make herself available at break and lunchtimes if you needed further help and you could email her at any time and she would reply. I loved this level of support from a very caring teacher.

A favourite feature of the school: I really enjoyed my experience of six years at High School. There was really good relationships between pupils in other year groups and such strong relationships with staff. I felt staff had a genuine level of care about me as a person and an individual, and as we entered the senior school, this care also showed itself as respect. I liked being treated with care and respect.

CASE STUDY: SLOW LEADERSHIP OF TEACHING AND LEARNING

Title: The Slow Leadership of keeping Learning and Teaching the Main thing

General Area: Teaching is Learning

Author: Mark Healy, Deputy Head Teacher and Learning and Teaching Lead

Classroom teaching is a nuanced craft that involves interlinking many cognitive processes and decisions. To reduce to an arbitrary checklist of competences would merely traduce the collective value of the skills, knowledge bases and accrued wisdom that we hold within our community. However, there are guiding principles that we believe are valuable to highlight as key provocations. Crucially, developing a shared understanding and language of the WHY and HOW we might improve is a central tenet of keeping Learning and Teaching on centre stage. Questions we have generated and sought to respond, include:

- How do we enact and investigate our overarching learning and teaching priorities within our own context?

- How well do our findings resonate and correlate to a wider corpus of research literature? How can we even find and access wider findings in order to prevent an academic sarcophagus from developing over our community of learning?

- How aware are teachers and pupils at St Andrew's that research discourse is available to them that could have a potentially strong impact on what they do on a daily basis?

- How are these findings shared, translated, interpreted beyond the esoteric few in order to provide a 'lingua-franca of learning and teaching' that is accessible and understood?

- How do we define an evidence base? What do what works and what doesn't even mean?

- How do we develop a research meta-language that can be accessed and critically evaluated? Then link wider results and conclusions to our context in our school, against the inquiry findings we have produced?

- How do we create a set of overarching principles of effective practices that does not engender prescription and orthodoxy BUT still leaves the humanity and nuance of human relationships and transactions to be evident?

- How do we create leadership of these processes beyond systems of hierarchy and designation?

- How do we create collaborative and joint professional development process that are not 'top down' uniformed observations that highlight deficits based on misconceptions (e.g. the erroneous use of learning Styles in revision guides or pupils writing Learning objectives for EVERY lesson)

- How do we do all of this without it being viewed and enacted as additional layers on what we already do i.e. How are we Making Professional Learning Space available?

- How do we resist the valorisation of teacher roles and 'caped leader' becoming a damaging shibboleth that becomes little to anyone?

- How do we create a sustainable culture that is not an echo chamber of SLT voices?

Asking these questions in itself, without replies, perhaps also helps illuminate a level of professional growth that is not merely performative-driven in nature. It also perhaps helps highlight that although a particular classroom method may be effective, without explaining why that may the case is a classic example of cognitive dissonance in action. Edu tourism and voyeurism sits completely at odds with our professional learning. To that end, our six years of

CASE STUDY: SLOW LEADERSHIP OF TEACHING AND LEARNING

deliberate focus on research informed approaches OPENLY resists the implementation of quick-fix, short term interventions and paid credence to purposely developing a culture of collaborative professional inquiry that seeks to join many dots of professional learning. Rather, we are developing systems, structures and scaffolds that seek to codify the in-house knowledge that we gather via collaborative inquiry with the knowledge and expertise of professional researchers. As Marilyn Cochran Smith asserts, 'What is missing (*Handbook of Research on Teaching*, Wittrock, 1986) from the handbook are the voices of teachers themselves, the questions that teachers ask, and the interpretive frames that teachers use to understand and improve their own classroom practices.'

A Picture of our current Learning Rainforest @SAHS

Our journey to becoming more research aware and research informed community aims to be a fully inclusive process. Restricting to our Learning and Teaching group (L&T) merely cements a body of esoteric knowledge that benefits the few, only. Explicit within this process is a realisation that learning and teaching is complex and we need to place multiple lenses on what effective may look like, and then enact these to inform our strategic improvement priorities. A single snapshot can only pixelate a picture of effective learning and teaching to a specific focus. What we are also attempting is to create time and space in our 'constellation' of learning and teaching to join up our dots of professional learning to create a high-definition picture.

The most important rationale that informs this praxis is that the WORDS become LIVE in the classroom, that we have started to enact the strategies and interventions of self-improvement in our classroom practice. Our nodes of learning include:

- A mobile staff development library that contains over 150 books and a similar number of relevant research articles, blogs or newspaper articles. This visits each faculty/dept. once every two weeks for staff to browse and chose. Most, but not all, reflect and support professional dialogue with our learning and teaching priorities of homework for Learning, Memory for Learning and Collaborative inquiry for Learning.

- Blog Friday; a selection of research articles, summary bulletins or blogs that seeks to promote dialogue and inquiry into our own classroom practice and context. Examples vary in range from 'Do Learning Styles Really Exist' to 'Bill Rogers and key tips for Behaviour Management'. They support the work and dialogue of our Learning and Teaching priorities but are not mutually exclusive to such a narrow topic band.

- TeachMeets & INSETs: We have created a culture where the knowledge and provocations we gain of our own context, placed side by side with wider literature and research, is presented to staff at regular intervals. This can be communicated via Blog Friday, but we hold three internal, entirely voluntary TeachMeets per year. This is a vibrant and expanding forum that allows dialogue to extend beyond L&T or TLC members only.

- In-House CPD: We do not impose CPD/PRD targets in our community, they arise from dialogue between colleagues. They are not rigidly set by strategic priorities but of course an overlap is welcomed. However, more personal areas of interest around professional learning is equally valued. To support this, we run our own in-house CPD programme, in tandem with external events. Courses include an aspiring middle leaders course, behaviour management course and Memory for Learning course.

- CPD IS NOT a single event, done 'to' a teacher. We take this maxim very seriously and we also invite colleagues to recommend professional reading to support learning. Similarly, we recognise that we 'don't know everything' and we have a very healthy culture of external speakers to support our CPD. This includes collaboration with local colleagues, colleagues from Higher Education and partnership with schools and institutions, colleagues from SCEL, and colleagues from England and International Schools

- We have a very vibrant and energetic Learning and Teaching group and Teacher Learning Communities group. Colleagues use this forum to further inquire and enact key L&T priorities. This is a wonderful example of slow leadership as reading and discussing key literature is accorded as much importance as any other facet of professional development.

- We also started a Saturday morning CPD for Charity event, whereby four guest speakers provide CPD for a nominal ticket price and all proceeds are given to charity. It allows us to walk the words of our values, supporting local charities whilst providing a rich forum for dialogue and thought.

CASE STUDY: SLOW LEADERSHIP OF TEACHING AND LEARNING

Memory for Learning
AN EVIDENCE-BASED APPROACH TO SUPPORTING LEARNING AND TEACHING

ST ANDREW'S HIGH SCHOOL

Memory is the residue of thought and learning requires a change in long-term memory.

WILLINGHAM, D., 2010

Working Memory acts as a form of mental workspace, providing a basis for thought.

BADDELEY & EYSENCK, 2015

Memory for learning has three main parts – how we put in (encode), where we put (store) and how we bring back to our awareness (recall).

EYSENCK, 2012

Working Memory is thought to have limited capacity of four chunks of information; we need to optimize to help learning.

COWAN, N., 2005

Attention is not solely related to classroom management; it is a vital cog in the process of learning and encoding information.

ANDERSON, 2015

Distribute learning; a little done often is better than longer, massed practice. Space it out.

BJORK & LANDAUER, 1978

Retrieving information through testing is a more effective technique than restudying.

ROEDIGER & KARPICKE, 2006

Allowing pupils to self test not only improves retrieval but directly improves learning.

KORNELL & SON, 2009

Retrieval based strategies are varied; free recall and practice quizzing are effective as are coupling pupil-generated quizzes with teacher tests.

BAE & REDIFER, 2016

Some learning techniques are more effective than others; testing and distributed practice is better than highlighting and rereading.

DUNLOSKY et al, 2015

Retrieval Practice and Low Stakes Testing
THE TESTING EFFECT IN EDUCATION

ST ANDREW'S HIGH SCHOOL

What does the term Testing Effect mean?

1 Simply put: testing. The retrieval of a given piece of information from memory increases the long-term retention of that information, a phenomenon often called *Testing Effect*. This can be used to support learning rather than just assess learning.

Roediger & Karpicke, 2006

So, testing is only important when we seek to recall information?

2 No. Testing, although commonly associated with improving retrieval strength from LTM, may also be contingent on memory success at encoding (How we *put in* from our senses) and should be used also *during* teaching, not only at an *end point*.

Marsh & Wing, 2013

Can low stakes testing help deal with performance anxiety?

3 Yes. Frequent low stakes testing, where pupils self mark and/or self generate tests may help reduce performance anxiety and stress. This is in part due to the confidence pupils gain from successfully and regularly recalling information as well as from their ownership of developing their own learning.

Hintze & Rapp, 2014

Can retrieval practices have a role to play in how we study *outside* class?

4 Although most students prefer rereading or writing a summary when preparing for an exam, research has shown that actively retrieving information through testing can be a far more effective study technique.

Carrier & Pashler, 1992 | Karpicke, Butler & Roediger, 2009

Are there any widely held beliefs we should challenge?

5 Yes, in terms of metacognition, we need to raise an awareness that low stakes testing is a means of assessment (Indirect Effect) *but* also that successful retrieval directly improves learning (Direct Effect).

Kornell & Bjork, 2007

Is there any research on the testing effect and working memory capacity?

6 Yes, but not extensive. Administering frequent low states test and using different variations may have strong benefits in learning for all, despite individual differences in working memory capacities.

Bertlisson & Stenlund, 2017

Is there any research on the testing effect and working memory capacity? CONTINUED

7 Retrieval practice during learning, when accompanied by simultaneous feedback of correct answers, may afford greater advantage for pupils with lower working memory capacities.

Aagarwal & Roediger, 2016

Does retrieval practice just mean teachers setting tests for pupils to answer?

8 No, retrieval practice is not one unitary strategy. What then can variations look like and which are more effective? Free recall and multiple choice quizzes (MCQ) can be effective strategies and combining pupil generated quizzes (MCQ) and teacher practice quizzing with free recall can have significant benefit.

Bae & Redifer, 2018

What testing principles would be effective when using textbooks?

9 Ask pupils to create test questions as they read texts.
Stop at the end of sections, test themselves on their own questions.
Mark their own responses & "right wrongs" by self where possible.
Review the questions they have generated with the questions at the end of the chapter given in the textbook.

Bugg & McDaniel, 202 | Roediger, 2017

Retrieval; is this the silver bullet for learning and teaching in my class?

10 It is OK to help scaffold during retrieval practices as *actually* retrieving information and content is necessary to reinforce retrieval strength.

Learning Scientists, 2017

Some lessons will be better than others, at different times, on different days. We are continually striving towards creating a culture whereby improving is not seen as a deficit. It is seen as a natural enactment of a professional learning community that recognises that *Teaching IS Learning*.

MARK HEALY
DEPUTY HEAD TEACHER AND
LEARNING AND TEACHING LEAD

CASE STUDY: SLOW LEADERSHIP OF TEACHING AND LEARNING

'Everything works somewhere, nothing works everywhere' to quote Dylan William. What does that actually mean in terms of what we do in the classroom? Perhaps that quality of implementation, systems, structures and cultures will mediate the effectiveness of any intervention, no matter how strong and robust the research. This is why our memory for learning and retrieval practice processes have been shared and developed in collaboration with staff, pupils and parents, over a three year period. We have books that allow access to Psychological language without the need to have formally studied Psychology. These include 'How We Learn', 'Making it Stick' and 'Why Don't Students Like School?'. We have tried to distil a meta-language from the abstruse to easily understood across the entire community of learners. In addition, we have blog articles from the Learning Scientists, Deans for Impact and research papers from Baddeley (The Episodic Buffer, A new component of Working Memory, 2000) Eysenck (Individual differences in Attention, 2010) and Dunlosky et al. (Practice Tests, Spaced Practice and Successive relearning: Tips for classroom use and for guiding students' learning, 2015) to help support the efficacy of any intervention or strategy linked to Memory for Learning.

We also have provided parental workshops to explain key factors such as retrieval practice or spaced learning in order to create a sense of fluidity between key messages in school and how these are reinforced at home. Such CPD and reading opportunities have also been extended to our Cluster Primary colleagues in order to create a sense of seamless dialogue and meta-language between primary and secondary stages. Key strategies of foci will be:

- Memory and Retrieval Practice (Years 1–3 Foci)
- Spaced Practice & interleaving (Years 1–3 Foci)
- Feedback & Differentiation (Year 3–4 Foci)
- Dual Coding (Years 4–5 Foci)

In addition, we have provided the opportunity for all our parents, staff and pupils to access a guide to effective strategies for Learning from the Dunlosky et al. study (2013) 'What Works, What Doesn't'.

Within our learning community, there is a recognition that a unitary lens of Cognitive Science focused solely on how we learn and what constitutes an evidence base is not the ONLY level of analysis available. Reducing learning and teaching to results from laboratory experiments or field experiments is valuable but not merely in itself. Experimental methods generally have participants that are adults and may take place in lab conditions – we do not ASSUME uncritical translation into our classrooms. However, aspects of memory for learning, such as Ebbinghaus' Forgetting Curve (1880) has a credible degree of research that is robust and well replicated. As such, providing examples of retrieval practice, e.g. MCQ (multiple-choice questions) to pupil generate quizzes, as staple starters in all classes should help improve retrieval strength and accessibility. Regular Low stakes testing may also help reduce levels of anxiety in more formal, higher stakes testing (see poster). Importantly, there is also a consistent structure for implementing low stakes quizzing as an integral focus of learning and teaching in the class, not an addendum of testing.

The implementation of any whole school priority focused on learning and teaching needs to be 'slow and deliberate'. Scaling our architecture involves so many different yet interlocking facets of change, from first exposure to staff to implementing consistently in classrooms across the school. In a world of constant shifting sands, it is also a process of 'reframing hearts and minds' around the efficacy of why change may be beneficial. This is not to traduce teachers as willing participants of change, rather to highlight that change is so constant in schools, punctuated by damaging fads at times, that filtering out desirable change is a complex dialogue.

We have certainly not found the Rosetta Stones that unlock attainment to all; what we have done however is recognised that one priority of learning and teaching per year is a threshold layer of complex change that should not be exceeded. We have focused an entire year on 'what makes effective feedback?' in the class as our current priority, and 'slowing the word down' certainly helps to better formulate responses to this seemingly simple four word question.

Link to Learning Rainforest:

'Making Space for Sustainable growth' – slow leadership and development of the collective intellectual capital of our own school at our pace and within the context of our priorities.

'Fertile ground & Establishing the conditions' – One full year spent reading, learning and evaluating research papers, book chapters and blogs in order to contextualise to our school, our colleagues and our pupils within our community.

'Enrich from with-in' – Forums and protected space that provides opportunities for dialogue and the richness of friction of views to be both articulated and welcomed.

'Enrich from with-out' – Iterations of our internal voices with from visiting colleagues. Helps to challenge our biases and also support our contentions.

'Diversity of Thought' – Gathering a wide collective of views in order to constantly reframe 'why' we were engaging in such a long process of professional development & what success may look and feel like in our community.

'Diversity of Behaviours' – we equated excellent to consistently good classroom teaching without the desire to impose an orthodoxy of teaching. There was no unitary 'St Andrew's way' lesson and we resisted that direction with passion

'Stages of Maturation' – Professional Growth and development was not a uniform and linear bar for all teachers, and rightly so but it needed an overarching culture and rationale not merely individual strengths of personality.

'Secure roots, flourishing results' – resist the fad of educational voyeurism and zeitgeist picking, we deliberately resourced professional development in key ways – knowledge capital, decisional capital and organisational capital of time and space. We had to know not just *how* we could prioritise learning and teaching but *why* we were doing so. Hegemonic diktats of imposed school practices rarely fall as seeds on fertile ground.

CONCLUSION

After reading through the 30 entries of *The Learning Rainforest Fieldbook*, it seems sensible to stand back to consider what it all adds up to. What have we learned? Are there any general messages; some common themes; some overarching conclusions? I was tempted just to leave this to readers to decide for themselves, but let me suggest the following.

Curriculum is a broad concept and schools are wonderfully ambitious about it.

School life can be such a fabulously rich experience. This is probably my overriding conclusion. Reading all the student profiles, you get a flavour of what school life can offer to young people across the world. Not only do schools provide a wide-ranging subject-based curriculum, inspiring students to explore the world in myriad ways, they also foster wonderful relationships and give students the opportunity to engage in an incredible array of activities: sports, theatre visits, field trips of all kinds. Curriculum is a broad concept; learning takes many forms – and I think the scale of the ambition inherent in our view of what a good education looks like comes through strongly.

Values and beliefs are major drivers.

It's fascinating to me how quickly a school's values come to the fore in the way they tell their own stories. *Fieldbook* isn't a collection of neutral, technical descriptions of processes and outcomes. When left to write freely, the contributors' instinct is usually to communicate their schools' wider goals and values as part of their narrative. Schools are values-driven places; they have a strong sense of purpose that is necessary as a motivating force for all that they do. We work in education because it matters – and it matters that we do it as well as we can. This means teachers and leaders are ready and willing to go to great lengths in terms of time, energy and resilient determination to push themselves forward. I find it hugely inspiring.

Schools operate in hugely different contexts but still have much in common.

The 30 schools in *Fieldbook* are an eclectic collection – deliberately so. I wanted to capture a broad range of educational contexts. However, it's clear that context plays a major role in shaping schools' opportunities, challenges and priorities. Comparing schools is a dubious pursuit at the best of times and here, it's not really wise or possible at all. The key thing is for schools to understand their contexts well and to capitalise on every opportunity as they face their specific challenges. I love the quirky distinctiveness that schools have – whether it's Gordonstoun in Moray or St Columba's in Dublin, Penrice in Cornwall or Les Quennevais in Jersey, St Matthias in Tower Hamlets or Huntington in York. Obviously, some contexts provide more inherent advantages and it's important for schools to count their blessings at the same time as striving to provide models for what is possible in an educational setting. It's also the case that even when schools are poles apart in terms of funding, facilities and levels of disadvantage, they all have a great deal in common; many of the elements of any great school are similar regardless of context and I think there's value in sharing ideas, whatever context they come from.

Teacher development is complex and highly individual.

It's certainly true to say that the 30 *Fieldbook* schools are likely to represent a skewed sample in relation to their focus on professional learning because that was a major factor in my selecting them to be included in the first place. However, I have been hugely impressed by the extent to which schools pursue professional learning with real determination and commitment. Several of the case studies describe the process of taking ideas from research and assimilating them into their routine practice. The NQTs at Turton, the teachers at Lebanon Evangelical, Tanya Douglas at Chace, John Tomsett at Huntington and the Oldham College story all capture this complexity. Ideas don't always work; they need to find form in the specific classroom contexts that teachers operate in and there's the need for a degree of persistence to make ideas stick. What's so wonderful is that these processes are being explored and developed with such rigour and tenacity so that individual teachers are motivated and supported to make real shifts in their practice. If we don't get our CPD systems sorted, schools can't improve – and the Learning Rainforest cannot thrive.

Evidence-informed wisdom is a powerful concept.

It's hugely encouraging to hear how schools are embracing research engagement as part of their school improvement work. The Markethill case study on English mastery is a great example of this, as is Helen Ralston's story about assessment at The Rise School – to name just two. Across the *Fieldbook* schools there are numerous examples of teachers and leaders seeking out ideas and solutions that are evidence-informed but that also then need to be woven into their contexts and take account of teachers' experience and values. It's the synthesis of first-hand experience and research evidence that leads to wisdom – and I'd say the Learning Rainforest that I've explored has wisdom of this kind in abundance.

Changes in curriculum and assessment require time and deep thought.

A common characteristic of the schools that have reached a point where they are delivering an excellent education – great teaching, a rich curriculum, effective assessment practices – is that they have done so over a long period of time. The professional culture at Saffron Walden or Heathfields, the assessment systems at London Academy, and the curriculum thinking at Turton, Parliament Hill, Huntington, St Andrews International and St Matthias have all taken many years of careful, deliberate, continuous review and improvement. There are no quick fixes – at least, not in established schools that achieve a level of quality that is sustained over time. In discussions, a common feature of these schools is that their leaders have had a clear vision for the long-term goal but are very pragmatic about timescales. This has the effect of making changes that are deep and sustainable because of the high level of understanding and buy-in built across the staff body over time.

The Learning Rainforest metaphor has both practical use-value and symbolic power.

When I wrote *The Learning Rainforest*, I didn't really expect the metaphor of the trees with their three-part structure to be picked up beyond providing a loose framework for discussing a set of ideas about curriculum, assessment,

ACKNOWLEDGEMENTS

and teaching and learning. However, I'm now much more confident that the three elements can help people to take their practice forward, either as an evaluation tool or as a planning tool. As I outlined in the introductory chapter, the three parts lead into distinct sets of questions that schools can ask about themselves:

How well do we **establish the conditions** for great learning? Do we provide the right kind of nurturing environment? Have we designed a curriculum that is rich, broad, challenging and inspiring? How well do we support teachers in their professional learning?

How effective are we at **building the knowledge structure** in our subject disciplines? Is the curriculum well sequenced to allow for secure schema-building, blending rich learning experiences with a knowledge-rich philosophy and strong emphasis on fluency and building long-term memory?

How extensive are our students' opportunities for **exploring the possibilities** for learning via a rich diet of 'Mode B' activities, building on the knowledge they've acquired to produce fabulous work in multiple forms?

Amongst the *Fieldbook* entries are schools that have used the Learning Rainforest structure more directly than others but all of them have found that it resonates in one form or another. I think that the power of it lies in the fact that it allows schools to place emphasis on one element more than others at different phases of their development without it ever being a question of picking one path over another. It's not about whether you do attend to each part or not; it's a question of how well you attend to them. There's room for everyone in this inclusive model and I'm excited to see that schools with quite different perspectives on the surface are equally at home, expressing their ideas through the Learning Rainforest concept.

The *Fieldbook* is the result of the fabulous efforts of a lot of different people – there are well over 100 different contributors and I'm deeply grateful to each one of them for the part they've played in bringing the book together.

With so many people to liaise with, the book couldn't have happened at all without the support of Sara Stafford. In the early stages she communicated with each of the school contributors, keeping in touch with them as they worked on their entries and keeping track of the whole enterprise.

I'm delighted that my friend and fellow explorer of the Rainforest, John Tomsett, agreed to write the foreword and I'm grateful for his unwavering support and encouragement for the book and much more besides over recent years.

I'm grateful to Alex Sharratt, Oliver Caviglioli and Caroline Derbyshire for helping me to give shape to the *Fieldbook* concept. I'm forever indebted to Oliver for his magnificent work with all the general styling, the profile pictures, map graphics, the cover image and all the original Learning Rainforest images. His rapid turn-around on such a major undertaking was quite amazing. I'm also hugely grateful to Rebecca Bafico for her fabulous design work. She is the person who took the text from each school and formatted the entries patiently, one by one, producing the wonderful final versions in the book – often after lots of detailed exchanges back and forth. Thanks also to Jonathan Woolgar for his final editing.

More broadly, I'd like to acknowledge all the people who have invited me into their schools over the last two and a half years. It continues to be a profound privilege to see the fabulous work people do and I consider myself lucky to have had the opportunity to work with thousands of committed teachers and hundreds of brilliant school leaders. If I ever write a second *Fieldbook*, I would certainly be spoilt for choice in selecting the schools to make a contribution.

Finally, as ever, I want to say a huge thank-you to my lovely family – Deb, Daisy and Sam – for all the things that matter the most.

As I have described in the St Stithians entry, in order to give something back for all the support I have received from teachers and schools around the world, I have agreed with John Catt Educational Ltd that we will contribute 15% of revenue from the sales of *The Learning Rainforest Fieldbook* to St Stithians Thandulwazi Maths and Science programme, created in 2005 to improve the quality of Maths and Science teaching and learning in public high schools. The details of the programme are on page 117. All the money raised will have a direct impact on the education of a great many children in Johannesburg and I'm delighted that the collective efforts of all the *Fieldbook*'s contributors have put us in a position to support Thandulwazi in this way.

BIBLIOGRAPHY

Allison, S. and Tharby, A. (2015) *Making every lesson count*. Carmarthen: Crown House.

Barton, C. (ed.) (2019) *The researchED guide to education myths*. Woodbridge: John Catt Educational.

Beames, S. (2018) *The nature and impact of Gordonstoun School's out-of-classroom learning experiences*. Edinburgh: The University of Edinburgh. Retrieved from: www.bit.ly/2kST4cy

Berger, R. (2003) *An ethic of excellence*. Portsmouth, NH: Heinemann.

Christodoulou, D. (2016) *Making good progress? The future of assessment for learning*. Oxford: Oxford University Press.

Didau, D. (2016) *What if everything you knew about education was wrong?* Carmarthen: Crown House.

Didau, D. and Rose, N. (2016) *What every teacher needs to know about psychology*. Woodbridge: John Catt Educational.

Enser, M. (2019) *Teach like nobody's watching: the essential guide to effective and efficient teaching*. Carmarthen: Crown House.

Massey, R. (2019) *From able to remarkable: help your students become expert learners*. Carmarthen: Crown House.

Myatt, M. (2018) *The curriculum: gallimaufry to coherence*. Woodbridge: John Catt Educational.

Robinson, M. (2013) *Trivium 21c: preparing young people for the future with lessons from the past*. Carmarthen: Independent Thinking Press.

Robinson, M. (2016) *Trivium in practice*. Carmarthen: Independent Thinking Press.

Robinson, M. (2019) *Curriculum: Athena versus the machine*. Carmarthen: Crown House.

Rosenshine, B. (2012) 'Principles of instruction: research-based strategies that all teachers should know', *American Educator* 36 (1) pp. 12–19, 39.

Sherrington, T. (2019) *Rosenshine's principles in action*. Woodbridge: John Catt Educational.

Shimamura, A. (2018) *MARGE: a whole-brain learning approach for students and teachers*. PDF available from www.bit.ly/2UEi1IB

Sumeracki, M. and Weinstein, Y. with Caviglioli, O. (2018) *Understanding how we learn: a visual guide*. Abingdon: Routledge.

Thom, J. (2018) *Slow teaching: on finding calm, clarity and impact in the classroom*. Woodbridge: John Catt Educational.

Willingham, D. (2009) *Why don't students like school?* San Francisco, CA: Jossey-Bass.

Young, M., Lambert, D., Roberts, C. and Roberts, M. (2014) *Knowledge and the future school: curriculum and social justice*. London: Bloomsbury.